A

NEW PLAN

of the Borough of

READING,

1840,

THE ROYAL BERKSHIRE HOSPITAL
1839–1989

The Royal Berkshire Hospital 1845, from a painting by W. F. Poulton

THE
ROYAL
BERKSHIRE
HOSPITAL
1839~1989

MARGARET RAILTON

MARSHALL BARR

THE ROYAL BERKSHIRE HOSPITAL

*This book is dedicated to the numerous
people whose names do not appear within
its pages who, through their skill, hard
work and compassion, have done so much to
shape and develop the work of the Hospital
over the past 150 years.*

First published in 1989 by the Royal Berkshire Hospital
© Copyright Margaret Railton and Marshall Barr 1989

ISBN 0 9514373 0 5

Typeset in 11 on 12 pt Baskerville by Columns of Reading
Printed by the University Printing House, Oxford

CONTENTS

LIST OF ILLUSTRATIONS

PART I

PART II

ACKNOWLEDGEMENTS

I would like to thank the Royal Berkshire Hospital and the Reading Pathological Society for giving me access to their libraries and archives; Miss Enid Forsyth (District Librarian) and Mrs Margaret Coleman for their help and for obtaining various publications and reports; Mr Lionel Williams (Head of Department of Medical Illustration) for his skill and patience in providing and reproducing many of the illustrations.

I would also like to thank Miss Daphne Phillips, her successor Mrs Margaret Smith and the staff of the Reading Reference Library for making available the old newspaper files and other relevant records; Dr Peter Durrant and the staff of the Berkshire Record Office for allowing me access to various local, Poor Law, County and Borough archives; Miss Susan Read of the Reading Museum for her help with photographs in the Museum's collection; the Editors of the *Reading Chronicle* and *Reading Standard* for their interest and permission to reproduce their photographs (listed below); Mr I. H. Parr (Estates Information Officer, West Berkshire Health Authority), Mr Marsh and his successor Mr Ward (Technical Services Department, Reading Borough Council) for providing old plans; Mr Robert Johnson for drawing the plan of the early Hospital; Mr Keith Parker of the Science Museum, for his assistance with the old medical instruments and ambulances; Mr Sidney Gold for his help with Joseph Morris's architectural drawings.

In addition I would like to thank the following people who have given me their time, advice and information: Mr Willoughby Cashell, Dr Basil Hill, Mr Gordon Bohn, Dr A. J. Reed, the late Dr George Burfield, Mr David Goodwin, Sister Ruth Clark, Dr A. Barr, Mrs Sheila Copsey, Mr J. Weiss, Miss Jane Rendall, Mr Bob Lacy, Miss J. C. Targett, Mrs E. M. Holloway, Mr E. Harris, Mr A. Carlisle, Mr Harry Edwards (Morris Register), Mr M. Fellowes-Freeman (Dunedin Hospital), Mrs Iris Binstead (Branch Administrator, Berkshire Branch of the British Red Cross Society) and Mrs Elaine Cook (County Secretary, St John Ambulance Brigade, Berkshire).

Finally, I would like to thank my co-author, our editor Miss Moyna Kitchin and our graphics designer Mr Chris Harper for their support, and also my family and friends for their great tolerance during the period of research and writing of Part I and the Epilogue of this book.

Margaret Railton

I would like to thank the following people for their assistance in the preparation of Part II of this book: Gordon Bohn, Tom Boulton, the late George Burfield, Hugh Calvert, Geoffrey Cashell (particularly), Basil Hill, Frank Hampson, Conrad Latto, George Patey, Donald McWilliams, Frank Naylor, Les Parcell, Alan Thorp, Geoffrey Weston, John Dykes, Eric Clark, Harry Sellwood, Claude Arent, Una Spanner, Evelyn Aust, Rosemary McIlvenna, Margaret Thorngate, Charles Robinson, Lorna Palmer, Olive Knight, C. F. Taylor, Doreen Thomas, Emily Charlotte Pickering, Gill Griffiths, Clifford Thomas, Olive Clark, Gladys Morgan, Edmund Burton, Janet Reynish, Mary Seymour and Elvis Fappiano.

I am especially indebted to Lionel Williams for his work in preparing many of the photographs used in Part II of the book.

Finally, thanks to my family for their patience; and for her skilled typing a special thanks to Mary, my wife.

Marshall Barr

The authors would like to thank the following people and organisations for their kind permission to reproduce the illustrations on the pages listed below:

Local Studies Department, Reading Reference Library: First endpaper, pages 3 and 134 (bottom);

Mr W. A. Benyon and the Berkshire Record Office: Frontispiece and page 26 (top);

The Librarian, Reading University Library: Page 6;

Mr R. Johnson: Page 46;

Science Museum, South Kensington, London: Pages 65, 107, 121 and 210 (centre right);

Technical Services Department, Reading Borough Council: Page 93;

British Architectural Library, R.I.B.A., London: Pages 95, 99 (top left and right);

Estates Department, West Berkshire Health Authority: Pages 103, 155, 161 and 206;

Reading Museum and Art Gallery: Pages 125, 260, *Berkshire Chronicle* collection 226, 228 (bottom left and right), 229 and 230 (top and bottom);

Institute of Agricultural History and Museum of English Rural Life, University of Reading (Lewis and Dann collection): Page 157 (top);

Walton Adams Studios: Pages 157 (centre left and right, bottom) and 159 (top, centre and bottom);

Francis Frith Collection: Page 163;

The *Reading Standard*: Pages 168 (top left and right), 184, 200 (top) and 207 (top left and right);

Mrs E. M. Holloway: Page 168 (centre);

Mrs A. Longstaff: Pages 170, 173, 177 and 179;

The Reading Newspaper Company Ltd, *Berkshire Chronicle*: Pages 183, 210 (top right), 226, 228 (bottom left and right), 229, 230 (top and bottom), and 248, *Reading Mercury*: 228 (top left and right);

C. E. May and Son: Pages 202, 204 (bottom), 231, 274 and 282;

Morris Register: Page 210 (bottom);

Royal Commission on the Historical Monuments of England: Page 242 (top and bottom);

Photo Reportage, London: Page 310;

Architects Design Partnership, Henley: Page 344 (top, centre and bottom);

Martin Airpics: Second endpaper.

All other illustrations are from the archives of the Royal Berkshire Hospital.

PART I

THE VOLUNTARY HOSPITAL

by

MARGARET RAILTON

The Royal Berkshire Hospital 1839

PROLOGUE

The formal opening of the Royal Berkshire Hospital took place on Monday May 27th, 1839 with great ceremony and rejoicing. This notable day brought the people of Reading and the neighbourhood in their hundreds to watch the occasion with pride and anticipation. An imposing building had been completed; an ambitious enterprise was about to become a reality.

The Committee formed to arrange the details of the occasion had been instructed to make the ceremonial as impressive as possible with 'due care for the preservation of order throughout the day'. The local newspapers had suggested that a public dinner 'might be beneficial . . . and provide a spirit of harmony'.

The Committee had more elaborate plans. The day would start with Divine Service at St Lawrence's Church, after which a procession would go to the Hospital for the formal opening ceremony. In the afternoon a dinner would be held at the Town Hall with the High Sheriff in the chair and numerous county dignitaries acting as stewards.

Every edition of the local papers in the intervening weeks contained items relating to the opening. The *Reading Mercury* anticipated 'a gala day of no ordinary character' and advertisements urged those who would like to attend the Town Hall dinner to obtain tickets without delay at a cost of 5/- (excluding wine). The Philanthropic Society would also be taking part in the ceremony and published details of their 'Line of Procession'. They advised that a dinner would be provided at the Peacock Inn for 'those brothers who wish to dine together on the occasion', with tickets at 2/6d each and the dinner 'on table at half-past three precisely'.

Monday, May 27th proved to be a bright, sunny day and from early in the morning people from the surrounding districts began to arrive in the town. Practically all the local shops and businesses were closed for the day to enable as many people as possible to attend the celebrations. As eleven o'clock approached, the bells of St Lawrence's Church were ringing and the members of the congregation began to arrive for the service. The church was filled with those who had been instrumental in the establishment of the Hospital, including the High Sheriff and the Mayor and Corporation of Reading who arrived in state.

The service was conducted by the Revd J. Ball, Vicar of St Lawrence's, and the sermon was preached by the Revd G. Hulme of Holy Trinity Church, who had been closely connected with the commissioning of the Hospital. He took as his text St Matthew's Gospel, Chapter 4, Verses 24 and 25: 'And His fame went through all Syria, and they brought unto Him all sick people that were taken with divers diseases . . .' Mr Hulme delivered an impressive oration which lasted some forty minutes, interrupted, as noted by the *Times* correspondent, by noisy cheers from the impatient crowds assembled outside. At the end of the service a collection of some £65 was taken in aid of the Hospital funds.

By the time the service was over the area around the church was crowded with spectators and those who were to form the procession. Over 2,000 Sunday School children had been assembled as well as children from the local charity schools. These were to head the long procession to the Hospital, preceded by a 'band of music'. The Sunday School children, six abreast, were followed by the Girls of the Green School and the Boys of the Blue School, four abreast. Then came the choristers in the charge of Mr Binfield, the benefit clubs and the members of the Philanthropic Society resplendent with their own band, banners and insignia. Behind came those associated with the building of the Hospital; the Clerk of Works, the architect and the builder. After them were the surgeons and physicians of the town, the Vice Presidents and Board of Management of the Hospital (complete with wands), the Hospital Treasurer and Secretary. The final section of the procession consisted of local dignitaries: the Borough Magistrates, Town Councillors, Aldermen, Mace Bearer, Town Clerk, the Mayor and Town Sergeants. As this great assembly moved off its length stretched almost to the Hospital. In its wake came some thirty carriages of the 'nobility and gentry'.

The route was from the Market Place, up London Street and into London Road, the whole length of which was lined with cheering spectators. As the procession approached the Hospital, volleys of guns were fired and, as the *Reading Mercury* recorded: 'The view of it in the London Road from the Hospital to the Crown Inn was remarkably pleasing; every balcony and window being crowded with fair spectators and the wide, handsome road thronged with apparently the whole population of the town.' As the procession entered the Hospital gates the band took up its position and the school children, choristers and other members of the procession assembled at the foot of the Hospital steps. A great number of visitors joined the gathering, paying the 1/– charged for admission to the Hospital grounds.

By this time it was about two o'clock and the Hospital Secretary announced that the Revd George Hulme was about to offer a prayer. The assembled company fell silent. Mr Hulme, standing under the portico beside the massive Ionic columns, 'delivered a most solemn and appropriate prayer with great emphasis and feeling'. There followed the singing of the old One-Hundredth Psalm 'All People that on Earth do Dwell'. The forecourt resounded with the voices of the large gathering of some 3,000 people, accompanied by the band and the Reading church choirs. Few could have been left unmoved as the concluding blessing was

PROGRAMME OF THE
PROCESSION
ON THE OCCASION OF
THE OPENING
OF THE
ROYAL BERKSHIRE
HOSPITAL,
On *MONDAY*, May 27th, 1839.

DIVINE SERVICE will commence in St. Lawrence's Church at Eleven o'clock, when the Rev. G. HULME, M.A.. will preach a Sermon for the benefit of the Hospital; after which the Procession to the Hospital in the London Road, will be arranged in the following order :—

The Children of the Sunday Schools, six abreast, the Girls taking the lead.

The Girls of the Green School, four abreast.

The Boys of the Blue Coat School, four abreast.

THE CHORISTERS UNDER CHARGE OF MR. BINFIELD.

The Band of the Philanthropic Society.

The Members of the Philanthropic Society with Flags.

The Benefit Societies of Reading.

Band of Music.

The Contractor and the Clerk of the Works.

The Architect.

The Resident Surgeons of Reading.

The Physicians.

The Vice-Presidents and Board of Management with Wands.

The Treasurer.

The Secretaries.

The Clerk of the Peace.

The Borough Magistrates.

The Two Marshalmen in their Cloaks carrying their Staves.

Borough Treasurer.

The Town Councillors.

The Aldermen.

The Mace Bearer.

The Town Clerk.

The Mayor.

The Town Sergeants.

The Carriages of such of the Nobility and Gentry as may be pleased to attend, who are requested to join the Procession from Friar Street.

It is requested that the Schools be assembled in the Forbury at Twelve o'Clock, to be arranged in proper order, to proceed into the Market Place and take their places in the line of Procession to be there formed as soon as Divine Service shall be over.

All persons, whether in the Procession or not, on being admitted within the gates will be expected to produce an Admission Ticket or pay One Shilling at the Gate; except the Sunday School Children with their Teachers, and the Bands, and the Members of the Philanthropic Institution; the latter will pass through the grounds and go out at the West Gate.

This arrangement is made in order that the ground may not be inconveniently crowded; and the surplus of the receipts, if any, after defraying the expences of the day, will of course be appropriated to the funds of the Hospital.

The Interior of the Hospital will be reserved principally for Ladies.

Admission Tickets within the Gates may be obtained, price One Shilling, of Messrs. RUSHER and JOHNSON, King-street; Mr. BURGESS, Broad-street; Mr. SNARE, Minster-street; Mr. LOVEJOY, London-street; Mr. BLACKWELL, London-street; Mr. CRAPP, Castle-street; Mrs. RUGMAN, Oxford-street; Mr. THOMAS, Broad-street.

DINNER at the TOWN HALL at THREE O'CLOCK—The Members of the Amateur Musical Society, under the able superintendance of Mr. Venua, have kindly consented to afford their valuable and gratuitous assistance in contributing to the harmony on that occasion. Tickets to be had of Mr. Golding, Hall-keeper, Friar Street; and of Mr. Lovejoy, Bookseller, London Street, FIVE SHILLINGS each. An early application is requested for the convenience of all parties.

R. WELCH, PRINTER, DUKE STREET, READING.

3

followed by the singing of the National Anthem, and the announcement that the Hospital would be open to receive accident patients the following day.

There was great cheering and each of the children was given a bun; some 2,200 buns were distributed. The visitors were then allowed into the Hospital 'which they entered in dense crowds and appeared unanimous in their admiration of the whole arrangements and fitting up'. As the *Berkshire Chronicle* reported: 'It was not until a late hour of the evening that the gates of the Hospital were closed; and we are happy to add that the festivities of the holiday terminated without the occurrence of a single accident to mar the prevailing pleasure and satisfaction which appeared to be enjoyed by all present on this memorable occasion.' The Committee would be well content.

After the opening ceremony at the Hospital the members of the Philanthropic Society and benefit clubs dispersed to their various meeting places. The members of the Philanthropic Society gathered at the Peacock Inn and, after playing the National Anthem, a subscription was raised for the bells of St Lawrence's Church to be rung.

At 3.30 some 60 members sat down to their dinner at the Philanthropic Lodge room. The addresses delivered were pronounced excellent, 'both appropriate to the business of the day and the furtherance of the Institution'. Other celebrations were held in the town at the Woolpack, the Bell and the Elephant, and 'the satisfaction which the day had afforded was warmly expressed by all'.

These gatherings were by no means as lavish or fashionable as that taking place at the Town Hall, but the members of these societies and benefit clubs were all too aware of how greatly the Hospital was needed by those who were not in the fortunate position of being able to contribute to its establishment.

By three o'clock about 300 guests from all parts of the county had assembled at the Town Hall for the grand public dinner to celebrate the opening of the Hospital. A gallery had been built at one end of the hall for the 150 ladies who would join the company for the toasts and speeches. The orchestra and the Amateur Music Society, who were to provide the music under Mr Venua and Mr Binfield, were seated at the opposite end of the hall. After the High Sheriff of the county, Mr M. G. Thoyts of Sulhamstead House, had taken the chair and the Revd G. Hulme had said Grace, the assembled company proceeded to enjoy an excellent cold dinner of 'poultry, ham, shell fish, lamb etc. and jellies and confectionary of every description'. At the end of the meal the ladies filled the gallery and were greeted by loud cheers. The Amateurs then sang 'Non Nobis Domine', all glasses were replenished and the toasts and speeches began.

Altogether 29 toasts were proposed covering everyone associated with the founding and commissioning of the Hospital and those who would be responsible for its future welfare. The newspapers devoted column after column to reporting the occasion, with details of the toasts, the eloquent speeches made in reply and the music that was played at appropriate points throughout the proceedings.

The High Sheriff began by proposing the health of Her Gracious Majesty the Queen, who had kindly consented to become Patroness of the Institution. The singing of 'God Save the Queen' was followed by toasts to the Queen Dowager (Queen Adelaide), members of the Royal Family and other dignitaries, interspersed with cheering, singing and rousing music.

The Marquess of Downshire then proposed the health of the High Sheriff who had done so much to bring everyone together 'when this great work of benevolence and charity, the Royal Berkshire Hospital, was advanced and promoted'. Enthusiastic cheering filled the hall followed by the 'Huntsman's Chorus' from *Der Freischultz*.

The High Sheriff, after returning his thanks, proposed 'the only bumper toast' he would call that evening, 'success and prosperity to the Royal Berkshire Hospital'. Great cheers and the 'Charity Hymn' by Mr Venua signalled the approval of all present.

The next toast was to Lord and Lady Sidmouth who had so generously given the land on which the Hospital was built. This was followed by one to Mr Richard Benyon de Beauvoir, President of the Hospital, who had donated £3,000 towards its establishment.

After 23 toasts and replies the ladies, who were about to retire, were requested to remain a few minutes more while the health of the 'Marchioness of Downshire and the Ladies of Berkshire' was proposed. This prompted even greater cheering and the toast was drunk with 'uproarious applause', during which the ladies retired. The madrigal 'Down in a Flow'ry Vale' was sung and 'rapturously encored'.

There remained but five toasts to complete the evening and after those to the architect and builder of the Hospital, the High Sheriff finally proposed 'prosperity to the Town of Reading and the County of Berkshire'. Great cheering and the singing of the National Anthem brought the proceedings to a conclusion at a quarter past eight.

While all these festivities were taking place, large gangs of men were working a few miles away on the construction of the line for the Great Western Railway. Among them was George Earley, a labourer aged 15. On Thursday, May 30th he was in charge of a wagon train when the horse that was drawing it knocked him down and he was thrown under the wheels. He sustained a compound fracture of the upper arm of such severity that his arm was later amputated at the shoulder.

George Earley was the first patient received at the Royal Berkshire Hospital and the operation performed as a result of his accident was believed to be one that had not been attempted in the town for over 60 years. The work of the Royal Berkshire Hospital had begun.

To the Nobility, Gentry, Clergy, *and all others, who either inhabit, or have any property in the County of* BERKS.

Gentlemen,

IT would be an *affront* to your *kind dispositions* to make any *Apology* for my present *Address*, which is design'd to give *you* the *truest Pleasure*, and your indigent afflicted Neighbours a *generous* Relief.

The noble Examples set us at *Winchester, Exeter, Bath, Bristol, York,* and *Northampton,* should stir US up to *Emulation* ; and the *deplorable Condition* of many afflicted (and perhaps in some Degree *neglected* POOR, calls upon us, with a *most persuasive* Earnestness, to erect a COUNTY HOSPITAL.

The *Motives* hereunto are not to be enumerated in this *short* Address, nor is it needful when directed to *compassionate Englishmen*, and benevolent Christians. Difficulties will indeed appear at *the first* View of such a Proposal, but *surely* cannot discourage those who recollect, that an Hospital has *not long since* been established at *Northampton* in less than six Months ; it may *possibly* be accomplished even *sooner* here, since we can *at once* adopt those *admirable* Statutes which have, with many *additional* Improvements been *so very lately* compil'd from the Rules of *all* other Hospitals by the *worthy* Gentlemen of *Northamptonshire,* and which will be by the *assured* Blessing of Providence, a *lasting* Monument of their *publick* Spirit, *indefatigable* Zeal, and *tender* Concern for the Welfare of the distress'd.

We have *NATIVES* of Berkshire, and *many others* fond of this *delightfull* County at so *commodious* a distance from *London,* who are Men of *Generosity, Activity,* and *Abilities*; consequently there can be no Room to doubt, but this *Good,* this Godlike Scheme MIGHT take Root, and extend as *Happily,* be conducted, and regulated as *Wisely* at *READING,* as in *any other* part of this *generous* Kingdom ; and more especially as *we* have the *peculiar* Advantage of the *Royal Palace* at *WINDSOR* surrounded with the Seats of *Nobility,* as well as *Gentry,* the *splendid* appearance of the Ladies at their *frequent,* and *celebrated* ASSEMBLIES in *READING,* the *great* Subscription for the Support of our *Horse-Races* there, amounting to an hundred and fifty (nay sometimes *three* hundred) Pounds *per Annum,* are *undeniable* Proofs of the *Affluence* and *Generosity* of this County ; and I may venture *with great Confidence* to affirm that the *Ladies* alone, since Tenderness is their *distinguish'd* Characteristick, will raise a very *considerable* Sum to animate so *noble,* so *comprehensive* a Charity ; and the Encouragement of the Tradesmen at *Newbury, Abingdon, Hungerford, Faringdon,* &c. &c. in *General,* and in *particular* at *Reading* (a Town *so* famous for it's Wealth and Trade by the *vast* Benefits of a *navigable* River) will *undoubtedly* be very great ; since not only Humanity, but their own *Interest* must spur them on to approve themselves *true* Friends to the County Hospital, and to act *with Unanimity* for the Support of it.

Gentlemen,

I *humbly* hope this GENERAL ADDRESS will not be regarded as a *romantick* Invitation to an *Impracticable* Attempt, nor the Prosecution of this *laudable* Design be delay'd by *needless* Inquiries WHO WAS THE AUTHOR OF IT ? 'Tis sufficient to know, that he will be a SUBSCRIBER, and is a *sincere* Well-wisher to Mankind of *all* Ranks, Parties, and Denominations— who has neither *Ambition* nor *Interest* to gratify, in promoting this Proposal ; nothing to tempt him to it, but *natural* Compassion for the *diseas'd* Poor of his *native* County ; a full Conviction that the Charity he recommends is *most extensively* useful, and the heart-felt Joy arising from the *silent* Approbation of his own Conscience in *this* Endeavour to introduce it among you.

I am, Gentlemen,

With all due Deference and Respect,

Your very humble Servant,

A NATIVE of BERKSHIRE.

P. S. If *this* Proposal meets with its *deserv'd* Encouragement, it is presumed *the Clergy* of all the *chief* Towns will properly recommend it (as has been customary at other Places) from their Pulpits, and that the Nobility, and *leading* Men of *all* Parties (for CHARITY can surely be *confined* to *none*) will *unanimously* agree to advertise in the *Reading* Papers a publick Meeting at the County Town of *Reading,* and *then* appoint a *select* Committee to draw up *proper* Arguments for the *effectual* Recommendation of this *Glorious* Charity, to be dispersed thro' the *whole* County ; after which they will *of Course* consult on a *convenient* Method of collecting Subscriptions, and executing *all other* Requisites towards the *happy* Establishment of so *beneficent* an Undertaking to the *perpetual* Good and Honour of *Berkshire.*

N. B. *Whereas several may object* to the Expence of removing Patients from the distant *Parts of the County.* I must beg Leave to remark, that 'twill bear no Proportion to the Charge of maintaining *them at home, that many Carriages come every Market Day to Reading, and if a poor Labourer dies, his Wife and Children must be a Burden to the Parish.*— So that it may *reasonably* be expected, that all *Persons who have any Relation to this County will entitle their poor Neighbours to receive such Help in the Time of their greatest Distress, as neither Money, nor Friends can procure them any where but in these charitable Foundations.*

Extract from *The Gentleman's Magazine,* December 1743

1

THE FOUNDING
OF THE HOSPITAL

The possibility of establishing a hospital in the Reading area had been raised on various occasions from the early eighteenth century but the idea had never gained enough support to make it a reality. The medical facilities of London, only 40 miles away, combined with those at the Winchester Hospital, founded in 1736, and John Radcliffe's Infirmary, founded in Oxford in 1770, were believed to be sufficient and close enough to offer help to the people of Berkshire.

There had, indeed, been great developments in establishing hospitals in London. The dissolution of the monasteries by Henry VIII had removed the care of the sick and the poor from the hands of the Church and religious foundations, and throughout the country alternative ways had to be found to fill this need. In London itself, St Thomas's and St Bartholomew's Hospitals were re-established from their religious foundations but in Reading the care given to the sick by the monks of the Abbey and the Grey Friars had never been replaced by a comparable institution. One reason had been the lack of resources. Reading had produced no Thomas Guy whose wealth had founded Guy's Hospital in 1725, nor had there been philanthropic groups such as those who had established the Westminster Infirmary in 1719 and St George's Hospital in 1733. In the eighteenth century eleven hospitals were founded in London, 37 in the provinces and nine in Scotland. Many of these establishments had become renowned teaching hospitals and, with the medical centres which had grown up in the universities, they provided the basis for the advancement of medical knowledge and the training of physicians and surgeons.

By the beginning of the nineteenth century a large number of well-qualified physicians and surgeons were available to give medical advice and treatment throughout the country, and the medical establishment as it is known today had begun to take shape. The College of Physicians had been founded in 1518, and this had been followed by the United Company of Barber-Surgeons in 1540 and the Society of Apothecaries in 1617. By the nineteenth century the surgeons had broken away from the barbers and a separate association, the Royal College of Surgeons, was founded in 1800. In 1818 the Apothecaries Society was given the right to examine and license those who wished to become general practitioners and in 1832 the

Provincial Medical and Surgical Association was formed, which was the forerunner of the British Medical Association.

There were three physicians and seven surgeons in practice in Reading at the turn of the nineteenth century. At that time there was not a single medical treatment or surgical procedure which could not be undertaken outside a hospital. There were no anaesthetics, no X-rays, or complicated life-support machines. If the patient had the facilities and could be given warmth and attention at home, there was no need for the sick to go to hospital. The services of the medical profession were readily available to those who were able to pay.

Since Elizabethan times the care of the poor had rested in the hands of parish officials and a series of Poor Laws enacted over the years determined how those in need were to be looked after. 'Parish relief' was administered through the overseers of the poor in each parish and it was their decision how help should be given to those who they believed to be deserving. A rate was levied in every parish for the maintenance of the poor and those who were unable to support themselves were removed to the parish workhouse. Here their basic needs were provided, and this included medical treatment from local doctors who attended the sick at these institutions.

It was extremely difficult for the poor who were not cared for in the workhouse to pay for medical treatment. These were the people who relied on physical fitness in order to maintain themselves and their families and who had no savings on which to draw in times of crisis. Those working in the factories and on the farms were especially exposed to accidents and illness; they laboured in all weathers, often ill-clothed and with homes that provided only minimal warmth and food. At that time the state provided no sick pay, no unemployment benefit or pensions for the elderly. For those who could not work there was no income. The Church and charitable bodies assisted where they could but their help was far from adequate. Friendly Societies and Benefit Clubs were established, and those who were able to contribute regularly received a small sum of money in times of sickness. Unless they were seriously ill and confined to bed, the ordinary men and women usually continued to work but were frequently without any medical help to ease their condition.

In 1802 a group of physicians and surgeons, supported by local clergy and eminent people, had founded the Reading Dispensary financed by private subscription. Here the 'industrious poor of the town' could obtain free medical advice and treatment from honorary physicians and surgeons on the recommendation of a subscriber. A few beds were later made available at the Dispensary House in Chain Street, but this was basically a surgery with occasional home visits and not a hospital.

When the Dispensary was first established the population of Reading was under 10,000, and within a short time 400 patients were being treated each year. Thirty years later the population had increased by over 50 per cent to almost 16,000 and by 1835 the Dispensary was treating about 800 patients each year. It was becoming increasingly obvious that further medical help was needed for this section of the population, not just in Reading itself, but also in the surrounding districts.

In the meantime innumerable problems had developed with the administration of the Poor Laws and often those supported by the parish were seen as faring better than those who were working. In 1834 the Poor Law Amendment Act was passed and this was to remain in force for almost 100 years until it was superseded in 1929 by the Local Government Act.

The New Poor Law system combined several parishes in an area to form a 'Union' administered by a Board of Guardians with its own workhouse for those who were unable to look after themselves. Others who were not infirm could be helped by 'outdoor relief'. The cost of this was still to be defrayed by a poor rate raised by the overseers in each parish. In Berkshire twelve such Unions were formed and in some instances parishes in adjoining counties were combined with others in Berkshire for ease of administration. In Reading the three parishes of St Giles, St Mary's and St Lawrence were joined to form the Reading Union.

The administration of the New Poor Laws caused great hardship. The old and infirm who could not be supported by their families were still looked after in the workhouses, but the most stringent rules were applied to prevent the able-bodied from receiving parish relief. This came at a time of high rural unemployment and the plight of these families was pitiable.

The Proposed Establishment of a Hospital

On February 23rd, 1836 a Committee, under the chairmanship of Dr Thomas Ring, submitted a report to a Special Meeting of the Governors of the Reading Dispensary on *The Proposed Establishment of a County Hospital in Reading or its Vicinity.* Much work had been done by the Committee before they drew up their report. The general consensus of opinion appeared to be in favour of building a hospital, as it was now recognised that the Winchester, Oxford and London hospitals were not able to supply the needs of Berkshire.

In the past some of the local medical practitioners had not been in favour of establishing a hospital in Reading, fearing that their own practices would suffer as a result. Later they became more enthusiastic as they realised the great possibilities such an institution would afford, both for the benefit of the community and for their own professional work.

Canvassing of opinion had been going on for some time and much of this behind-the-scenes work was done by one person. Mr Edward Oliver was a quiet, unassuming man with a mission. He had retired from his job as a Managing Clerk at a London bank but through the fraudulent conduct of a trustee had lost all his savings. He was now living in Reading and supporting himself and his family on a small pension. When the idea of the hospital was raised by a local surgeon, Mr George May, Sr, in 1830, the proposal met with opposition. Mr Oliver, however, was so convinced of the need for a hospital that he continued to raise the subject, not only by writing to the local papers but also by walking throughout the County to canvass support. His persistence twice gained him an audience with King William IV at Windsor. It was later said that without Mr Oliver the hospital would never have been built when it was.

Dr Ring's Committee was able to report to the Governors of the Reading Dispensary that they thought 'the time is fully come to propose the erection of a hospital for the benefit of the poor and afflicted of this large town and opulent and Royal County'. They recommended that £1,000 should be given by the Dispensary for the purpose, and 'the remainder of the funds be appropriated for the future annual expenditure necessarily arising from such an establishment'. At that time the Dispensary had £5,350 invested in three per cent stock besides the Dispensary House, valued at £900. The annual income from the dividends on the stock was £160 and in 1835 the subscriptions had amounted to £115 6s.

The Governors of the Dispensary were in full agreement with the Committee's proposals and formally resolved that it was 'desirable that a County Hospital be established in Reading or its vicinity' and that £1,000 should be given from the Dispensary funds. The meeting was then told that Mr Richard Benyon de Beauvoir of Englefield House had said that he would donate £1,000 towards the erection of a County Hospital provided the plan of such a hospital met with his approval.

With the offer of these two generous donations the prospect of building a hospital seemed very hopeful, but the approval and financial backing of the affluent members of the County would be required before all the necessary funds could be obtained. It was therefore agreed that a letter should be sent to Sir Henry Russell of Swallowfield, the Foreman of the Grand Jury, asking for support and, if thought expedient, a County meeting would then be called.

The Grand Jury was a body of between twelve and twenty-three eminent people of the County who were summoned by the Sheriff at every Court of Assize and Borough Sessions to investigate the various indictments being presented at these courts. They were all influential people and their approval would be invaluable in obtaining the support that was necessary for such an undertaking to succeed.

Three days later, on February 26th, Sir Henry Russell reported that the Grand Jury had given their 'cordial concurrence' to the idea and suggested the Committee's letter should be referred to the Magistrates of the County and others at the next Quarter Sessions to be held on April 8th at Newbury. Meantime 500 copies of the Committee's report were printed and circulated to the magistrates, clergy and 'other suitable persons belonging to the County'. The Committee itself increased its numbers and now consisted of the seven members of the original Dispensary Committee plus the Mayor of Reading, the Revd George Hulme, James Wheble Esq., Dr Bailey, Dr Smith and Sir Henry Russell. A Sub-committee was formed of five members to look for a suitable site on which to build the hospital.

Numerous letters of support were arriving and following the

Newbury Quarter Sessions the magistrates declared 'their desire to promote the success of the undertaking'. A public meeting was called for Saturday, April 30th in the Town Hall of Reading, duly advertised in the local papers, and 1,000 circulars were distributed to the 'nobility, gentry, clergy and others' inviting them to attend.

The public filled the Town Hall for the meeting held on April 30th. The audience was described as 'one of the most respectable ever assembled within its walls' and the large number of 'elegantly dressed females' was particularly noted. The four members of Parliament for the County and the Borough were present as well as many magistrates and 'other leading gentlemen connected with Berkshire'.

The Mayor, Mr H. Hawkes, opened the proceedings by saying he had no doubt that the result of the meeting would be the establishment of a hospital worthy of the Royal County. The chair was then taken by Mr Robert Palmer MP who told the meeting of the support the idea of a hospital was receiving and that several most generous donations had been received already as well as promises of others. Mr Richard Benyon de Beauvoir's gift of £1,000 was greatly applauded and the meeting was informed of the help which could be given from the funds of the Reading Dispensary.

Eight resolutions were then passed, each being proposed and seconded by eminent local people who delivered eloquent and stirring speeches in their favour. At the end of the meeting it had been agreed:

1. That a Hospital should be established in the vicinity of Reading.
2. That a humble solicitation be submitted to their Majesties that they will be graciously pleased to become the Patron and Patroness of the Institution.
3. That Richard Benyon de Beauvoir Esquire be requested to accept the office of President.
4. That William Stephens Esquire be requested to act as Treasurer and C. S. Robinson Esquire and Mr Henry Letchworth as joint Secretaries of the Institution.
5. That the purchase of the ground, the erection of the buildings and the support of the establishment be provided by voluntary contributions.
6. That a book be opened forthwith for contributions towards the erection of the Hospital and that similar books be deposited at the banks of the towns enumerated in the following list, and circulated through the County and the adjacent districts: Abingdon, Basingstoke, Farringdon, Henley, Maidenhead, Newbury, Reading, Wallingford, Wantage, Windsor, Wokingham.
7. That a Committee, of whom five shall form a quorum, be appointed to determine the site of the Hospital and to treat for the purchase of the ground, and to frame a code of regulations for the general conduct of the establishment; and that the Committee do consist of the Members of the County, the Members for Reading, R. Benyon de

Beauvoir Esquire, and the Members of the Committee that has already been sitting to promote the object of the present Meeting, with power to add to their number.

8. That a General Meeting of Subscribers be held at the Town Hall at Reading on Thursday, June 9th at 12 o'clock to receive the report of the Committee and to consider any further recommendations that their inquiries may suggest for the benefit of the Institution.

The meeting had achieved its objectives and by the end of the afternoon £4,850 had been subscribed. The way was now clear to proceed with the establishment of the Hospital.

The Search for a Site

The Sub-committee which had been appointed to find a suitable site for the Hospital reported that they had found three possibilities. It was agreed the owners would be approached to see if they would be prepared to sell about four acres of land and on what terms.

The Chairman, Sir Henry Russell, wrote to all three owners but without success. In the case of the first he wrote not only to Lady Sidmouth, who had inherited the land at the eastern extremity of the town as part of the Earley Estate from her father, Lord Stowell, but also to her husband, Lord Sidmouth, a former Prime Minister, Home Secretary and Speaker of the House of Commons. Lady Sidmouth replied to Sir Henry's letter by return saying the proposition was 'very objectionable to Lord Sidmouth and myself'. They would, however, contribute towards the building of the Hospital.

The next General Meeting of Subscribers, which was held on June 9th, was given an encouraging report by the Secretary. Their Majesties had graciously agreed to become Patron and Patroness of the Hospital and His Majesty had commanded that the building should be called the 'Royal Berkshire Hospital'. Furthermore His Majesty would grant an annual donation of fifty guineas from the Privy Purse. The subscriptions towards the building now stood at over £8,000; only the selection of the site remained to be settled.

It was to be another three months before a site for the Hospital was obtained. Advertisements were placed in the papers asking for offers of land of between two and three acres. Several sites were investigated, ranging in price from £383 to £500 per acre, but none appeared particularly suitable. On August 24th Sir Henry Russell received a letter from Lord Sidmouth, dated the same day:

'My dear Sir,

I wrote my former letter to you with reluctance and regret. I write this with great pleasure. Today I have heard that there is very considerable difficulty in finding a proper and suitable site for the intended County Hospital. It will be an extreme satisfaction to Lady

Sidmouth and myself to remove this difficulty and we request that the piece of land belonging to the Earley Court property may be applied to the purpose for which it is thought to be particularly adapted.

I have the honour to be with great regard, my dear Sir,

Yours faithfully,

Sidmouth'

When writing to Lord Sidmouth to convey their cordial and grateful thanks, the Committee enquired 'by what means they may become acquainted with the price of the land and how soon they may obtain possession of it . . .'

Lord Sidmouth replied: 'The piece of land, which is thought the best adapted to that purpose, is offered by us for acceptance and not for sale.' Lord and Lady Sidmouth's generous offer was formally accepted at a General Meeting of the Subscribers held on September 9th.

Later in the month Lord Sidmouth informed the Committee that if additional land should be required, it could be obtained, as 'on no account should the Institution in its appearance or usefulness be limited for want of an appropriate quantity of land.'

Designs and Estimates

By the end of September 1836 a plan of the land had been made showing the almost square four-acre plot. The surveyor, Mr Hawkes, reported that the site was nearly level and the soil was dry gravel. At the beginning of October an advertisement was placed in the Reading papers, the London *Express* and *Oxford Journal* as well as in the *Times*, *Herald* and *Chronicle*, asking for designs and estimates for the building. A competition would be held and architects were requested to submit their plans by December 13th with a motto attached and 'accompanied by a letter having a like work of distinction containing the address of the party forwarding the design'. A prize of £50 would be given to the architect whose design won most approval; £30 for the second and £20 for the third. If, however, the architect whose plans were chosen was also instructed to supervise the building, his prize would be forfeited. Sixteen points were noted in the specification, one of which was that the building was to be of brick cased throughout in Bath stone. It should face the London Road at a distance of 100 feet and occupy a central position from east to west; the cost of the building should not exceed £6,000; it should accommodate 60 beds in wards besides suitable apartments for the 'officers of the Institution' and be capable of enlargement to contain 100 beds; the Royal Arms were to appear on the front of the building and the whole to be constructed to give an 'appearance of completeness' especially in the front but 'admitting without violence to its architectural character'.

Mr George Basevi, an architect of Savile Row and the designer of Belgrave Square, was appointed at a fee of six guineas per day plus expenses to help the Committee with the judging. It was agreed that any plans costing more than £6,000, or submitted without estimates or including the name of the architect and without a motto, would be eliminated. Out of 55 entries, 24 failed to fulfill the conditions, leaving 31 in the contest. Nine of these were shortlisted by Mr Basevi and on December 13th the results of the competition were announced.

> First, two plans 'SPIRO' and 'CONFIDO' which won £50.
> Second, 'TACERE TUTUM EST' which won £30.
> Third, 'I was sick and ye visited me' which won £20.

The winning plans had been entered by Mr Henry Briant of Reading. His first plan 'Spiro' was a Greek design and the second, 'Confido', was Gothic. The second plans were by Mr W. Newham of New Kent Road in London and the third were by Mr Inman of Eaton Square, London.

Mr Briant was asked if he could adapt the plans of 'Confido' to contain some of the 'excellences' of the former design 'Spiro'. Within a few days Mr Briant produced his amended plans and these were submitted to Lord Sidmouth and Mr Richard Benyon de Beauvoir for their approval. By the end of the first week of January 1837 both gentlemen had expressed themselves 'entirely satisfied' with the Committee's recommendation.

In February the plans entered for the competition were exhibited at the Town Hall for one week. The request of the Reading architects for such an exhibition had been agreed provided that any of Mr Briant's plans which might be needed for making drawings and specifications for builders would be on show for three days only.

By early in February, Mr Briant had completed his specification for the builders and was authorised to advertise in the London and County papers for tenders to be submitted by March 25th. Seven quotations were received for the building work, three for the plumbing and one for the ironwork. The tenders of three Reading firms were accepted, Mr Plumley's of £7,820 for the building, Mr Darter's of £848 for the plumbing and Messrs Wilder's of £709 for the ironwork, making a grand total of £9,377. Mr Thomas Rumble of Great Marlow was appointed Clerk of Works for a fee of two and a half guineas a week plus 4/6d for lodging to superintend jointly with Mr Briant 'the performance of the works'.

In the middle of April the Treasurer announced that the subscriptions now amounted to £9,744 5s 6d. Mr Plumley was authorised to start digging the foundations and the Committee turned their thoughts to the ceremony of laying the foundation stone.

The Foundation Stone

Lord Sidmouth was invited to lay the foundation stone at a ceremony to be held on June 21st. The events of the day, accompanied by Masonic honours, would include a service at St Lawrence's Church followed by a procession from the Forbury to the Hospital for the ceremony of laying the stone. A public dinner would be provided at the Town Hall at 4 p.m., with tickets costing 5/–, at which the principal subscribers would be asked to act as stewards.

An inscribed brass plate was obtained for fixing to the foundation stone; a glass case was ordered to display the coins and documents to be deposited beneath it, as well as the silver trowel to be used at the ceremony itself. The arrangements for the day were finalised: a band was engaged; the programme of the procession was drawn up and the Mayor and Corporation were 'respectfully invited to attend'.

A series of events then completely altered all these plans. The participation of the Masons was withdrawn when it was realised that Lord Sidmouth was not a Mason. Lord Sidmouth himself then became ill and the High Sheriff, the Earl of Abingdon, agreed to take his place. The final blow came with the death of King William IV on June 20th and notices were hastily inserted in all the local papers postponing the ceremony, planned for the following day.

The occasion was then advanced to the next month and the inscription on the brass plate was altered to read:

> The foundation of the Royal Berkshire Hospital was laid on Saturday 13th May in the year of our Lord 1837 and in the seventeenth year of the reign of His Majesty King William the 4th under whose generous patronage and that of his Royal Consort Queen Adelaide the Institution is founded.

The date referred to the laying of the first brick of the foundation by Master Edmund Letchworth, the son of the Committee Secretary.

These plans also had to be postponed and it was reluctantly agreed that any idea of a special ceremony would have to be abandoned.

Today, over 150 years later, this brass plate recording the laying of the foundation can be seen above the main staircase in the entrance hall of the Hospital where it was placed, without any ceremony, some months after the Hospital had opened.

Building and Equipping the Hospital, August 1837 to December 1838
Over the next twelve months the Committee was fully occupied with matters associated with the building. At the very beginning there had been problems when the Clerk of Works reported some bricks unfit for use and some stone was not well prepared, but this caused only minor delays.

In September 1837 a more serious incident occurred when allegations were made about unsatisfactory building work. Mr Plumley, the Clerk of Works, was accused of allowing brick nobbles to be put into walls and plastered over instead of using solid brick. The Committee investigated the matter in detail and were convinced the allegations were false and expressed themselves 'fully satisfied' with the manner in which the work was being executed. In order that the subscribers should be made aware of what had happened, they directed that a statement of the facts of the

15

incident should be made public by being published in the local papers.

The winter of 1837–38 was long and hard. The Kennet and Avon Canal, which was used to transport materials to the site, was frozen over for some time and could not be used. At the quarries, severe frosts damaged large quantities of stone which had been prepared for use in building the portico. Even after the weather improved the canals were so crowded with coal barges that the stone barges could not get through.

At this time the Great Western Railway linking London to Bristol was still in the course of construction. Work had begun early in 1836 but the line had only reached as far as Maidenhead in June 1838 and the section to Twyford was not completed until the following year. In the meantime heavy and bulky goods were transported by water and the difficulties caused by bad weather became all too apparent. The railway line which could have helped with the building of the Hospital was not completed to Reading until 1840 and the entire length to Bristol was not finished until two years after the Hospital had opened. By the end of March 1838 these delays meant that an extension of four months was required for the completion of the building.

Various problems cropped up as the work proceeded and some, as in the case of the operating theatre, required alterations to and adaptation of the original plans. Dr Ring drew attention to the confined state of the theatre and the need for more and better lighting. The corridors leading to the operating room were too narrow and a staircase impeded the entrance. The corridors were widened, an additional window was built and a special type of staircase installed. Folding doors were then attached to the theatre entrance and an inclined plane fixed to enable patients to be wheeled in and out with ease. Other alterations included combining the library, museum and study into one room instead of having the three originally planned.

Dr Cowan recommended that the walls of the wards should be washed in a drab colour rather than white and that they should be painted up to a height of about five feet. The building was insured for £5,000 through the County Fire Office, the premium of £39 7s 6d being considered rather higher than normal owing to the greater risk involved with an unfinished building.

It was then time to consider the fixtures and fittings. Mr Hoggard and Mr Letchworth were asked to examine the 'internal arrangements of the London hospitals' and 'report on what may appear necessary for the establishment'.

In September 1838 they reported to the Committee that they had:

'. . . visited the following hospitals in London, viz, the Westminster, St George's, St Thomas's, Guy's and the North London for the purpose of obtaining all requisite information respecting the various and best methods of fitting up in every department the Royal Berkshire Hospital. In the wards will be wanted iron single bedsteads with hair mattresses, blankets, sheets and rugs for coverlets. These last it is recommended should be similar to those in St George's Hospital, of a light blue (being most cheerful) with the name of the hospital worked in. Besides these will be required a large table, two or three benches, a strong coal chest to contain at least a sack of coals, an iron fixed in the wall over each bed with a rope suspending from it to enable patients to assist themselves in changing their position, a small shelf over each bed to put on nourishment or medicine, a grate with hot closet attached to keep the nourishment warm, two or three saucepans and a kettle.

A box about 18″ × 15″ should also stand by each bed to contain the wardrobe or other property of the patient.

In the kitchen a smoke-jack, range with oven, a large elm dining table, benches, dressers fitted up under the windows, one sufficiently strong to cut up meat on, with scales, shelves, etc. around; one iron boiler small for gruel etc. In the scullery, two iron boilers with copper covers, a steamer for potatoes fitted to one, the place intimated for the third boiler to be left for the purposes of carrying off the steam, a plate rack.

Laundry to be fitted up if washing is not done by contract.

Presses, closets, shelves, etc. to drug cellar.

Bread room, larder, wine cellar and linen closets.

Hot and cold water to be conveyed to each washing place.

Baths to be made of zinc.

Gas not to be used in the wards.

Dispensary to be fitted up as an apothecary's shop.

The furniture in the various rooms to be plain with a little deviation for the Committee room – a large table and twenty-four chairs of oak pattern recommended, after a design in character with the building, in that case the skirting and the door should be painted accordingly, a suitable carpet also required.

In the operating theatre – a table for operations and a red oilcloth for the floor.'

The Committee unanimously adopted the report and appointed a Sub-committee to execute the recommendations and equip the Hospital.

Details concerning the kitchen, the laundry and the method of warming the building were all meticulously investigated to ensure that the best results were obtained. A firm in Leicester was engaged to prepare a report and estimate for warming the hall and passages. The wards would be heated with coal fires. A kitchen range with spit and rack which would also provide hot water for the general use of the Hospital was selected at a price of 30/–, which included maintenance for the first twelve months. A firm of engineers in Brighton was approached to advise on fitting up the laundry, wash-house and the construction of the 'drying apparatus'.

Water had to be connected to the building and the water company gave a quotation of £20 per year, supplies to start from the date of the opening of the Hospital. The drainage was by means of cesspools which had been included in the architect's original plans. Estimates for supplying gas were also obtained. That of the Gas Light Company of 7/– per 1,000 feet was accepted.

There were still innumerable other items to be attended to. The stock from the sale of a druggist's effects was acquired at a cost of £32 18s 6d. Shutters were put on the inside of the post-mortem room and the physician's room was partitioned to enable a waiting room to be made. The land around the building itself still had to be put in order, and three members of the Committee were put in charge of superintending the laying out of the grounds. A carriage shed was constructed near the west entrance, the ground was made level between the main gateway and the London Road and lamps were fixed up to light the front of the Hospital and the forecourt.

Administration and Staffing
At a General Meeting of the Subscribers held at the Town Hall on February 4th, 1839, the Committee reported satisfactory progress with the building and equipping of the Hospital. The original estimates for the building and the boundary walls had been for £7,820 but with the various alterations and additions, it was expected the final figure would be about £12,000. To date the subscriptions with interest amounted to £13,264 9s 11d. It was believed the Hospital would not be ready for opening before May. It was anticipated that it would cost about £2,000 a year to maintain and run the Hospital when it was fully working and support for its future maintenance was required. Her Majesty Queen Victoria had generously taken over the Patronage and had promised an annual donation of 50 guineas.

The Committee concluded its report by saying that they were confident that 'the liberality which has raised the walls of the building will prove an unfailing spring to supply its yearly wants and diffuse its blessings around the county.'

In order to obtain an adequate income it was agreed that books would be opened at all the banks in the County to receive annual subscriptions and benefactions. There were no Government or local grants available in those days and the Royal Berkshire Hospital would be entirely dependent on voluntary contributions, not just for its establishment but for its maintenance, payment of staff and future expansion.

The subscribers approved a recommendation that the Hospital and the Reading Dispensary should unite. The question of staff was also discussed and it was decided that within three months a Medical Officer who would perform the duties of House Surgeon, Apothecary and Secretary would be elected. Those eligible to vote would be all those who subscribed two guineas per annum or 30 guineas in one sum, such payments to have been made one week prior to the election. As ladies would not be attending they were 'to have the privilege' of voting by proxy.

The next three months, until the opening of the Hospital, were almost entirely concerned with approving the rules and regulations, the election of a Medical Officer and the proposed union with the Reading Dispensary. It was not until two months later, after six adjourned General Meetings, that on April 4th the subscribers could resolve unanimously that 'the statutes, rules and orders as now agreed be confirmed'.

Election of a Resident Medical Officer

The three-fold duties of House Surgeon, Apothecary and Secretary required of the Resident Medical Officer must have appeared daunting even to those attending the meeting on February 4th when it was agreed that should these duties 'appear too onerous the Committee would be empowered to appoint temporary assistance to dispense the medicine'. The local papers reporting the meeting the following Saturday also printed two letters addressed to the Governors and Subscribers of the Hospital. One was from Mr Isaac Harrinson and the second was from Mr Edward Boulger. Both were Members of the Royal College of Surgeons and Licentiates of the Apothecaries Society, and both were offering themselves as candidates for the position of Resident Medical Officer at the Hospital. It was decided that the election should take place on Monday, April 15th at Reading Town Hall and the poll would be open from 12 to 4 p.m. The salary of the successful candidate would not begin until the opening of the Hospital.

At this point the rules relating to the appointment and duties of the Resident Medical Officer had not been finally confirmed, though no doubt the candidates would have been familiar with what was expected at similar institutions. In the event the House Surgeon was required to be unmarried, to have good testimonials and be a member of one of the colleges of surgeons and also of the Apothecaries Society. Besides board and lodging at the Hospital he would receive a salary of £60 per annum. He would instruct up to two apprentices, if there were such, for which he would receive an additional £10 a year for each apprentice. The House Surgeon would also act as Hospital Secretary until such time as the Court of Governors appointed a separate Secretary. He would be expected to receive accident and emergency cases by both day and night, keep records for all in-patients and out-patients received and discharged, keep a book of the patients' diets, prepare and supervise the preparation of all medicines, visit the wards each morning and report to the physicians and surgeons. He would be in charge of all the medical stores, pharmaceutical apparatus and surgical instruments belonging to the Hospital. He would bleed and do 'all common surgical offices' when required by the physicians and surgeons and, if necessary, visit out-patients in their homes and be available to vaccinate out-patients if requested. On days when the clergy were not attending the Hospital he would read prayers in the main wards in the mornings.

Mr Harrinson's and Mr Boulger's letters were published in the Reading papers each week until the election, as were the various testimonials which had been received on their behalf. Mr Harrinson submitted 16 excellent testimonials including one signed by 10 physicians and surgeons of the Reading Dispensary. Mr George May, a Reading surgeon, wrote that Mr Harrinson had been his assistant for nearly four years, and that: 'By his uniform conduct and character and high professional attainments, I believe him to be eminently qualified to fulfill the important duties of House Surgeon at the Royal Berkshire Hospital.'

Mr Edward Boulger also submitted 16 testimonials, one of which was from the physicians and surgeons of the Surrey Dispensary and another from Sir Astley Cooper, Sergeant Surgeon to Her Majesty. Like Mr Harrinson, he had attended the Webb Street Medical School where he was apprenticed to Mr George Pilcher, and many of those who taught him wrote enthusiastically of his ability. He had studied in Paris for a while and two of his testimonials were from surgeons whose courses he had attended on anatomy and surgery. Both candidates were well qualified for the position of House Surgeon at the Hospital.

On March 9th a letter from Mr Harrinson addressed to the Governors and Subscribers was published withdrawing himself as a candidate for House Surgeon, as he had now entered into partnership with Mr George May. One candidate alone remained and at the election on April 15th a show of hands unanimously agreed to the appointment of Mr Edward Boulger to fill the office of House Surgeon, Apothecary and Secretary to the Royal Berkshire Hospital.

Proposed Union with the Reading Dispensary
The original report delivered by Dr Ring's Committee to the Governors of the Reading Dispensary in 1836 had suggested that the funds of the Dispensary should be used for the maintenance of the proposed Hospital. Nothing further appears to have been decided until December 1838 when a special General Meeting of the Governors of the Dispensary resolved unanimously that: 'The estate and effects of this Institute should be annexed to those of the Royal Berkshire Hospital for the purpose of carrying on a united Institution as a Hospital and Dispensary.' The meeting then set up a committee of five Governors to confer with the Hospital Committee to make all the necessary arrangements.

At the Annual General Meeting of the Reading Dispensary held the following month in January 1839 the Committee gave details of the arrangement which they recommended 'in consequence of a union of the two bodies'. The main points referred to the privileges subscribers to the Dispensary should enjoy compared to those subscribing to the Hospital, and also the recommendation that the physicians and surgeons of the Dispensary, in recognition of their 'valuable gratuitous services', should be appointed to the same situation in the Hospital.

These recommendations were by no means unanimously accepted.

Some people felt this would mean the Dispensary would be 'interfering' with the running of the Hospital, and others voiced most strongly the view that a hospital with 50 beds did not need the large staff of three physicians and six surgeons. It was suggested that three physicians and three surgeons would be adequate for the Royal Berkshire Hospital. At this time all the medical officers at the Dispensary were honorary physicians and surgeons; they received no salary for their work at that institution nor would they do so at the Hospital. Their private practices provided their means of remuneration and funded their work at the Dispensary. A similar position at the Hospital was sought after as a means of obtaining wider medical experience, with facilities for research and treatment difficult to find elsewhere.

In spite of these differences of opinion a majority of both the Dispensary and Hospital subscribers voted to accept the recommendations for the union of the two institutions. However, when it was suggested that such a union might not be legal, the Dispensary Committee and also Mr Edward Vines, Jr, a solicitor who had raised this legal point, decided that it would be wise to take Counsel's opinion.

On February 20th, 1839 a most crucial meeting of the Dispensary Governors and Subscribers was held in the Town Hall to discuss the legal opinions. When it became evident that in the present circumstances it would be 'unsafe' to transfer the Dispensary property and funds to the use of the Hospital, the following resolution was moved:

'In consequence of the establishment of the Royal Berkshire Hospital it is no longer desirable to keep on foot the Dispensary as a separate Institution, that the subscriptions therefore be discontinued or transferred to the Hospital, that the property be transferred to the Hospital, that the trustees be requested so to transfer it and, if necessary, application be made to the Court of Chancery to sanction such a transfer.'

This produced a heated discussion and Mr Vines's amendment to abandon the proposals was defeated by a considerable majority. The original motion was 'triumphantly carried'.

Following the decisions taken at this meeting, a petition was drawn up and presented to the Court of Chancery in April asking that the Reading Dispensary might be authorised to transfer its funds and property to the Hospital or that the petition might be referred to the Master to consider. Mr Vines and others against the petition submitted their objections. It had been hoped that the case would be heard within a short time, but owing to various delays the petition did not come before the Vice Chancellor until June 3rd, by which time the Hospital had already been opened.

The delay in deciding the legality of the union of the Dispensary and the Hospital caused considerable difficulty with the appointment of the permanent medical staff. On Dr Cowan's suggestion it was arranged that the medical staff from the Dispensary would act as provisional staff to the Hospital until the decision of the Court of Chancery was obtained. These appointments could then be confirmed if the union took place; otherwise a public election would be held. In the meantime the Hospital would not be 'materially inconvenienced as regards medical assistance by the delay of the law'.

On May 4th it was decided that the formal opening of the Hospital would take place on Monday May 27th. This left just over three weeks in which to organise the occasion and to complete all outstanding business concerning the Hospital itself.

A sub-committee was appointed to arrange the opening formalities and celebrations. All the plans which had been so meticulously worked out for the ceremony of laying the foundation stone could now be put to use for the Hospital opening. Those who had not been repaid for their cancelled dinner could use their 5/– tickets at the dinner planned to celebrate the opening. There would be a service at St Lawrence's Church with a sermon preached by the Revd George Hulme and all the excitement of a procession to the completed building. The Hospital would be declared open with solemnity, dignity and a sense of occasion.

The First Court of Governors
In the meantime there were still administrative matters to be attended to. On May 6th a special meeting, chaired by the Mayor, was held in the Town Hall to elect officials for the management of the Hospital. This was the first 'Court of Governors' and those eligible to attend were subscribers of 30 guineas or more, termed 'Life Governors', and annual subscribers of two guineas or more, who were termed 'Governors'. Those who had been a Governor one day before the time of voting were eligible to vote at this election of officers.

The meeting appointed Lord Sidmouth and Richard Benyon de Beauvoir Esq. Vice Patrons and Lady Sidmouth Vice Patroness in recognition of their great generosity to the Hospital. Later, Mr Richard Benyon de Beauvoir also accepted the office of President.

Twelve 'noblemen and gentlemen' were elected Vice Presidents and this was followed by the election of the Board of Management. This consisted of the President, Vice Presidents and Treasurer as ex-officio members and 18 Governors, nine of whom had to be residents of Reading. Many of those elected to the Board of Management had been actively engaged in the establishment of the Hospital and some were also associated with the Reading Dispensary. They were all distinguished people in various fields including banking, the law and the Church, and their wide range of experience would be of great service in the running of the Hospital. The Board would meet each week and its duties would include the admission of in-patients besides all matters concerning the running of the Hospital, the conduct of its officers and servants, its government and finance. One third of their number would be replaced at the Annual Court each year.

From this point the Board of Management took over the administration of the Hospital, but it was agreed that the Committee which had been in charge of building and equipping the Hospital would continue to meet until 'the whole works undertaken by their order were completed and the accounts passed and settled'.

Election of a Matron
The Board of Management met three times before the Hospital was opened. Their first meeting was concerned with the appointment of a Matron. Six candidates had applied since the position was advertised the previous month. Two of these were excluded, as they did not meet the condition that applicants should be unmarried and have no family commitments. The duties of the Matron included being responsible for all the hospital goods and furniture, being in charge of inventories, diet sheets and patients' effects, organising the provisions and supervising the nurses and servants. She had charge of the keys of the outer doors of the Hospital and was responsible for seeing that they were kept locked at stated times. She had to supervise not only the conduct of the nurses and servants but also the patients, to see that none were absent, that they knew the rules and attended Chapel if fit to do so. If the clergy were not available she would say prayers in the women's wards each morning. She was required to sleep in the Hospital and never be absent at the same time as the House Surgeon. She would be paid a salary of £30 a year in addition to her board and lodging at the Hospital.

The testimonials of two of the candidates were published in the papers. Mrs Sophia Hogg submitted seven testimonials in support of her application. Many of these referred to her work at St George's Hospital, London, whose Matron, Miss Steel, gave her an excellent recommendation. She had known Mrs Hogg for nearly 20 years and during that time 'had an opportunity of witnessing her intelligence and superiority in the management of domestic affairs'. She believed that there were 'few women who could compete with her in economy and the superintendence of a public establishment'.

Mrs Mary Cox had been working under the Matron of the Radcliffe Infirmary, Oxford, for six months and was able to enclose a most impressive list of testimonials 'from the medical men of the Hospital and from the most respectable characters in Oxford and its neighbourhood'. The Revd Vaughan Thomas, B.D., noted 'her attention to her moral and religious duties' and Mr C. Wingfield, Surgeon, felt the Royal Berkshire Hospital would be 'fortunate if they obtained the services of Mrs Cox'. A third letter signed by no less than 41 eminent Oxford people, ranging from the Vice Chancellor of the University to the surgeons at the Radcliffe Infirmary, the Master of Balliol and Thomas Badcock, Wine Merchant, stated quite simply: 'We the undersigned beg leave to recommend Mrs

23

Treasurer's Report of the Receipts and Disbursements on account of the Building Fund.

RECEIPTS.	£	s.	d.	£	s.	d.
Subscriptions received during the Year 1836	9744	5	6			
Ditto .... ditto 1837	1500	12	6			
Ditto .... ditto 1838	1138	6	0			
Ditto .... ditto 1839	35	4	0	12418	8	0
Surplus of Grand Jury Dinner	7	2	6			
Lectures by Dr. Cowan	19	7	6			
Surplus of Oratorio and Ball, by Mr. Binfield	80	0	0			
B. Clark for Rent of part of Garden	1	18	0	108	8	6
Difference of Interest and Premium on India Bonds purchased and sold,	842	16	4			
Difference of Interest & Premium on Exchequer Bills purchased & sold,	21	6	5	864	2	9
				£ 13,390	19	3

WILLIAM STEPHENS, Treasurer,

DISBURSEMENTS.	£	s.	d.	£	s.	d.
Building Account.						
James Plumley, amount of Contract	7820	0	0			
Henry Briant, commission on ditto	391	0	0			
Thomas Rumble, Clerk of the Works	304	19	0	8515	19	0
Extra Work on Building Account.						
James Plumley for mason's work	1671	9	1			
W. S. Darter, for plumber's work to hot water apparatus, baths, &c.	476	10	10			
W. S. Darter, for painting	63	11	4			
T. Lawrance, for carpenter's work	134	14	4			
Huntley, for iron work, 2l. 2s.; Paint, 1l. 19s.	4	1	0			
H. Briant, for commission on extra work	109	9	0	2459	15	7
Premiums for plans	50	0	0			
G. Basevi, jun., consulting architect	30	13	0	80	13	0
Insurance of building				39	7	6
Furniture and fittings for hospital				1246	14	5
Printing, advertising, stationery, and books				157	11	11
Garden.						
Turf, shrubs, and laying out the garden	146	17	3			
J. Plumley, for mason's work	3	10	0	150	7	3
J. Trendell, for silver trowel and engraving ditto				8	7	0
Brass plate and engraving ditto				10	17	0
F. Hawkes, for valuations				6	5	2
J. J. Blandy, and W. Chisholme, for law expences				151	0	7
Messrs. Williams and Palmer, for coals				12	15	9
H. Briant for sundries, 8d. 1s. 6d.; T. Rumble, for ditto, 4l. 1s.				12	19	6
W. Golding, for use of Town Hall				8	5	0
Incidental payments by the committee				15	17	5
Stock and crops, and injury to crops on land	108	16	0			
Fixtures in cottage pulled down	12	7	0	121	3	0
Balance in hands of Treasurer				393	0	2
				£ 13,390	19	3

We, the undersigned, the Auditors of the Royal Berkshire Hospital, do hereby certify, that we have examined all the items in the foregoing Account, which we find to be correct, and that there is a Balance of three hundred and ninety-three pounds and two pence in the hands of the Treasurer.

Witness our hands this 23rd day of April, 1840,

THOMAS HOGGARD,   ROBERT RHODES.

Mary Cox of this City as a fit and proper person to be appointed Matron of the newly established infirmary in Reading. She has for many years had the sole management of her mother's house, the Kings Arms Inn, Oxford, and she is in our opinion highly qualified to discharge the duties of the above-mentioned office.'

The Board of Management elected Mrs Hogg who obtained 16 votes as against Mrs Cox who obtained six.

It was decided that for the time being the domestic establishment would consist of two nurses, one for the men's ward and one for the women's ward, each of whom would be paid £12 per year. There would also be a cook with wages of £15 a year and a housemaid who would be given £8 a year. A porter would also be necessary, and he would receive £20 a year and be supplied with a hat and coat. They would all obtain board and lodgings at the Hospital but would be required to supply their own tea and sugar. A gardener would also be employed for a wage of 15/– per week. As well as his outside work, he would be expected to make himself generally useful in the house.

Two days before the Hospital was formally opened an advertisement was placed in the local papers. The Board of Management would receive applications for the situation of porter, cook, housemaid and nurses on Tuesday, June 4th at 11 o'clock at the Hospital. 'None but parties having the most undeniable testimonials will be treated with.'

All was now ready. The Hospital would open with a resident staff of the House Surgeon and the Matron and a provisional honorary medical staff of three physicians and six surgeons. The Hospital would be brought into service gradually. Accident cases only would be admitted from Tuesday, May 28th and a week later on June 4th general admissions and out-patients would be received. The ceremony and rejoicing of the formal opening would provide a suitable climax for all the work of the past three years and give recognition to the generosity of the many people who had made it possible to build the Hospital. On Tuesday, May 28th 1839 the long and challenging working life of the Hospital would begin.

PATRONESSES.

HER MOST GRACIOUS MAJESTY THE QUEEN.

HER MAJESTY THE QUEEN DOWAGER.

VICE PATRONESS.

THE RIGHT HONOURABLE VISCOUNTESS SIDMOUTH.

VICE PATRONS.

THE RIGHT HONOURABLE VISCOUNT SIDMOUTH.

RICHARD BENYON DE BEAUVOIR, Esq.

PRESIDENT.

RICHARD BENYON DE BEAUVOIR, Esq.

VICE PRESIDENTS.

MARQUIS OF DOWNSHIRE	R. PALMER, Esq. M.P.
SIR H. RUSSELL, Bart.	T. RING, Esq. M.D.
HON. GENERAL BRODRICK	W. STEPHENS, Esq.
G. H. ELLIOTT, Esq.	J. WALTER, Esq.
REV. G. HULME	J. WHEBLE, Esq.
W. MOUNT, Esq.	REV. S. W. YATES

BOARD OF MANAGEMENT

(Elected May 6, 1839)

M. G. THOYTS, Esq. *High Sheriff*	E. HODGES, Esq. *Mayor of Reading*
REV. H. C. CHERRY	C. S. ROBINSON, Esq.
H. CLIVE, Esq.	CAPTAIN MURRAY, R.N.
R. J. T. PERKIN, Esq.	T. HOGGARD, Esq.
W. MERRY, Esq.	Mr. ALDERMAN GARRARD
REV. J. E. AUSTEN LEIGH	Mr. ALDERMAN RICKFORD
H. GREENWAY, Esq.	Mr. W. BLANDY
G. BEAUCHAMP, Esq.	Mr. H. F. LETCHWORTH
CAPTAIN GARTH, R.N.	Mr. RHODES

The early Hospital and its first officials

2

THE EARLY YEARS
1839 TO 1855

ESTABLISHING THE SYSTEM

There were two admissions to the Hospital during the first week and both were the result of accidents on the Great Western Railway line. Had the Hospital wanted to select as its first patient someone who would provide medical interest, surgical challenge and human drama they could not have found a more suitable case than that of George Earley.[1] The injury to his arm (a compound comminuted fracture of the humerus) made amputation at the shoulder necessary, and after consultation it was agreed by the medical staff that Mr Young should perform this operation.

In those days operations were seldom undertaken. Apart from the pain for the patients in the absence of anaesthetics, the danger of death from shock, loss of blood or infection made a successful outcome by no means a certainty. The operation was performed on Thursday May 30th in the new operating theatre furnished with its strong table and red oilcloth on the floor. With no prior scrubbing-up or sterilisation of instruments, no anaesthetic, no masks, gowns or rubber gloves, Mr Young amputated George Earley's arm at the shoulder joint with a mixed circular and flap incision, assisted by the House Surgeon and watched by an audience of all the medical men of the town.

George Earley was a strong 15-year old. The papers described him as a 'fine youth', and two days after the operation they were able to report that the patient was progressing favourably and doing as well as could be expected. Nine weeks later he was able to leave the Hospital with the Board of Management pronouncing him 'a most excellent character'. Medical interest and public approbation had been secured quite dramatically with this first admission to the Hospital.

James Wetman's admission, with a fractured leg, the day after George Earley's operation, was less spectacular. Nevertheless this accident, caused by the fall of a mass of earth, demonstrated once again to the subscribers and public alike, through the medium of the local papers, how important a hospital could be in the life of a community.

The following week the Hospital was open for the reception of both in-patients and out-patients. At this stage only two wards were opened and a

The first page of the In-patients Admission Book, 1839

male nurse, Alfred Cotton, was appointed to Benyon Ward for men and Nurse Hollis was put in charge of Victoria Ward for women. As more patients were admitted, two other nurses, Nurse Maskell and Nurse Page, were employed and Sidmouth Ward was brought into use as the second men's ward and Adelaide the second women's ward. The ground floor wards became surgical wards and those on the first floor, medical wards.

It was to be several months before the Hospital became fully operational. In the second week only one in-patient was admitted and the following week there were a further eight. By the end of July a total of 59 in-patients had been received, with a maximum of 38 patients in the Hospital at any time. Of these admissions 49 were men and ten were women, 46 were surgical cases (ten of which were railway-line accidents) and 13 were medical cases. The patients came from a wide area with a great variety of complaints, ranging from heart disease, meningitis, neuralgia, ulcerated legs, impetigo, aneurism and tumours. Three operations were performed, all of which were amputations as a result of railway-line accidents.

The out-patients during this period were less numerous and by the end of July there were 29 on the books. Twenty-four of these were men and five were women, 17 were surgical cases and 12 were medical. Once again there was a large number of railway-line accidents and, of the 11 treated, three were suffering from gunpowder burns. As with the in-patients, they came from a wide area with a great variety of illnesses and injuries, including diseased kidneys, fever, contusions, fractures, heart complaints, conjunctivitis and hepatitis. One case of 'hypochonderiasis' was diagnosed.

To obtain admission as either an in-patient or out-patient, applicants had to be deemed 'worthy objects of charity' and be recommended by a benefactor (someone who gave a lump sum to the Hospital) or an annual subscriber. An exception was made for accidents and cases of emergency which were admitted day and night without any recommendation.

The privilege of recommending patients for treatment was linked directly to the sum donated or subscribed:

Benefactors giving	*Annual subscribers giving*	*In-patients sponsored per year*	*Out-patients always on the books*
15 gns	1 gn	0	1
30	2	1	1
45	3	1	2
60	4	2	2
75	5	2	3

The physicians and surgeons of the Hospital had the same privilege as an annual subscriber of two guineas. Ministers making congregational or parochial collections of over four guineas had the same right of recommending patients as an annual subscriber of two guineas. The

ADMISSION TICKET FOR IN-PATIENTS.

TO THE BOARD OF MANAGEMENT OF THE ROYAL BERKSHIRE HOSPITAL.

GENTLEMEN,

I recommend for examination _____

of the parish of _____

whom I believe to be a real object of Charity, and desire _____ *may be*

admitted an IN-PATIENT of the Hospital, if duly qualified.

Age ...... *Subscriber's Name* _____

Occupation ...

How long ill ... *Residence* _____

_____ *day of* _____ 18 _____

This Ticket must be sent with the Patient on a TUESDAY MORNING, by Eleven o'clock; if presented later than Eleven o'clock, it cannot be attended to.

It is requested that Subscribers will direct the Patients to be sent in as clean as possible; and every Patient is expected to bring sufficient change of Linen, or a Guinea in lieu thereof.

Subscribers are earnestly requested to ascertain that they have vacancies before they give recommendations.

All Subscriptions are to be paid in advance, and be understood to commence on the 1st January in each year, and no Subscriber's recommendation can be acted on, while his or her Subscription is in arrear.

By the Rules of the Hospital, no Person labouring under confirmed Consumption, primary Venereal Symptoms, Confirmed Epilepsy, Measles, Scarlet Fever, Small Pox, Itch, or Whooping Cough, or apprehended to be in a dying state, or judged incurable; no Persons disordered in their intellects, no children under seven years of age, except in cases of severe accident, or requiring surgical operation (or except upon a special report of the examining Physician or Surgeon, when the Board may, if they think fit, admit any such case), and no woman in an advanced state of pregnancy can be admitted as In-patients, or, if inadvertently received, be allowed to remain; neither, without the unanimous consent of the Board, shall any case of club-foot be admitted; and all cases of secondary Syphilis shall be specially reported by the Medical Officers to the Board before admission.

Subscribers are earnestly requested, previous to sending in very severe cases, to take the opinion of some medical man in their neighbourhood, as to the fitness of the case for Hospital treatment.

N.B.—Linen Rags will always be deemed an acceptable present.

(left margin, rotated:) This Ticket must not to be used for Begging a Change of Linen with them. Patients must bring

---

President and Vice Presidents were required to be benefactors of at least 75 guineas or an annual subscriber of five guineas.

There were other stipulations for those wishing to be treated in the Hospital. No applicants would be considered who were in a position to pay for their treatment. No one would be admitted as an in-patient who could equally well be treated as an out-patient. No one would be accepted as an out-patient who was already in receipt of parochial relief or who was a living-in servant. Again, an exception to these conditions was made in cases of accident and emergency but if these patients were able to pay for their treatment it was expected that the Hospital would be reimbursed.

Certain conditions and illnesses were also excluded. Consumption, primary venereal diseases, confirmed epilepsy, smallpox and patients with itch came into this category. Also those 'apprehended to be in a dying state', the incurable, the mentally sick and children under the age of seven (except in severe accident cases or those requiring surgical operations). Women in an advanced state of pregnancy were most definitely not to be accepted as in-patients and if by any chance one were admitted she should be removed as quickly as possible. Maternity work was not the concern of the Hospital but of parish midwives, and if necessary local doctors were able to attend cases of difficult childbirth.

People wishing to be admitted as in-patients were required to attend the Hospital on Tuesdays at 11 a.m. where the House Surgeon and honorary medical staff for that week would examine them and, if they were thought suitable, would recommend them for admission to the Board of Management who held their weekly meetings that day. Each patient had to bring a special form of admission signed by the recommender who stated that he or she believed the applicant to be a proper object of charity. A second part of the form was addressed to the Treasurer and had to be signed by a person of substance who promised to pay all expenses which might arise from the removal or burial of the patient. Those to be admitted were expected to come to the Hospital as clean as possible and to bring with them a change of linen or one guinea in lieu.

Out-patients were seen at the Hospital on Mondays, Wednesdays and Saturdays between 10 a.m. and 11 a.m., when they would be examined by the honorary physician and surgeon attending that day. They were required to bring a similar form of recommendation and also a pint bottle and gallipot, or pill box, for their medicines.

Treatment having been completed, Rule 74 was applicable: 'When in-patients are discharged cured or greatly relieved, they shall be enjoined by the Chairman of the Board to return thanks to Almighty God in their respective places of worship, and also, whether relieved or not, to the persons who recommended them to the Hospital, for both of which purposes printed papers shall be delivered to them.' A similar letter of thanks was also given to out-patients on their discharge. Anyone failing to obtain these papers was entered in the records as being 'irregular', and classified with those who had been dismissed for bad conduct or who had left the Hospital without authority. Rule 74 was regarded as being of great importance.

The Hospital Building

The Hospital in 1839 consisted of the front block facing the London Road with the main entrance at the top of the steps as it is today. Behind this were two wings, each containing two wards running from north to south. The Hospital had been designed to keep the male and female patients completely apart with separate wings, bathrooms and walks in the grounds. The men's side of the Hospital was situated in the East Wing with Benyon Ward on the ground floor and Sidmouth Ward above. The women's side was the West Wing with Victoria Ward on the ground floor and Adelaide Ward above. All four wards were named after the first benefactors.

The Hospital had been planned to accommodate 60 patients and be capable of enlargement to 100. At the beginning only 50 beds were made available with a maximum of 14 in each of the four wards. There were also other rooms which were capable of being used as small wards for eye patients, for bleeding or for any special requirement which might occur.

The front building contained the surgeons' and physicians' consulting and waiting rooms, the Dispensary, the House Surgeon's rooms, the Matron's rooms, the staff dining-room, the Secretary's room, the porter's room, the stores and the servants' bedroom. In the basement area on the east side was the laundry with washroom, coppers and drying equipment. On the west side was the kitchen area with larder, cellar, bread room, pantry and scullery.

Halfway up the main staircase from the entrance hall was the door to the room used by the medical staff as a library, study and museum. Today all that remains of this room is the handsome door with brass handles and decorations which leads to the organ loft of the chapel. Below the library, reached by a door which now leads to the chapel itself, was the post-mortem room and, next to it, the mortuary.

There were two stairways on each side of the building leading from the basement to the ground floor and first floor. The operating theatre was at the back of the building on the east side between the stairs and Benyon Ward. It was a small, bare room, lit mainly by light from the roof. In the middle was the operating table and on one side an area in which those watching the surgeon could stand or sit.

The Board Room was at the front of the building on the first floor above the entrance hall. It was an impressive room capable of seating 24 people round the table, and it was here that the Board of Management held their weekly meetings. The building had been well designed for its purpose and once in use lived up to all expectations.

The Role of the Board of Management
The Board of Management met each week on Tuesday mornings. Between 10 and 20 members normally attended with Mr Richard Benyon de Beauvoir, the President of the Hospital, taking the chair at most of the meetings. This Committee was answerable to the Governors and was the centre of administration. It ensured the efficient running of the Hospital with due regard to the resources available and the various demands that had to be met.

Each year two members were nominated Auditors and were put in charge of examining the books and accounts prior to these being passed for payment by the Board. Each month two other members were appointed Visitors and it was their duty to inspect the Hospital at least once a week and to note the condition of the establishment, its cleanliness, the efficiency of the staff and servants. A list of eight questions was drawn up which were to be asked and a special Visitors' Book was supplied for a brief report to be made after each inspection. Two ladies, who were also Governors, were asked to inspect the women's wards. White wands were supplied to enable the Visitors to be identified. The Visitors' Book was produced at the weekly Board meetings, the contents noted and, if necessary, acted upon. The whole Board inspected the Hospital every three months.

One of the first tasks of each Board meeting was to authorise the admission of those patients who the House Surgeon and medical staff recommended should receive treatment. Two beds were always kept available for accident cases. After every meeting the Board sent the local papers a list of the number of patients admitted and discharged and the total remaining in the Hospital. It was important that the public should know what was happening in the Hospital, and the local papers were glad to add their own reports of any interesting admissions, especially in cases of accidents.

The House Surgeon was required to keep a special Journal which was also produced at each meeting. In this were kept particulars of admissions, including those coming through accidents or emergencies between the weekly Board meetings, and details of those cases fit to be discharged. Any drugs, appliances or instruments requested by the medical staff had to be entered in this book and could only be purchased with the sanction of the Board. Should one of the medical staff have obtained something without permission, he was usually left to pay the cost. Registers of daily admissions of in-patients and out-patients were also kept by the House Surgeon and over the years more details were added, so that useful statistical information could be obtained and trends noted in various illnesses and treatments.

After a patient had been in the Hospital for eight weeks a report had to be submitted to the Board by the medical staff to determine whether the treatment was being successful and worth continuing. If a cure was unlikely the patient was usually discharged. If the patient remained, monthly reports were required thereafter.

The medical staff were expected to report their meetings to the Board but it soon became evident that they were not prepared to do this, though they would let the Board know of anything important that arose. Case books were also kept, and it was a matter of debate whether these belonged to the Hospital or to the individual doctors.

The Board advertised for tenders for the supply of provisions and drugs. Quarterly contracts were negotiated for most items except coal, milk and drugs, which were obtained through annual contracts. Prices were competitive and the Board was very particular about the quality of the goods supplied. The Visitors frequently reported that certain items were not up to standard and the supplier was immediately contacted and often changed. In 1839 beer was bought for 1/– a gallon, bread at 7¾d per 4-lb loaf, milk at 9½d a gallon, meat at 6d per pound and best Bath coal at 25/– per ton delivered. Over the next 15 years there were certain variations in price owing to trade and harvest problems, and in 1855 the Hospital was paying 10d per gallon for beer, 8d for a 4-lb loaf of bread, 7d for 1 lb of

QUESTIONS.

1.
Was every part of the house and premises clean and in good order? or in what parts did you observe any neglect in this respect?

2.
Did every person appear to be in his proper place, and in the regular discharge of his proper duty? or where did you observe any irregularity or confusion?

3.
Did the provisions appear to be wholesome and good, and properly kept? Did you examine the bread and beer?

4.
Did you ascertain whether the provisions were properly weighed and distributed according to the directions of the Medical Officers?

5.
Were the beds in proper condition, and the table of regulations hung up in each ward?

6.
Did you enquire from the patients themselves, and when they were under no restraint, whether they had any cause of complaint?

7.
Did you require the House Surgeon and Matron to attend you? and did you enquire whether any instance of irregular conduct, either on the part of the patients or servants, had come within their knowledge? and what answers did they give to these or any other questions you put to them?

8.
Have you any observation to make? On what day did this inspection of the Hospital take place?

VISITORS' OBSERVATIONS.

Tuesday 11th Jan.y 1842

Having been appointed as Visitor for the Month

Seeing my absence from home & without any previous knowledge it was not in my power to attend till this day to provide a substitute

[signature] Chas. C. Brickham

Wednesday 12th Jan.y

attended at the Hospital this morning. Mr Potter gave Mr Horgan & Mr Rhodes [illegible] when it was [illegible] upon that the whole of the [illegible] made in the hospital should be laid [illegible] for what the establishment should be [illegible] with the [illegible] of labour for our method [illegible] & instructions were given from Mr Potter accordingly

[signature] Chas. C. Brickham

Thursday 13th Jan.y 1842

The Water Tank over the little Vestry burst and the ceiling falling upon the Cork it stopped the underneath [illegible] at the moment it was considered very [illegible]

Saturday 15th

A Woman admitted in the Victoria Ward very severely burnt & since time & then was brought in from [illegible] his arm [illegible] dreadfully cruelly [illegible] by Machinery—

The Boy Collin not yet discharged

in other respects all going on favorably

[signature] Chas. C. Brickham

Tuesday 18th Jan.y 1842

The House Surgeon states that it would be very desirable that [illegible] should be laid on in the [illegible] company as an emergency occasions they are much in [illegible] for sufficient light—[signature] Chas. C. Brickham

Thursday 20 Jan.y

visited the Ward the Lady [illegible] inspected Adelaide & Victoria Wards & found all satisfactory

[signature] Chas. C. Brickham

Saturday 22nd

Mr Hozgard & self visited the Ward & found all correct

[signature] Chas. C. Brickham

J. NASH, PRINTER, READING.

Extract from the Visitor's Book, January 1842

meat, 8d for a gallon of milk and 26/– for one ton of best Newcastle coal. Altogether £496 was spent on provisions in 1839 with 304 in-patients being treated and in 1855, when there were 748 in-patients, this had increased to £1,112.

For many years most drugs and items for the Dispensary were obtained from London but wherever possible local chemists were used for certain items, with those subscribing to the Hospital sharing the custom between them. In 1841 it was decided that the Great Western Railway would no longer be used to bring the supplies from London as Josey, the carrier, could do the job for 1/6d per hundredweight and deliver the empty packages back to London free of charge. Road versus rail was an issue even in those days.

By 1855 the local chemists had become more competitive in their prices and frequently the main annual contracts were given to Mr Cooper instead of the London suppliers. The annual dispensary bill in 1855 was £341, having been £397 in 1839, when there were additional expenses including £130 for a chest of surgical instruments.

Reports and records were kept of practically every aspect of hospital life. The Matron was required to keep a Provisions Book noting every item obtained and the number of people fed in the Hospital each week. She also had to keep separate records of the consumption of beer, potatoes, meat and dripping. Other hospitals were frequently contacted and used for comparison. The Royal Berkshire Hospital, with 50 beds, was found to be using as much soap as the Radcliffe Infirmary which had 120 beds, and the meat consumption at one time was between 100 per cent and 200 per cent greater than that of the Charing Cross Hospital. The Board of Management kept a tight hold on all expenditure and the Matron's books had to be produced at every meeting.

The Board itself kept minutes of all its meetings and at the Annual Court of Governors, with the Treasurer and the House Surgeon it submitted reports summarising the work of the Hospital over the previous twelve months.

The Reading Dispensary Petition
On June 3rd, 1839 the Petition of the Reading Dispensary concerning the transfer of its funds to the Hospital came before the Vice Chancellor in the Court of Chancery. The outcome was eagerly awaited, as the additional capital and income from the Dispensary would be a great help to the Hospital and also the difficulty of appointing a permanent medical staff could be resolved. In the event, the Vice Chancellor dashed all hopes that such a union could ever take place or that the Dispensary funds could be transferred from the one body to the other. He pointed out that it was not in the power of the Court to authorise such a transfer, that it could not be referred to the Master and indeed, under the rules of the two institutions and because of the manner in which the Hospital had been founded, it was impossible that the two could unite. The Governors of the Dispensary had

no power to authorise the extinction of their charity nor to transfer its funds to the Hospital.

The hearing was widely publicised in the local papers. Many people had predicted such an outcome and much bitterness and recrimination resulted. A meeting of the Dispensary Governors was called for June 25th at which their solicitor, Mr J. J. Blandy, reported on the Vice Chancellor's decision. Following this, the Dispensary Chairman formally notified the Board of Management of the outcome. The Board immediately arranged for a Special Court of Governors to be held at the Town Hall on July 29th for the purpose of electing the permanent medical staff of the Hospital.

Election of the Medical Staff

As soon as the proposed union of the Dispensary and the Hospital had been called into question in February 1839, it was realised that an election might have to be held to appoint the medical officers of the Hospital. Within three weeks various surgeons had written to the Governors of the Hospital stating that they intended to offer themselves as candidates should an election prove necessary. All these letters were published in the local papers, and there followed a series of events which, compared with today's methods of appointing staff to the Hospital, can only be described as remarkable.

By mid-March letters of application for the surgical posts had been received from four prospective candidates: Mr T. B. Maurice, Mr George May, Mr F. A. Bulley and Mr T. L. Hinton. The first three were surgeons at the Dispensary and later formed part of the provisional surgical staff when the Hospital opened. Mr Hinton was not associated with the Dispensary but he sent with his letter 12 testimonials which he had used the year before when he was an unsuccessful candidate for one of the Dispensary surgical posts. During the next two months all these letters were regularly published in the local papers and were joined by others from Mr Samuel Harris, Mr John Sutton and Mr T. C. Wood. Mr Workman alone stated that he was not a candidate:

At one time there had been much discussion about the number of medical staff which would be needed at the Hospital. When the rules were finally approved in April it had been decided that the 50-bed hospital should have a medical staff of three physicians and three surgeons. All these would be honorary medical officers and would retain their private practices and other medical work in the town or neighbourhood.

Once the result of the hearing was made known and the date for electing the medical staff was announced for July 29th, the activity of the candidates gathered momentum. Early in July Dr Pritchard Smith, Dr Cowan and Dr Woodhouse, already working in the Hospital as the provisional staff of physicians from the Dispensary, wrote to the Governors saying that they would be ready to form part of the permanent staff. They would not take part in a personal canvass. As they were the only candidates for the three physicians' posts a canvass would have been unnecessary and, in any case, all three were well known with local practices in the area.

Those interested in obtaining the surgical posts re-wrote their letters stating that they were now formal candidates. Three of the original seven withdrew leaving Mr Maurice, Mr May, Mr Bulley and Mr Hinton in the contest.

Over the next month the papers published letters and statements from the candidates, their committees and other interested parties drawing the attention of those eligible to vote to the merits of the respective candidates. The Board of Management in the meantime checked credentials and satisfied itself that all four surgical candidates were well qualified and were Members of the Royal College of Surgeons. The three physicians were all Doctors of Medicine and Dr Pritchard Smith was also a Fellow of the Royal College of Physicians.

It had been decided that in the first election of medical officers those who were subscribers to the Hospital Building Fund of £1 or more prior to February 4th, 1839 and all annual subscribers to the Hospital of £2 or more prior to June 25th, 1839 were eligible to vote. This produced an electorate of some 800 people. Many felt that it was unfair that a Building Fund subscriber of £1 had a vote when an annual subscriber of the same amount did not. The Hospital Secretary published details of all the rules relating to the election and notified the eligible voters to attend the Town Hall at 10 a.m. on Monday, July 29th. Those subscribing £1 to the Building Fund as well as a £2 annual subscription could only have one vote. Two scrutineers were appointed and the ladies were informed they could vote by proxy. The poll would close at 5 p.m.

Mr Maurice, Mr May and Mr Bulley had all been in practice in Reading for many years and all were surgeons at the Dispensary. Mr Maurice had been in practice for 25 years and had succeeded Mr Sherwood, an eminent surgeon, at the Dispensary 13 years before. Mr May, aged 40, had been in practice for 17 years, most of which were as a Dispensary Surgeon. Prior to that he had qualified at Edinburgh University and worked at Guy's and St Thomas's Hospitals. Mr Bulley had been a Dispensary Surgeon for 10 years. Before he came to Reading he had worked at Guy's Hospital for six years and had also done much work among the poor in the local Poor Law Unions. Mr Hinton was not so well known locally, and before coming to Reading had worked in the Radcliffe Infirmary and St Bartholomew's Hospital.

On July 3rd the campaign took an unexpected turn. The Committee conducting the election of Mr Hinton drew attention to the fact that their candidate was the only 'pure surgeon' practising in the County. They believed that only such a surgeon would be eligible to work in any of the London hospitals, and that out of the three surgeons to be elected for the Royal Berkshire Hospital one, at least, should come from this category. Furthermore they wondered if Berkshire should be the only county in the kingdom to reject the claims of this invaluable class of the medical profession.

Mr Bulley and his Committee were incensed and pointed out that Mr Bulley had undergone precisely the same examination at the College of Surgeons as a 'pure surgeon'. It was only the feeling that this limited examination alone was insufficient to justify him in undertaking the complicated and difficult cases frequently occurring in general practice which determined him to extend his studies.

A notice was then published, addressed to the subscribers of the Royal Berkshire Hospital from a subscriber to both the Dispensary and the Hospital, to which there was no reply:

'In an advertisement emanating from Mr Hinton's Committee, inserted in the *Reading Mercury* of last week, great stress is laid on that gentleman's peculiar claims to your suffrages, in consequence of his being, as therein designated, "a pure Surgeon", – meaning, of course, that ignorance of the other important branches of Medical Science, necessarily implies a super-eminent degree of skill in Operative Surgery; this by no means follows – as a knowledge of the human constitution, the state and condition of the Patient, the mode of treatment required previous and subsequent to the performance of an operation, ought always to be taken into the account, and form the serious subjects of the Surgeon's consideration, on whom the success of the measure, and oftentimes the life of the Patient depends. Surely, then, the knowledge resulting from a regular education and practice of the other branches of Medical Science, so far from detracting from, must greatly add to, the recommendation of a Candidate. Now in our Town, there are three Candidates, gentlemen of long standing, high respectability, and undoubted skill – their devotedness to their respective Patients, and unremitting attentions to the Poor, have for a long series of years been under our immediate observation, and in very many instances been the subject of our admiration and gratitude. Surely, then, they have an equal degree of Surgical Skill, and more practical knowledge than that of Mr HINTON, though they happen to range in a wider field, and possess a more extended knowledge of the other branches of Medical Science. This may confidently be said of the three Candidates, Messrs MAURICE, MAY and BULLEY.

It may not perhaps be known to all the Subscribers to the Hospital, that these Gentlemen have been regular attendants at the Medical Dispensary for upwards of Ten years, during which time many Surgical Cases of great difficulty and danger were placed in their hands; and the poor suffering Patients, by their means and Surgical Skill, have been restored to health and strength – they do and will remember their services with tears of gratitude, being their only reward, and all the poor have to bestow.

Surely, then, with three such unexceptionable Candidates for the appointment, would it be consistent – would it not rather be an act of injustice and ingratitude, to exclude either of these, and elect a

Gentleman who, however respectable or skilful, is comparatively a stranger amongst us, and of whom little is known except by his written Testimonials.'

On July 29th the Town Hall was a hive of activity all day. The Special Court was chaired by Mr Robert Palmer, M.P., and at 10 o'clock quickly got down to business. Dr Pritchard Smith, Dr Cowan and Dr Woodhouse were unanimously elected the three physicians and a ballot was then called to elect the surgeons. Until the close of the poll at 5 o'clock there was a steady stream of electors with the four candidates and their supporters doing all in their power to obtain every possible vote. Electors from the country had been advised beforehand that everything would be done to help them to get to the poll, and by the end of the day 762 people had voted, 514 in person and 248 by proxy.

The final state of the poll was: Mr May – 599; Mr Maurice – 524; Mr Bulley – 458; Mr Hinton – 256.

The result was announced the following day and an account was included in the local papers at the end of the week. All the candidates published notices to the electors thanking them for their support and those who had been successful hoped that in the discharge of their duties they would continue to merit the confidence reposed in them. Such an election was never to be held again in the history of the Hospital.

STAFFING AND FUNDING

When the Hospital first opened a cook, kitchen maid, housemaid and gardener were engaged and as more patients were admitted, additional staff were required. A porter was appointed at £20 a year with board and lodgings in the Hospital and was given a blue coat with a red collar and a hat bound with gold lace. A laundry maid was engaged at £12 a year who would also wash the patients' clothes and a barber was employed at £10 a year to shave the patients and cut their hair.

The Board of Management expected the same efficiency and behaviour from the servants in the Hospital as they demanded in their own homes. Incidents of impertinence, disobedience and stealing frequently occurred and the jobs of many were of short duration. Drink and absence from the Hospital without permission were constant problems. A daily allowance of 1½ pints of beer was given to all the staff, including the nurses, but when it was realised that bottles were being brought into the Hospital, thorough searches of all parcels and baskets were regularly carried out. No servant or nurse was supposed to leave the Hospital without permission from the Matron, who in turn was required to notify the Board in writing of anyone missing by day or night. When a porter's lodge was built in 1842 at the west entrance in Redlands Road, it was easier to keep a check on illegal exits and illicit bottles. In the meantime the porter was given an extra pint of beer a day to lessen his desire to obtain supplies from the Row Barge opposite and the cook, 'in consequence of the heat in the kitchen', was given an extra half pint daily.

Disputes between the servants were always referred to the Board. On one occasion the laundry maid was accused of using abusive language when the porter had given her a vapour bath and he then refused to give her another. Both parties were brought before the Board. The laundry maid was admonished for her language and the porter told to obey orders; if the House Surgeon ordered a bath it was to be given.

The servants and nurses were expected to supply their own tea and sugar, but when it was realised that this did not apply to an errand boy who had been engaged at 2/6d a week, there was great ill feeling. The Board resolved the problem by giving the boy a rise of 6d a week and made him supply these items like the rest.

In spite of tight discipline, the women servants declared that they would not sleep in a room on the women's side of the house as it was 'too dull'. They were told in no uncertain terms that the choice was theirs – sleep there or be dismissed.

Over the years these problems became less numerous, although there were still dismissals for improper behaviour between the staff besides stealing and drunkenness. As the Hospital increased in size the Board became less involved with such incidents, which were then handled by the Matron alone.

When Sidmouth and Adelaide wards were brought into use within a few weeks of the Hospital opening, other nurses were needed to supplement the two originally appointed. Applicants were required to supply testimonials when interviewed by the Matron but frequently those applying came from the Union workhouses and were sorry characters.

The role of the nurses in the first half of the nineteenth century was completely different from that of today. They cleaned the wards, served the meals and kept an eye on the patients. They had no qualifications and their only medical duty was to see that the patients took the medicines prescribed by the medical staff. On average they were paid 5/– a week with board and lodgings in the Hospital.

It was not long before the Matron pronounced the male nurse, Alfred Cotton, to be inefficient and 'not a proper person for the appointment'. She believed a woman nurse would be much more satisfactory for the patients. The House Surgeon reported that Alfred Cotton had been negligent in his duty and had fallen asleep when put in charge of a patient in the eye ward. He was dismissed, and the Matron was instructed to engage an efficient replacement.

Finding good nurses was extremely difficult and many were engaged who were quite unsuitable for the job. Nurse Butler was employed although she could neither read nor write, and the House Surgeon was requested to see that the proper medicines were given in her ward. Nurse Wells from the Bradfield Union could neither read nor write but was considered suitable as a night nurse and under laundry maid. Nurse McCormack from the Reading Union workhouse proved totally incapable while Nurse Isabella Jones, who could read and write, was found to be partial to drink. She was discovered intoxicated and eventually dismissed for stealing spirits from the Dispensary. A nurse from the Oxford workhouse left without leave and never returned, and another was engaged until it was realised that she had previously been a barmaid at a nearby public house. One nurse engaged for Sidmouth Ward was found to be almost blind and quite incapable of looking after the patients.

There was a constant change of staff with women being employed part-time to fill the gaps at 1/– a day or 1/6d for day and night attendance. There was, however, a core of two good nurses and Nurse Hollis and Nurse Maskell stayed in the Hospital for many years. Nurse Hollis was put in charge of Benyon Ward, the busy accident ward, and her intelligence and efficiency earned her an additional £1 a year in salary and a pension of 6/– a week when she retired in 1849. By the end of the first year, besides the Matron, there were four nurses employed in the Hospital and in 1855 when there were almost twice the number of patients, their number had been increased to no more than five nurses and one night nurse. The salaries had, by that time, risen to £20 a year for the Benyon Ward nurse and £14 for the junior nurses.

The House Surgeon and the Matron

There were six House Surgeons and four Matrons appointed at the Hospital between 1839 and 1855 and the day-to-day responsibility of running the Hospital was largely in their hands. Problems in the early years were not confined to the servants and nurses. When originally appointed, the House Surgeon, Mr Boulger, was also required to fill the post of Apothecary (Dispenser) and Secretary. As the number of patients increased it was not long before his workload became so heavy that the Board of Management decided to employ a temporary assistant in the Dispensary and Gabriel Ward was engaged at 5/– a week. Shortly after this, Mr Pidgeon's offer to help as an Assistant Secretary with no salary was gratefully accepted and the Board dismissed Gabriel Ward without reference to Mr Boulger. The House Surgeon was indignant and said he must have the same assistance as before, with someone employed solely in the Dispensary and capable of making infusions and concoctions and spreading plasters. He refused to accept a compromise with an errand boy to help in the Dispensary and tendered his resignation, which was accepted. A week later, after expressing his deep regret and accepting the Board's suggestion, the resignation was suspended but it was to be a further two months before Mr Boulger's position in the Hospital was confirmed and his suspension lifted. Errand boy Fox was employed at 2/6d a week to go on errands, clean the surgery and make himself generally useful. The Board had demonstrated that whatever position a member of staff might hold, its authority was paramount.

In 1841 the duties of House Surgeon, Dispenser and Secretary became three quite separate appointments and the House Surgeon was able to give all his time to the treatment of patients. To begin with Mr Pidgeon had not requested any salary, but early in 1840 he accepted the position of Assistant Secretary and Collector with a salary of £20 a year plus 2½ per cent of all subscriptions received by the Treasurer. This became a fixed salary of £52 10s in 1841 and by 1855 the full-time Secretary was receiving a salary of £125 a year.

The physicians and surgeons suggested to the Board in 1841 that a full-time Dispensary Assistant should be employed. Mr May explained that the patients were suffering as the House Surgeon was not having enough time to dress their wounds and on days that out-patients were seen it was increasingly difficult. The Board agreed that an Assistant Dispenser should be appointed to attend daily between 10 a.m. and 3 p.m., except on Sundays. He would be given a salary of £30 a year without board and lodgings and 'should be capable of reading physicians' prescriptions, well accustomed to compound medicines and not require constant superinten-dence'. The London hospitals were approached without success, but eventually an interview was arranged for Mr Huxley, a 'surgery man' from Chatham. When he never arrived enquiries were made and it transpired that after he had left Chatham, he had started drinking on the road, became intoxicated for three days and then returned home. The situation was then advertised and from eighteen applicants, Mr Byfield was selected and started his job in November 1841. From that time onwards the duties of House Surgeon, Dispenser and Secretary were separated.

The Matron's duties were comparable to that of a housekeeper. She was required to supervise the patients and domestic staff and take responsibility for all the provisions and catering. As with the nurses, no particular medical knowledge was needed but ability to deal with sick and injured people was essential. Mrs Hogg remained in the Hospital until 1846 when ill health caused her resignation. For some months the Secretary acted as House Steward during her illness, but when Miss Pritchard was appointed he relinquished all these duties to her.

Miss Pritchard was one of 62 applicants when the post of Matron was advertised in *The Times*, the *Morning Herald* and the local papers at a salary of £40 a year. She had been Matron at the Northampton Asylum and she supplied testimonials from Lord Radnor and the Mayor and Justices of Northampton, besides the Board of Management of Abingdon Abbey Asylum.

Mr Boulger left to go into private practice in Reading in 1840 and was succeeded by Mr James Dunn, who held the position for nine years. He had acted as a locum for Mr Boulger; his testimonials were excellent and he was a Member of the Royal College of Surgeons and Apothecaries Company. Both Mr Dunn and Miss Pritchard left the Hospital in 1849, having secretly married six months before. This information was quite astounding to the Board, who found it impossible to agree to their remaining. They left with the thanks of the Board and testimonials expressing satisfaction for their work at the Hospital. They were succeeded by Mrs Hunt and Mr Moxhay.

Mr Moxhay, aged 28, was one of eight applicants for the post of House Surgeon and one on the short-list of three. He had studied in London under Mr Pilcher and at St Thomas's Hospital. After qualifying he had started his medical career at the Surrey Dispensary, followed by private practice in London. He had had to give this up after three years after suffering a haemorrhage of the lungs. Upon recovery he had become a ship's surgeon on a large passenger ship for two voyages to India. At a Special Court of Governors held on May 29th, 1849 he was unanimously appointed to the post after the other two candidates withdrew 'in consequence of the medical staff having united their influence in favour of Mr Moxhay'. Mrs Hunt was one of five applicants answering the advertisement for Matron and both she and Mr Moxhay took up their appointments at the end of June 1849.

When Mrs Hunt became ill and had to resign in 1850, Mrs Dunn (Miss Pritchard), whose husband had recently died, applied for the post and was interviewed by the Board. By this time she had a small child and although she offered to hire her own nurse to look after the baby, she was not prepared to allow him to sleep out of the Hospital and for this reason the Board felt they could not reappoint her. Mrs Tillbrook, the second choice of candidate before the Board the previous year, was appointed at a salary of £50 a year and was Matron at the Hospital until 1860.

Mr Moxhay was an excellent House Surgeon and it was with much regret that the Board of Management accepted his resignation after five years when he left to go into private practice in 1854. He was succeeded by Mr Drew who, within a few months, also left for private practice and Mr Eubulius Williams was appointed in his place. This last appointment was made by the Board of Management, since it had been decided that in future House Surgeons would no longer be elected by a Court of Governors.

Over the years the House Surgeon and Matron gave stability and continuity to the work of the Hospital and made it possible for the physicians and surgeons to effect many cures and advance new techniques and surgical skills. In the 15 years since the Hospital was opened, the salary of the House Surgeon had remained unaltered at £60 a year and that of Matron had increased from £30 to £50 a year.

The Chaplain

For several months when the Hospital first opened there was no official Chaplain and the Revd George Hulme and other members of the local clergy undertook to look after the spiritual health of the patients and staff. There was no chapel at that time and on Sundays those patients who were fit enough attended a service held in the Board Room.

Early in 1840 the Revd John Field was appointed Chaplain. This was not a full-time post, and Mr Field was given a salary of £50 a year. He took a service in the Hospital on Sundays and Thursdays, read prayers and gave a short address in Benyon Ward and one for the women's wards each week. He was expected to visit all the wards at least twice a week and 'afford spiritual assistance to any of the patients who might desire it'. Mr Field was requested to submit quarterly reports to the Board and in his first he noted the thankfulness of the patients and their good conduct.

When the Board of Management gave their annual report to the Governors in 1842 they pointed out that while appointing a Minister of the Established Church, it should not be forgotten that the Hospital was always open to Ministers of other religions 'whose special services may be required by any of the inmates'. At that time in Reading, as elsewhere, there were several dissenting churches and chapels and the literature and tracts of the non-conformists were highly disapproved of by the Established Church. Mr Field's feelings were no exception and he stressed to the Board the importance of seeing that the literature read by the patients was suitable. All papers and tracts were vetted by him, as were the books placed in the library which he formed for the use of the patients.

Mr Field was Chaplain until 1845 and during this time he had a great influence on the life of the Hospital. He was a far-sighted and sympathetic man. In 1841 he suggested that a Samaritan Fund should be established as he had noted the problems and difficulties that could arise when patients left the Hospital and returned to their homes. Often the good done in the Hospital was undone through lack of food, warmth and clothing. In many cases patients were in need of surgical appliances which they could not afford, and unless these could be supplied there was great hardship and suffering.

Mr Field's proposal was put to the Board who set up a small Committee to look into the question and to investigate the rules of St George's Hospital Convalescent Fund and similar societies attached to the Radcliffe Infirmary and the Middlesex Hospital. It was felt that it would not be possible to establish such a fund without the sanction of a Court of Governors. It was suggested that the Chaplain should go ahead on his own with 'such voluntary assistance as he may be able to obtain in furtherance of so benevolent an object'. Mr Field took their advice, and the Convalescent Fund was established in the autumn of 1841 through the generosity of public subscribers.

Over the years the Convalescent Fund became indispensable to patients leaving the Hospital. With its help they were able to obtain such items as trusses and wooden legs, besides help with food, clothing and fuel. The Hospital Chaplain managed this Fund until 1865 when, with the agreement of the Governors, it was taken over by the Board of Management. It continued to operate until the National Health Service was established in 1948.

In 1844 Mr Field drew attention to the need for more accommodation in the Hospital for Divine service, and the Secretary was instructed to write to 11 provincial hospitals to enquire about their arrangements. Seven hospitals replied and their answers appear to have satisfied the Board that a chapel should be included in any plans adopted to enlarge the Hospital. By the end of that year plans for enlarging the Hospital had been drawn up and include a small chapel at the back of the building behind the library and post mortem room, linked to the main wards by covered ways.

Mr Field resigned as Chaplain in 1845 as his work as Chaplain of the County Gaol was greatly increasing and it was no longer possible for him to hold both positions. The President, Mr Richard Benyon de Beauvoir, wrote to Mr Field expressing the grateful thanks of the Board for all the work he had done for the patients and with the Convalescent Fund. The chapel was completed in February 1846 a few months after the Revd Francis Trench had been appointed the new part-time Hospital Chaplain.

By 1852 the number of patients had greatly increased and it became apparent that a full-time Chaplain was required. To fund this appointment, Mr Richard Benyon de Beauvoir gave a donation of £1,000 to the Hospital with the stipulation that the Chaplain should be a member of the Church of England and that he should hold no other cure of souls. A salary of £70 a year would be provided from the income of the donation. In January 1854, Mr Shewell, a bachelor aged 33 from Collumpton, was elected by the Board as the Hospital's first full-time Chaplain.

Hospital Expansion

Within two years of the opening more accommodation became necessary and in 1841 ten extra beds were brought into use, bringing the total to 60. This did not require any additional building as this expansion had been catered for in Mr Briant's original plans. But it was not long before still more beds were needed, and in May 1842 the Upper Ward was brought into use, making a total of 70 beds. This was almost the limit that could be put on the building and with three additional beds in July 1844 all available space had been exhausted.

In October 1844 it was decided that the enlargement originally contemplated when Mr Briant produced his plans should now be carried out and the two wings at the back would be extended to accommodate a further 40 patients. At the same time a chapel would be built behind the library and post morten room. A public subscription was launched and although well supported, it did not provide sufficient funds to enable the whole work to be completed at once. It was decided to build the chapel and extend the west wing, as the cost of this could be met with the money already raised.

Mr Briant, the original architect, was no longer in practice, having decided to take Holy Orders. In 1842 he had written to the Hospital expressing a desire to carry out any alterations or extensions but at that stage none was contemplated. Mr Rumble, who had worked on the original building and who had designed and built the porter's lodge at the Redlands Road entrance in 1842, had no difficulty in carrying out the extension in

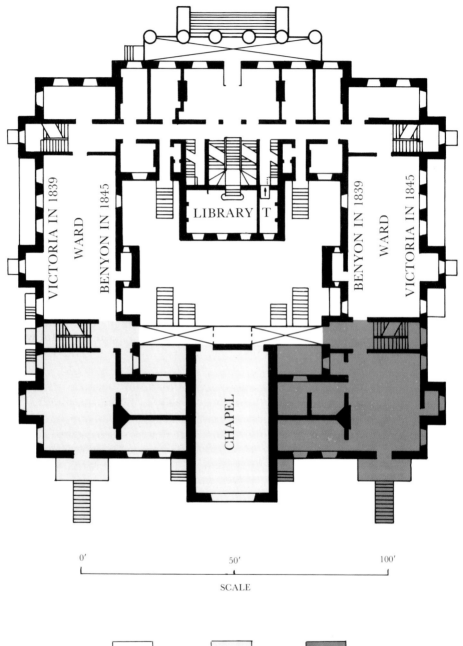

VICTORIA IN 1839

WARD

BENYON IN 1845

LIBRARY T

BENYON IN 1839

WARD

VICTORIA IN 1845

CHAPEL

0'   50'   100'

SCALE

HOSPITAL
IN 1839

EXTENSION
1844/45

EXTENSION
1849/50

T

THEATRE

Plan of the Hospital showing expansion between 1839 and 1855 (Drawn by R. Johnson from Board of Health Map 1853 and O. S. 1879)

conformity with the original designs and he also produced a plan for the chapel. Mr Plumley's tender was accepted and the work was completed in April 1845 at a cost of £2,716, bringing the number of beds to over 80.

This expansion provided two large and four smaller wards on the existing west wing which accommodated the women patients in Victoria and Adelaide wards. However, the problem at that time was the lack of beds for the men and it was therefore decided that the two wings would be transposed. The women's wards, Victoria and Adelaide, went to the east wing and the men's wards, Benyon and Sidmouth, to the now greatly extended west wing.

By 1849 the women's wards had become very overcrowded and additional beds were urgently required. Once again a public appeal was launched and sufficient funds were raised, including a generous donation from Queen Victoria, to enable the east wing extension to be built with room for a further 20 beds. At the same time it was decided to enlarge the laundry, which by now was working to full capacity and was under considerable strain. In April 1850 the work was completed at a cost of £1,600. Within 11 years the Hospital had almost doubled in size.

The Funding of the Hospital
It had been anticipated that the cost of running the 50-bed Hospital would be about £2,000 a year when it was fully operational. At the end of the first financial year on March 25th, 1840 this estimate proved to be fairly accurate. In the 10 months since the Hospital opened £1,990 had been spent with 304 in-patients and 270 out-patients being treated. Over the next 15 years these figures increased substantially and in 1855 the Hospital, which by then had been extended to 90 beds, treated 748 in-patients and 968 out-patients at a cost of £3,168. As more beds were brought into use and more out-patients treated, additional income was required and there was a never-ending problem of obtaining sufficient funds.

Everything possible was done to encourage people to become annual subscribers, but by 1855, with 588 subscriptions totalling £1,634, this source provided only about half the necessary income. Any legacies or donations of over 30 guineas were put into a separate endowment fund in the hope that the interest would eventually be sufficient to meet the ordinary annual expenditure. From 1844 executors who were responsible for money to be applied for charitable purposes were made life Governors for bequests of 30 guineas or more.

Many contributions were made each year apart from annual subscriptions. The Great Western Railway Company gave £105 in 1839 besides an annual subscription of 10 guineas. In that year 61 of the 86 accidents taken to the Hospital were the result of injuries received by those building the railway line. When the Reading to Reigate railway was being constructed in 1848, the Southern Railway Company and its contractor also contributed to the Hospital funds.

The clergy and ministers were urged to make congregational

collections on behalf of the Hospital, but these tended to fluctuate in the first few years and the Churches only gradually became regular contributors. Collecting boxes were placed round the town and in the banks. In the Hospital itself visitors were asked not to give gratuities to the staff, but to place donations in the boxes instead. Special occasions produced donations and in 1839 a public discussion, chaired by Dr Cowan, between the Independent Minister, Mr Legg, and Mr Robert Owen, on 'The Evidence of Christianity' raised £56 11s for the Hospital. In 1842 a special County Ball was held to celebrate the christening of the Prince of Wales and the proceeds, some £148, were sent to the Hospital. It became fashionable to send the proceeds from the County and Hunt Balls to the Hospital, and in 1845 a Hospital Ball was organised which in later years became an annual occasion in the town.

There were many donations from individuals showing the high regard in which the Hospital was held. The profits from a book, *The Philosophy of a Happy Futurity*, were received by the Hospital. Former patients sent contributions and thanks offerings, ranging from several pounds to 'a poor widow's mite' of 1/–. It was not uncommon for conscience money to be sent: 'family fines for late rising, £2 5s'; 'self-imposed fine for furious driving 10/–'; 'self-imposed fine for cruelty £1'. Fines for trespass, injury, cruelty and poaching were often directed to the Hospital, as well as others for 'misconduct'. Contributions were sent from across the County and all were gratefully received.

Reading at this time was expanding rapidly and the advent of the Great Western Railway added to its prosperity as a centre of agriculture and commerce. There was a great variety of industries in the town, including a silk factory, an iron foundry, carriage makers, breweries and instrument makers. There were also more recent family businesses such as Huntley and Palmer and Sutton's, which were becoming very successful enterprises. The men and women working in these factories became increasingly aware of the benefits of the Hospital following accidents at work. In 1843 a mechanics meeting agreed that five young girls should collect weekly subscriptions of 1d in aid of the Hospital, and altogether £5 was raised. The Hospital was much in favour of this and arranged for special cards to be printed for 'Penny Collections'. In 1845, when £7 had been raised, the Hospital was asked if the privilege of recommending patients could be conferred from money raised in this way. The Windsor District of Oddfellows, with a donation of £14, had asked the same question, and it was decided that any person who made an annual collection of not less than six guineas on behalf of a group should have the same privileges as an annual subscriber of two guineas.

Workmen at their separate factories made collections but it was difficult to raise as much as six guineas. The workmen at Messrs. Barrett, Excell and Andrew's factory raised £1 7s in 1846 and those at the Katesgrove Foundry managed to collect four guineas in 1848. Collectors at the County Gaol in 1846 had almost raised six guineas when their collection box was broken open and the contents removed. These collections were the beginning of treatment being obtained for individuals in a group on their own recommendation rather than through an independent subscriber who might have been their employer, their vicar or the owner of their homes. In 1855 the Katesgrove Foundry workers were the only group who had managed to raise the necessary six guineas, but the idea had taken root and in subsequent years other groups at their places of work were able to raise enough money and become regular subscribers on their own account.

The maintenance of most patients admitted to the Hospital was covered by the subscriptions of the people who recommended them. Servants of Governors, however, were treated as in-patients only if their employers agreed to pay 12/- a week. Cases of accident and emergency which were admitted without any recommendation were always expected to contribute if they could afford to do so. At this period up to 200 accident and emergency cases were being admitted each year, and the cost of their maintenance, without the benefit of a recommender's subscription, was a drain on the Hospital's limited finances. When such patients belonged to a benefit club they were asked to give a proportion of their sick pay to the Hospital each week, taking into consideration the demands of any family left at home without a wage earner. In 1849 William Keen was receiving 9/- a week from a Winkfield Club and he agreed to pay 2/- a week. William Newport paid 5/- of the 10/- a week he received from the Duke's Head Benefit Club. Samuel Carpenter was a cabinet making earning between 24/- and 26/- a week; during his illness the Mechanics Benefit Society allowed him 12/6d a week, and 10/- of this was paid to the Hospital. It was always stressed that treatment was free and these payments were contributions towards the maintenance of the patient in the Hospital.

The Poor Law Unions

In many cases the Poor Law Unions became involved, as often those who met with accidents or emergencies had technically made themselves casual paupers, so becoming the responsibility of the parish in which they had gained settlement. In such instances the Hospital requested that the Unions should pay 7/- a week for the maintenance of each patient, or pay an annual subscription to defray the cost. Understandably, the Unions were unwilling. A great deal of time was spent in writing to the Guardians and each case was keenly argued, with the Unions denying it was their responsibility and declining to pay. Bradfield was the first Union to agree to these payments of 7/- a week and by 1841 they were joined by Wokingham and Easthampstead. Hartley Wintney said they subscribed to the Winchester Hospital and would not enter any agreement with the Reading Hospital. In March 1842 the Poor Law Commissioners, whose attitude had been far from clear on the subject, sanctioned payments by the Unions for accident cases admitted to the Hospital. This by no means ended the controversy as, in many instances, the Unions did their utmost to prove settlement had been gained in another parish. When Thomas Bozier, aged 15, was admitted with a compound fracture of the arm caused by a wagon passing over him, the Wokingham Union refused to acknowledge him as a casual pauper of Shinfield, claiming that the boy had been taken to his master's residence in another parish before going to the Hospital.

The Poor Law Unions were very slow to become annual subscribers to the Hospital. In 1840 the Hungerford Union asked how many in-patients could obtain treatment for an annual subscription of 10 guineas if no out-patients were admitted. When told that the rules allowed five in-patients per year and five out-patients always on the books, they declined to subscribe, saying that the Salisbury Hospital would accept ten in-patients for this amount.

The Reading Union refused to pay 7/– a week for accident cases or to subscribe to the funds of the Hospital. In 1842 the Guardians arranged for three local doctors to attend the paupers in the three parishes of the Union. They were paid between £40 and £70 a year with an additional 10/6d for every difficult maternity case. With such arrangements the Reading Union felt unable to contribute to the funds of the Royal Berkshire Hospital.

Wallingford was the first Union to become an annual subscriber in 1842, followed by Cookham in 1845, though neither continued their subscriptions every year. In 1855 Hartley Wintney, Highworth and Swindon, and Hungerford were the only ones to appear on the subscription list.

Problems also arose when accident or emergency patients died in the Hospital and there was no one able to pay for the removal and burial of the body. Those who were recommended for treatment always came with a surety for such an event but accident and emergency patients had no similar cover. The Minute books record the desperation of these situations and show the working of the Poor Law system at its very worst. Bodies were left in the Hospital mortuary for up to two weeks awaiting collection, with no Union willing to admit responsibility. The Hospital was frequently driven to arrange for the burial of the body and then the battle continued about who was to pay.[2]

The case of Eliza Franklin in 1847 was similar to many others but was particularly distressing as it concerned a small child. She was admitted to the Hospital on April 13th suffering from severe burns from which she died on May 1st. Her father could not afford to remove the body and have it buried and he applied to the Bradfield and Reading Unions, both of which refused to help. On May 4th the Hospital Secretary was instructed to write to the Reading Union telling them that the body must be removed and buried immediately. If they refused, the body, after due notice, would be taken to the Relieving Officer's house and left there. An amendment altered this last decision to read that if nothing had been done by May 6th, the child would be buried by the Hospital for decency's sake. Eventually

Eliza Franklin was buried by the Hospital, but it was more than two months before the wrangling eventually ended when the Bradfield Union agreed to meet the expenses of the child's burial.

The Board of Management was so incensed by this incident that they asked for legal advice. They were told that in such a case they should demand the expense of burial from the Guardians of the Union in which the Hospital was situated. Should this not be met, the Hospital could take action for repayment. In October of that year this opinion was confirmed and from that time such incidents seldom occurred and the Reading Union became liable for the payment of all these burials.

At the time of Eliza Franklin's case there were about 80 beds in the Hospital and patients were coming from all over the County for treatment. The resources of the Hospital were greatly overburdened; waiting lists were growing, and there was a danger that wards might have to close and staff be dismissed through lack of funds. Two public appeals saved the situation temporarily but still the numbers wanting treatment increased. Every 10 extra beds required an additional annual income of £300, and this was not easy to find. By 1853 the number of out-patients had risen to 1,660, and it was decided that some financial limitation would have to be imposed. In future out-patients whose weekly earnings or those of their family were more than 18/– would not be treated. This limitation would not apply to in-patients or to out-patients who were members of Friendly Societies or benefit clubs making annual subscriptions to the Hospital. The Board felt bound to take these measures 'both for preserving the funds of the Hospital for the benefit of the poorer classes and also in justice to the medical men whose private practice is in danger of being infringed on'.

The Board went to great lengths to consider the circumstances of every applicant, to note any special problems and the financial demands on the family as a whole. In many instances the rule was relaxed to admit cases in extenuating circumstances. Tradesmen and artisans with their wives and families were usually not admitted: for example Stephen Ivins, a bricklayer earning 21/– a week and Robert Messenger, the son of a journeyman carpenter earning £1 per week, were turned down. Sarah Walter's husband was a master cooper and she, like Ann Emmetts whose husband was a cabman and eating-house keeper, were 'not allowed'. Richard Hill was a journeyman plumber earning 3/6d a day but was only able to get work on three or four days a week in winter. He was admitted. Richard Lowe was a journeyman wheelwright earning 18/– a week with a wife and five young children. He too was admitted. The effect of this new rule was very noticeable and the number of out-patients fell by almost a half with 968 being treated in 1855. This eased the immediate financial position, but the Board was never able to relax its efforts to secure an ever-larger income to keep the Hospital working to capacity and to meet the demands of the increasing numbers seeking admission.

THE MEDICAL STAFF, PATIENTS AND TREATMENT

For many months after the Hospital opened the enthusiasm which had been exhibited by the medical staff to obtain their posts was not matched by an equal enthusiasm on the part of the 'deserving poor' to go there for treatment. The sick in the area had never been treated in such a place before and to many the building appeared awesome and frightening, a mixture between a church and a mansion. Being admitted to the Hospital was an intimidating experience, especially if it was far from home.

The system of admission through the recommendation of a subscriber had its limitations. The knowledge of the parish clergy was invaluable in finding those in need of medical help and putting them in touch with subscribers to give them the necessary tickets of admission. However, it will never be known how many patients were the reluctant recipients of tickets from employers, vicars and people in authority, or how many people wished to be admitted but knew of no one to recommend them. In one case Viscount Chelsea recommended a patient who refused to be admitted on two occasions, and it was noted that 'the man was at work and applying some quack medicine to his wound'. Admission of patients with untreated fractures which had taken place weeks or months beforehand and illnesses of long duration show that those needing treatment were not always obtaining it, but whether by their own choice or not will never be known.

At the end of the first year the Annual Court of Governors was told that 'the prejudice held by the poorer classes had been dissipated by the kindness and skill of the medical officers', and certainly the numbers applying each week for admission show that by then there was no shortage of applicants. The success of the Hospital in helping the many accident cases who were injured in the construction of the Great Western Railway and the publicity this received did much to allay the fears of the sick and bring reluctant patients to the Hospital.

When applying for admission, patients would be seen by the House Surgeon and by one of the physicians or surgeons in attendance that week who would then be in charge of the case. Once in the wards the nurses took over and the patient was allocated a bed, a locker for clothes and, if fit enough, was expected to assist with the work in the ward. Few of the nurses had any experience of hospitals and, with the frequent changes in nursing staff, the wards were often as strange to them as to the patients themselves.

The wards were sparse with high ceilings, bare wooden floors and iron bedsteads. At one side a coal fire provided the only heating and at the end there was a closet for washing. There were two bathrooms in the Hospital, one for the male patients and one for the female patients. Blinds covered the windows and folding screens could be put round the beds if privacy was required. Lighting was provided at first by oil lamps, but these were shortly replaced by rush lights and candles. The wards were functional and severe.

All food was prepared in the kitchen and patients were strictly forbidden to bring anything in apart from tea, butter and sugar which they had to provide for themselves. Every bundle and parcel was examined to make certain that neither the patients nor their visitors brought in additional food and drink. Four different diet tables were drawn up by the medical staff and, although it was pointed out to them that the Radcliffe Infirmary had more frugal diets, they considered it economical to provide a liberal diet as it would, in many cases, hasten the recovery of the patient. Items like eggs, cheese, chicken, fish, broth and beef tea were recommended on many occasions in addition to the main diets and these were referred to as 'fancy diets'.

Diet Tables

EXTRA DIET
Breakfast: ½ pint of tea or coffee with sugar and milk.
Dinner: 4 days – 9 oz meat roast (weighed with bone before dressed), ½ lb of potatoes
3 days – 9 oz meat boiled, ½ lb potatoes.
Supper: ½ pint of gruel and milk or same of broth.
14 oz bread per day for men and women (later reduced to 12 oz for women)
1 pint beer for men, ½ pint beer for women.

ORDINARY DIET
Breakfast: ½ pint tea or coffee with milk and sugar.
Dinner: 6 oz meat roast as per extra diet, ½ lb potatoes.
Supper: Same as for extra diet.
14 oz bread per day for men, 12 oz bread for women
½ pint beer daily for men and women.

MILK DIET
Breakfast: ½ pint milk.
Dinner: 4 days – 1 pint rice milk
3 days – ½ pint bread or rice pudding.
Supper: ½ pint milk
12 oz bread daily men and women.

FEVER DIET
½ pint tea morning and evening with sugar and milk.
7 oz bread daily, barley water ad lib.
(later altered to 6 oz bread)
Arrowroot, etc. to be specially directed.

At certain hours each day, patients who were fit enough were able to take exercise in the Hospital grounds where the male and female wings had their separate walks. By June 1840 it was noticed that patients were leaving the Hospital during the day and 'complaint was made of the frequency of in-patients being permitted to go out of the Hospital and of the late hours at which they returned.' After this no in-patient could leave without permission in writing from their physician or surgeon, countersigned by the House Surgeon. On no account should they be out after 4 p.m. between 1st September and 1st May and after 6 p.m. for the rest of the year. This did not appear to be satisfactory, and the following year the rule was tightened so that no in-patient was allowed to go beyond the grounds except in urgent cases. Visiting hours were limited to 15 minutes on two afternoons a week, although it would appear that at this time these rules were not very strictly kept.

Most patients were glad to accept the help of the Hospital but expressions of thankfulness and gratitude were by no means voiced by all and many never stayed to complete their treatment. There were complaints about the quality of the beer, the toughness of the meat and the freshness of the bread. Joseph Shaw is noted in 1839 complaining about the bread and 'leaving the Hospital without his discharge'. Others just disappeared without giving a reason. James Shelton left at his own request 'being very discontented but without giving any cause of complaint'. Some just did not want to be there; they did not like the treatment and discharged themselves against medical advice. Occasionally, even accident patients are recorded as having climbed over the wall and disappeared during the night.

Many patients were told to leave by the medical staff. There were numerous instances of patients being discharged for misconduct, failing to take their medicines, being rude, using bad language, and especially of being 'discontent' – a condition which was regarded with great disapproval. One male patient was dismissed for passing improper notes to a woman patient and two others were told to leave for smoking and drinking in the middle of the night. Another was discharged 'in consequence of creating a disturbance from an eager desire to leave the Hospital'. Mary Ann Whiting of Victoria Ward displayed very bad behaviour and was finally dismissed when she 'spoke very irreverently of the Bible and otherwise greatly misconducted herself'. The behaviour of some patients was believed to be the result of mental problems. These people were quickly discharged and their disruptive influence removed.

The Visitors on their regular inspection of the wards were in a position to receive complaints both by and about the patients, and in some instances it was at their instigation that a patient was dismissed. The Visitors made certain that the wards were kept clean and were properly run and in 1840, following reports of some wards being filled with smoke when the fires were lit, the Board arranged that 'machinery' should be used to sweep the chimneys instead of employing 'climbing boys'. The local clergy and Chaplain also visited the wards regularly and not only helped the patients spiritually but also gave books to those who could read and later also slates for their use in writing. In spite of minor upheavals, the wards ran on a smooth routine with the nurses in attendance, the Matron and House Surgeon organising, supervising and giving treatment and providing a suitable environment in which the work of the physicians and surgeons could be carried out.

Treatment

It is difficult to imagine being treated in a hospital without all the medical and surgical facilities which have now become commonplace. No practitioner today would welcome the thought of working in the Hospital as it was 150 years ago – no means of combating infection, no X-ray or Pathology Departments to call upon; no anaesthetics, or drugs for the control of pain. Whereas successful amputations were an achievement in 1839, comparable operations today are for the replacement of diseased organs and the reinstatement of severed limbs with micro-surgery. The first medical staff of the Hospital could never have visualised such advances.

The early Victorian physicians and surgeons at the Hospital were essentially general practitioners, and it was to be many years before medical knowledge and scientific advances brought about specialisation in various branches of medicine. Some of the medical staff showed particular interest in certain conditions and were especially successful with some types of treatment, but this was the extent of specialisation at that time. Each year the House Surgeon prepared tables showing the total number of in-patients and out-patients admitted during the previous 12 months and the number that died, were relieved or cured, and gave a list of the various conditions treated and the number of operations that had been performed. These tables show the success in the treatment of the wide variety of surgical and medical cases that were admitted to the Hospital during the early years.

Very few operations were carried out at that time and only 11 were performed in the first year. By the end of 1855 a total of 402 operations had been carried out with an average of 26 in each year. A case of surgical instruments costing £130 was one of the first purchases in 1839 and gradually more instruments were added. Some were specially made or hired for particular operations. There was no sterilisation of instruments though occasionally it would be noted that they were to be cleaned by Messrs Weiss or that Mr Botley would sharpen the knives. Lighting was a problem in the theatre and gas light was installed within three months of the opening. This was still not good enough, and special two-branch candlesticks were obtained to give additional light. When an operation was to be performed a board was hung up in the hall giving the nature of the operation, the name of the surgeon and the day and hour at which it would take place. With so few operations being performed the medical fraternity was interested in attending and an audience could always be expected.

Special equipment such as a ring bolt for reducing fractures was obtained and, in 1850, the more elaborate Luke's Ring Bed, complete with straps and rings, was purchased from Messrs Weiss for four guineas. Items like a strong chair and a Hanwell Jacket, purchased from the Middlesex Asylum, were all part of the necessary equipment. There were no

Name	Age	State	Occupation	Nature of Injury	Nature of Disease	Cause of Injury, &c.	Date of Operation	Stage: Primary	Stage: Secondary	Stage: Disease	Locality	Incision: Circular	Incision: Flap	Result: Cured	Result: Died	Duration of Treatment after Operation
Jarvis, David	27	Single	Navigator	Compound fracture of Elbow, left		Run over by waggon	Aug. 28, 1839	2 hours			Above Elbow	1		1		34 days
Bolton, John	30	Single	Railroad-labourer	Fracture of Humerus, in two places		Run over by railroad-truck	Jan. 7, 1842	3¾ hours			Above Elbow	1		1		63 days
Cox, John	50	Married	Carter	Compound fracture of Leg, above ankle		Run over by waggon	Oct. 11, 1840		0 days		Above Knee	1		1		76 days
Johnson, Geo.	33	Single	Railroad-labourer	Compound fracture of Leg, right		Run over by train	Oct. 6, 1841	12 hours			Below Knee	1		1		87 days
Lench, John	57	Married	Labourer	Compound fracture of Femur, right		Run over by waggon	Aug. 24, 1839	6 hours			Above Knee	1			1	2 days
Morris, John	21	Single	Railroad-labourer	Laceration of Hand and Wrist		Explosion of gun	Dec. 24, 1841	5 hours			Fore-arm	1		1		60 days
Blake, George	30	Single	Farm-labourer		Disabled Knee; absorption of Cartilage	Sprain	Sept. 5, 1843			1	Above Knee	1		1		51 days
Cox, Ann	23	Single	Servant	Severe burn, 4th degree			Oct. 26, 1843				Shoulder-joint	1		1		130 days
Edmonds, D.	0				Diseased Knee, right, of 2 years standing		May 5, 1843			1	Above Knee	1		1		65 days
Preen, John	11			Wound through Shoulder-Joint		Gun shot wound	Aug. 16, 1843	4½ hours			Shoulder-joint	1		1		36 days
Hackett, Anthy.	21	Single	Conductor on rail.		Diseased Knee, right		Nov. 18, 1843		9 days	1	Above Knee	1		1		93 days
Parker, William	34	Single	Carpenter	Compound fracture of Tibia and Fibula		Fall from ladder	July 1, 1843		9 days		Above Knee	1		1		11 days
Withers, John	30	Married	Carter	Compound fracture of Tibia and Fibula			Aug. 30, 1843	7 hours			Above Knee	1		1		31 days
Shepherd, Mary	10	Single	Servant		Onychia of great Toe; diseased bone		Jan. 23, 1843			1	Great Toe	1		1		43 days
Jones, William	15	Single	Railroad-labourer	Laceration of right Knee and Foot		Run over by waggon	Sept. 5, 1839	4½ hours			Above Knee	1		1		38 days
Siterwell, Rich.	33	Married	Labourer		Necrosis; Tibia	Wall fell on him	Oct. 12, 1842	2 hours		1	Below Knee	1		1		22 days
Gutteridge, W.	55	Married	Publican	Laceration of Hand		Explosion of gun	Nov. 28, 1842	2 hours			Above Knee	1		1		35 days
Hum, Frederick	17	Single	Clerk	Laceration of Hand			Feb. 6, 1844				Fore-arm	1		1		40 days
Hatt, Caroline	21	Single	Field-labourer	Severe Burn			Jan. 16, 1843				Above Elbow	1		1		44 days
Wheeler, Wm.	30	Married	Tailor	Laceration of Hand			Jan. 18, 1841	5 hours			Fore-arm	1		1		43 days
Herver, Joseph	35	Single	Labourer	Compound fracture of Radius and Ulna			Jan. 15, 1842	Within 24 hours			Upper third of Fore-arm	1		1		43 days
Cooper, James	30	Single	Carpenter	Laceration of Hand		Bursting of gun	March 12, 1844	2 hours			Thumb	1		1		95 days
Heath, James	13	Single	Railroad-labourer	Compound fracture of Tibia and Fibula			June 26, 1839	Within 24 hours			Thigh	1		1		140 days
Coxhead, James	20	Single	Labourer	Laceration of Hand		Machinery	July 9, 1840	Within 24 hours			Ring and middle Fingers	1		1		35 days
Stacey, John	27	Single	Garden-labourer	Laceration of Hand		Bursting of gun	Jan. 6, 1841				Finger	1		1		34 days
Baldwin, John	0			Lacerated wound of Thumb, left		Bursting of powder-flask	Jan. 22, 1842		12 days		Thumb	1		1		32 days
Real, Elizabeth	20	Single	Servant	Compound fracture of Tibia and Fibula		Upsetting of a coach	June 27, 1841	16 hours			Below Knee	1		1		110 days
Bozier, Sladrach	14	Single	Labourer	Fracture of Humerus; compound, comminuted, with laceration		Machinery	Aug. 7, 1841	Within 24 hours			Near Shoulder-joint	1		1		92 days
Green, William	23	Married	Labourer		Ulceration of cartilage of Femur in the Knee-Joint		May 5, 1841			1	Above Knee	1		1		174 days
Kittleby, James	32	Single	Bargeman	Contusion of little Finger		Bursting of gun	Aug. 27, 1843	Within 24 hours			Finger	1		1		42 days
Lambden, Jos.	28	Married	Labourer	Laceration of Hand			Oct. 15, 1843	Within 24 hours			Finger	1		1		36 days
Frith, Henry	40	Married	Navigator		Inflammation of absorbents; Sloughing of integuments of Finger	Prick of finger whilst handling weeds	Jan. 7, 1843			1	Finger	1		1		38 days
Brown, James	42	Married	Wheelwright	Laceration and fracture of Finger		Machinery	Oct. 13, 1843	1 hour			Fingers	Mixed		1		47 days
Early, George	16	Single	Railroad-labourer	Compound, comminuted fracture of Humerus			May 27, 1839	2 hours			Shoulder-joint	1		1		9 weeks
Pearson, Stephen	54	Married	Scavenger	Compound fracture of Leg		Run over by waggon	Feb. 16, 1841				Above Knee	1			1	12 days

Average duration of Treatment of each Case ... 60 days.

Table of amputations 1839–1844, from Mr May's *Statistical Report*

anaesthetics until the use of ether in 1847 and, until then, Hanwell Jackets, brute force, opiates and alcohol were the only means of keeping the patients still and alleviating pain. Mr May recorded an occasion when a young boy of nine was insecurely tied and moved during a lithotomy operation which unfortunately resulted in the death of the boy.

In 1845 Mr May delivered a paper at the Anniversary Meeting of the Southern Branch of the Provincial Medical Association which was held at Reading. It was entitled 'A Statistical Report on the Surgical In-Patients of the Royal Berkshire Hospital from its Establishment in May 1839 to May 1845'. This report gives detailed tables of the various surgical cases, their treatment, duration and outcome as well as a short introduction with remarks about certain more important operations. The high proportion of successful treatments on the 1,291 surgical cases in those first six years, with a death rate of little more than four per cent, was noted 'to contrast most favourably with that of the large hospitals of England and the Continent'. A total of 96 operations were performed in this period, nine of which resulted in death – a rate of 10½ per cent. Fractures, some necessitating amputation, dislocations, eye conditions and cataracts, the removal of tumours, lithotomy operations and operations for hare lips and cleft palates are among the long list of cases treated. Three cases of fractures of the skull resulting in trephining operations were recorded. One of these concerned a patient called Richard Woolley, who was admitted to the Hospital on December 24th, 1841.

On that day, an appalling accident occurred on the Great Western Railway line at the Sonning Cutting when a down luggage train ran into a fall of earth on the track. Eight passengers were killed and 19 others were taken to the Hospital, some suffering from very serious injuries. This was the first emergency the Hospital had experienced and every member of the staff and all the servants were called upon to assist with the casualties. Seven were able to leave the Hospital within a short time but the other 12 were more severely injured with fractures, dislocations and lacerations. Richard Woolley was treated for a compound fracture of the skull, but the trephining operation was not successful and he died five days later. Eliza Barnes, a young girl in her twenties, remained in the Hospital for several years and eventually went to live with one of the nurses, supported by an allowance from the railway company. The publicity obtained for the Hospital did much to show how valuable its services had become. A letter published in the *Berkshire Chronicle* noted 'the first-rate medical aid and surgical skill, the most tender and careful nursing, joined to the greatest cleanliness and the most benefiting diet, not to speak of the great spiritual aid and comfort administered by the very able and zealous Chaplain.'

The early Hospital contained a great variety of equipment, much of it strange by today's standards but some still very recognisable. Water beds were frequently used, the first one being presented to the Hospital in 1839. In 1845 it is noted that one costing eight guineas was obtained 'complete with all modern improvements' including mattress, legs and headboard.

Triangular pillows were bought in 1843 and Hooper's water pillows were obtained in 1851 and were found to be invaluable. Patients were often in hospital for months on end and this equipment did much to help and prevent bed sores.

Sulphur and vapour baths were installed soon after the Hospital opened and special pumps were connected to the warm baths for the treatment of diseased joints. In 1841 Duval's steam apparatus, costing £7 19s, was given to the Hospital and in 1846 the House Surgeon devised a hot-air apparatus for giving baths in bed which was considerably cheaper than the one being manufactured at the time. In 1848 a cold water douche for diseases of the rectum was fitted in one of the bathrooms.

Electrogalvanic treatment was popular as the application of electric current was found to be beneficial, bringing comfort and helping the circulation in a great variety of cases. The first electro-magnetic machine with galvanic battery was purchased for £5 in 1840 and this was later replaced by a more powerful one. By 1849 a greatly improved apparatus had come on the market and the Hospital was presented with this equipment.

The application of fomentations (from Mr Hall of High Wycombe), iodine plasters (from Ewens of London), mustard and bread poultices were commonplace, as well as the use of leeches. The Board of Management seldom interfered with anything that was requested by the medical staff, but in 1844 they drew attention to the fact that over the previous five years the Radcliffe Infirmary, with double the number of patients, had used about a quarter of the number of leeches used at the Royal Berkshire Hospital. These were by no means inexpensive and in 1844 nearly £25 was paid for the 2,450 leeches used in the Hospital. There is no record of the medical staff making any comment on the subject, but the consumption of leeches fell from a peak of 2,800 in 1842 to 1,125 in 1848 and after that date they were no longer itemised in the accounts.

Various appliances were obtained for the support of the body, as many conditions which can now be cured by operations could then only be relieved by the use of surgical appliances. Trusses, abdominal supporters, supports for ovarian tumours, instruments for supporting the head, the wrists, the knees, the feet and the spine were all obtained. Irons and Dr Little's shoes for club feet, shoes with iron supports and shoes with springs in the soles were regularly in use. In 1840 the first Knox's Revolving Bed, price 17 guineas, was bought for patients with spinal injuries, and later special Liston's splints were used for treating fractures. Crutches and wooden legs were also required and the first patient to need such appliances was James Heath, who had a leg amputated within a month of the Hospital opening. Like George Earley, he was a young boy working on the construction of the Great Western Railway line and an accident resulted in his admission with a compound fracture of the tibia and fibula. Mr Bulley operated immediately and James Heath was fit enough to leave the Hospital about five months later. Being the first case to require a wooden leg, the Board of Management went to great lengths to find out where such appliances could be obtained.

St George's Hospital bought wooden legs below the knee at 18/– and above the knee at 25/–, crutches without handles at 21/– a dozen and with handles at 42/– a dozen from Sheldrake and Biggs of Leicester Square. Mr Smith, a surgical instrument maker, could supply legs below the knee at 10/– and above the knee at 25/–, and knee caps at 8/– each. Messrs Weiss of London sent an excellent leg, costing two guineas, complete with leather coverings and fittings. This was regarded as very expensive, so Mr Emery of Reading was asked to make a copy and produced one costing 10/– without any fittings. James Heath in the meantime was ready to leave the Hospital and a minute dated November 19th, 1839 notes that 'the boy James Heath was removed to the Union Poor House this day. He had the wooden leg by Weiss, the one made by Emery being too heavy for him – the difference in weight 13 oz.' Mr Emery eventually managed to make wooden legs which were lighter in weight and over the years many were supplied to the amputees in the Hospital. In 1848 he produced an artificial leg with foot attached costing around £9, but when the Board found similar appliances cost £14 from Mr Grossmith in London and £8 15s from Messrs Weiss, it decided they were all too expensive and wooden legs would continue to be obtained. The supply of a hook for an amputated arm is recorded for the first time in 1842 and in 1847 wooden arms with crooks were recommended for two patients.

Burn cases were numerous and Mr Bulley took a particular interest in these. He found treatment with a mixture of treacle and warm water to be most beneficial and he published several articles on the subject, giving details of this method compared with others. Burns from gunpowder explosions and clothing set on fire were most common and remarkable success with this treatment was obtained. The admission of patients with severe burns caused great distress among the other patients and one instance is recorded of hysterical fits and convulsions resulting from the horror of such a case.

There were also many cases of eye infections and diseases which were of great interest to Mr May. A separate eye ward is noted from an early date and later, when this room became the House Surgeon's sitting-room, the eye patients were put in one of the small wards which had been included in the Hospital extension.

Cases of iritis, amaurosis and purulent ophthalmia were all admitted immediately as it was feared that any delay might cause the patients to lose their sight. Cataract operations were performed with a high percentage of success, as well as operations for staphyloma and artificial pupil. Glasses were supplied to cataract patients and also convex lenses for patients with defective sight. Cases of squinting were always treated as out-patients. In 1854 an ophthalmoscope was obtained at a cost of 15/–.

Many children were admitted to the Hospital, although those under the age of seven were only accepted following accidents or emergencies or if

TABLE OF CASES OF BURNS TREATED IN THE ROYAL BERKSHIRE HOSPITAL.

(*From January*, 1845, *to January*, 1848.)

Communicated by F. A BULLEY, Esq., Surgeon to the Hospital.

Date of Burn.	Sex.	Age.	Parts which were burnt.	Treatment.	Days Treated.	Results.
1845 Jan. 7	F	4	Arm	Flour	13	Died Jan. 20, 1845
Dec. 5	F	3	Lower part of the face and both arms	Flour	2	Died Dec. 7, ..
1846 Oct. 7	F	17	Arms, neck, and face	Tepid treacle and water	131	Discharged Feb. 16, 1847
Oct. 19	F	6	Right side of the body	Flour	8	Died Oct. 27, 1846
Dec. 4	F	10	Head, back, abdomen, and legs	Simple dressing	—	Died same day at two o'clock.
Dec. 8	F	9	Neck, &c.	Tepid treacle and water	104	Made out-patient March 23, 1847
Dec. 15	F	4	Face, arms, and shoulders	Simple dressing	8	Died Dec. 23, 1846
Dec. 31	F	6	Neck, &c.	Tepid treacle and water	82	Made out-patient March 23, 1847
1847 Mar. 2	M	—	Leg	Tepid treacle and water	18	Cured, March 20, 1847.
Mar. 13	M	3	Face, neck, & breast	Flour	15	Died Mar. 28, 1847
Mar. 19	M	4	Abdomen	Simple dressing and Ung. Plumb.	73	Cured June 1, ..
April 3	F	10	Abdomen, arm, and thighs	Flour	28	Died May 1, ...
June 11	F	3½	Right side, arm, and leg	Simple dressing	5	Died June 15, ..
Aug. 13	F	14 mos.	Chest, face, and arm	Tepid treacle and water	31	Cured Sept. 14, 1847
Sept. 14	F	4	Arm and forehead	Ol. Lini, and Aqua Calcis	56	Cured Nov. 30, 1847
Dec. 2	M	10	Arms and chest	Tepid treacle and water	82	Relieved & made out-patient, Feb. 22, 1848
Dec. 27	M	31	Body and extremities	None	—	Died immediately

(from *Prov. Med. and Surg. Journal Vol. XII 1848*)

in need of surgery. Fractures, dislocations, burns and eye infections were all quite common and in most cases the mothers were allowed to remain to nurse their children. Several successful operations for hare lips and cleft palates were carried out. One performed in 1840 required the help of Mr Bewley, the dentist, and with his assistance Mr May was able to insert an artificial palate. In 1843 another child was operated on for contraction of the jaw from burns. The operation was regarded as an experiment, but the mother consented and a special appliance for the operation was made by a London firm. Children were admitted for the removal of calculus from the bladder (lithotomy), division of tendons, removal of tumours and trephining following fracture of the skull, all with a remarkable degree of success.

Foundation of the Reading Pathological Society
In June 1841 the medical officers of the Hospital submitted a report to the Board of Management saying they were 'desirous of forming a society for the discussion of professional subjects and the collection of morbid specimens in conjunction with the Practitioners of the Town and neighbourhood and they would feel obliged to the Board of Management if they could concede to them the use of the Museum Room for this purpose.'

The Board of Management were very glad to allow this and on July 13th, 1841 the Reading Pathological Society held its inaugural meeting at the Hospital and one of the oldest medical societies in the country was founded. At the monthly meetings papers were read, specimens exhibited and discussions took place. It became a centre for the exchange of ideas and stimulated thought and research in all fields of medicine. The Society exists to this day, and over the years has contributed greatly to the advancement of medical knowledge and interest.

In 1844 the Pathological Society and the Hospital combined to purchase their first microscope. It was obtained from Messrs Carpenter and Westley at a cost of £61 10s and was pronounced a 'very powerful and most excellent instrument'. The value of this purchase was demonstrated not only in the increased interest in the examination of post-mortem tissues but also in the resulting information produced at the meetings and published in the medical journals. At this time Mr May, Mr Bulley and Dr Cowan were submitting articles to various medical publications on interesting cases admitted to the Hospital and their treatment. Dr Cowan was particularly interested in medical statistics and published an article on a form of register for use in hospitals, dispensaries and private practice. The collection of data and information on cases was becoming increasingly important to enable publication of such articles as Mr May's report on the surgical cases in the Hospital. The registration of births, marriages and deaths had recently been made compulsory, and the collection and study of population statistics as well as medical statistics were beginning to assume considerable importance. Dr Cowan also published a book called *The Bedside Manual for Physical Diagnosis* and within the Hospital itself a very interesting collection of medical books was being assembled.

Medical Progress
The medical staff took a great interest in different types of treatment. 'Accupuncturation' needles were obtained in 1842 and the following year Mr Bulley requested to be allowed to try the effects of 'Animal Magnetism or Mesmerism' on an in-patient. Many impressive results had been recorded of the effects of mesmerism with patients having undergone major operations without feeling any pain. Mr Bulley later withdrew his request and it is not known whether he ever tried this technique or not. Dr Cowan

had always been interested in phrenology and this was put to a good practical use when a skeleton, price £8, was purchased for the Hospital with the proceeds of one of his lectures. Dr Woodhouse was particularly interested in galvanism and gave talks and lectures on this subject besides supervising this treatment in the Hospital.

New instruments and apparatus were appearing all the time and two pieces of equipment, invented by Mr Bulley, were particularly highly thought of and were specially made by Messrs Weiss in London. The first was an apparatus for treating poplitoeal aneurisms by compression. The medical staff were unanimous in their approval and recommended its purchase by the Hospital in 1846. Five years later a special splint which he had invented for the treatment of fractures of the thigh bone occupied a prominent position in Weiss's cabinet at the Great Exhibition of 1851, and was the subject of papers published in the medical journals. Among his many other surgical inventions was a tourniquet for arresting the flow of blood through the subclavian artery in shoulder joint operations and a uterine compress to stop haemorrhage during and after labour.

One particularly interesting case combined the use of a new apparatus with the only recorded occasion of a difference of opinion among the medical staff. In May 1845 George Wicks, a farm labourer aged 30, was bitten by a horse and suffered a compound fracture of the left ulna. He was attended by his local doctor but four months later the fracture had not united and he was admitted to the Hospital under the care of Mr Bulley. For six months various treatments were carried out 'which included in succession friction, mercury, compression with rest, the hot douche, strong tincture of iodine externally and a seton between the ends of each bone'. As this had no effect and 'a strong leathern band having failed to assist him', George Wicks said he would agree to amputation if nothing else could be done.

On March 24th, 1846 Mr Bulley sent a letter to the Board of Management stating that a difference of opinion existed between him and his colleagues. They recommended the removal of the ends of the fractured bone but he favoured amputation. At that time no operation would be performed, except in an emergency, without a prior consultation of all the surgical staff. Mr Bulley said he could not perform the operation favoured by his colleagues as it was 'against his natural judgement', and for this reason he would like to hand the case over to someone else. It was agreed Mr May should take over and the operation was performed in April 1846.

Mr May submitted a description of the operation to the *London Medical Gazette* and noted the use of a rotary saw supplied by Mr Weiss and a special apparatus designed by the House Surgeon, Mr James Dunn. This enabled the arm to be placed in a suitable position with the required pressure for the period following the operation. Six weeks later the wounds were healed and the apparatus was taken away. After 18 weeks the patient left the Hospital. The operation had proved to be a complete success and George Wicks was able to return to work in his turnip field.

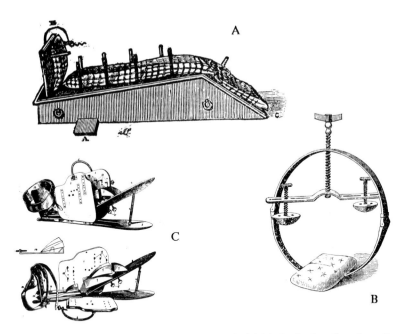

Early instruments and apparatus (not drawn to scale): (a) Mr Bulley's splint, from *Prov. Med. Surg. Journal III, 1841;* (b) Mr Bulley's instrument for treating poplitoeal aneurism, from *Med. Times XV, 1847;* (c) Mr Dunn's apparatus, from *London Medical Gazette,* 1846

On January 19th, 1847 the medical staff recommended to the Board of Management that an ether inhaler should be obtained and Messrs Weiss were asked to send one on approval. The previous year the first use of ether as an anaesthetic had been demonstrated in the Massachusetts General Hospital and on January 2nd, 1847 an article had been published in *The Lancet* describing its use in an operation for tooth extraction. On February 1st, 1847 Mr James Dunn, the House Surgeon, exhibited Hooper's apparatus for inhaling ether at a meeting of the Pathological Society and said he had used it on two occasions of tooth extraction with great success. The Hospital records do not note the use of ether in operations at that time and although it must have been a welcome relief to the patients and an assistance to the surgeons, the suppression of pain in itself does not appear to have been considered of great significance.

Later that year on November 10th, 1847 a historic paper was read by Dr James Simpson of Edinburgh University on *A new anaesthetic agent as a substitute for ether.* Chloroform had arrived. Two weeks later Mr May 'presented a sample obtained from Hooper Operative Chemist of Pall Mall' at the meeting of the Pathological Society. At that time he had no experience of using it and only knew what had been written in the various papers. In December Mr May operated on a young girl with a diseased toe in the Hospital, and was able to tell the members of the Pathological Society at their next monthly meeting that he had obtained perfect anaesthesia in 90 seconds by pouring a few drops of chloroform on to a handkerchief and holding it under the patient's nose. She had felt no pain and the operation was successful. It was not long before simple masks were being used to administer these anaesthetics and later more elaborate ones were made which incorporated a sponge. In 1851 the Hospital purchased a special 'apparatus for inhaling chloroform' and gradually the range and scope of surgical procedures was extended.

Infection and Sanitation

The need to isolate certain cases and have special wards was frequently confronting the Hospital and the Board of Management consulted the medical staff on how these matters could best be dealt with. One of the first problems in this area did not come within the bounds of medical opinion as it concerned 'Females of Immoral Character'. A sub-committee was formed which included several members of the clergy and they advised that special wards would not really be practical, but whenever possible these patients should be separated within the wards and the Matron's and House Surgeon's attention should be 'directed especially to the subject'.

The possibility of a separate ward for fever cases was raised but it was considered unnecessary as 'no evil could result from mixing fever patients indiscriminately with the others'. Erysipelas, a virulent streptococcal infection, was quite another matter and frequent outbreaks in 1848 made a special ward necessary from time to time to enable the main wards to be cleaned, ventilated and whitewashed. Similarly when there was an outbreak of smallpox in 1849, patients were isolated in Adelaide Ward until the infection was over.

Cholera was another worry, but fortunately Reading escaped without suffering a major epidemic. The Board of Management consulted other hospitals on the subject and decided that they would not admit such cases but would prescribe medicine to them as out-patients. They were not prepared to appropriate part of a wing, bricking up all access to the rest of the building, as had been done at the Winchester Hospital, but agreed with Salisbury that it was better not to admit any cholera cases at all. Dr Cowan did not agree with this decision but the Board stated quite firmly that: 'The admission of cholera cases . . . being a question of management, it was quite competent for the Board to decide upon it and believing that decision to be a sound one, the resolution would not be reconsidered.'

Following the passing of the Public Health Act in 1848 a Board of Health was set up in Reading. Much concern had been expressed about the sanitary state of the town, with its dirty streets, bad water supplies and drainage, poor housing and overcrowded conditions. The incidence of fever, epidemics and chronic illness had been noted and reports were drawn up with recommendations to remedy the situation.

The medical staff and Board of Management had been all too aware of the need for good drainage and water supplies, and as the Hospital increased in size, problems arose with drains that smelt and overflowing

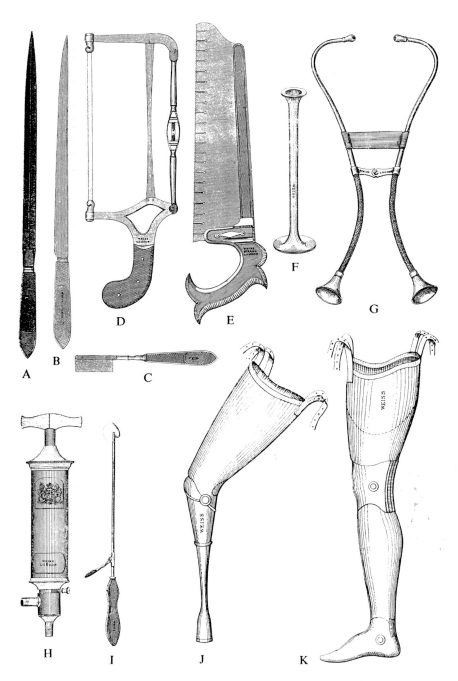

Early surgical instruments and appliances, from the *Catalogue of Surgical Instruments, Apparatus, Appliances etc, manufactured and sold by John Weiss & Son, 1863* (not drawn to scale): (a) Double-edged amputating knife; (b) Liston's knife for flap operation; (c) Saw for trepanning and necrosis; (d) Butcher's saw for amputation and re-section; (e) Amputating saw; (f) and (g) Stethoscope; (h) Stomach pump; (i) Needle holder; (j) Socket leg; (k) Artificial leg.

cesspools. Quantities of linen, provisions and other articles were found to be blocking the drains and printed notices were hung up in the water closets forbidding any articles being thrown down which might cause blockages. In 1846 the overflowing cesspools were replaced by a barrel drain which flowed directly into the canal, and this improved the situation at the Hospital itself. Later, special taps were fitted so that water for cooking and drinking could be obtained straight from the main and not through the lead pipes from the lead cistern. The only occasions on which the Board of Health had any direct dealing with the Hospital was when the Inspector of Nuisances had cause to complain of the pigsties which were kept in the Hospital grounds.

In 1849 the medical staff drew up a report on the sanitary conditions of the Hospital and included recommendations for the improvement of the ventilation in the wards. Apart from being better for the health of the patients, good circulation of air did much to combat the unpleasant smell from suppurating wounds, gangrene, infected burns and ulcers. Mr Bulley had noted that one of the benefits of his burn treatment with treacle and water was to lessen the dreadful smell from the injured flesh. Until the cause and means of combating infection were discovered, such conditions were all too common. Metallic iodine in bottles covered with muslin and placed in the beds was found to lessen the smell. In 1852 a quantity of Irish peat charcoal was given to the Hospital with instructions on how it should be used to combat odour. This was of little help, and bottles of deodorising fluid, fresh air and scrubbing with carbolic soap were found to be the best methods of alleviating the problem.

Before the East Wing had been completed there was severe overcrowding in the women's wards. There were frequent outbreaks of erysipelas and to add to the problem the wards were reported to be infested with bugs. Bedsteads were dismantled, cleaned and painted with a special preparation (as used in the County Gaol) and gradually the problem was overcome. Each year whitewashing of the wards and cleaning of bedsteads had to be undertaken to keep the situation under control.

The need for fresh air had always been appreciated by the medical staff and apart from outdoor exercise which was recommended for the patients, additional benefits were suggested on several occasions. In 1843 it was recommended that one of Mr May's patients, a conductor on the G.W.R. who, before his accident, had been constantly in the fresh air on the journey between London and Reading, should be 'driven out when the weather was favourable' as he was greatly missing being out of doors. In 1848 Mr Bulley arranged that William Hammond, who had a diseased joint, should be sent to Upper Caversham 'to get a change of air in the country', and later patients were occasionally sent to Margate Infirmary for a period of convalescence. The Earl of Radnor's idea of sending them to Torquay was dismissed as being too far away and too expensive.

With overcrowding, outbreaks of erysipelas and bugs, conditions in the wards were far from ideal for some time. The number of patients in the

Hospital had almost doubled since 1839 and the number of nurses had only risen by two. There were frequent complaints by women patients of ill treatment and cruelty by the nurses. Anonymous letters were sent to the Board about the nurses' behaviour and several patients, having left the Hospital, were at great pains to say how badly they had been treated. This adverse publicity was taken very seriously and every incident was investigated in detail, but on most occasions it was believed the allegations could not be substantiated. The chief complaint was that patients were being made to scrub the wards when they were not fit to do so. It was the nurses' duty to keep the wards clean and they were allowed to call on the patients who were fit enough to help. The scrubbing of floors became such an issue that however much the ill-treatment allegations were refuted, it became obvious that some changes had to be made. In 1853 the Board decided that special cleaning women would be employed as scrubbers and from that point the complaints by the women patients became less frequent and the morale on the wards improved.

There were very few complaints about the medical treatment of the patients, but one which was made in 1855 was put in a letter and sent to the *Reading Mercury* for publication. The paper notified the Board of Management and sent them a copy. The writer complained of inattention by the House Surgeon to a patient admitted with a strangulated hernia. He had been operated on the day after admission but had died two days later of peritonitis. A full enquiry was held by the Board and all the details of the case examined. Mr Maurice noted that the operation had been severe and protracted and all the medical staff were in agreement about the treatment prior to the operation and believed nothing different should have been done. The letter was never printed and the complainant expressed himself fully satisfied with the explanation given by Dr Smith on behalf of the Board. Public relations and communications were as important then as they are today.

Public Esteem

The high regard in which the Hospital was held caused others, besides the poor, to wish to be treated there. In 1844 Mr May asked if the wife of Mr Gosling of High Bridge Wharf could be admitted as a private patient. The Board was adamant that: 'It was contrary to the rules of the Hospital to admit respectable persons as private patients.'

Over the years it became noticeable that some treatments could be carried out more easily and successfully in the Hospital. This was particularly the case with certain operations which the surgeons preferred to perform in the theatre rather than in patients' homes. In 1851 Mr Charles Blandy asked if the son of Mr J. Y. Willats could be admitted. He had a stone in his bladder and his surgeon, Mr Maurice, believed the case 'capable of deriving great advantage from admission to the Hospital and if it was decided to operate on him, his chance of recovery would be greater in the Hospital than out of it.' The matter was discussed by the Board and a

HOUSE SURGEON'S REPORT.

GENERAL STATEMENT OF CASES OF IN-PATIENTS AS ENTERED AT THE TIME OF ADMISSION.

ACCOUNT OF IN-PATIENTS, For the Year ending Dec. 31st, 1855.

Remaining in Hospital, 31st December, 1854 ... 53
Admitted during the year } 695 { Medical 296 / Surgical 399
Total 748

Account of In-Patients discharged.
Cured ... 318
Relieved ... 104
Relieved and made out-patients ... 188
Not benefited ... 32
Irregular ... 3
To Lunatic Asylum ... 1
To Jail ... 1
Died ... 21
Died within a few hours of admission, from the immediate effects of injuries ... 12
Remaining, Dec. 31st, 1855 ... 680 ... 68
Total 748

Number of In-Patients admitted from Commencement.

In 1839-40 ..	304	In 1848-49 ..	634
1840-41 ..	392	1849-50 ..	609
1841-42 ..	431	1850-51 ..	666
1842-43 ..	400	1851-52 ..	695
1843-44 ..	480	1852-53 ..	665
1844-45 ..	544	1853-54 ..	717
1845-46 ..	537	1854(9 mo.)	542
1846-47 ..	607	1855 ..	695
1847-48 ..	605		
		Total	**9,564**

ACCOUNT OF OUT-PATIENTS, For the Year ending Dec. 31st, 1855.

Remaining on the books, 31st December, 1854 ... 61
Admitted during the year } 911 { Medical 459 / Surgical 448
Total 968

Account of Out-Patients discharged.
Cured ... 500
Relieved ... 127
Made in-patients ... 13
Not benefited ... 20
Irregular ... 27
Died ... 3
... 798
Remaining, Dec. 31st, 1855 ... 170
Total 968

Number of Out-Patients admitted from Commencement.

In 1839-40 ..	270	In 1848-49 ..	977
1840-41 ..	412	1849-50 ..	1066
1841-42 ..	549	1850-51 ..	1156
1842-43 ..	680	1851-52 ..	1326
1843-44 ..	790	1852-53 ..	1443
1844-45 ..	892	1853-54 ..	1477
1845-46 ..	970	1854(9 mo.)	975
1846-47 ..	1092	1855 ..	911
1847-48 ..	947		
		Total	**15,933**

Nervous System.
Cerebral diseases ... 7
Hemiplegia ... 11
Paraplegia ... 1
Hypochondria ... 1
Hysteria ... 6
Chorea ... 8
Neuralgia and sciatica ... 3
Spinal irritation ... 6
Debility ... 6

Organs of Sense.
Diseases of ear ... 2
Ophthalmic diseases ... 25
Cataract ... 3
Disease of Tongue ... 1

Blood & Vascular System.
Diseases of heart ... 13
Pericarditis ... 6
Chlorosis and anæmia ... 31
Fever ... 4
Rheumatism ... 44
Scrofula ... 4
Secondary syphilis ... 4
Diabetes ... 2
Varicose veins ... 5

Respiratory System.
Laryngitis ... 1
Bronchitis ... 25
Pneumonia ... 7
Pleurisy ... 1
Phthisis ... 19
Emphysema ... 1

Digestive System.
Gastric ailments ... 28
Diseases of bowels ... 11
Hernia ... 7
Intussusception ... 1
Fistula ... 4
Peritonitis ... 3
Ascites ... 8
Diseases of liver ... 6

Genito-Urinary System.
Diseases of kidneys ... 6
Diseases of bladder and prostate ... 10
testis, &c. ... 6
Extravasation of urine ... 2
Retention of urine ... 10
Stricture ... 4
Hydrocele ... 4
Stone ... 4
Uterine diseases and derangements ... 29
Ovarian dropsy ... 1

Glandular System.
Bronchocele ... 3
Diseases of breast ... 6

Cutaneous Diseases ... 10

Bones, Joints, & Limbs.
Diseases of cranium ... 1
sternum ... 1
spine ... 8
pelvis ... 1
tibia ... 1
hip ... 7
thigh ... 3
knee ... 28
leg, ankle, and foot ... 28
elbow ... 2
arm & hand ... 11
Ulcers of leg ... 41

Diseases of uncertain seat.
Tumours ... 12
Abscess ... 22
Nævus ... 5
Malignant disease ... 4
Cancer ... 2
Ulcers (excluding those of leg) ... 1

Hemorrhages.
Hemorrhage from lungs ... 3
stomach ... 2
bowels ... 2
nose ... 1

Injuries.
Various contusions ... 30
Burns and scalds, wounds ... 24
Fracture of thigh ... 10
leg ... 9
leg, comp. ... 3
compound ... 15
both legs, comp. ... 1
foot, compound ... 1
skull ... 7
spine ... 3
jaw ... 1
clavicle ... 1
rib ... 3
humerus ... 1
compound ... 3
forearm ... 1
compound ... 1
hand, compound ... 1
Dislocation of shoulder ... 1
elbow ... 1
wrist ... 1
ankle ... 1
Injuries to spine ... 7
head ... 6
Cut throat ... 2
Burnt with lime ... 1

OPERATIONS DURING THE YEAR.
Amputation of thigh ... 1
leg ... 2
foot ... 1
fingers and toes ... 6
Removal of tumours ... 5
Operation for hernia ... 3
cancer ... 2
fistula ... 1
Puncture of bladder by the rectum ... 1
Operation for hydrocele ... 4
ovarian dropsy ... 1
Total ... 27

NUMBER OF ACCIDENTS AND EMERGENCIES Received as In-Patients.
Accidents ... 127
Emergencies ... 39
Total ... 166

MINOR ACCIDENTS AND CASUALTIES, Treated as Out-Patients.
Accidents ... 131
Casualties ... 85
Total ... 216

vote was taken. It was decided that the patient would be admitted as a case of emergency and the Hospital would require to be reimbursed at a rate of two guineas a week. Mr Willats was the first private patient to be admitted to the Hospital and on his discharge paid a bill of four guineas and became a subscriber of one guinea a year.

Regard for the Hospital was expressed in other ways. In 1854 the Reading Medical and Chirurgical Society, which had been formed in 1824, offered the Hospital their library, consisting of about 1,000 volumes. The library would become the property of the Hospital and no expense would be incurred on its transfer. Dr Burnett of Alton also offered the Hospital his museum containing some 100 specimens. Dr Cowan and Mr May suggested that if these collections were accepted, the post-mortem room and mortuary could be moved to a separate building in the Hospital grounds and the vacated room turned into a museum. The room above, which was used as both a library and museum, would then have more space to house the library. It was noted that the removal of the post-mortem room and mortuary from the main building would be highly desirable from a sanitary point of view.

These suggestions were adopted and the new post-mortem room was built at a cost of £135, the new museum was fitted up and the library equipped with extra shelves and a new Turkey carpet costing £18 15s. By April 1855 the alterations were complete. Following their next monthly meeting, the Secretary of the Pathological Society wrote to express thanks 'for the much improved and very excellent accommodation the Board has so liberally afforded them'. Today this collection of books forms a very important and interesting part of the library of the Pathological Society but, unfortunately, Dr Burnett's museum was disposed of nearly 50 years ago.

In 1854 the Vice Patron and first President of the Hospital, Mr Richard Benyon de Beauvoir, J.P., D.L., died at the age of 84. His great interest and generosity had extended beyond the building of the Hospital and from the early years of its development until quite recently he had chaired practically all the meetings of the Board of Management where his guidance had been invaluable. He was succeeded as President by his nephew, Mr Richard Benyon, M.P.

The year 1855 witnessed two changes in the Hospital. One was the decision that tea, butter and sugar should in future be supplied by the Hospital for all the patients as well as a better supply of towels and soap. It was anticipated that this would cost an additional £180 a year, but would be a great improvement on the present arrangement. Breakfast and tea would be made by the nurses on the wards, instead of in the kitchens, and a supply of tea pots was specially ordered.

The second change came through the resignation of Mr George May, the Senior Surgeon, who had been on the honorary medical staff since the Hospital opened. This was the first change to take place among the surgical staff. In 1845 Dr Edward Wells[3] had been appointed one of the honorary physicians in the Hospital following the retirement of Dr Pritchard Smith, but for over 15 years the honorary surgical staff had remained the same.

The Board of Management accepted Mr May's resignation with deep regret. His work in the Hospital had been invaluable and he was greatly respected by patients and staff alike for both his skill and compassion. The Board proposed that he should be nominated 'Surgeon Extraordinary' at the next Court of Governors.

Six candidates applied for the vacant position of Honorary Surgeon and the election took place at a Special Court of Governors held in July. One of the candidates was the former House Surgeon, Mr Moxhay, and another was Mr George May, Jr, son of the retiring Surgeon. Mr May produced diplomas in arts, medicine and surgery as well as numerous certificates and testimonials from the professors and surgeons at King's College Hospital. His application noted that he had become a Fellow of the Royal College of Surgeons by examination in 1851. Before that time it was customary to be made a Fellow by election.

Mr George May, Jr was elected the new Honorary Surgeon to the Hospital and at the same Special Court an alteration was made to the rules. In future:

'Every physician and surgeon who shall have filled their respective offices in the Hospital for 15 years may after their resignation be elected respectively "Consulting Physician" and "Consulting Surgeon" to the Hospital and, as such, shall be called in to all general consultations of the Faculty but they shall not interfere in any manner with the usual business of the Hospital.'

Mr George May became the first Consulting Surgeon to the Royal Berkshire Hospital on the same day that his son was elected an Honorary Surgeon.

Only weeks later Mr Edward Oliver, who had done so much to bring about the establishment of the Hospital, died in Benyon Ward at the age of 72. He had been knocked down by a Huntley and Palmer horse-driven van in London Street some days before. Details of the accident and the inquest that followed his death appeared in the papers with tributes to all the work he had done on behalf of the Hospital. Many people then and later believed that Mr Oliver's work had never received the recognition it deserved. One Minister wrote: 'If any man of wealth had incurred half the personal toil and sacrifice there would have been no end to his praise.' Mr Oliver lived to see the Hospital grow to almost double its original size and watched it fill the role that had been expected of it by its founders. Since its opening, the Hospital had treated 9,564 in-patients and 15,933 out-patients with many remarkable cures effected and operations performed.

The same papers that carried the tributes to Mr Oliver blazoned the news of the fall of Sebastopol. This victory heralded the end of the war that had been fought in the Crimea for the past two years. Before long Miss

Florence Nightingale, who had been nursing the sick and wounded in the Crimean hospitals, would return to England. The Royal Berkshire Hospital, with many others, would be influenced as a result of her work.

NOTES

1   The operation was described by Mr George May in the *London Medical Gazette*, 1842, Vol. 1, p. 49.
2   The cost of a funeral at the Reading Union at that time was 16/8d, 12/– for an elm coffin with a shroud and 4/8d for the fees of the clergyman at St Giles. It cost the Hospital 35/– for a nearby undertaker to bury patients who died with no one to pay for them.
3   Dr E. Wells, M.A., M.D., OXON, F.R.C.P. Fellow of New College, Oxford and Radcliffe Travelling Fellow, Oxford. Licentiate of Royal College of Physicians, London. Studied also at St George's Hospital.

3

EXPANSION, RE-ORGANISATION AND MEDICAL ADVANCE 1856 TO 1886

Over the next thirty years there were many changes at the Hospital but the most fundamental of them all were those made in reorganising the Nursing Department and in improving the sanitary conditions.

In August 1856 Miss Florence Nightingale returned to England from the Crimea and was greeted with the admiration and respect of the whole nation. Through her tireless work among the sick and wounded, she had demonstrated the importance of good nursing and what could and should be done to improve nursing standards and hygiene in both military and civilian hospitals. Many months before her return to England a special fund had been set up in London and this enabled the Nightingale School and Home for Nurses to be opened in 1860 at St Thomas's Hospital. Her book *Notes on Nursing* was published the same year, and in 1867 she wrote a paper on *Suggestions for the Improvement of the Nursing Service in Hospitals and on the Methods of Training Nurses for the Sick Poor*. Over the years she imparted her views and knowledge with force and clarity, and slowly but surely her suggestions were put into practice in hospitals throughout the country.

It was to be several years before these ideas and methods were adopted at the Royal Berkshire Hospital. In the meantime, the day-to-day routine continued much as before with the conditions of patients, nurses and servants leaving much to be desired. Although the employment of scrubbers at £9 a year had taken some of the hardship out of the work of both patients and nurses, there were still complaints from all quarters.

Many difficulties could be attributed directly to the character of the Matron. Mrs Tillbrooke was an aggressive woman with strong opinions and a short temper. Although firmness and discipline were needed in the wards and below stairs, she was not blessed with tact and frequent outbursts caused much unpleasantness with few people being left unscathed by her behaviour. A new House Surgeon, Mr Langdon, took up his duties in 1856 but within two months he had resigned, as the Matron had interfered with his work and he could not put up with her 'habitual temper'. The next House Surgeon, Mr Fernie, also crossed swords with the Matron and the Board were forced to draw her attention to the rules of the

Hospital. Time and again the Board were told of nurses and servants handing in their notice and of patients complaining of the Matron's unkindness and intolerance. On one occasion, Mrs Tillbrooke was advised to be 'very cautious' in her conduct after she had called one patient wicked and misguided because she was a Catholic. Such an atmosphere surrounding the Matron could not fail to have an effect on the staff and patients throughout the Hospital.

The nurses had little free time and even less privacy. They were overworked, tired and often ill. Since the enlargement of the Hospital, they had been given small partitioned cubicles in their wards instead of sleeping in a dormitory. This meant that they were seldom able to get away from the patients and the atmosphere of the wards. There were frequent complaints of their harshness, ill-temper, bad language and drunkenness from patients who had left the Hospital. All were investigated, but it was almost impossible to substantiate the claims as patients still in the Hospital were not prepared to say anything against the nurses who were looking after them.

Typical of such incidents was the complaint of Mrs Wells who, having been sent home as incurable, told of a patient being badly treated, struck and forced to do too much work. She also said that the ward was very noisy at night with songs being sung to the accompaniment of a concertina played by the nurse. The patient in question was called before the Board and confirmed that she lit the fire, swept out the ward and scrubbed the lockers, but insisted that she did no more than she could. She had not heard the nurse use bad language or seen her strike a patient, and any complaint about songs was incorrect as only hymns were sung. The nurse said these complaints were quite untrue and the woman who made them had come into the Hospital in a neglected and dirty state. She had attended her knowing how ill she was and had felt for her suffering. Once again, the Board could only state that they were satisfied there were no grounds for complaint, but perhaps they wondered.

In 1858 the complaint of a member of the Board of Management that Mr Sherwell, the Chaplain, was not complying with the rules concerning his duties was taken very seriously. The Board agreed that the spiritual state of the patients had been neglected and the Chaplain resigned. His successor was more attentive and also tightened up on the servants attending services in the chapel, discouraging their former practice of attending churches in the town.

The medical staff drew attention to the fact that the recommended diets were not being given to the patients. There was a lack of vegetables, the beer was not good, and boiled meat was being given daily instead of being alternated with roast. New diet tables were drawn up, a better quality of beer was ordered at 1/– a gallon and porter, which then cost 1/6d a gallon, was to be used as sparingly as possible. No servant should be given porter unless under medical treatment and female patients should only be given half a pint of beer each day.

The Hospital in 1862, showing extensions

The main difference between the diet tables of 1839 and those of 1858 was the halving of the quantity of meat supplied. The original criticism of too much meat being given compared with other hospitals had been noted. More bread and ½ lb butter per week as well as free tea and sugar were now included.

The nurses complained that their food was always cold when they received it. They were given permission to cook their own dinners in the wards after the patients had been fed, thereby adding to the smell and lack of ventilation.

While there were constant changes among the nursing and domestic staff between 1855 and 1860, as well as the appointment of a new House Surgeon and Chaplain, there was only one change among the honorary medical staff. In 1856 Mr T. B. Maurice resigned and was made a Consulting Surgeon. He had been on the medical staff since the Hospital opened and his retirement was greatly regretted. A special Court of Governors was called to elect his successor and two candidates, Mr Charles Vines and Mr William Moxhay, applied for the vacant post of Surgeon. Mr Moxhay was no stranger to the Hospital, having been House Surgeon from 1849 to 1854 when his ability and energy earned him much respect among the medical staff, the nurses and the patients. When the poll closed he had obained 175 of the 228 votes cast. It may well have been his remark after he was elected Surgeon that he had noticed a great laxity of discipline in the Hospital from the highest to the lowest that caused the Board of Management to consider the reasons behind the many problems. In 1860 Mrs Tillbrooke left the Hospital and Miss Williams succeeded her as Matron. Although many difficulties still remained, the atmosphere improved and the Board were able to turn their attention to problems of another kind.

Building Extensions 1861–66
Since 1855 the number of patients being treated at the Hospital had risen steadily each year and in 1860 there were 789 in-patients admitted and 86 operations performed besides the 1,423 out-patients treated. Ever greater demands were being made on the Hospital as the population of Reading and the surrounding district was increasing rapidly. For some time there had been a shortage of beds and a waiting list had been drawn up. Certain cases could expect to be in the Hospital for months on end and by today's standards the turnover was very slow, with the average length of treatment being about five and a half weeks.

In the spring of 1861 it was decided that additional wards should be built and also convalescent day rooms, which would ease the pressure on the wards and make it quieter for the severely ill who could not leave their beds. A local architect, Joseph Morris, was asked to submit designs. The first idea was to build out from the middle of the two southerly wings, but this was abandoned in favour of extending the front of the building. The plans produced by Joseph Morris provided two wings, one to the east for female patients and another to the west for male patients, each of which contained a convalescent day room on the ground floor and a ward for ten patients above. He skilfully made use of different levels so that the new wings complemented the original building and retained the visual emphasis on Henry Briant's imposing entrance.

Thirteen tenders were submitted for the work and that of a London firm, Messrs Sharpington and Cole, was accepted. A public appeal raised the necessary £5,451 very quickly and work was started in July 1861. In May 1862 the building was complete and Alice and Albert Wards were opened for the reception of an additional 20 patients. The convalescent rooms were made as attractive as possible with prints on the walls and periodicals such as the *Illustrated London News* provided for the patients to read. The Hospital rules were altered to allow cards, dice, dominoes and similar games to be played in these day rooms, although playing for money was strictly forbidden. The new wards were described as airy and cheerful and the Board confidently noted that with a total of 100 beds the Hospital would be adequate to meet requirements for many years to come.

In 1863 it was decided that the Board of Management would subscribe to the Metropolitan Servants Institution in High Holborn. For one guinea the Hospital would be sent as many nurses and servants as were required during the year and would also be saved the nuisance and expense of advertising in the papers. By this time seven nurses were employed, one on each of the six main wards, and a night nurse, as well as occasional temporary help. All were paid £16 a year except the Benyon Ward nurse, who received £20. The Matron's salary had remained unchanged at £50 a year. The domestic staff consisted of the cook, housemaid, kitchen maid, laundress, assistant laundress and two scrubbers.

On June 8th, 1863 Mr Holmes, the Assistant Surgeon at St George's Hospital and Dr Bristow of St Thomas's Hospital were sent to inspect the Royal Berkshire Hospital on behalf of the Health Department of the Privy Council. This was the first inspection the Hospital had experienced, and after nearly four hours the authorities were informed that the inspectors were 'much pleased with the building and the general arrangements'. The following year in an article in the *Medical Times and Gazette* Dr B. W. Richardson noted that the staff was insufficient compared with what was demanded in similar institutions. He also drew attention to the water closets and sinks adjoining the wards. These points were to receive much attention in the years to come.

By 1865 there was once again a shortage of beds and the male convalescent day room was turned into a temporary ward for ten patients. Joseph Morris was asked to prepare plans for a further enlargement of the Hospital. It was agreed that Benyon and Sidmouth Wards would once again be extended southwards to provide an additional twenty beds, ten on each floor, with a gardener's cottage under the southern end of the building. There would be no basement between the cottage and the present end of the ward and the walls would be carried on arches to enable the free passage of air in the central court. The tender of Messrs Wheeler of Reading was accepted and the following year the work was completed and the Hospital enlarged to provide 120 beds, 70 for male patients and 50 for female patients. No public appeal had been made and the total cost of just over £2,000 was met from Hospital funds. Charles Ferreby was engaged as gardener at 14/– a week and given the newly built cottage as unfurnished accommodation. With additional patients now being admitted, it was decided that the time had come to increase the medical staff and to appoint an Assistant Surgeon. At the Annual Court held in February 1866, Mr O. C. Maurice, a former House Surgeon from 1860–62, was unanimously elected to this new office.

The Re-organisation of the Nursing and Domestic Staff 1866–1871
Since Miss Williams had been appointed Matron, the management of both the nursing and domestic staff had improved, but the nurses supplied by the Metropolitan Servants Institution were very similar to those obtained before and none was properly trained.

Early in 1866 a request was received by the Board of Management, the outcome of which was to have a profound effect on the re-organisation of the nursing staff. The Board were asked if 'a very respectable person' could attend the Hospital daily for a few weeks to learn to do dressings. She had been offered a job as a village nurse by a gentleman in Cornwall and was keen to gain some practical experience. The Board approved, and Mr Moxhay on behalf of the medical staff commented that 'it was worth a trial' and 'likely to be a means of extending the usefulness of the Hospital'.

This venture opened up new possibilities and one month later a small committee was formed 'to investigate the practicability and advisability of training nurses to let out or for the purpose of supplying the Hospital when vacancies occur.'

The Committee's enquiries were extensive and brought to light most forcibly the fact that fundamental changes would have to be made in the nursing arrangements of the Hospital. The days of the women from the workhouse were over, and in future only properly trained nurses should be employed. The Board of Management gave Miss Williams three months' notice to leave and agreed to engage a Superintendent to take over the entire management of the nurses and to act as Matron. The original question of training nurses for work outside the Hospital was left unresolved in view of the more urgent need to reorganise the existing nursing arrangements.

Miss Nightingale's institution, the Liverpool Training Institution and Dr Falconer of the Bath Home for Trained Nurses were approached for advice and information. Several 'kind and invaluable' letters were received from Miss Nightingale herself.

The Board were impressed by Dr Falconer and the Bath Home and in June 1866 entered an agreement whereby the Home would supply the Hospital with one trained Superintendent Nurse and three trained nurses.

The Superintendent would receive a salary of £70 per year, one nurse £30 a year and the other two nurses £20 a year. The Bath Home would also send their own probationers to be trained in the Hospital. They would be given board, lodging and laundry, would receive no salary but should they later be engaged as nurses in the Hospital, they would be paid £20 a year. The Superintendent and nurses would be regarded as the permanent nursing staff and would be subject to the Hospital rules and regulations. The Superintendent would have complete control over the wards, the nurses and the female servants and would manage the kitchen department, but not the purchase and delivery of provisions. Neither the nurses nor the probationers would be called upon to do scrubbing or 'any menial duties whatever'. They would be given at least two weeks' holiday a year. The Hospital would pay the Bath Home direct, who in turn would pay the salaries of the nurses.

In August 1866 the new Superintendent, Miss Smith, arrived from the Bath Home with three trained nurses and on the same day Miss Williams and four nurses left the Hospital. Within a week Miss Smith asked for three more nurses to be obtained immediately as well as additional kitchen and laundry staff. In a short time the nursing staff had been increased to ten besides the Superintendent and the Visitors were noting 'a visible improvement in the general management of the wards'. The period of transition was not completely smooth and one disturbance was recorded in Adelaide Ward 'to the prejudice of the new nurses'.

Several changes were made throughout the Hospital, including a rise in wages for all the domestic staff. A special dining-room was provided for the nurses and cooking was no longer allowed in the wards. A library was formed for the nurses with periodicals such as the *Illustrated London News* besides books on nursing. On the wards toys and games were obtained for the children and a simpler form of prayers was read each day. The storage of splints and instruments was re-organised and a special splint room was made for the storage of the large variety which would now always be available. The suggestion that prescriptions should be hung above the patients' beds was not adopted as the medical staff objected to their prescriptions being 'exposed'.

Within three months Miss Smith became ill and the Sidmouth Ward nurse was put in charge during her absence. Problems arose once again on the wards and it became noticeable that there was a division of authority between the Hospital and the Bath Home. To add to the difficulties, it was found that probationers were being supplied to the Hospital instead of trained nurses. In December 1866 it was decided that the arrangement with the Bath Home would be terminated. Another Superintendent and a completely new staff of nurses would be obtained from elsewhere and the Hospital would in future run its Nursing Department independently of any other institution.

Miss Nightingale, among others, was approached by the Committee in their search for a new Superintendent and she wrote to the Chairman with advice. Unfortunately neither this nor any former correspondence with the Hospital has survived. In the meantime Miss Smith had recovered and decided not to return to the Bath Home. She applied for the job of Superintendent and was re-appointed at her former salary of £70 a year. Another nurse was asked to stay on and additional trained nurses were obtained through the South Audley Street Institution in London, all of whom were paid a salary of £20 a year.

Gradually the Nursing Department was brought to full strength and additional help was obtained with assistant nurses engaged at £10 a year. Altogether a staff of ten nurses was employed as well as probationers. Each nurse was supplied with material to make two jackets and skirts each year, these clothes to be considered the property of the Hospital. The probationers were given such outer clothing as Miss Smith considered necessary. In 1869 the nurses were given their own bathroom instead of using the one attached to Alice Ward. The following year the sleeping accommodation of the Benyon and Sidmouth nurses was improved when their cubicles and the ward bathrooms were transposed. Those nurses not sleeping in the wards were given a dormitory in the Hospital. When the nurses' salaries were raised to £22, increasing by £2 a year to £26 a year, each nurse was required to provide her own clothes and the probationers were given £4 a year in lieu.

Benyon Ward, the busy accident ward, now employed two nurses, but as they were constantly under pressure a servant was sent to help with the more ordinary tasks. The difference in status between the nurses and servants had by now become most obvious. The Board noted that the nursing staff were 'greatly superior in education and intelligence to those who were previously employed'. Furthermore, it was believed that owing to their duties they should be given a better diet than that of the ordinary servants; indeed, the Committee noted quite firmly: 'They should be considered superior to the servants and treated with consideration and respect.' Miss Smith was relieved of her duties of managing the household and devoted all her time to the Nursing Department. The Secretary took on the duties of a House Steward and with the Housekeeper ran the household side of the Hospital, making the organisation of the nursing and domestic staff entirely separate.

Better organisation and training did not necessarily mean happier nurses and patients, and one incident led to a very different aspect being noted. Problems had arisen when certain visitors were allowed on the wards out of visiting hours. Miss Smith believed this to be unnecessary, saying the patients were never lonely or in need of comfort and sympathy. The Chaplain felt quite differently, and wrote: 'The Head of the Nursing Staff (under whom the others are now little more than dumb machines) so coolly repels the kind offers of those who would minister to the relief of the sufferers and treats the patients and speaks of them rather as animals to be watched and tended according to prescribed rules than as our fellow sufferers.' Was this to be the price of a better nursing system?

A House Committee was formed in July 1869 to deal with domestic matters and to be available to any member of the household who might wish to contact them. This Committee consisted of four people appointed by the Board of Management; they met once a month and had the power to engage and dismiss the male servants and to pay the wages of all the nurses and servants. Early in 1870 they were responsible for revising the rules for the in-patients and clarified points concerning the behaviour and work expected of patients in the wards.

Under the sixteen detailed rules, patients were required to behave correctly, not to use improper or abusive language, nor to swear. They were not permitted to smoke in the wards or to gamble. They were not to put any coal on the fire or to stir it after it was made up, nor to open and shut windows or touch the blinds. They were to keep silent during visits of the medical staff and in the presence of officers of the institution. Rule 4 stipulated: 'Such patients as are able shall assist in nursing the patients or in doing such work as the House Surgeon or Superintendent may require with the approbation of the medical attendants. Every such patient who shall refuse to assist shall be reported to the weekly Board of Visitors.' Visiting times were limited to Wednesdays and Saturdays between 2 p.m. and 3 p.m., except by special permission. Patients could only have two visitors at a time and anyone detected bringing in food or drink would not be allowed to visit again except with permission. Friends and relations living in the country could visit on Sundays if their work prevented them visiting during the week, but anyone who came during the week could not come again on Sunday.

The following year, in 1871, the House Committee was asked to draw up a report on the domestic arrangements in the Hospital. Various difficulties had been arising and once again many of the problems resulted from the attitude of the Matron. Miss Smith was efficient but cold and intolerant. Patients had complained that they were made to stand while she was in the room. On the household side poor food, bad cooking, dirty dishes, badly washed linen and frequent changes of servants had all been noted. Letters telling of the care of some nurses were outweighed by others pointing out instances of neglect or unkindness. When the House Surgeon, Mr Royds, tendered his resignation he was asked to reconsider and offered a rise in salary. He replied that no amount of salary would induce him to stay so long as Miss Smith was there.

The House Committee contacted several hospitals about their domestic organisation and found that many had experienced difficulties similar to those of the Royal Berkshire Hospital. They recommended that the office of Housekeeper should be abolished; a Superintendent should be appointed to take over the management of both the Nursing Department and the Household Department and that she should be a fully trained nurse. Two nurses should be selected by the Superintendent to be responsible to her for the general management of the medical and surgical wards respectively with a slight increase in salary. A 'person of superior class' should be engaged as cook who, under the control of the Superintendent, would take charge of the kitchen department.

This scheme, the House Committee believed, would not incur any increase in expenditure and the Board of Management had no hesitation in agreeing to the recommendation. The situation of Superintendent was advertised and Miss Smith resigned. In June 1871 Miss Baster, the Superintendent of the Eye and Ear Infirmary at Bradford, was appointed Superintendent at a salary of £70 a year. Under her guidance and authority the Hospital entered a new period of expansion which included the re-organisation of the Out-patients Department, the consideration of a convalescent home and the establishment of a private nursing scheme.

The Out-Patients Department

Since the opening of the Hospital out-patients had been seen three times a week on Mondays, Wednesdays and Saturdays. It had been arranged that one surgeon and one physician should attend on these days so that each of the honorary medical staff was required to see the out-patients once a week. These duties were not popular with the surgeons and in 1849 when Mr Moxhay was the House Surgeon it became usual for him unofficially to see the out-patients on behalf of the surgeons. In 1854 it was found that whereas all the physicians attended the out-patients, among the surgeons Mr May never came, Mr Bulley rarely did so and Mr Maurice only attended in case his opinion should be needed. The Board noted that the rules had become very relaxed and required that they should be kept in future.

The out-patients' days remained unpopular with the surgeons and when Dr Cowan gave up attending in 1865 the medical staff asked if the Monday clinic could be stopped so that that day could be kept clear for operations and consultations. The Board were reluctant to do this, and wondered if the appointment of an Assistant Medical Officer would ease the problem. As the medical staff could come to no agreement on this point the Board investigated the possibility of arranging with the Reading Dispensary for the out-patients to be seen there instead of at the Hospital. The Dispensary, however, was short of space and was unable to help the Hospital at that particular time. A compromise was then reached and it was agreed with the medical staff that the duties of the Assistant Surgeon, who was about to be appointed, would include attending on out-patients' days as well as assisting at operations and in cases of emergency. When Mr O. C. Maurice was elected Assistant Surgeon in 1866 the Board stressed that they hoped the medical staff would continue to see the out-patients and not regard Mr Maurice's appointment as a substitute for their own attendance.

In 1868 Mr Bulley retired and was made a Consulting Surgeon and Mr O. C. Maurice succeeded him as an Honorary Surgeon. The office of Assistant Surgeon was left unfilled. Later that year Dr Cowan died and Dr Richard Shettle succeeded him as Honorary Physician. The Out-patients

Department was still causing problems with large numbers attending on each of the three days. Up to 100 patients would fill the entrance to the Hospital and the surrounding corridors. The noise of so many people and the risk of infection being brought to the building caused some anxiety. For the patients themselves there were such long delays that it was decided that refreshments should be provided. Tickets costing 2d were made available from the Hall Porter, and this enabled one pint of soup and bread to be obtained.

The medical staff were still very keen that the Monday out-patients' day should be stopped and Dr Wells put their views once again before the Board. It was decided that the Monday clinics would be stopped for a trial period of one month and a record should be kept of the number of patients attending on the other two days and of how long they had to wait. The results of the trial showed that on Wednesday May 27th, 78 medical cases and 66 surgical cases attended out-patients. The hall, waiting rooms, stairs and passages were filled with the 144 patients. At 5 p.m. there were still at least 20 patients waiting to be seen and it was 6 o'clock before the last left for home. One patient had walked from Goring Heath intending to go home with the carrier. She was kept waiting so long that she missed her lift and had to walk home, getting there at 10 o'clock at night. There was no argument now with the medical staff. Mondays would be retained as an out-patients' day. A Committee was formed to look into the whole organisation of the Department.

The Committee produced a report with long-term and more immediate recommendations. They believed that at some time in the future patients from Reading and nearby would be seen at the Reading Dispensary, 'a charity with precisely similar objectives and now only wanting funds to increase its work', and patients from further afield could be seen at dispensaries to be established in the surrounding villages. This would leave the 'more peculiar' cases to be dealt with in the Hospital. In the meantime they suggested out-patients should be seen daily except on Sundays and three Assistant Medical Officers should be appointed to attend each day in rotation. A new and separate Out-patients Department might be built in the grounds of the Hospital.

Although the Board were willing to adopt these recommendations, the medical staff were not. They believed the problems had been exaggerated and basically what was needed was an Assistant Dispenser as they felt the difficulties were caused by delays in making up the prescriptions. One additional Assistant Medical Officer was all that was needed and this would be equal to the requirements of the Hospital for some time to come. The Board bowed to the opinion of the medical staff. An Assistant Dispenser would be employed on out-patient days and a Special Court was convened to appoint an Assistant Medical Officer. On September 15th, 1868 Mr F. Workman was appointed to this new office with the same privileges and duties as that of Assitant Surgeon.

The job of Assistant Dispenser was of short duration and in May

1870 the Board decided that for an additional 1/– a week the errand boy would help the Dispenser on out-patient days. Mr Hadwen was given a rise in salary to £80 a year, provided he did his job satisfactorily, and was given his dinner at the Hospital on out-patient days.

It was also suggested that the appointment of a dentist would be beneficial. He could attend on out-patient days to draw teeth and perform any other dental operations required. Although the medical staff agreed there would be advantages in such an appointment, they believed a dentist should only attend when requested by them, otherwise there might be 'inconveniences' between the House Surgeon and the dentist. It had been quite normal for the House Surgeon to extract teeth on out-patients' days and the first use of ether in the Hospital had been on such occasions. At other times the surgeons had obtained the assistance of local dentists for operations such as cleft palates but the time had not yet come for a dentist to be appointed to the medical staff of the Hospital.

One suggestion made by the Committee in 1868 was taken up again two years later. It was agreed that a suitable building should be erected in the Hospital grounds to accommodate the Out-patients Department. By 1870 this now urgent need coincided with other plans for extending the Hospital.

The Convalescent Fund
In 1865 the administration of the Convalescent Fund, which had been in the hands of the Chaplain since its formation in 1841, was transferred to the Board of Management. By this time the number of patients applying to the Fund for assistance had increased so considerably that it was believed the administration would be made easier if the Board took over. All applications would be put before the Board by the House Surgeon and any assistance to be given from the Convalescent Fund could then be arranged as each case was considered. The Fund would be kept entirely separate from the finances of the Hospital and yearly accounts would be included in the Annual Reports. As this new arrangement would involve additional work for the Secretary, his salary was increased to £150 a year. The Fund was still financed by donations and special annual subscriptions but whenever possible applicants were asked to contribute what they could afford.

The need for the Convalescent Fund in 1865 was as great as it had been when it was first established. Social conditions had not changed in the intervening years and the problems of the poor remained the same as they were before. It was to be many decades before there was an appreciable improvement in the overcrowded houses with poor sanitation, inadequate food and lack of warmth and clothing. Conditions for the poor in Reading, a rapidly growing industrial town, were even more unfavourable than those in the surrounding rural areas. Tuberculosis and rickets were all too common and conditions which can now be helped by surgery could then only be alleviated by the use of supports and appliances. Without the help of the Convalescent Fund many patients would have been unable to obtain the equipment they needed and it is not difficult to imagine the suffering of those with unsupported hernias, children unable to walk without irons or the amputees without their wooden limbs.

Applications to the Convalescent Fund were considered by the Board of Management at their weekly meetings. Details of the help needed were followed by a discussion of the financial position of the patient and family concerned. These records are a catalogue of the poverty of the time.

It was particularly difficult for patients who were out of work to pay for their appliances. These were sometimes so expensive that even patients who had a wage earner in the family could not afford the cost. Artificial arms at 35/–, artificial legs at 30/–, irons at £5, shoes for club feet at £2 and Jury masts for patients with Potts disease at five guineas were beyond the means of most. When Sarah Ford, whose husband earned 11/– a week, needed an artificial leg and foot her parish came to her help. The Vicar raised part of the money needed and the Convalescent Fund paid the difference.

Requests for artificial eyes were not granted but spectacles costing 2/– a pair were frequently supplied. An application for artificial teeth in 1869 was allowed and the Convalescent Fund agreed to pay the three guineas Mr Liddon, the Dentist, said he would charge for a set.

There was no ambulance at that time and on many occasions the 'Flyman' was paid to take a patient home. By 1869 these payments had become so numerous the Board had to draw the line and say that in future fares home would only be paid in exceptional circumstances.

The Board of Management with its administration of the Convalescent Fund was the forerunner of the hospital almoner. Occasionally the records describe certain cases in detail and show the feeling of compassion combined with the need for thrift as week after week applications for help were received. When William Fry walked from London to Reading in search of work in 1867, he arrived so exhausted and with such injured feet that he was admitted to the Hospital. When he was fit enough to leave it was discovered that his uncle, with whom he had been living in London, would not have him back. The Board arranged for the boy to be given a job at the biscuit factory and in the meantime gave him 1/6d and arranged to pay the 2/– for his first week's lodging.

When Ebenezer Blandy had both his legs amputated he was recommended 'some mechanical contrivance to enable him to move about'. It was decided that to begin with he would be provided with leather pads and a pair of crutches. Attention was drawn to the distressing nature of the case and it was pointed out that help would be needed when the boy returned to his home. The Board agreed to allow 5/– a week from the Convalescent Fund for his support for one month and this would be given to the Vicar of his parish to be distributed as he thought best. Nearly three months later the boy was recommended a pair of wooden legs. These would be supplied by the Convalescent Fund as the boy's father was a labourer earning 14/– a week and with a family of four children could not afford the cost. But, to the surprise of the Board, the Blandy family refused the wooden legs and asked if the £3 could be put towards a pair of cork ones with feet attached. The Board decided that if the recommended wooden legs were not acceptable the Convalescent Fund could not be used to supply 'ornamental' ones instead. Such a request was unnecessary and extravagant and could not be allowed.

It was decided in June 1869 that the Convalescent Fund could be used for sending scrofula and similar cases to institutions for convalescence or to places which were specially adapted for their condition. Annual subscriptions were sent to the Royal Sea Bathing Infirmary at Margate, which had been established in 1796 by a Quaker physician, John Coakley Lettsom, for children suffering from tuberculosis, and also to the Eastbourne Convalescent Hospital. This enabled patients from the Royal Berkshire Hospital to be sent there on a regular basis.

It was felt that other patients would also benefit from a period of rest before returning to their work. It was suggested by the Chairman at the Annual Court in 1871 that a small convalescent home might be established in connection with the Hospital and it was believed that such a scheme would be sympathetically received by the public. Early the next year Mr Hibbert of Braywick Lodge, a Vice President and generous supporter of the Hospital, offered £1,000 towards the building of a convalescent home in the neighbourhood of Reading to be run in connection with the Royal Berkshire Hospital. A Committee was formed to investigate the feasibility of Mr Hibbert's proposal.

This offer came at a time when other developments at the Hospital were also under consideration. When the new system of nursing was adopted in 1866 it was hoped that at some time a group of nurses trained at the Hospital could be formed to provide private nursing in the town and neighbourhood. The various problems encountered during the reorganisation of the Nursing Department delayed the establishment of such a scheme and it was not until 1870 that the Board of Management decided that they should proceed with this plan whenever possible.

In parallel with this was the urgent need for better out-patient facilities, and in July 1870 it was finally agreed that a separate building should be erected in the Hospital grounds to accommodate both the out-patients and the private nursing staff. This decision coincided with more problems in the nursing and domestic departments and it was not until the spring of 1872, when the Hospital was running smoothly under the new Superintendent, Miss Baster, that it was possible to consider this next stage of development. It was at this point that Mr Hibbert made his offer.

There was never any doubt that the building of a convalescent home would be of great benefit but after much consideration the Committee concluded that for financial reasons they could not recommend the idea and with very great regret Mr Hibbert's most generous offer was declined. It was suggested instead that the convalescent day wards should be retained and to relieve the pressure on the Hospital the female wards should now be extended to correspond with the male wards which had been enlarged in 1866. Any additional building should be to provide accommodation for private nurses and the Out-patients Department.

The New Buildings 1872–73

By July 1872 Mr Joseph Morris, the architect, had produced plans for the enlargement of Victoria and Adelaide wards to provide an additional 20 beds. He had also designed two single-storey buildings to be erected in front of the Hospital for the Private Nurses and the Out-patients Department. The style blended well with the original building and complemented the wings which he had designed just over ten years before. The Board of Management approved the plans, tenders were obtained and a public appeal for funds was launched. Within weeks Messrs Clarke and Co.'s tender for the building work was accepted, a Clerk of Works was engaged and the building began. The Lodge Porter was given 1/6d a week as the new out-patients' building would deprive him of his garden.

By 1873 the building was well under way. Various alterations were made to improve the laundry facilities and in the spring the grounds were laid out and furniture and fittings ordered.

The Out-patients Department was on the west side, parallel to Redlands Road. It provided a large waiting room, a dispensary, consulting rooms for the surgeons and physicians, changing rooms and facilities for the performance of minor operations.

The Nurses' Home was on the east side and corresponded in size and style to the out-patients' building. It contained eight separate bedrooms, one large sitting-room, kitchen and bathroom. In January 1873 the House Committee drew up rules for the administration of the Private Nursing Scheme and Miss Baster started to look for suitable nurses. Early in July a notice was placed in the local papers that trained nurses were ready to be sent out for private nursing, and by the middle of the month the Private Nursing Scheme was in operation.

The total cost of the new buildings, including furniture and fittings and the laying out of the grounds, was £6,196. About half this sum was raised by donations to the Building Fund and the remainder was taken from the sale of stock. This expenditure had enabled the Hospital to be enlarged to provide 140 beds, 70 for each sex, the convalescent wards had been retained, and the Out-patients' Department had been made entirely separate from the main building with greatly improved facilities. In addition, a Private Nursing Scheme had been established which from the outset was to prove a great success.

In the meantime Dr Wells had asked that his out-patients' duties should be given to someone else. The Board decided that the time had come to appoint an Assistant Physician, as the Hospital was now greatly enlarged and this new officer would be able to help on out-patients' days. Mr Workman, the Assistant Medical Officer, was made Assistant Surgeon and a special Court elected Dr John Shea (the Medical Officer of Health for Reading) the new Assistant Physician. In anticipation of their increased duties the House Surgeon, Mr Galpin, was given a rise in salary of £20 to £100 a year and the salary of Miss Baster, the Superintendent, was increased to £90 a year. Both were able and efficient and the Board of Management were reassured that at last the Hospital was running well and the problems of the previous years were over.

The Private Nursing Scheme

The Winchester Hospital in 1869 was one of the first to adopt a private nursing scheme and its success and method of organisation were influential in the establishment of the scheme at the Royal Berkshire Hospital. The object of the new Department was to provide well-trained nurses for private families at a set scale of charges and also eventually to make the same service available either free or at a reduced rate to the poor of the town and neighbourhood. The nurses would be trained in the Hospital and would be available to assist on the wards if not engaged in private nursing. They would be housed at the new Nurses' Home quite separately from the nurses employed at the Hospital. Miss Baster would be in charge of the scheme and applications would be made to her for the services of the private nursing staff. Medical and surgical cases would be charged one guinea per week; fever and infectious cases £1 11s 6d per week and, although mental cases were not usually to be undertaken, the charge in such instances would be two guineas per week. The nurses would be paid by the Hospital with board, lodging and laundry provided either at the Nurses' Home or by the families employing them. Special regulations were drawn up, including the requirement that at the end of each case the Superintendent should be notified by the family of the conduct and efficiency of the nurse employed.

At the end of 1873, when the scheme had been in operation for about six months, a profit of £62 18s 3d had been made. The eight nurses had been constantly employed and their services had been greatly appreciated in every case. In 1875 it was decided that the scheme should be extended to the poor, either at a reduced rate or gratuitously as circumstances dictated. Except in emergencies, the Board would decide on the charge to be made and it was noted that the rules requiring the nurses to be maintained by the family they were attending should be strictly adhered to. In March 1875, at the request of the Revd O. Slocock, a nurse was sent to look after a poor woman at Greenham for one month free of charge. Other cases followed with nurses being sent to poor families in Reading and the surrounding towns and villages at either a reduced rate or at no charge at all. By 1876 the scheme was working so well with nurses being sent to attend both the poor and those who could afford to pay that the salaries of the nurses were increased to £24 a year, rising by £2 a year to a maximum of £34. Occasional gratuities were now allowed on the recommendation of Miss Baster, and the profits were paid into a separate Private Nursing Fund.

The Private Nurses were dedicated people. Without question or hesitation they attended all types of cases in every sort of circumstances. In some instances it was discovered that the families were so poor they could not afford to feed and maintain the nurses who were attending them. Nurse Woodford found she could obtain no food with the family of the old lady she had been sent to care for. Another nurse sent to a boy with typhoid fever found the patient and the rest of the family all sharing one room. Both nurses had to return to the Hospital each day for food and rest. Nurse Cox was sent to two typhoid cases in Brightwell free of charge. When she returned to the Hospital she was given one guinea from the Nurses' Fund for 'having cheerfully borne the personal discomfort that could not be prevented'. Mental cases could be especially difficult. One nurse was sent to the Reading Gaol to attend a female prisoner with a mental disorder, and Nurse Giles spent six months attending a mental case, at the end of which she was given a gratuity of £5. The strain on the nurses was considerable and it was not uncommon for them to have to go to the coast for a period of rest at the expense of the Nurses' Fund.

Very occasionally there were problems, as in the instance when Nurse Williams was sent to attend a case at Prospect Park and arrived in a state of intoxication. Such cases were quite exceptional and letters of appreciation of the kindness of the nurses were constantly being received. Lady Swinbourne of Holmwood, Shiplake, was so grateful for the help the two nurses had given during her husband's illness that besides the fees, she gave a donation of £20 to the Nurses' Fund, £20 to the Convalescent Fund and a further £10 to Nurse Woodford.

The Board of Management were delighted with the success of the scheme. In 1877 about 100 cases were attended by the Private Nurses and year by year the number increased. Not only was the scheme self-financing but the need for and benefits obtained from professional nursing care were being demonstrated to rich and poor alike. In the words of the Chairman, it was hoped that 'the former style of ignorant and inefficient old women may rapidly disappear and be replaced by respectable, humane, kindly women who are properly trained and take an interest in their duties'. The Private Nurses were pioneering the new system of nursing beyond the hospital wards.

Conditions on the Wards
Miss Baster supervised both the nursing and household departments with care and efficiency and ensured the smooth running of the wards, the Outpatients Department and the Private Nursing Scheme. The Hospital now consisted of 10 main wards – the original Benyon, Sidmouth, Victoria and Adelaide wards with their four extended back wards, Albert and Alice wards – as well as the two convalescent day wards and seven small side wards leading from the two southern wings.

The wards had changed very little over the years. John B. Jones in his *Sketches of Reading* described them in 1870 as clean and airy, with the

Group of Hospital staff, *c*1880

women's wards decorated with biblical texts and pictures. They were still heated by open coal fires and lit by candles. A request in 1872 that gas lights should be installed in the wards was rigorously opposed by the medical staff, who felt that such a system could not be recommended and should be limited to the other areas of the Hospital. A staff of eight trained nurses and eight probationers looked after the patients and a nurses' room was attached to each of the main wards as before.

The rule which limited the admission of children to those over six years old except for cases of emergency or those requiring surgery was relaxed in 1869. Special cribs were obtained and before long the number of young patients had increased considerably. In November 1874 Miss Baster pointed out that there were 15 children under six and a further ten between six and ten years old now in the Hospital, 'all suffering in such a way that they are fretful and often cry for hours after their dressings'. She suggested a separate children's ward would be better for all concerned. It was agreed that Alice Ward would be the most suitable as it was cheerful and away from the other wards. The children were transferred and Alice Ward became the first children's ward in the Hospital. It was described as more of a nursery than a ward with toys and games and a cheerful atmosphere that belied the sickness of its inmates.

The expansion of the Hospital put increasing pressure on everyone who worked there. The post of Assistant Dispenser requested by the medical staff in 1868 had been of short duration and since 1870 the errand boy had been the only help available to the greatly overworked Dispenser. All the medicines for the in-patients and out-patients were prepared by Mr Hadwen and on Saturday, June 14th, 1872 a dreadful mistake was made. Mary Ann Corps had been admitted suffering from uterine disease and had been prescribed a sedative containing chloral hydrate to be taken each night. On the night in question the dose was administered as usual with disastrous effect, for within half an hour the patient was dead. It was discovered that inadvertently prussic acid had been substituted for chloral hydrate. Mr Hadwen was suspended and a full investigation carried out. The jury at the inquest returned a verdict of accidental death with the recommendation that additional assistance should be given to the Dispenser as they believed he was 'over-pressed by the great numbers of cases for which he had to dispense, especially on out-patients' days'. The medical staff told the Board they had complete confidence in Mr Hadwen and on the recommendation of the House Committee, he was reinstated three weeks later. Special arrangements were made in the two Dispensaries to keep the poisons in fluted bottles under lock and key and an Assistant Dispenser was obtained from Bradley and Bliss, the chemist. When this assistant was dismissed for misconduct with a female servant, the Reading Board of Guardians was approached. It was arranged that the Dispenser at their pauper dispensary would attend the Hospital three times a week for £30 a year. The employment of the errand boy at 1/– a week had proved, quite fatally, to have been a false economy.

Various non-medical facilities were gradually obtained for the patients. In 1872 Miss Baster suggested that chairs should be purchased to take patients to and from the bathrooms. When it was found that the 'Bath chairs' cost four guineas each, the carpenter was asked to fit four wheels on strong wicker chairs as this would suit the purpose at a fraction of the cost. Newspapers were supplied to the convalescent wards in 1872, although two years before the Chaplain at that time had been strongly against the suggestion, saying they would do unmentionable harm and he could not speak of the evils that arose 'with a taste for daily penny papers, apart from the positively hurtful matters often found in them.' The next Chaplain organised a better supply of books for the patients' library, having pronounced those available as rather dull.

The Prince and Princess of Wales (the future king Edward VII and Queen Alexandra) visited Reading in 1870, and at the request of the medical staff the patients were allowed to watch the procession from the convalescent wards and a specially erected platform in front of the Hospital. This was the first recorded special occasion for the patients. In 1873 a 'Magic Performance' was given to the patients and staff and was such a success that it was followed by concerts and similar events from time to time. Mr Moxhay was very enthusiastic about such occasions and organised a 'Musical Entertainment' in 1874. A suggested performance of 'Box and Cox' was not considered suitable but the offer of the Reading

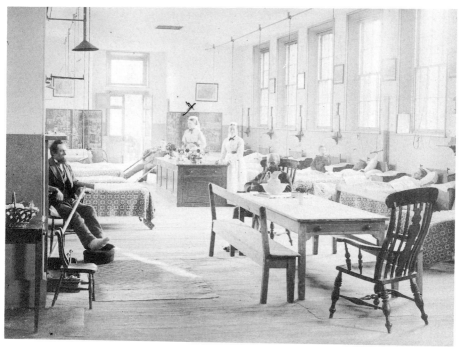

Benyon Ward *c*1880

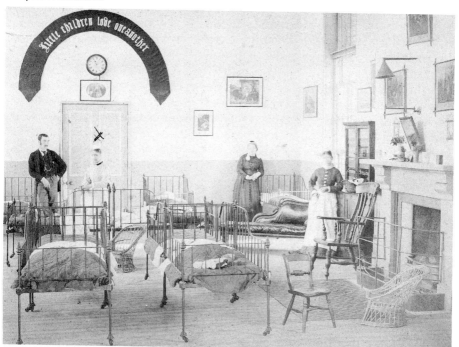

Alice Ward *c*1880

Rifle Volunteer Band to play in the Hospital grounds was accepted. From 1883 it became quite usual for such outdoor concerts to be given in the summer months.

Sanitary Conditions

The improvements that had taken place in the nursing system and in the organisation of the domestic establishment had not been matched in the sanitary conditions of the Hospital. The 'objectionable', 'dirty and unwholesome' system of water closets and sinks at the end of each ward which Dr Richardson had noted in 1864 was still in use ten years later. In 1870 earth closets on wheels were provided for Benyon Ward patients who could leave their beds but were unable to go to the lavatories and the number of bathrooms in the Hospital had by now been increased to four. John Jones's description of the clean and airy wards did not mention the smell that permeated everywhere, as offensive drains were commonplace.

The quality of water from the main was good but often the supply was inadequate. Alexander Ford complained in 1870 that on admission he had been given a bath in which seven patients had bathed before. His complaint was investigated and confirmed. The porter said it took about ten minutes to fill the bath and the same time to empty it. On some occasions the supply stopped altogether, and men had to be employed to pipe and carry water to the tanks in the building. In 1874 an old well was re-opened and dug deeper and a forcing pump was used to obtain water when the main supply became inadequate or stopped. The following year the procedure was resorted to again and it was to be some while before these problems were eventually overcome.

Following the outbreaks of cholera in the 1830s and 1840s, much thought was given throughout the country to the need for a good water supply and proper sanitation. The causes of disease and the reason for its spread were not fully understood at this time. A connection between cholera and the water supply had been convincingly demonstrated by John Snow in 1849 and the report made to the Reading Board of Health in 1850 spelt out what should be done to improve the sanitary state of the town. Progress in this direction was slow, and it took two further Public Health Acts in 1872 and 1875 to organise the local Sanitary Authority and give it the legal power to complete these and other recommendations.

The Act of 1872 provided for the appointment of Medical Officers of Health and Sanitary Inspectors in every sanitary district, and the Reading Urban Sanitary Authority appointed Dr John Shea to the former office. The following year he was appointed Assistant Physician to the Hospital where his knowledge, advice and authority were to prove invaluable in the improvement of the sanitary conditions of that building. Water closets, sinks and bathrooms were repaired or replaced with better systems with levers and cisterns. Better connections were made with the outside drains and special vents inserted for the escape of foul air. The Hospital became linked with the main drainage in 1876 after the town sewer was installed

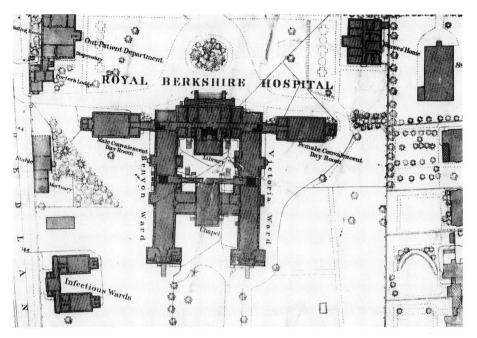

Plan of the Hospital in 1879 (reproduced from O.S. map 10″ to 1 mile, Reading edition 1879)

and gradually over the following years the sanitation was improved. The complaints of neighbours of the offensive smell of the pig stye and manure heaps in the Hospital grounds seemed insignificant by comparison but when the Board was threatened with prosecution, it was agreed that this profitable sideline should now be given up and the 'pig account' was closed.

There were also other more basic problems concerning the disposal of used bandages and dressings and the burial of amputated limbs. Dr Shea, as Medical Officer of Health, was consulted and recommended that bandages should be burnt in the furnaces (previously they had often been flushed down the drains) and that the amputated limbs should be buried in a pit of quicklime at least three feet deep. It was anticipated that at some point burial in the Hospital grounds would no longer be practical, at which time an undertaker would have to arrange for the disposal of such limbs.

The Infectious Wards 1875

It was usual for patients developing infectious illnesses while in hospital to be isolated. From time to time there were cases of mumps, measles, chicken pox, scarlet fever and, more seriously, cases of erysipelas. By 1875 the incidence of this last infection was increasing and the surgeons had become loath to operate. Dr Shea confirmed the opinion of the medical staff that a separate building was now required for infectious cases. He drew attention to the danger of erysipelas, stressing that in most instances it proved fatal.

What caused such outbreaks was not yet known, but Dr Shea believed that cleanliness, isolation and good ventilation were vital in preventing its spread, as well as the disinfection of wards, beds and bedding when outbreaks occurred.

Mr Joseph Morris was asked to draw up plans for a separate building with male and female infectious wards. Sharpington and Coles's tender of £3,038 was accepted and it was decided that the cost would be met from the sale of Hospital funds. Until the new wards were ready an isolation hut specially built in the grounds would be used. The treatment of venereal disease was also considered, but it was decided that those patients should be referred to the special Lock Hospitals in London.

The new West Ward, a one-storeyed building behind the Out-patients Department on the western boundary with Redlands Road, was completed early in 1878 and the first two cases, of erysipelas and scarletina, were transferred there from the Hospital. Over 100 years later this building is now used for medical records but its external appearance has hardly changed.

When the West Ward was opened the medical staff recommended that an Assistant House Surgeon should be appointed as the work of the House Surgeon was now more than one person could perform efficiently. In May 1878 Mr Graham was appointed with a salary of £50 a year and the stipulation that his duties would include looking after the medical library. When he succeeded Mr Carlyon as House Surgeon, the Board decided that his successor need not be fully qualified. A student who had finished his hospital studies and was waiting to pass his final examinations would be appointed without salary, but would receive board and lodging at the Hospital. A completely new non-medical appointment at a salary of £40 a year would also be made of an Inspector of Mechanical Apparatus who would regularly inspect the buildings, the sanitary apparatus, water supply, gas lighting, heating and other equipment.

Expansion and Building 1879 to 1883

A great deal had been achieved in the improvement of the organisation and sanitary conditions of the Hospital but much still remained to be done. In 1879 Miss Baster reported that the nursing staff was inadequate for the increased work of the Hospital. The Private Nursing Scheme, which now employed ten nurses, was very successful and needed to expand. In addition the servants were badly lodged and scattered about the Hospital in rooms that were confined and unhealthy. There was an urgent need for more accommodation for both the nurses and the servants.

These matters coincided with a request by Mr May, Sr that greater attention should be paid to cleanliness throughout the Hospital, and he cited a recent article in *The Lancet* on the subject. There were three main areas where improvement was necessary. The floors of the wards had become thin and worn and difficult to clean. Mr May recommended dry rubbing instead of scrubbing and that the floors should be specially prepared for this purpose. The offensive smell from the dissecting room gave rise to much complaint and he believed this work should now be removed from the building itself. Thirdly, good circulation of air and ventilation were needed both inside and out to prevent the rise and spread of infection. The quadrangle behind the central building had become very constricted with the Chapel and side wards. Mr May believed that the site of the Chapel should be changed, the kitchen and laundry removed from the basement and as much open space as possible obtained around the building to enable a free circulation of air.

Mr May's suggestions and Miss Baster's report were considered very seriously and it was acknowledged that alterations were necessary both for sanitary reasons and for the efficient running of the Hospital. Mr Joseph Morris, who had now gone into partnership with Mr Stallworth, was asked to draw up plans for the largest building operation yet undertaken by the Hospital. The smaller items such as the removal of the dissecting room and the re-flooring of the wards with teak were started almost immediately, but the rest of the programme needed much planning and a Building Committee which included the Chaplain was set up to go into all the details and cost.

The following year, in July 1880, it was agreed that the Nurses' Home would be raised by another storey to provide accommodation for 17 Private Nurses as well as probationers. An additional block would be built on the south side of the Nurses' Home to accommodate the Housekeeper and 22 servants. The laundry would be removed from the basement and placed on the south end of the servants' dormitories. This would form a wing on the north-east side and would be connected to the main building by a closed way along the south wall of the female convalescent ward. The

Nurses' Home and servants' wing

Out-patients Department would also be raised another storey to correspond with the Nurses' Home and would provide rooms for a new museum and library. The chapel would be removed from its present position and the side wards from the south wings would be reduced to one-bed wards to enable the quadrangle at the back of the building to be opened up. The present museum and library would be converted into a chapel with an operating theatre and small ward above. The kitchen would have minor alterations to prevent the smell of cooking entering the wards and the present laundry would be converted into a staff dining room.

Joseph Morris once again produced plans that provided style and symmetry to the building, with the new addition blending perfectly with the older wings. Tenders were obtained for all the work, including the installation of the most modern steam machinery in the laundry, pitch-pine fittings in the library and a special lift to the new operating theatre. In April 1881 tenders amounting to nearly £16,500 were accepted and the work began. Parnell and Son were to carry out all the general building work, Kimberley of Banbury the library fittings and Sheppard of Reading would build the chapel, alter the side wards and kitchen and convert the laundry to a dining-room. Outside, Holden and Son, of the Crown Nurseries in Reading, were to convert the kitchen garden to recreation grounds with grass, trees and shrubs and when the building work was completed the front would be drained and laid out neatly in a similar way with grass and shrubs.

The First District Nurse

It was to be almost 18 months before the building work was completed. In the meantime the Private Nurses, who were now 13 in number, moved out of their Home to temporary rented accommodation at 26, Portland Road. Their work had been steadily increasing over the years and in 1881 a new demand was made on their services.

A committee had been formed by the clergy, non-conformist ministers and doctors of the parishes included in the Deaneries of Reading and Sonning to look into the question of nursing the poor in their own homes. The Revd J. Brown of Wokingham asked if the Hospital could supply trained nurses for a specific district, the salary and expenses to be paid by the Committee of the district concerned. In particular a nurse was requested for the town and neighbourhood of Wokingham. The Hospital were quite prepared to make such an arrangement and asked for a fee of £12 10s per quarter exclusive of providing lodging, fuel and light for the nurses. It was believed that quite apart from the nursing duties, it was an opportunity for instructing the poor on matters of health, diet, cleanliness, cookery and treatment of simple cases of illness and accident. In September 1881 Nurse Williams was sent to Wokingham as the first District Nurse for a trial period of six months. It was arranged that she would work daily under the instructions of the Wokingham doctors and would not be confined to any particular case. The experiment proved a great success and after six months Mr Brown believed the necessary money would be forthcoming to enable the services of a District Nurse to be obtained again in the autumn. This was indeed the case and from that time it was customary for a District Nurse to be sent to Wokingham to assist in the area throughout the winter months. A valuable extension to the services of the Private Nursing Scheme had been established.

Medical Matters

Changes also occurred among the medical staff. Following the death of Dr Woodhouse early in 1879, a Special Court elected Dr John Shea Honorary Physician in his place. Dr Woodhouse had been one of the original Honorary Physicians and had given 40 years of service to the Hospital, where he was greatly liked and highly regarded. The office of Assistant Physician was not filled as it was decided that with the increased work of the Hospital two additional Assistant Surgeons should be appointed instead. Mr J. H. Walters and Mr H. G. Armstrong were elected and with Mr F. Workman made up the team of three Assistant Surgeons. A new rule was drawn up concerning consultations and it was decided that 'no important operation shall be performed without the previous consultation of the whole staff but it shall remain within the discretion of the surgeon in charge of the case to limit the examination of the patient to the consulting surgeons, the physicians, surgeon and assistant surgeon of the patient concerned'.

Alterations were also made in the use of stimulants and from September 1879 'spirits or wine', 'beer or porter' were not included on the diet sheets but were only given to patients when specifically ordered by the medical staff. The consumption of liquor by the staff and patients had been a matter of concern. The case of Edward Starke in 1869 was exceptional but during the six months he was in Hospital following a knee joint excision operation it was discovered that he had consumed nearly 50 bottles of brandy and 25 bottles of port in addition to his daily beer allowance of 1½ pints. Quite apart from the belief, which was increasingly gaining ground, that daily consumption of beer and porter was unnecessary and often harmful, the cost of supplying the liquor was becoming very high. In 1877 £3 a year had been offered to the nurses and servants in lieu of their daily beer allowance. Out of the 30 employees all except two or three had accepted the money and within a year all had done so. In 1873 an all-time record of £403 had been paid for liquor in the Hospital, only slightly lower than the total expenditure on drugs and chemicals for that same year. By 1878 this had been reduced to £252 and with the removal of stimulants from the diet cards in 1879, the total cost was reduced to £174 and by 1886 this had been reduced by a further £50.

The First Ambulance Service

In 1882 it was decided that an ambulance should be obtained for the Hospital. This would save patients suffering the often dreadful journeys by cab or wagon and in cases of accidents and serious illness would enable them to be lifted straight out on to a stretcher without being too disturbed.

A new ambulance had recently been made in London and this was inspected at the London Hospital. A second type, the 'newest carriage' belonging to the St John Ambulance, was also seen. Dr Howard's ambulance costing 60 guineas was chosen, although the medical staff had expressed many doubts about having such a service attached to the Hospital. The ambulance was horse-drawn and had sides fitted with sliding shutters. The one chosen for the Hospital was varnished (painting cost an extra £5) and it was agreed any wording necesary would be painted on the sides after delivery. A lean-to shed was built to accommodate the new vehicle and an agreement made with Edward Targett of London Road for the supply of a horse at a rate of 1/3d per mile. A list of rules was drawn up for the operation of the service and copies sent to the medical men, Boards of Guardians, Police Stations and railway station masters within a 15-mile radius of the Hospital. In September 1882 the new ambulance had its first call when it was sent to collect a woman with typhoid fever from Whitchurch. So began a most valuable service which it is now difficult to imagine once never existed.

The New Buildings
Most of the new building work had been completed by the end of 1882 and on January 23rd, 1883 the Bishop of Oxford attended the Hospital for a service to dedicate the new chapel. Joseph Morris's design has remained almost unaltered to this day and now, as then, the handsome Victorian interior with the seven stained glass windows representing the Crucifixion and the six miracles of healing make it a place of peace for those who visit it in times of sorrow or anxiety. The new museum and library were used by the Pathological Society for the first time at their meeting in September 1883 when a special letter of appreciation was sent to the Board of Management for the 'handsome accommodation' that had been provided for them. Like the chapel, the library has hardly changed over the years. The splendid collection of medical books is still housed in the original cases lining the walls from floor to ceiling and much of the furniture which was specially designed for the room is still in place. The original turkey carpet has long since gone but the Victorian fireplace, complete with large-faced clock, still looks over the room which has provided the venue for the meetings of the Pathological Society and a place for quiet study for over 100 years. The museum was housed in the room adjoining the library in glass-fronted cases lining the walls and remained there until the collection was disposed of some 50 years ago.

It was a great sadness that Mr F. A. Bulley, whose special splint was one of the exhibits in the museum, did not live to see its new location nor to attend the meetings of the Pathological Society in the new library. On April 21st, 1883 he died suddenly at the age of 74 outside the new operating theatre which had been completed some months before. He was one of the

Top left: The laundry; *Top right*: The chapel; *Bottom*: The library

original Honorary Surgeons elected when the Hospital opened and was a most able and skilful operator. In 1868 he had been made a Consulting Surgeon and until his death had remained involved and interested in all the work of the Hospital.

The completion of the new building was of great benefit to the work of the Hospital and the Chairman of the Board believed that 'never before did the arrangements so nearly satisfy the requirements of modern sanitary science'. The total cost was met from the sale of Hospital investments and the Treasurer was hopeful that this capital would be replaced within a short time by the legacies which were so generously left to the Hospital.

The Outbreak of Smallpox

The routine of the Hospital was dramatically interrupted early in March 1884 when four cases of smallpox broke out in Victoria Ward. By the end of March there were 13 cases, seven isolated in the infectious wards and six in the female convalescent ward. Stringent measures were brought into operation by Dr Shea and the Board of Management temporarily handed over its duties to the House Committee. Patients, servants and nurses were all vaccinated, no new cases were admitted and visitors were banned. Gradually patients who were fit to leave were sent home and by the end of April only 28 patients, including the smallpox cases, were left in the Hospital. As the Out-patients Department was separate from the main building there was no danger of infection and the clinics continued as usual. No new cases of smallpox developed after March 21st and by the beginning of May all the cases were able to leave the Hospital. Dr Shea drew up a report of the outbreak for the Sanitary Authority and an abstract appeared in the local papers.

Before the Hospital re-opened it was necessary to disinfect the building and the bedding. The buildings were disinfected by sulphur under the supervision of the Inspector of Nuisances for the Borough of Reading and all mattresses of smallpox patients were burned under the supervision of the Inspector of Nuisances of Wokingham Rural Sanitary District. All the female wards and infectious wards were whitewashed and bedding disinfected with chemically saturated steam at a temperature of 300°F. The outbreak had been contained and had not spread beyond the female wards. Dr Shea and the Hospital were congratulated on dealing with the situation so efficiently, and it was decided to take sensible precautions and limit the admissions of visitors when the Hospital re-opened on June 24th.

Financial Demands and Public Support

When it was agreed that a convalescent home attached to the Hospital was not a feasible proposition, the Board decided to extend its work of sending patients to homes and institutions elsewhere.

Convalescent homes were also opening near Reading and in 1873 two young boys recovering from knee joint excision operations were recommended by Mr Moxhay to convalesce at a home in Tilehurst. By 1886 annual subscriptions amounting to £14 10s were being sent regularly to six convalescent homes on the coast and at Tilehurst. In that year 49 annual subscribers provided an income for the Convalescent Fund of £91 10s and from this and donations (including £25 from a concert held in Twyford), £9 was given to patients leaving the Hospital, £59 was paid for instruments and appliances and £47 for patients to be sent to convalescent homes. From an income of under £150 a remarkable amount was achieved, and the aims of the Convalescent Fund to supplement and make permanent the work of the Hospital were successfully fulfilled.

The expansion that had taken place between 1856 and 1886 made great demands upon the financial resources of the Hospital. Nearly £35,000 was spent on the extensive building programme during this period and the cost of running the Hospital rose steadily with the increasing number of patients treated and nurses and servants employed. The annual expenditure of £6,000 in 1886 was double that of 30 years before. All these demands were met through the generous support of the public.

Annual subscriptions still provided the largest item of income and in 1886 nearly 800 people, including Queen Victoria, subscribed £2,482 in sums ranging from one guinea to several hundred pounds. By 1886 practically all the Poor Law Unions of Berkshire as well as some from the neighbouring counties had become annual subscribers. Many Friendly Societies such as the Foresters Lodges and the Oddfellows and smaller benefit clubs also subscribed annually. Workers from local factories and businesses collected among themselves and annual subscriptions were received on behalf of the iron workers, the hands at the Biscuit factory, the railway line employees, the gas company and members of the Co-operative Society, besides many others.

The Churches also provided a substantial income for the Hospital. In 1886 147 churches of all denominations contributed £1,176 from their collections. In 1881 the Reading churches decided to set aside a special Sunday in October as a 'Hospital Sunday', when all collections would be paid to the funds. This became an annual event and five years later 25 local churches contributed on that day.

All the subscribers, the representatives of the various groups of workers and Friendly Societies as well as the clergy and ministers making church collections, had the privilege of recommending patients for treatment in proportion to the amount they subscribed. As Governors they attended the various Courts, were able to vote for the election of medical officers and could elect and be elected members of the Board of Management. A much wider range of people was now able to influence the administration of the Hospital.

The proceeds from concerts, lectures and exhibitions as well as donations large and small all helped the Hospital funds and enabled the ever-increasing financial demands to be met. Gifts in kind were frequently sent and it became customary to send flowers, fruit and vegetables from Harvest Festival Services direct to the Hospital. Game and poultry were also sent, with one donor stipulating that the hares were for the officers and the rabbits for the patients! Books, linen and clothing were also received and in 1885 for the first time a list of gifts was published in the annual Hospital report. Each Christmas the gift of decorations for the wards and presents for the patients demonstrated the bond between the Hospital and the public whose support maintained its work.

Medical Developments

In this mid-Victorian period medical and scientific research in Britain and Europe was beginning to provide answers to the hitherto baffling questions of the cause of disease and infection and its method of transmission. The work of Louis Pasteur (1822–95) overturned the belief that foul air or bad humours were the cause and in 1864 he convincingly proved the existence of micro-organisms as the cause of decomposition. Joseph Lister applied Pasteur's work to infection in surgery and in 1866 demonstrated that the use of carbolic acid destroyed these germs and provided an 'anti-septic' to combat infection.

This discovery was of immense importance and in October 1867 Mr George May, Sr told the Pathological Society meeting that he had used carbolic acid with good effect in an operation for a compound fracture. He had used one pint of carbolic acid mixed with three pints of castor oil, whereas Lister had recommended a weaker solution using linseed oil. This antiseptic treatment was extended to ulcers when Mr May applied linen soaked in a solution of sulphrous acid over the sore and covered it with foil. This had checked the suppuration and little discharge had occurred. The use of carbolic acid combined with a spray, which produced a fine vapour of carbolic over the operating area, was most successful and enabled surgery to be extended to within the abdominal and thoracic areas of the body. Operations were made safer and greatly increased in number and more dangerous procedures such as ovariotomy, colotomy, laparotomy and tracheotomy were carried out with remarkable success.

Panorama of the Hospital 1883

Mr O. C. Maurice specialised in ovariotomy operations and in 1870 special instruments were obtained when the first of these was performed in the Hospital. A nurse was sent from London to look after the second patient in 1872 as complete quiet and special nursing were essential, but unfortunately in this instance the patient did not survive. Greater success was gradually obtained and the mortality rate for this operation was reduced to 25 per cent in 1886. Of the 30 ovariotomy operations performed in the Hospital between 1870 and 1886 one third of the patients had died.

In 1881 opinion among the medical staff differed about the point at which such operations should be performed. Mr Moxhay believed they should be delayed until the condition became one of 'grave inconvenience or a serious danger to life'. Dr Wells, however, thought that the earlier the operation was done the more likely it was to be a success. With the antiseptic treatment making operations safer there was less hesitation in undertaking them early. Mr Maurice said he always tried to use the antiseptic system 'in its entirety'. Not only were carbolic sprays used but instruments were soaked in a carbolic solution and antiseptic dressings applied.

Mr Moxhay specialised in operations for the excision of joints. He had performed knee joint excisions before the arrival of the 'antiseptic treatment' but with its use such operations were performed more frequently and with greater success on hips, shoulders and ankles as well as knees. Mr Moxhay noted he was able to operate on bones for deformity

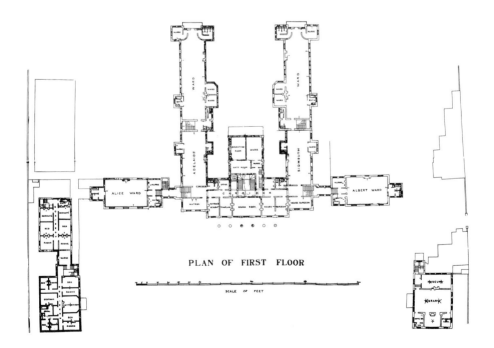

PLAN OF FIRST FLOOR

SCALE OF FEET

without any pus forming, which before 'would have been most hazardous and a nasty prolonged suppuration would have taken place'. Such operations saved patients from amputations, and in an article on knee joint excisions Mr Moxhay remarked on the quality of life obtained by these patients compared with the likelihood of a girl with a wooden leg getting married or a man with a pin leg being able to dig his garden.

The combination of anaesthetics and antiseptic precautions revolutionised surgery, although anaesthesia was by no means without its problems. By 1864 chloroform had been used at least 800 times in the Hospital and no deaths had resulted from its use. When discussing the types of apparatus and the use of both ether and chloroform at a Pathological Society meeting in 1880, Mr May, Sr remarked that the question was 'whether the poison (chloroform) should be used at all and not what form of apparatus should be used'. Furthermore he believed a great proportion of the medical profession 'condemned its use'. But there was no question of giving up anaesthetics. Nitrous oxide gas and bichloride of methylene as well as ether and chloroform were used in the Hospital and developments were also made in the use of local anaesthetics.

In 1882 the first chloroform fatality occurred in the Hospital when Daniel Lever died while being given chloroform by the House Surgeon for an operation for the amputation of a finger. The verdict at the inquest recorded that the patient died from weakening of the heart accelerated by chloroform and the jury noted that every precaution had been taken and no one was to blame. The case was discussed in detail by the Pathological Society. Dr Wells preferred ether to chloroform and felt that patients should be made aware of the danger of the latter. Mr May, Jr recommended an injection of morphine and atropine before giving ether. Mr Armstrong mentioned the use of bichloride of methylene and the benefit of elevating the legs and lowering the head of the patient. Dr Shea felt that all anaesthetics had some degree of danger and Mr May, Jr believed the question was to find the least dangerous. Mr Walters mentioned the benefit of a cup of strong beef tea given to the patient about 1½ to 2 hours before an operation, and the use of sphygmographic tracings were noted in checking the condition of the heart.

The medical staff expressed their confidence in the House Surgeon administering anaesthetics as he was a qualified medical practitioner. However, the case had attracted much publicity and the Revd Charles Eddy wrote to the Board protesting that stricter procedures should be observed. A member of the medical staff should always be present at operations and the House Surgeon should not administer anaesthetics alone. Mr Eddy believed the confidence of the subscribers and the poor had been shaken by the incident and unless something was done the support of the clergy for the Hospital might not continue. It was agreed that in future, except in emergencies, a member of the medical staff would always be present at an operation under anaesthesia. A few years later it was discovered that minor operations using chloroform were being performed within the wards and the medical staff agreed that they would, as far as practicable, conduct such operations in a separate room.

In spite of these incidents and the doubts attached to the use of chloroform, the number of operations performed each year continued to rise and the mortality rates remained extremely low. New and dangerous operations still caused loss of life but in 1886 of the 136 operations performed only 11 resulted in death; one herniotomy out of six, one ovariotomy out of four, three abdominal sections out of five, and one lithotomy operation out of two. All three tracheotomy patients died as well as the only colotomy patient and the patient whose tongue had been removed. The 125 other patients undergoing surgery had all survived. With anaesthesia and antiseptics, patients could be operated on without pain and for a variety of conditions that previously would have been considered inoperable. Much had been achieved since 1839 when only 11 operations, all without anaesthetics, had been performed in the Hospital.

The cause of cancer and the method of treatment were of much concern as many cases were admitted to the Hospital. In 1857 Mr Bulley noted that he was generally able to distinguish by the microscope the 'disintegrated cancerous blood' from healthy blood and he read a paper on the local treatment of cancer with caustics. He believed 'a dycrasy of the blood was the original cause of cancer and that the broken down globules are either imparted in the vessels, constituting non-malignant tumours, or extra vascular, constituting malignant disease'. He felt that if the condition of the blood was corrected by 'certain vegetable infusions' the disease could be cured. Baths and friction to improve the condition of the skin would also help. Mr George May said he thought along similar lines but differed in that he believed that the cell theory was the explanation of the cause. Ordinary cells reproduced themselves but cancer cells 'multiplied themselves more numerously'.

Developments in other directions also took place with an apparatus for blood transfusion being shown to the Pathological Society by Mr May in 1863. Twenty years before he had given small transfusions of blood by using a syringe. Nothing was known of blood groups at this time and the discussion questioned whether blood should be warmed or kept at ordinary temperatures to delay coagulation. Mr May believed that blood transfusions should be used more often – a far cry from the days when bleeding a patient was considered a cure for many conditions.

In 1870 skin grafting was being attempted and a pair of skin grafting scissors were obtained by the Hospital. Mr May, Jr had tried transplanting a small piece of skin to the site of a burn on the abdomen, but the experiment had not proved successful. In 1881 the first 'plastic' operation in the Hospital was performed on the eyelid and was followed by similar operations in the two succeeding years.

Research was meanwhile being carried out by Robert Koch in Germany to extend Pasteur's work and enable the germs responsible for particular diseases to be identified. The first bacilli to be discovered were those of tuberculosis and anthrax. A paper read to the Pathological Society in 1882 described these discoveries and the medical staff noted the importance of this advance. A new microscope and the necessary equipment for staining tubercle bacilli were acquired by the Hospital. New horizons were opening up in the understanding of disease. In 1883 Robert Koch identified the microbe which caused cholera. Pasteur had now directed his research towards the prevention of disease and the discovery of vaccines for immunisation. In 1885 he found a vaccine which immunised against rabies. This was not only an extension of Jenner's work on smallpox in 1794, but his research did much to explain the previously unknown reason why such vaccination was effective.

New instruments and equipment were constantly being obtained at the Hospital. In 1872 Mr Bulley invented a double tourniquet for the treatment of popliteal aneurism and this as well as his earlier tourniquet and his special splint were obtainable from Messrs Weiss in London. The first tonsil guillotine was obtained in 1866, although in earlier years Mr May had declared in no uncertain terms that he did not agree with the use of such an instrument. Syringes for subcutaneous injections obtained from 1871, rubber gloves for post mortem examinations from 1880, test apparatus for sugar from 1881 and 500 temperature charts from 1886 were just a few of the items acquired. New and more powerful equipment was purchased for the much-used Galvanic treatments besides skeuasma magnetic belts and bands much favoured by Dr Shettle for patients with rheumatism. At the instigation of Mr Maurice a professional 'Rubber' was employed in 1884 to instruct the nurses in massage. In 1886 he also suggested that the Hospital should be connected to the new telephone system. The reluctance of the Board was overcome when the South of England Telephone Company offered a donation of £2 a year to the Hospital so long as the £10 a year rental agreement existed. The Hospital was connected and given the number of Reading 31.

The British Medical Association had been formed in 1855 and early the following year, at the suggestion of Mr May, a meeting was held at the Hospital to discuss forming a local branch. In July 1856 the first Reading Branch meeting was held at the Great Western Hotel, nearly 30 years before the formation of an Oxford Branch in 1885. Various Medical Acts were passed over the years, the first of which in 1858 established the General Medical Council. From 1859 under its auspices an annual Medical Register was compiled. In the Hospital all applicants for medical posts were then required to be 'registered' practitioners. The Council also had the power to withdraw registration of any practitioner who was in breach of the conduct expected in the profession, thereby establishing a standard both in learning and of behaviour.

The death of Mr George May, Sr in 1884 was followed by those of Dr Wells and Mr Moxhay in 1885. Mr May had been the Senior Surgeon when the Hospital first opened and on his retirement in 1855 he was made the first Consulting Surgeon. He was a founder member of the Pathological

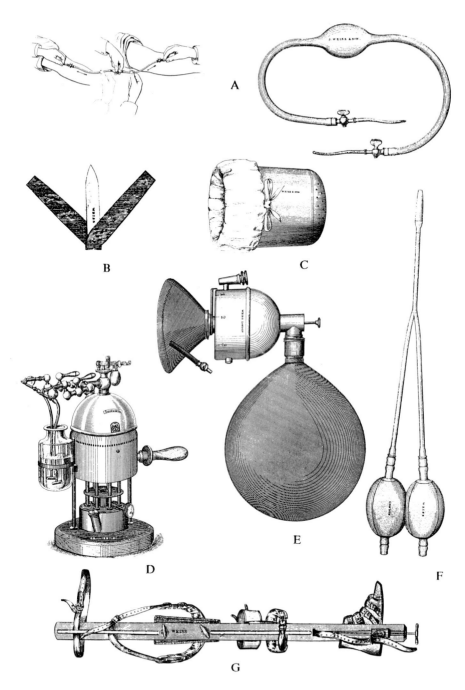

Some surgical instruments and apparatus, from Weiss's *Catalogue of Instruments, 1889* (not drawn to scale): (a) Transfusion apparatus; (b) Bleeding lancet; (c) Inhaler for ether or chloroform; (d) Antiseptic spray apparatus; (e) Ether inhaler by Clover; (f) Bellows by Richardson for artificial respiration; (g) Mr Bulley's splint

Society in 1841 and its President from 1851 until his death. Dr Wells had been elected Honorary Physician in 1845 following the retirement of Dr Pritchard Smith and for a short time was President of the Pathological Society before his death. Mr Moxhay became an Honorary Surgeon in 1856 following the retirement of Mr T. B. Maurice. All three were highly regarded, both personally and professionally. Mr Moxhay was succeeded by Mr A. S. Royds and Dr Wells by Dr H. French Banham.

By 1886 all the original surgeons and physicians at the Hospital had died. With the now greatly increased number of subscribers eligible to vote for the appointment of the honorary medical staff, it was decided a new system would be adopted. A special Elective Committee consisting of six Governors from Reading and six from the neighbouring districts would in future act with the Board of Management to elect new members of the medical staff. No canvassing would be allowed and testimonials should be sent to the Secretary 10 days before an election. How different from the election of the original staff in July 1839 with its committees, the canvassing and the hundreds of voters at the Town Hall. The surgeons and physicians elected that day pioneered the work of the Hospital and had lived to see great medical and scientific progress. Their successors, with a now greatly enlarged Hospital and a new system of nursing, took over with the promise of even greater advances in the years to come.

4

THE END OF THE CENTURY
1887 TO 1899

Queen Victoria's Golden Jubilee in 1887 was celebrated on June 21st in towns and villages throughout the country. The Hospital flew the Royal Standard in honour of its Patroness and provided a special dinner, tea and entertainment for the patients to mark the occasion.

The Victorian era was one of great expansion in Reading. In the fifty years since the Hospital had opened the population of the town had more than trebled to nearly 60,000. The population of Berkshire in the same time had increased by some 70,000 to 225,000, almost one quarter of whom lived in Reading. This great influx to the town, with the development of better communications and the expansion of industry, made ever-increasing demands on the resources of the Hospital. Although the number of annual subscribers had risen steadily over the years the income obtained from this source, as well as from legacies, donations and church collections, was insufficient to meet the financial requirements. Some means of obtaining further financial support from the wider general public would have to be looked for.

In 1886 a member of the Board of Management, Mr Hibbert of Braywick Lodge, suggested that the Hospital should consider establishing a 'Hospital Saturday' collection. These occasions had been held for many years in Birmingham, Liverpool, Manchester and London. Mr Hibbert had recently started them with much success in Windsor and Maidenhead for the local hospitals there.[1]

On July 16th, 1887 the first 'Hospital Saturday' was held in Reading. A total of £172 was collected and the Hospital was greatly encouraged by the result. The following year £239 was raised with additional collecting boxes being placed at the locks along the river between Goring and Maidenhead. The tradition was also established of the Reading Temperance Band playing in the Hospital grounds during that evening. 'Hospital Saturday' collections were an annual event in Reading from 1886 until 1899 when in that year a special Hospital appeal was launched. These collections usually amounted to between £250 and £300 on each occasion and proved a valuable addition to the Hospital funds. Hospital Saturdays made the needs of the Hospital known to a far wider range of people and enabled many to contribute who could not afford to become annual subscribers.

The growth of commerce and industry had led to the formation of many Trade and Friendly Societies in Reading and the surrounding area. By 1887 a large proportion of these had become annual subscribers to the Hospital and received admission tickets for their members. These Societies fully appreciated the benefit of the Hospital to the ordinary working people and recognised that good health was the most valuable commodity their members could possess.

In 1886 the Henley local Trade and Friendly Societies held a parade in aid of the Hospital funds and the following year one was also held in Wokingham. The first Reading Hospital parade took place on Sunday, April 29th, 1888 and was organised by a special committee of the Amalgamated Friendly and Trade Societies of the area. Nearly 3,000 people took part in the procession and included the Oddfellows Lodges, the Foresters Courts, the Hearts of Oak, the Railway Servants Society, the Rechabites, the Carpenters and Joiners Society, the United Patriots and the four Buffaloes Courts.

Practically the whole town turned out that afternoon to watch the enormous procession. The parade, with banners flying and accompanied by no less than five local bands, marched from the Market Place and Friar Street round the town to return some two hours later. Special services were then held at St Lawrence's Church and in the Town Hall. The sermons paid tribute to the invaluable work of the Royal Berkshire Hospital. The collections made along the route with boxes, and also with bags on long poles for window collections, resulted in £84 being sent to the Hospital.

During the following years the number of towns and districts holding Hospital Sunday parades increased steadily. In 1900, 17 different parades were held and £400 was collected for the Hospital. The success of these occasions resulted in the abandonment of the Hospital Saturday collection. By 1914 as many as 27 parades were being held and about £600 was being sent to the Hospital each year. By today's standards these sums may appear small but they formed about 6½ per cent of the total income of the Hospital and were by no means insignificant. The organisers on their part obtained admission tickets for their members in respect of the collections which had been made.

In many towns, including Reading, the Hospital parades became a regular annual event and were held right up until 1948. The services of local bands, which were now becoming more numerous, were called upon to accompany the long processions. With their brightly coloured uniforms, the rhythm and melody of their music, the bands had a remarkable drawing power and did much to encourage the people to contribute along the route. These parades probably did more than anything else to bring the needs of the Hospital to the attention of the general public. People in towns and small villages alike looked forward to the day of the parades when the enthusiasm and generosity of all concerned provided a visible as well as a financial link between the Hospital and the community it was serving.

Medical Appointments

The great increase in the population of Reading had led to a corresponding rise in the number of medical practitioners in the area. By 1887 there were almost 40 physicians and surgeons in Reading alone, compared with about half that number in practice when the Hospital first opened. Practically all were in private practice, several in addition holding honorary appointments such as those at the Hospital and at the Reading Dispensary. Several were employed on a part-time basis by the Poor Law Guardians and others were engaged as medical officers by benefit clubs and the larger factories. In 1867 when a new Reading Union Workhouse was built at Battle a medical officer was appointed to be in charge of the attendant infirmary. The Sanitary Authorities appointed their first Medical Officer of Health, Dr John Shea, in 1873 and he also became a member of the honorary medical staff of the Hospital.

In 1879 the Friendly Societies of Reading amalgamated to form a Medical Association with contributions from members of nine different societies paying the salary of a full-time practitioner. This appointment, apart from the resident staff of the Hospital, was one of the very few which was not combined with general practice.

For all these practitioners the Hospital was the place to which they were able to refer their poorer patients for further advice and treatment. It was also an institution which offered great opportunities to those who became members of the honorary medical staff. Such a position greatly increased the experience a physician and surgeon could obtain; it added to his reputation and carried prestige held by no other medical appointment in the area.

In September 1887 the death was announced of Dr John Shea. He had been on the medical staff since 1873 besides being Medical Officer of Health and in 1879 had been elected Honorary Physician on the death of Dr Woodhouse. The appointment of his successor would be made by the Elective Committee on November 1st after due advertisement of the vacancy in the local and medical papers.

Early in October Mr Richard Benyon, President of the Hospital, received a letter signed by 28 practitioners of the area asking that the physician to be elected should be sufficiently well qualified for them to refer their patients. A Fellow or at least a Member of the Royal College of Physicians was requested. Since the election of Dr Wells F.R.C.P. in 1845, no physician appointed to the Hospital had, they believed, held qualifications suitable for the position. News of this letter reached the local papers and also *The Lancet* and resulted in much publicity. The Board's reply that it was not their duty to appoint a consultant physician for the doctors of the area did not end the discussion. The *Reading Observer* believed that the request indicated 'without doubt, that something more than now exists is, in the opinion of these gentleman, needed on the staff of the Royal

Berkshire Hospital'. *The Lancet* extended the issue by drawing attention to the appointment of surgeons to the Hospital over the past years.

The rules of the Hospital required that an Honorary Physician should be a medical graduate of one of the universities of Great Britain or Ireland whose name was on the medical register. It was also necessary that he should not practise or be in partnership with anyone who practised pharmacy, surgery or midwifery. The election of members of the honorary medical staff by an Elective Committee had only been in effect since 1886. Prior to this all such appointments had been made by a Court of Governors. The new procedure meant that the testimonials of all candidates must first be submitted to the medical staff, who would then provide a short list of candidates to the House Committee, who in turn would submit their recommendation to the Elective Committee. This consisted of the Board of Management and twelve specially appointed Governors. The influence of the medical staff at the beginning of this procedure was considerable and their opinion carried much weight.

There were three candidates for the post of Honorary Physician and the medical staff recommended two for consideration. On the day of the election one of these withdrew, leaving Dr Moody Ward the only candidate. He was well qualified with an M.B. and had glowing testimonials, but he also held the post of Medical Officer at Huntley and Palmer's factory and in this capacity practised pharmacy and surgery. A majority of the medical staff believed this made him ineligible as a candidate, although he had intimated in writing that he would conform to the Hospital rules should he be elected. A suggested postponement of the election was over-ruled and on a majority vote Dr Moody Ward was appointed Physician.

News of the election reached the local papers which declared the medical staff had been inconsistent in first recommending a candidate and then withdrawing their support. As *The Lancet* said, a candidate had been appointed 'in opposition to the recommendation of the medical staff but to the satisfaction of the large body of practitioners who interested themselves in the election'. Anonymous letters were published and many articles appeared in the papers and *The Lancet* with various implications and demands for an explanation.

Over a month later, following continuing public criticism, a letter was published by Mr Benyon on behalf of the Board of Management and Dr Shettle on behalf of the medical staff, in which the situation was satisfactorily explained. The election of Dr Moody Ward had highlighted the interest taken by the public and medical profession alike in the administration of the Hospital. It had also shown that the role of the press was extremely influential in bringing certain matters to the attention of its readers and that the Royal Berkshire Hospital in all things was subject to public scrutiny.

One of the articles in *The Lancet* had drawn attention to the election of the surgeons at the Hospital and noted:

'A fact of importance should be recorded in reference to the appointments at this Hospital. For many years we are informed it has been the custom to appoint to the surgical staff those who are either the descendents of former surgeons or those who have been pupils to one of the surgeons, or those who have been in partnership with them or their successors. This custom, whether accidental or intentional, has been rarely deviated from for a period of more than 25 years except in the case of minor temporary appointments. The effect of such a custom is to shut out from the Hospital able men from among the practitioners of the Town and elsewhere and naturally tends to discourage highly qualified men from becoming candidates when a vacancy occurs at the Royal Berkshire Hospital.'

This had indeed been the case and in January 1888 one of the Governors, Mr Leveson Gower of Bill Hill, Wokingham, gave notice that he would ask for three resolutions to be placed on the agenda of the Annual Court:

1. That no two members of a firm or family be on the active staff at the same time, excepting under special circumstances.
2. No medical or surgical officer to be more than 20 years on the active staff or after 60 years of age.
3. The Hospital to be made departmental.

Mr Leveson Gower had noted *The Lancet* article and others in the papers and believed these resolutions should be discussed in the best interests of the Hospital, its patients and also the medical practitioners of the area.

The first two motions were discussed but gained little support in the ensuing vote and the third was not even seconded. The overwhelming opinion was that there was no reason to change the working of the Hospital. Mr George May added weight to the discussion by saying he could not recall a single appointment during the past 49 years in which the best man had not been chosen. He agreed with another speaker that in a town like Reading there was the tendency for the best practice to obtain the best partners and it was therefore not inconsistent that the Hospital should find its honorary staff came mainly from one practice or include several members of one family. The matter had been raised, found unacceptable and it was to be a further eleven years before the subject was discussed again and changes were made in this aspect of Hospital administration.

The influence of the medical staff became increasingly important in the administration of the Hospital. For many years they had advised the Board on the choice of candidates for House Surgeon and Assistant House Surgeon and since 1886 provided the short lists for the honorary staff appointments. They were also an innovative body advising on the appointments necessary in the expanding Hospital and the duties relating to such positions. On their suggestion new surgical and medical facilities were introduced and their specialised knowledge enabled the Board of

Management with its lay members to keep the Hospital abreast of medical advances. Only rarely did the Board of Management make a decision which was contrary to the advice of the medical staff.

In 1889 the procedure for the Elective Committee was simplified and members of the honorary medical staff were added to that electoral body. In 1894 the Hospital rules were altered to enable one physician, one surgeon and one assistant surgeon, chosen by the medical staff, to be appointed to the Board of Management each year. Two years later the rules were altered again. All the physicians and surgeons became ex-officio members of the Board of Management and the role of the medical staff now ceased to be purely advisory in the administration of the Hospital.

The Expanding Hospital

To mark the Hospital's Jubilee in 1889 a special appeal was launched in aid of its funds. Some £2,000 was raised, including £500 from the President, Mr Richard Benyon. It was agreed that this money should be put towards extending the accommodation. The Hospital, which had opened with 50 beds, had almost trebled in size over the fifty years but even so, the 144 beds were still inadequate to meet demands. It was noted in April 1889 that over the previous 12 months nearly 150 patients, mostly women, had been turned away for lack of available beds. It was decided to equip the female convalescent ward with ten beds for female patients. Although at first a temporary measure, Jubilee Ward remained in existence and helped to meet the need for additional accommodation.

Ten extra beds did not eliminate the waiting list and other means were needed to make more beds available. Subscriptions to the various convalescent homes were doubled to enable more patients to complete their treatment elsewhere. It was arranged for patients to be admitted on two days a week instead of one and discharged on three days instead of two, thereby vacating beds as early as possible. Waiting lists were drawn up and urgent cases were given priority. Those living at a distance were asked to find out in advance if beds were available for their admission. A close watch was kept on 'overtime patients', those who had been in the Hospital for over eight weeks, to see that none was kept in who could be discharged. In the winter of 1889/90 an influenza epidemic struck Reading and the need for beds was so great that in February 1890 notices were placed in the local papers advising that only emergency cases could be admitted.

In the spring of 1890 Mr Joseph Morris was asked to produce plans for an additional 14 beds. It was then found that the funds available were not sufficient to meet the cost, nor was the Hospital's income adequate to maintain the extra beds. Reluctantly all ideas of increasing the accommodation had to be postponed. The overcrowded state of the Hospital was recorded almost every week. In September 1890 the Revd H. C. Littlewood of Goring informed the Hospital that his Harvest Festival collection would be sent elsewhere as all too often patients from his parish were not admitted for lack of room. Two years later the Revd F. T. Wethered of Hurley wrote

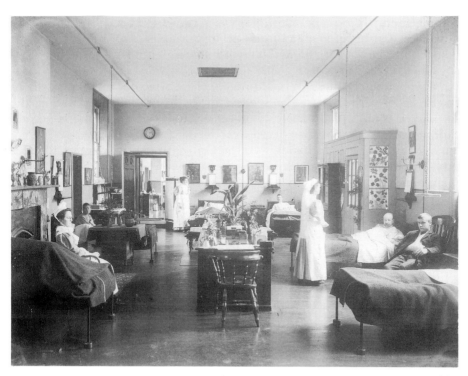

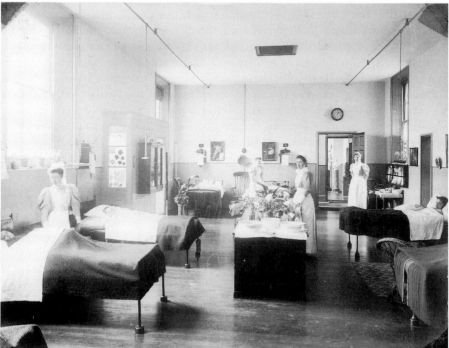

Two of the wards

more bluntly: 'I do not know how you can expect any support from Berkshire parishes if you can't take in urgent cases. Lay this before your Board. Enlarge your Hospital. Have you now a right to appear as a county hospital? It is a farce.'

Unfortunately there were still insufficient funds for any enlargement and instead various alterations were made to make better use of the accommodation already there. Jubilee Ward was turned into a second children's ward, the Casualty Department and the Dispensary were removed from the main building to the Out-patients Department with an extra room added to the physicians' side and a dark room for the examination of eye and throat cases. The vacated dispensary room in the main building was then converted to a consulting room for the medical staff.

The large increase in the number of patients being treated, combined with the advances being made in medical, surgical and nursing skills, resulted in a period of great change and adaptation at the Hospital.

In 1888 it was decided that the Assistant House Surgeon should in future be a fully qualified practitioner. Not only would this enable him to take over the House Surgeon's duties in his absence but he could also administer chloroform and be of greater help to the medical staff. The appointment would be for six months with a salary of £50 a year. The House Surgeon's appointment would in future be for one year only instead of for an indefinite period as before.

By 1893 the work of the Hospital had expanded so greatly that on the recommendation of the medical staff the Board decided there should be three resident medical staff instead of the present two. The House Surgeon would be appointed for six months and be eligible for re-election either as House Surgeon or House Physician with a salary of £60 a year. A House Physician and Pathologist would be appointed as above also with a salary of £60 a year. A qualified Assistant House Surgeon and Chloroformist, who would be unsalaried, would be appointed for six months but eligible for a further six months' residence either as House Surgeon or House Physician. In no case should the period of residence exceed one year. This latter post remained unpaid until 1899 when a salary of £30 a year, later increased to £50, was included.

In the meantime there had been changes among the honorary medical staff. In 1889 Mr George May resigned, having been on the staff for 34 years, and was made a Consulting Surgeon. The Senior Assistant Surgeon, Mr J. H. Walters, was elected the new Surgeon and Dr L. Guilding was appointed Assistant Surgeon in his place. In 1891 Dr Banham resigned after six years on the staff and was succeeded as Physician by C. W. Marriott, M.R.C.P. Dr Marriott was the only candidate and had previously had a large private practice in Leamington. Dr F. Hawkins was appointed Physician following the death of Dr Moody Ward in 1893. Mr Royds resigned in 1894 and Dr Maurice took his place as Surgeon and Mr Roberts was elected Assistant Surgeon to succeed him.

When Dr Shettle resigned in 1897, having been on the staff for 28 years, he was made a Consulting Physician and it was decided that, for the time being, no third physician would be appointed.

The Nursing Department

The work of the nursing staff was increasing and in 1889 an Assistant Matron was appointed with a salary of £50 a year. In 1890 an additional seven ward nurses and six private nurses were engaged. The extra accommodation needed for them was provided by raising the servants' dormitory another storey and the old laundry wash house was adapted to provide a nurses' dining room.

The nursing staff by this time also included one male nurse, the Assistant Porter having been appointed in 1878 to assist with delirious cases and to help in Benyon Ward. This was the first time since Alfred Cotton's dismissal in 1839 that a male nurse had been employed in the Hospital. His duties also included attending the post-mortem room, cleaning the surgical instruments and bathing male patients upon admission. For this he was paid a salary of £25 a year. In 1891 his post-mortem room duties were taken over by the Assistant Porter to enable him to have time to receive instruction in massage. In addition a list was obtained of male nurses who could be hired for special nursing when required at a rate of 3/6d per night, 3/– a day or 5/– for 24 hours.

There were 28 Private Nurses employed by the Hospital in 1890 and

Group including Miss Baster, House Surgeon Mr Ward and Assistant House Surgeon Mr Clowes, *c*1892

their services were constantly in demand. Not only was this Department self-supporting but it was also highly profitable. The services of the Wokingham District nurses were so appreciated that in 1888 the six-monthly appointment was extended to the full year. At the same time the Hospital agreed to supply a District Nurse to Camberley and Yorktown and also a nurse to the Marlow Sick Aid Society for a fee of £50 a year. Occasionally the Poor Law Unions asked for nurses and in 1894 the Farnham Union was supplied with one for a period of almost a year. From time to time nurses were supplied to Smith's Isolation Hospital in Henley and also the small Fever Hospital in Bridge Street, Reading, which was run by the Reading Town Council.

In 1890 the possibility of establishing District Nursing for the sick poor in Reading was raised and the views of the Hospital were requested. Nothing further happened until 1894 when the Revd E. J. Norris called the attention of the medical staff to the 'almost total absence of any system by which nurses can be trained and supplied at a low cost to the sick poor'. All too often it had been found that the poorer patients could not accommodate the Private Nurses supplied by the Hospital, nor could they afford to pay anything towards their maintenance. The need for such a service was undisputed; the debate was whether this should be undertaken by the Hospital or independently.

The medical staff advised the Board of Management to increase the number of Private Nurses and extend the service to enable maternity and other nurses to be supplied to the sick poor of the Borough and District. Further enquiries made it apparent that the training and employment of nurses to fill this role would not be self-supporting. It was believed such a scheme would go beyond the province of the Hospital, and it was suggested it would be more satisfactory if a Nursing Association were formed in Reading. Subsequently this organisation was established independently of the Hospital and became affiliated with Queen Victoria's Institute of Nursing.[2] In 1897 the Institute contacted the Board and offered to send nurses to attend any cases leaving the Hospital which might require their help. Their services were of great assistance both to the Hospital and its patients, enabling many to return to their homes sooner and thus releasing badly needed beds.

Although nurses had been trained at the Hospital for many years, receiving instruction from both the nursing and medical staff, no certificate of their efficiency had ever been given. By 1893 most hospitals of any standing were giving certificates and it was believed such an award would encourage the nurses. An examination at the completion of two years' training would be highly satisfactory for all concerned. In order that this should be established it was necessary to define the course of training, but while the matter was being considered other events occurred which had a profound effect on the Nursing Department.

In May 1895 a complaint made against a nurse was investigated by the House Committee, found to be justified and the nurse was asked to

Top: Group of Hospital staff *Bottom*: The Private Nurses

resign. The nurse's brother demanded an enquiry and it transpired that the House Surgeon who had made the complaint had not notified Miss Baster. The Superintendent wondered how she could be responsible for the work of her nurses when occasions of negligence and omission were not reported to her until two months later. She believed that if she had been alerted at the time the matter could have been satisfactorily resolved. The nurse resigned and the medical staff informed the Board that they, 'having considered the statements respecting the charges of inefficient nursing, are of the opinion that immediate steps should be taken with the view of reorganising the arrangements at the Hospital.'

Miss Baster resigned and the post of Lady Superintendent was advertised. The new Matron should be aged between 30 and 40, be a fully trained nurse with experience of hospital administration. The salary would be £100 a year with board, washing and apartments. A letter written and signed by Mr Benyon the President and Major Thoyts, the Chairman of the Board, was sent to Miss Baster. They expressed their great appreciation of all the work she had done for the Hospital in the 24 years she had been its Superintendent. It had been 'important work well done'. A pension of £75 a year was granted to her for life. In contrast the medical staff coldly minuted that 'no formal notice be taken by the staff of Miss Baster leaving the Hospital'. This lack of magnanimity was a sad conclusion to the work of a dedicated woman.

There were 55 applicants for the post of Superintendent. Miss Law, formerly Matron at the Mercers' Hospital in Dublin, was appointed and took up her duties at the Hospital in July 1895. Within months the nursing arrangements of the Hospital had been revised and the organisation of that Department was established for many years to come. Each ward would be in the charge of a sister with one staff nurse, one assistant nurse and one third-year probationer. Extra nurses would be used as necessary. The nurses would undergo a three-year period of training after which two types of certificate would be given, one noting the completion of the training and a second to be given after passing the training examination. The age of admission of probationers would be between 23 and 30 years unless varied by the Matron. All nurses would be expected to take the examination at the end of the course of instruction and no certificate would be given before the completion of the three-years' training. All contracts with the nurses would be for a period of three years.

No charge nurses or staff nurse would be sent on private nursing. The private nursing would be separate from the Hospital staff and although the Hospital could draw on the Private Nurses, they in turn could not draw on the Hospital nurses. Lectures would be given by Miss Law on bandaging, nursing and economy and by members of the medical staff on anatomy, physiology, surgical nursing and medical nursing. Lectures would also be given from time to time on galvanism. Nurses from other institutions such as the workhouse and the Helena Home would be able to attend these lectures.[3]

These arrangements required five additional nurses to be appointed to the Hospital staff. Mr Joseph Morris produced plans for five nurses' cubicles to be built over the Porter's Lodge at the Redlands Road entrance. In May 1896, Mr F. Whiting's tender of £625 was accepted and the work proceeded.

Innovations

There had been other developments within the Hospital. In 1890 a course of 'Ambulance Lectures' was started. Over a period of three months the medical staff gave lectures to the young men in the area who were interested in learning First Aid. This course was repeated for several years and those who attended included members of the St John Ambulance Association whose Reading Brigade Division was established in 1893.

In 1892 alterations were made to the rules for the use of the Hospital ambulance to enable others besides the patients to make use of its services. A payment of one guinea was required within the Borough with an extra charge of 1/– per mile beyond the boundary. If the porter or a nurse accompanied the ambulance an additional charge of 10/6d would be made.

After complaints that the original ambulance was draughty, an additional horse-drawn vehicle was obtained in 1896. Mr John Carter's model costing £100 19s, with 'Royal Berkshire Hospital' inscribed in a garter on each side, was purchased through the generosity of various friends of the Hospital. Its 'modern improvements' were much appreciated and both this and the older ambulance were in use for many years.

Telephones were installed in the wards connecting them to various parts of the building and electricity was suggested as a better means of lighting the Hospital. Although it was to be several years before this improvement was carried out, the superiority of electric compared to gas lighting had been acknowledged.

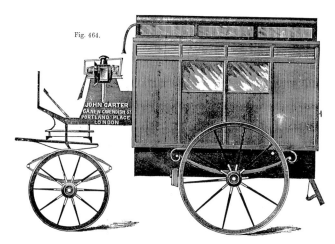

The new Hospital ambulance, 1896 (taken from Carter's *Catalogue of Invalid Ambulances 1902*)

In 1896 it was decided to appoint a Hospital photographer. In answer to an advertisement, Mr Dann's tender was accepted. The photographer agreed to 'undertake to attend at the Hospital for the purposes of photographing patients when required and find all photographic apparatus at the following terms – one ½-plate negative and three unmounted photographs 5/–; three or more negatives taken at the same time with three prints from each – per negative 3/6d. Above terms to include the indexing of negatives and prints and mounting of same in book. All negatives to be the property of the Hospital.'

In 1902 the contract was terminated when a secondhand camera was obtained and the medical staff decided to undertake their own photography. Several of Dann's photographs have survived and record the Hospital and its wards at the turn of the century.

The Appointment of a Dentist

The suggestion by the Board in 1868 that an honorary dentist should be appointed had received no support from the medical staff. The subject was raised again in 1892 and once more they believed such an appointment was 'not desirable'. Three years later, in spite of opposition from the medical staff, the Board set up a special Dental Committee and in June 1895 it was agreed that a consulting dentist should be appointed. He would attend cases referred to him by the medical staff, such patients being required to obtain out-patient's tickets. He would be required to be a licentiate in dental surgery or be similarly qualified and must be registered. He would be appointed by the Elective Committee with the privileges of a Governor subscribing two guineas a year while in office. The suggestion that the dentist should attend weekly to extract teeth and do stoppings was not accepted. In October 1895 the position was advertised and in November Mr A. L. Goadby was elected out of five candidates. It had taken the Board 27 years to bring this appointment about.

The Operating Theatre

When the new operating theatre was built in 1882, less than 100 operations were performed each year. Ten years later the number had more than doubled with 225 operations in 1893 and by the following year this had risen to 322.

The plan of the operating theatre, which had been built in 1882 to replace the original theatre on the ground floor, was not unlike the present E.N.T. theatre which now occupies the same site. With its ante-room, adjoining room 'for the use of patients after operations' and nearby lift, the layout was in principal quite similar. The ante-room at that time was not used as an anaesthetics room as most patients were put under chloroform before leaving the wards. Instead it was used for the storage of instruments and other items, the cleaning of which was in the charge of the male nurse. In 1894 the medical staff informed the Board of Management that the theatre was now 'insanitary, out of date and inconvenient'. Improvements were 'absolutely necessary', not to keep abreast of other hospitals but for the health and safety of the patients.

Aseptic surgery had developed following Robert Koch's discovery that hot steam could kill germs impervious to chemicals. The 'antiseptic treatment' had been overtaken and it was now realised that it was preferable to keep operating theatres germ free or aseptic rather than killing microbes already present. Both the theatre and its contents needed to be renewed and the medical staff pointed out that 'there are at present no means whatever of efficiently sterilising water, instruments and dressings'. They believed a completely new theatre should be built and suggested the site of the old chapel between the male and female surgical wards. The building could be partly underground to enable the roof of the theatre to be no higher than the bottom of the ward windows. The present theatre could then be used as an eye ward or for special cases.

The construction of a new theatre was financially impossible but the reconstruction of the existing theatre was feasible. A special fund was opened and Mr Richard Benyon immediately donated £1,000 towards the £2,000 needed. The medical staff advised on what would be required and Mr Joseph Morris drew up plans using the Leamington Hospital and the new theatre at the Middlesex Hospital as a guide.

There would be terrazzo dado and flooring throughout with polished plaster walls (the medical staff had suggested teak or parquet floors and walls lined with slabs of slate or washable paint). The rooms would be wired for electricity to enable such lighting to be installed whenever possible. In the meantime gas lighting would be used. The present basins and sinks would be replaced by large porcelain troughs with pedal taps. Two operating tables on wheels would be required 'so that the anaesthetic may be administered in the ante-room and the patient and the table wheeled in'. The second table would be in readiness for the next case, thereby saving time and a 'great sparing of alarm to many nervous patients'. Tables for instruments and dressings and cupboards would be made of metal with glass tops. A stand for lotions would also be needed 'capable of being raised and lowered so as to provide a continuous stream'. Sterilisers would also be required and the medical staff noted that at St Thomas's these had to a great extent displaced the use of antiseptics. They drew the attention of the Board to the great benefits both to the Hospital and the patients that resulted in the avoidance of suppurating wounds and the cost of the ensuing dressings.

Work began on the new theatre towards the end of 1895 and the male convalescent ward was used as a temporary theatre until Wheeler Bros had completed their work. In June 1896 the work was finished and a month later the surgical staff pronounced the theatre, complete with sun blinds, to be in 'fairly good working order'. Both the theatre and the instruments were put in the charge of Sister Hunter. It was agreed that whenever practicable notices of all operations would be sent out the previous day. Electric light, with a transformer, was installed in the theatre in 1899 as

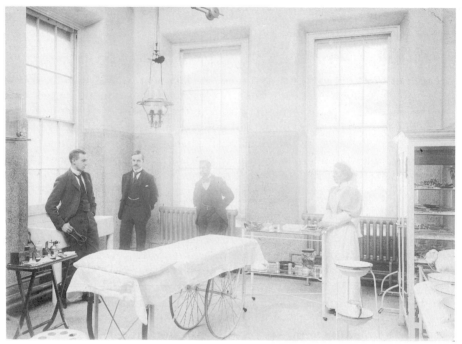

The new operating theatre, 1896

well as an electric cautery. A total of 1,020 operations were performed that year, including 212 minor operations. In 1901 a clock was provided and over the next few years various improvements were made to the lights, the sinks and the sterilising equipment. In 1904 a telephone was installed and in the ensuing years an additional nurse was provided and the theatre was kept up to date with the latest equipment. Masks, gowns and rubber gloves were gradually introduced and the transformation of the old theatre to one not unlike that of the present day was completed.

Jubilee Year and Huntley and Palmer Ward

On the completion of the operating theatre the male convalescent ward returned to its normal use. It was then suggested that this room should be used for septic cases which were not suitable for admission to the general surgical wards. It was equipped with six beds and made available to either male or female cases as necessary.

The following year, 1897, was Queen Victoria's Diamond Jubilee. An illuminated address was sent to Her Majesty on behalf of the Governors and the patients celebrated her reign of 60 years with a special dinner, tea and entertainment. Messrs Huntley and Palmer offered the Hospital a gift of £7,000 for the endowment of a ward to mark the occasion. It was decided that the male convalescent ward should be equipped with ten beds and a bathroom would be added. The ward would be called the 'Huntley and Palmer Ward' with a brass tablet bearing an inscription commemorating

Huntley and Palmer Ward

the endowment on June 22nd, 1897. The partners of Huntley and Palmer were made Vice Presidents and it was agreed that 'as far as is consistent with the rules of the Hospital, special cases recommended by Messrs Huntley and Palmer shall be retained in the Hospital for periods not exceeding the period specified in the existing rules of the Hospital'.

On December 14th, 1897 the ward was officially opened with members of the Palmer family at the ceremony. The following year it was decided that this ward and Albert Ward would both be used for septic cases, although it was agreed that the term 'septic wards' would not be employed.

There were other notable events in 1897 besides the Jubilee. The opportunity arose to purchase two houses in Craven Road adjoining the Hospital. Although they were not to be occupied for some time, their purchase enabled land to be obtained on which the Hospital could expand in future years. The price of £1,950 was to prove a good investment.

In July 1897 the death of Mr Richard Benyon was recorded with great sorrow. He had been President of the Hospital for 43 years, having been unanimously elected to succeed his uncle Mr Richard Benyon de Beauvoir. Like him, he had been a most generous benefactor to the Hospital and had interested himself in all its work, frequently chairing the weekly meetings of the Board of Management. He was succeeded as President by Lord Wantage, Lord Lieutenant of the County and Provincial Grand Master of the Freemasons of Berkshire. In 1870 as Robert James

Lindsay he had been instrumental in the formation of the National Society for the Aid to the Sick and Wounded which later became the British Red Cross Society.

Resignation of the Surgical Staff

On June 10th, 1897 the Board of Management received a letter from the honorary surgical staff tendering their resignation and stating: 'We feel unable to act as colleagues of Mr J. H. Walters.' Mr Walters asked for an explanation and was informed that the surgeons and assistant surgeons believed 'the treatment of his patients and the performance of his duties have been for some time such as to bring discredit upon the Hospital'. The Board of Management immediately formed a committee to enquire into these charges and appointed Sir Thomas Smith to act as assessor.

The report of the Committee was considered by the Board at their meeting on August 24th. Its conclusions noted that: 'The conduct of Mr Walters as shown by the enquiry ... is deserving of very strong reprobation as militating against the best interests of the Hospital and hope that this expression of opinion may influence him in his future conduct.'

A more strongly worded amendment was not carried. In this the strained relations between Mr Walters and his colleagues was mentioned with the resulting difficulty in carrying out this side of the Hospital work. Mr Walters's valued services over a period of 18 years were noted but it was suggested nevertheless that he might possibly 'sever his connections with this Institution'.

No record was made of exactly what Mr Walters did or did not do, but undoubtedly his conduct was deeply resented by his colleagues. A meeting of the medical staff on May 10th, attended by Mr Walters and all the surgeons who signed the letter, was minuted only as 'Re: surgical practice of Hospital'. No meetings of the medical staff took place between June 3rd and September 10th. No reference was made to the subject at any Pathological Society meeting during those months and Mr Walters's name does not appear among those present. Another medical society, the Reading Medical Club, had been formed in 1888 to 'foster good feeling in the medical profession and keep up a high professional tone', and Mr Walters was among its members. On June 3rd, 1897 a special meeting of the Club was called by Mr O. C. Maurice 'to consider various grievances and charges brought by some members of the Club against another member'. After some discussion it was agreed that the Reading Medical Club should be dissolved. The seconder of the motion was Mr J. H. Walters.

Possibly some reason may be found in a complaint made by an in-patient, Walter Bunt of Albert Ward, who had been admitted on March 6th with an ingrowing toe-nail. On March 16th the Board asked the medical staff to report on the complaint that he had been operated on without an anaesthetic. Walter Blunt was one of Mr Walters's patients.

The concluding paragraph of the Committee of Enquiry considered that: 'The other members of the surgical staff would have shown more regard to the welfare of the Hospital by some other proceedings than that of combined resignation of their appointments.' On September 7th the surgeons withdrew their resignations and expressed their sincere regret that the Board felt their action discourteous and inimical to the interests of the Hospital.

Mr Walters did not resign. He was an able surgeon and in 1903 he was made a Consulting Surgeon. His work was highly regarded both in the Hospital and by his private patients. These events of the summer of 1897 never reached the press, but their impact on all concerned within the Hospital was considerable.

Administrative Changes
In the six years covering the turn of the century some major administrative changes took place. Before this, the Prince of Wales visited the Hospital on June 11th, 1898, the first official royal visit the Hospital had received.[4] Accompanied by Prince Christian, Lord and Lady Abingdon, Lord and Lady Wantage and many others, the Prince was taken round the wards and 'expressed himself much pleased with all he saw'. The page with his signature in the visitor's book was afterwards mounted on vellum.

It had been hoped to establish a Prince of Wales Fund in association with this visit to raise money for the Hospital and £1,000 had been promised by Messrs Sutton. The Prince regretted that he could not allow his name to be used as it had already been given for a similar purpose in connection with the London hospitals[5]. It was decided to start the Royal Berkshire Hospital's fund under another name, and a further £1,000 was promised by Lord Wantage. A public appeal would be launched when a Committee of Enquiry, recently appointed to review the finance and administration of the Hospital, had made its report.

The Committee was still at work when complaints were received in the autumn of 1898 about the nursing standards in the Hospital. Matters came to a head on October 25th when Dr W. Maurice appeared before the Board and complained of the arrangements made for an operation on the previous night. No hot water had been available and the nurse in charge of the theatre, in Sister Hunter's absence, was incompetent. Dr Price confirmed the facts. A motion that the Matron should resign as she had failed to fulfill her duties was withdrawn. Another was carried which noted that she should have satisfied herself that everything was ready for the operation. She had been shown to be 'incompetent to conduct the Hospital'.

The Matron, Miss Law, requested that the word 'incompetent' should be withdrawn, as it would be prejudicial to her obtaining another job and would jeopardise her future career. After she had consulted her solicitor, the Board were eventually persuaded to withdraw the offending word, and Miss Law sent in her resignation to take effect in three months' time. A letter signed by 30 nurses asked that the resignation might be

Visit of the Prince of Wales, 1898

128

reconsidered but the Board said it had been accepted and the matter was closed. On January 10th, 1899 Miss Easton, Matron of the Royal Hospital for Women and Children in London, one of 47 applicants, was appointed the new Matron. The same day a Special Board considered the report of the Committee of Enquiry on the financial position and general administration of the Hospital.

The report was far-reaching; its conclusions and recommendations were startling. For many years the income of the Hospital had been insufficient to meet the expenditure and by the end of 1898 the annual deficit was £1,500. The total ordinary income that year was £6,632 and the total ordinary disbursements were £8,146. By this time the Nursing Department consisted of 26 private nurses and the Hospital staff of 8 sisters, 34 nurses and probationers besides the Matron and Assistant Matron. The total number of beds in the Hospital, with the addition of Jubilee and Huntley and Palmer Wards, was now 164.

The Committee compared the Royal Berkshire Hospital with 13 other provincial hospitals of similar size. It was at once apparent that patients remained in the Royal Berkshire Hospital far longer than in other hospitals, the average stay in the Royal Berkshire being over 40 days – 43.2 days for medical and 42.2 days for surgical cases – compared with 28 days elsewhere. Each bed at the other hospitals had on average thirteen patients a year; at the Royal Berkshire Hospital it was only eight. Although the total cost per bed per year (£57 12s) was no higher, the cost of treating two patients at the Hospital was the same as the cost of treating three elsewhere.

The report recommended that the length of time patients remained at the Hospital should be reduced. With efficient management in this direction there would be more beds than necessary. These should therefore be reduced to 110, with Victoria, Albert and part of Sidmouth Ward being closed. There was no evidence that anyone was now waiting for admission. The nursing staff could also be reduced to 27 nurses and probationers to provide a further decrease in expenditure. These measures were believed to enable a saving of £500 a year to be made.

It might seem surprising that no patients were now awaiting admission as only a few years before the overcrowded Hospital and lack of beds were frequently being noted. In the intervening years the 20 beds made available in Jubilee and Huntley and Palmer Wards had relieved the pressure. In addition the various cottage hospitals which had opened in the surrounding towns had enabled those who were less severely ill to be treated locally. Towns such as Newbury, Maidenhead, Marlow, Fleet, Abingdon and Wallingford now had small hospitals ranging in size from 17 beds at Newbury to 9 beds in Wallingford. In Reading itself the extensions to the workhouse at Battle in 1894 had included an enlarged infirmary with greater facilities, enabling more inmates to be treated there rather than in the Royal Berkshire Hospital. By 1899 all cases applying to the Hospital could now be admitted.

The report then turned its attention to the honorary medical staff and recommended that they should be elected annually adding: 'It is essential that the governing body of any institution should have absolute control over its staff.' Furthermore the Committee believed there should be an age limit for holding office on the working staff. Physicians should retire at 65 and surgeons at 60. 'Surgery requires the use of faculties which become impaired by age more quickly than those required of physicians. In surgery the hand and eye are not as efficient as they should be for delicate operations whereas in pure medicine it is the brain which is the principal factor in the treatment of the case and, as we know, this may remain unimpaired in its functional activity for a much longer period.' The members of the staff should cease to be ex-officio members of the Board of Management and 'all communications from them should be made in writing'.

It was also recommended that the honorary medical staff should attend on fixed days and hours. Each should attend at least twice a week and there should be no day (except Sunday) on which a member of the staff was not in the Hospital. An attendance book should be kept in the staff room in which 'each member shall enter the times of his attendance at the Hospital on each occasion'. Operations, except in cases of emergency, should be performed on fixed days and at fixed hours for each surgeon.

Recommendations for the allotment of beds were included as well as the suggestion that the appointments of all the resident medical staff should be for a period of less than one year. Rules for the resident staff, the Matron and others were all detailed. No part of the administration was excluded. The Committee believed that 'the staff should be chiefly concerned with the care of the patients and that the administration of the Hospital should be kept to the Board who are elected by the Governors for this purpose.'

In connection with uniforms it was recommended that: 'There should be a fixed distinctive uniform for sisters, ward nurses, probationers and private nurses which should be contracted for and served out at a fixed time on a scale to be decided on.' The nursing staff should also be allowed half a pint of beer or stout with their dinners if they so wished.

The concluding paragraphs of the report stated that the chief cause of the deficit could be attributed to the length of time patients remained in the Hospital and believed the recommendations detailed were the only remedy to the problem. As these would only save about £500 a year the Committee ended its report with the words: 'The Hospital therefore confidently appeals to the town and neighbouring county for increased support to enable it to continue and perhaps extend the benefits it is already conferring on the sick and maimed among our poorer brethren.'

The honorary medical staff, understandably, were totally against the report. It had been made by a Committee which contained no medical representatives. They were particularly incensed when a special committee, without any independent medical advisor, was set up by the Board to review the rules in accordance with the recommendations of the report. Mr

May, as Consulting Surgeon, was asked 'not to accept a position which might be antagonistic to your colleagues'. The staff would have preferred the rules to have been submitted to representatives of the Royal Colleges of Surgeons and Physicians on the General Medical Council. Instead they were told by the Board that they could move an amendment at a Court of Governors.

The Annual Court held on February 28th, 1899 discussed the report and the possibility of reducing the number of beds and closing wards. Dr Hawkins challenged the conclusions of the report. Dr Marriott pointed out that two of his patients had been in the Hospital for over a year with bad legs. Their length of stay could have been reduced to a matter of weeks had their legs been amputated. Instead they were treated and left the Hospital cured and able to walk. Statistics alone could not be used in discussing the closure of wards. Eventually the motion was carried that no beds would be closed without 'first laying the matter before a Court of Governors specially summoned for the purpose'. All the other proposals in the report were accepted.

In April 1899 such a special Court was convened and among other matters the rule was agreed that only consulting physicians and surgeons should be ex-officio members of the Board. The retirement of Mr O. C. Maurice, the Senior Surgeon, was announced. He had worked at the Hospital for nearly 40 years and was made a Consulting Surgeon. Dr Price, the Assistant Surgeon, was elected Surgeon in his place and Mr W. J. Foster, F.R.C.S., was elected Assistant Surgeon. The question of beds was also raised and it was noted that the number might be reduced to 122 with the closure of Albert, Jubilee and part of Sidmouth Wards. Since the last Court there had been between 20 and 30 vacant beds. In the meantime it was agreed a public appeal for funds would be launched before any action was taken to close the wards.

Much of the rest of the year was concerned with the alteration of some 94 rules to put into effect the recommendations of the report. Patients were discharged as soon as was medically possible, although this led to complaints of some being sent home who had hardly left their beds. The rule concerning the overtime patients was altered to four weeks instead of eight, with the stipulation that 'in the first Monday in every month a meeting of the whole medical staff should be held to consider the necessity of the further stay in the Hospital of such patients as shall have exceeded one month.' Furthermore the Chairman should report these meetings in writing to the Board, noting the names of those patients. This was considered by the medical staff to be almost inoperable, and an article in *The Lancet* said: 'We can only hope that no harm will accrue to the well-being of the Royal Berkshire Hospital from a too-great insistance upon the strict letter of the law in question.' Later that year it was suggested that two committees should be appointed, one medical and one surgical, to report monthly on overtime patients. Each committee would consist of two surgeons or two physicians and if they should not agree on any case the whole staff would then be consulted on the subject and a decision taken.

A special public appeal was launched in June and the donations received included one from Queen Victoria. In December a special dinner was held, presided over by Prince Christian, at which more generous donations were received. Altogether £11,831 was raised besides additional subscriptions of £700. The public had rallied and the immediate financial crisis was over.

By the end of the year the average length of stay of patients had been reduced to 29 days with a total of 1,550 patients treated in the year, 250 more than in the previous year. No wards had been closed and with five sisters and 31 nurses and probationers the number of nursing staff was only slightly reduced.

There were other notable events in 1899 besides the reorganisation of the Hospital and the appeal for funds. Electric lighting and cauteries were obtained for the theatre and Out-patients Department. The drainage was completely overhauled. Private Nurses were supplied to the Marlow and Abingdon cottage hospitals. The sister's bedroom in Victoria Ward was converted to a small ward and a side ward was made into a ward kitchen. This was the beginning of the removal of the nurses' bedrooms from the wards. Most important of all a Röntgen Ray apparatus was obtained and special departments were recognised.

X-rays and Special Departments

In 1895 Wilhelm Röntgen, Professor of Physics at Wuizburg, discovered X-rays and a translation of his findings was published in *Nature* in January 1896. Members of the Pathological Society were advised in April that at the next meeting 'the new photography would be demonstrated'. No other business would be transacted at the meeting and officials of the Hospital would be allowed to be present. The minutes of the Pathological Society record that on May 27th, 1896 G. J. Burch, Esq. M.A. 'delivered a most interesting lecture on the new photography. After first explaining the nature of the Röntgen Rays and how they were produced, the lecturer exhibited a number of lantern slides of Skiagraphs that he had previously taken.' Several Hospital patients were also photographed. In the case of one, showing an abnormality of one finger, the negative proved successful; in the other cases the exposure was too short. Mr Burch also demonstrated the use of the fluorescent screen.

The results were exciting and impressive and in January the following year the medical staff recorded that they hoped the Hospital would soon be in possession of its own apparatus for Röntgen photography. In May they recommended the purchase of the equipment to the Board of Management. It was not until July 1899 that the Board agreed to the purchase at a cost of £70 17s 9d. The apparatus was placed in the Casualty Department and a dark room was made in the basement of the building. In the meantime some sort of X-ray work appears to have been undertaken, as the accounts include items for radiographing in 1898 as well as in 1899.

This was the beginning of the X-ray Department and the importance this was to assume in the years ahead could not have been anticipated in those early days with the simple equipment then in use.

In 1899 the question of forming special departments in the Hospital was raised again. It had been eleven years since this had first been proposed by Mr Leveson Gower when his suggestion had gained no support. The subject came to the fore with the retirement of Mr O. C. Maurice. Dr Price had specialised in eye cases and with this in mind Mr May suggested the formation of an Eye Department. Later the proposal was extended and the medical staff supported the idea of both Ophthalmic and Aural Departments which they noted had existed for some time but without formal recognition. A joint committee of members of the Board and medical staff drew up a scheme to be put to the Annual Court for approval in 1900. It was believed it would improve the efficiency of the Hospital and would not entail any increase in the medical staff.

The Hospital ended the 19th century reorganised and in a stronger financial position. With the advance of scientific and medical knowledge, it was now ready to develop and 'extend its usefulness' into the century ahead.

NOTES

1 The Windsor Infirmary was opened in 1857 and the Maidenhead Cottage Hospital in St Luke's Road in 1879.
2 The Queen Victoria Institute of Nursing was founded through the generosity of Her Majesty in diverting a gift of £70,000 made by the Women of England on the occasion of the Golden Jubilee in 1887. This enabled a Fund to be established for the training of nurses to visit the poor in their own homes. In 1889 a Royal Charter was granted to the Institute and numerous centres of District Nursing became affiliated to it over the years.
3 The Workhouse Infirmary at Battle, Oxford Road, was built in 1867. The Helena Nursing Home, Brownlow Road, Reading, opened in 1878, for 'poor ladies with incurable diseases without friends or relations'.
4 The Prince of Wales had unexpectedly visited the Hospital in 1870 to have some grit removed from his eye when he was attending the Foundation Stone ceremony of the Reading School. The incident caused a stir at the time and the royal casualty emerged from the Hospital wearing a black eye patch.
5 The Prince of Wales Hospital Fund, founded in 1897 to commemorate the Diamond Jubilee in support of the London hospitals, was later to be known as the King Edward's Hospital Fund. It exists to this day, is a registered charity 'to encourage good practice and innovation in the management of health care by research, experiment and education, and by direct grants.'

The Hospital *c*1900

5

GROWTH OF SPECIAL DEPARTMENTS 1900 TO 1914

The 20th century was only in its second year when the deaths were announced of both the Patroness and President of the Hospital. Queen Victoria died in January 1901 and a letter of condolence was sent on behalf of the Governors to the new King, Edward VII. Later he and Queen Alexandra agreed to become Patron and Patroness of the Hospital, and thereafter annual subscriptions were received on their behalf from the Windsor State Apartment Fund. The date of the coronation celebrations had to be changed in 1902 when the King underwent an emergency appendix operation. Eventually the Hospital patients celebrated on August 11th with the Mayor providing a special tea and the Coronation Committee for the Aged Poor donating 40 bright new half-crowns to be distributed among the elderly patients.

The death of Lord Wantage was announced in June 1901. He had been President of the Hospital for only four years but in that time he had been an interested and generous benefactor. He was succeeded by Major Thoyts of Sulhamstead House.

The death was also announced in 1901 of Mr Charles Stephens, a Vice President who had been Treasurer of the Hospital for 35 years. He had been elected to this office on the death of his father, Charles Stephens Sr, who had succeeded his brother William Stephens, the first Treasurer of the Hospital. For a period of over 60 years the post of Treasurer had been held by the same family. Their work on behalf of the Hospital was recalled with gratitude at the Annual Court in 1901 when Mr Stephens was succeeded as Treasurer by Mr F. C. C. Barnett.

In the meantime the proposal for the establishment of special departments had been put to the Annual Court early in 1900 and the Governors had accepted all the recommendations of the Board of Management. Ophthalmic and Aural Departments would be established and the honorary medical staff would include both an ophthalmic and an aural surgeon. The Out-patients Department would consist of medical, ophthalmic, aural and general surgical departments under the charge of the physicians, ophthalmic and aural surgeons and the assistant surgeons.

Each department would hold its own regular clinics on particular days.

Dr J. A. P. Price was appointed Ophthalmic Surgeon and Dr G. M. Guilding (an Assistant Surgeon) was made his Assistant. By the end of 1900, besides the large number of out-patients seen at the weekly ophthalmic clinic, 62 eye patients had been admitted and 41 operations performed.

As Dr Price continued to act as a general surgeon as well as ophthalmic surgeon, no additional beds were allotted to him specifically for eye patients. For a short time in 1900 a special clinic was held to enable school children, whose parents were not earning more than 20/– a week, to have their eyes tested. When Dr Price was appointed doctor to the School Board later that year this particular clinic was discontinued. The reports of the Ophthalmic Department, produced each year from 1902 onwards, record the steady increase in both in-patients and out-patients receiving treatment.

Mr A. Roberts was appointed Aural Surgeon and Mr W. T. Foster was made his Assistant in addition to being an Assistant Surgeon. One out-patients clinic was held each week and four beds were made available for aural in-patients. Special reports were given from the end of 1900 showing the work of the 'Throat, Nose and Ear Department'. By the end of that year 77 tonsil operations had been performed on out-patients and 26 ear operations (including 11 mastoids) and 10 nose operations on in-patients. In 1901 it was agreed that the House Physician should be allowed to give anaesthetics for Mr Roberts in the out-patients clinic as the Assistant House Surgeon was not available at that time.

The work of the X-ray Department was also increasing rapidly. In 1900, within months of the new equipment being received, the Board of Management appointed Mr Green, the House Surgeon, to be the Honorary Röntgen Rayist for one year with the addendum that 'this should not constitute him a member of the Medical Staff'. This appointment did not meet with the approval of the honorary medical staff who believed it unnecessary, and a few months later it was rescinded. Mr O. C. Maurice, the Consulting Surgeon, had convinced the other members of the Board on behalf of the now unrepresented active honorary medical staff that a special person was not required. Instead it was agreed that Mr Foster, the Assistant Surgeon, would take charge of the Department with the House Surgeon working under his supervision. A fluoroscope and a box for slides were obtained and by the end of 1900 it was noted that the Röntgen rays 'were being used every day as a rule' and the apparatus was 'working satisfactorily'.

In 1901 a new apparatus for localising the effect of X-rays was obtained at a cost of £21 7s 5d and a new accumulator was bought for the Röntgen equipment. It was emphasised that radiographs must be taken with the consent of a doctor and not at the request of the patient alone.

The use of X-rays had now been extended beyond the diagnosis of fractures and bone abnormalities and, as Dr Hurry showed the Pathological

Society in 1901, radiograms could identify tubercular deposits in the lungs and aneurisms of the heart and aorta. A further lecture given by Dr Hugh Walsham showed 'the use of Röntgen rays in the diagnosis of thoracic disease'. X-rays were also beginning to be used as a means of treatment as well as diagnosis. The first report of the Department in 1902 shows that besides 175 cases radiographed, a further 12 were treated by X-rays for conditions such as lupus and cancer. The report added that in addition 'a large number of patients had been examined by the screen'. Owing to the great increase in the work of this Department the male nurse was asked to assist and his salary was raised by 10/– to 40/– a week.

The first report of the administration of anaesthetics was given in 1901, after which year all anaesthetics were recorded and all operations noted in an anaesthetics book. A total of 1,520 were classified under the type of anaesthetic used – whether gas, ether, gas and ether, chloroform or A.E.C. In 1902 the number had risen to 1,817 and included Somnoform for the first time. In 1903 the figures had increased to 2,217 and included details of the sequences of anaesthetics administered. What was not recorded were the deaths of two patients under chloroform and the effect of the reporting of the two inquests in the papers on the same day. The following week a letter was published in the *Reading Observer* from Arthur M. Barford, M.D., Administrator of Anaesthetics to the N.W. London Hospital, the Throat Hospital, Golden Square and the Royal Dental Hospital in London. He noted that the recent chloroform deaths were:

'. . . not the first to have occurred during the last few years, for which there must be a reason. The Hospital has of late made special departments for certain branches of medical practice and why is not the administration of anaesthetics included in the same? There is hardly a hospital in London which is without a special medical man to conduct this responsible and anxious work. Surely the authorities of the Royal Berkshire Hospital must be slumbering or before now they would have taken upon themselves this important step.'

The matter was of great concern to the Board of Management and Mr May suggested an Honorary Anaesthetist should be appointed. The medical staff did not agree and on their advice the only change made was that the Assistant House Surgeon should be called the 'Resident Anaesthetist' in order to 'give the public confidence'. Future appointments of Assistant House Surgeons would be made with special regard to the candidate's knowledge of this subject. In 1909 the appointment of Mr T. W. Milne was made conditional on his attending a course on anaesthetics. Two weeks with the anaesthetist at the Westminster Hospital would be accepted instead of the usual one month, provided a certificate of efficiency was obtained.

The dental work at the Hospital continued to increase with all ordinary cases being treated as casualties and out-patients' tickets being required only when the Dental Surgeon was consulted. In 1901, 423 patients had teeth extracted and in 1903 this had risen to 740. Mr Goadby requested a new apparatus for the administration of nitrous oxide gas as the Assistant House Surgeon was giving gas on average to between 15 and 20 patients each week. Later it was decided only extractions of two or more teeth warranted an anaesthetic and in this way it was hoped to limit the great increase in the use of anaesthetics in the dental work of the Hospital.

When the suggestion was made in 1893 that an Honorary Pathologist should be appointed, the medical staff had stated firmly that this was 'unnecessary and undesirable'. Instead, the House Physician first appointed that year was also required to act as a pathologist, but no special facilities were made available for his use. Dr Hawkins's proposal in 1894 that a laboratory should now be provided had met with no success. Most specimens requiring analysis were sent to London, and since 1898 the Hospital had paid a subscription to the Clinical Research Company to enable necessary examinations to be carried out in their well-equipped laboratory.

In 1902 it was agreed that more pathological work should be undertaken within the Hospital and various items of equipment were obtained. These included a rocking microtome at £5, an incubator at £6 4s, a centrifugal machine at four guineas and a new microscope at 13 guineas. The importance of this branch of medicine was only slowly being acknowledged by the Board of Management but they, like the honorary medical staff, believed there was no need for a special Pathology Department or even a laboratory to be established at that time.

Tuberculosis

In modern times, when the scourge of TB has largely been removed through the remarkable results of antibiotics, it is easy to forget the prevalence of this disease until the second half of the 20th century and the toll it took on adults and children alike. In 1890 Robert Koch, who had isolated the bacillus which caused tuberculosis, had produced a vaccine which he called Tuberculin. In 1891 Dr Moody Ward had used 'Dr Koch's Fluid' for the treatment of a number of patients in the Hospital. The results were inconclusive and, despite initial optimism, the treatment was eventually discontinued.

In September 1900 Dr Hawkins suggested the Hospital should use the open-air treatment on balconies, as used by Addenbrooke's Hospital in Cambridge, for patients in the early stage of pulmonary tuberculosis. Many wards in the Hospital now had balconies built on their south side and those in the medical and children's wards were adapted for this type of treatment. The most encouraging results were obtained. The Hospital Visitors, however, were frequently reporting that patients were out in the open in all weathers and the medical staff had to stress that this was indeed part of the treatment. Spittoons were provided for the patients on balconies and later, on the advice of the Medical Office Health, these were also

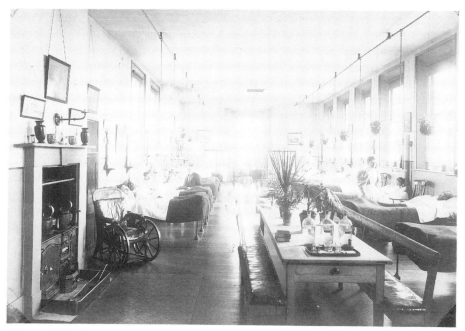

Sidmouth Ward

provided in the waiting-room and all prominent places in the Hospital in an attempt to prevent the spread of the disease.

When the effectiveness of this balcony treatment had been demonstrated, representatives from the Reading Union Workhouse at Battle inspected the facilities at the Hospital and established similar open-air balconies at the Poor Law Infirmary. In 1906 the Hospital arranged that all milk supplies would be sterilised and in 1910 it was agreed that only milk from herds free of TB would be given to the patients.

Near Reading Dr Esther Colebrook, the daughter of a former Mayor of Reading (later to be known as Dr Carling after her marriage to Henry Carling in 1904), had become interested in the open-air treatment of tuberculosis used in the sanatoriums on the Continent. In 1898 she undertook the treatment of a patient for a Reading doctor at a farmhouse near Peppard. Kingswood Farmhouse was later purchased in 1902 and the success of Dr Carling's work led to the founding of the Kingswood Sanatorium, with the addition of Maitland House. This was the beginning of what later became known as the Peppard Sanatorium and patients and staff from the Royal Berkshire Hospital were among the many who were treated there with great success.

The Nursing Department

The South African War had had little effect on the Hospital. In 1900 ten beds in Albert Ward had been reserved for sick and wounded soldiers at the request of the War Office and a charge of 3/– per day per patient had been agreed. In the event, no casualties were received and Albert Ward was returned to normal use. The male nurse considered volunteering for the Forces but was told his post would not be kept open for him. In June 1900 three nurses left to work as army nurses in South Africa.

Under Miss Easton the nursing staff were gradually increased and by 1902 numbered 46 to include the Matron, Assistant Matron, one Night Superintendent, seven sisters and 36 nurses and probationers. The Matron's salary had by now been increased to £125 a year since, on the retirement of the Housekeeper, Mrs Fry, Miss Easton had taken on her duties in addition to her own. The Assistant Matron's salary was £50 a year and that of a Ward Sister was between £35 and £45 a year. All the nursing staff now contributed to the National Pension Fund.

In 1901 the Private Nurses, 34 in number, were moved from the Nurses' Home in the Hospital to a house leased for them in London Road. When this lease expired in 1904 they moved to King's Road where two adjoining properties were made into one to accommodate them. The Private Nurses, although entirely separate from the Hospital nurses, continued to work in the Hospital when there was a shortage of staff or when any were not working on a private case. It was arranged that each year 5 per cent of their total gross earnings would be divided equally among them as a bonus in addition to their salary of between £35 and £45 a year. The demand for their services continued to increase and by 1904 a total of 44 were employed.

The removal of the Private Nurses out of the Hospital enabled the Hospital nurses to move into the vacated Nurses' Home. This improved accommodation at last enabled the remaining nurses' bedrooms in the wards to be dispensed with. All the nurses could now be given separate bedrooms and only a few probationers were left in cubicles within the Hospital itself. On the wards the vacated nurses' rooms were turned into small ward kitchens.

Alterations and Improvements

The reorganisation of the administration of the Hospital and the formation of special departments in 1900 was quickly followed by an inquiry into the condition of the Hospital itself. A firm of London architects, Messrs Young and Hall, specialists in hospital building, was asked to report on the arrangements in the Hospital and to advise 'in what way they fall short of the requirements of modern hospital practice'. Their recommendations were put before a Special Court of Governors in October 1901 but the total cost of £20,000 was considered far more than could be expended at that time. It was decided that no more than £16,000 should be spent, half from capital and half to be raised from the public.

Over the following two years work was carried out on improving and renovating the kitchens and the laundry; a Washington Lyon's steam disinfector was installed; the hot-water system was improved; Huntley and Palmer, Albert, Jubilee and Alice Wards were renovated with better

Albert Ward

sanitary fittings and floors; the isolation wards were improved, the theatre renovated and fitted with the latest sterilising equipment. A temporary corrugated iron building with 20 beds was erected between the laundry and Victoria Ward to accommodate patients while work was being done. The installation of electric light on the wards was now believed to be necessary, and by way of an experiment Mr May agreed to pay for this to be put in Benyon Ward at a cost of £98 10s.

Fund Raising
The public was asked once again to help by contributing to the building fund and to increase the annual subscriptions and donations. Additional income would be needed to replace that lost by the sale of invested funds. Mr and Mrs George Palmer made a most generous donation of £2,000 to the building fund and the Lord Lieutenant gave a further £500. Annual subscriptions were sought from previously untapped sources. One of those approached was the Commissioner of Woods and Forests as it was noted that 'the east end of Berks is unproductive to the Hospital, partly on account of Windsor Forest occupying much space'. An annual subscription of 15 guineas was obtained.

It was decided to ask for help from the working men of the town as it had been seen that in other areas many were supporting their local hospitals with weekly contributions. In May 1902 the Reading Work-people's Hospital Fund Association was formed, following much work by the Treasurer and a public meeting called by the Mayor. During the first seven months almost £500 was collected from employees in various factories and businesses in the town. Each firm had its own representative and tickets were given to them in proportion to the subscriptions raised. Those collecting three guineas or more would become Governors of the Hospital. Within a few years contributions of between £800 and £900 a year were being raised and the Association extended its work to include the nearby towns, with Sonning being the first to join. This source provided a significant increase in the ordinary income of the Hospital, and for the first time enabled regular contributions to be made by a specific group of people who were themselves eligible for treatment.

The whole subject of privileges to subscribers was reconsidered and it was arranged that those living at a distance of over seven miles, after eight months would be able to exchange their unused out-patients' tickets for that year for in-patient's tickets at a ratio of one in-patient ticket for every three out-patient tickets. Those making parish and church collections would have the same privileges as ordinary subscribers, something that had been requested for some time. In addition a subscription of 10/6d would provide one out-patient's ticket. The Reading Workpeople's Association was enabled to appoint three representatives each year to join the Board of Management. As with the Friendly Societies, the 20/- wage limit for out-patients being treated would not be strictly enforced provided the patients' tickets were countersigned by their club doctor or Secretary certifying that they were suitable for treatment.

It was also decided that a donation of £1,000 would cover the endowment of a bed in the name of a donor and £500 would endow a cot in a children's ward. If the money raised by a body such as a firm or a parish was not sufficient for an endowment, privileges would be granted in recognition of maintaining a bed or cot on the following scale:

50 guineas would give the privilege of a two-guinea
subscription for 10 years.
100 guineas would give the privilege of a three-guinea
subscription for 15 years.
200 guineas would give the privilege of a six-guinea
subscription for 20 years.

The idea of the endowment of beds had been raised many years before as the scheme had been adopted with success at the Windsor Infirmary. In 1893 a subscription of £21 was raised by the staff and children of the Kendrick School for Girls towards the maintenance of a cot in the children's ward, to be called 'The Kendrick Cot'. Every year since a similar sum had been received for its continued maintenance. In 1901 the children of the elementary schools in Reading raised £27 2s 3d to maintain a cot and both these contributions were continued for many years. For a short time contributions were also received for the maintenance of the 'Old Kendrick Cot'.

The first beds to be endowed were through the generosity of Miss

Mary Hall Pocock and Miss Martha Leggatt, who each gave £1,000 in 1903 to endow a bed in a female ward in perpetuity.

The Hospital had always been fortunate in receiving legacies. In 1902 they were left £1,000 by Mrs Julia Lloyd, the income from which was to be used for fitting up a room to be called 'The Lloyd Room' in memory of the late Capt. Ernest Boteler Lloyd of Silchester Hall. This room was to be available for the use of patients of 'gentle birth' who were unable to afford medical treatment in their own homes. Many who occupied this room gave small donations in appreciation of these facilities but the Hospital noted that only one third of the cost of this room was covered by the legacy.

Change and Expansion

In 1903 both the Matron, Miss Easton, and the Assistant Matron, Miss Hunter (formerly Theatre Sister), resigned because they wanted to move to Liverpool and set up home together. The Board regretted their leaving as the Nursing Department had been well organised and running smoothly over the past four years. Miss Gill, aged 40, trained at the Edinburgh Royal Infirmary, was appointed the new Matron. She had been Matron at the Edinburgh South African Hospital during the Boer War and had been decorated with the Royal Red Cross in recognition of her work there. In 1901 she was sent by the Colonial Office as a Matron to the South African concentration camps, where she remained until the camps were closed in November 1902. Miss Philp, who had also trained in Edinburgh and afterwards served in South Africa, was appointed Assistant Matron. Their arrival coincided with the beginning of a period of major change and expansion which was to last for several years.

By 1904 the population of Reading had increased by some 10,000 over the previous ten years. The number of patients being treated at the Hospital reflected this increase and in 1903 there were 1,813 in-patients and 4,317 out-patients, besides 627 accident and emergency cases and 16,199 minor accidents and casualties. The pressure on the resources of the Hospital, especially in the Out-patients Department, was considerable. Once again it was time to expand to meet the growing demands and to keep abreast of medical progress.

Before any structural changes took place certain administrative changes were made. In March 1904 various rules were amended by a Special Court. A motion calling for no physician or surgeon to be elected who held a Dispensary, Poor Law or Club appointment, was not carried. However, the qualifications needed by a physician were altered to stipulate that he should be an M.R.C.P. of London, or if a medical graduate of a university of Great Britain or Ireland it would be necessary for him to take the degree of M.D. within two years of election. The requirement that physicians should not be in partnership or practice surgery and pharmacy remained but midwifery was now excluded. It was also decided that no member of the honorary medical staff should hold more than one appointment at the Hospital except in special circumstances. No two members of a firm or partnership were to be on the medical staff at the same time. This did not apply to the consulting staff. The final suggestion made by Mr Leveson Gower in 1888 had now been carried out. The Court also agreed that in addition to the Ophthalmic and Aural Departments, a Skin Department should be formed. Beds would be assigned to these special departments and a special ophthalmic ward would be made. Two assistant physicians would be appointed to correspond to the assistant surgeons, to be in charge of the out-patients as well as septic and infectious cases. One would also be in charge of pathology and the other of skin cases. When a vacancy next occurred for a surgeon it would be left unfilled as two general surgeons were all the Hospital required besides the ophthalmic and aural surgeons.

The following month Dr W. T. Freeman was elected Assistant Physician in charge of skin cases and Dr G. S. Abram Assistant Physician in charge of pathology. Beds were allotted with four each to the Ophthalmic, Aural and Skin Departments, four each to the assistant surgeons and assistant physicians, and the remaining beds divided equally between the surgeons and physicians giving them 31 beds each.

The distribution of beds caused certain problems and Dr Abram, who was entitled to four beds as an Assistant Physician, found that Dr Hawkins refused to recognise his right to them. He maintained there was no precedence for beds once allotted to be taken away, as previously all beds had been distributed equally between the surgeons and physicians. Dr Hawkins's battle on this point lasted for many years with acrimonious letters from both him and his solicitor being received by the Board.

The first surgeon to retire after these changes were made was Mr J. H. Walters who had just reached the age of 60 and was made a Consulting Surgeon. He asked to be allowed to retain his beds in the Hospital as his appointment had been made prior to the rules on retirement. This was refused and the medical staff, for obvious reasons, were also not in favour of the retention of beds by the consulting staff.

With the new rule that no member of the staff could hold two appointments, Dr Price decided to retain his position as Surgeon and resign as Ophthalmic Surgeon. No election of a third surgeon would be made and later in the year Mr R. P. Brooks was appointed the new Ophthalmic Surgeon.

It was also decided that patients would be admitted and discharged every day except Sundays. This, it was hoped, would enable the beds to be used more efficiently and patients to be treated with less delay.

The increase in the administrative work of the Hospital had led in 1889 to the appointment of a clerk for the Secretary at a wage of 15/– a week. In 1892 the first typewriter was purchased for £21 but it was not until 1907 that the additional skill of shorthand was required. That year Frederick Cheer was engaged at 8/– a week with the promise that this would be raised to 10/– when his shorthand reached the speed of 80 words per minute.

In the meantime various sub-committees had been set up by the Board of Management: the House Committee in 1869, the Elective Committee in 1886 and a Finance Committee in 1899. There had also been a General Purposes Committee for a few months in 1900. In 1904 a Drug Committee was formed to be responsible for the ordering, stocking and storage of bandages, dressings, instruments, chemicals and drugs. It met each month and consisted of five members, two from the Board of Management and three from the honorary medical staff. At this time this was the only committee which included members of the honorary medical staff, although it had been agreed in 1902 that one member would be allowed to 'attend' the House Committee meetings. The influence of the honorary medical staff was to remain purely advisory and the administration was now firmly in the hands of the Board of Management as the representatives of the Hospital Governors.

The formation of a special Skin Department and ophthalmic ward, although approved in 1904, could not take place at this time as the necessary finance was not available. This was extremely disappointing to the medical staff concerned. A special Skin Committee had proposed a separate building to include baths for the Skin Department as well as electrical and other treatment for gout and rheumatism. Instead, skin cases had to make use of the special baths already provided in the wards and in the Out-patients Department, where between 50 and 60 skin patients attended weekly.

By the end of 1905 the medical staff were drawing attention to the 'inefficient and insufficient accommodation for eye patients, through which cases, often urgent, are frequently compelled to wait two months for treatment'. Later Mr Brooks reported that he had performed the last five cataract operations at his own expense outside the Hospital after these patients had been kept waiting many months for admission. An ophthalmic ward was urgently needed.

The Out-patients Department was now holding one dental, one skin, one aural, two eye, two surgical and three medical clinics each week. The great number attending included not only those with out-patient's tickets but also casual and accident patients. The numbers were now more than the facilities could accommodate. The Dispensary was inadequate and inconvenient and there was insufficient space for the examination of patients. In addition casual patients were being treated in the surgery of the main building. This was also used for light treatment and operations on septic cases which were inadmissible to the operating theatre. The one room was doing the work of three.

A great number of operations were also being performed in the Out-patients Department, including tonsils and adenoids. In addition parents were bringing their children for circumcision as casual patients without any ticket. This not only gave the Hospital much additional work but caused complaints from local practitioners who believed they were being deprived of patients who were able to pay for their services.

The application of the wage limit for out-patients had become very slack and it was agreed that this should be enforced more strictly with only those earning less than 20/– a week being eligible for treatment. The exception to this was still to be members of Friendly and Trade Societies and the Reading Workpeople's Association whose tickets were counter-signed by their own secretaries or doctors. Other patients would be asked if they belonged to a Dispensary or Club where they could obtain treatment. In 1907 the wage limit was increased to 25/– for married men or a widow with children and 20/– for the unmarried. In addition casual patients who wished to be seen a second time were required to produce an out-patient's ticket, and this limited the number of patients attending without any recommendation.

The Hospital was now able to give treatment which patients could not obtain in their homes. It was recommended that out-patients should not pay for treatment except when recommended by their doctors for a special course requiring special apparatus. A charge of five guineas would be made for a three-month course of Finsen's Light treatment and 10/6 for an examination by X-rays.

The suggestion that it might now be advisable to admit paying patients was reluctantly withdrawn as the Hospital had no space in which to accommodate them. Various requests were made for paying patients to be admitted for operations. One father who earned £220 a year offered payment for a hernia operation needed by his child. This was refused, but Mr Walters offered to operate at the patient's house 'for such fee as the father's income permitted'. Although paying patients as such were still excluded, the rules for reimbursing the Hospital if the patient could afford it gave a certain flexiblity and from time to time such cases were admitted in return for a substantial donation to the Hospital on discharge.

Pierre and Marie Curie's research on radioactivity resulted in the isolation of radium in 1902 and raised great hopes for advances in the treatment of cancer. In 1905 the medical staff recommended the purchase of radium for Hospital use and suggested that 'the Assistant Physician in charge of the Skin Department be responsible for its safe keeping'. The Board agreed to the request and a 'sufficient quantity', costing £32 2s 6d was obtained. Three years later a further purchase was requested costing between £10 and £15. The report of cases treated in the Skin Department in 1905 noted that radium had been used successfully in the treatment of lupus, rodent ulcer, naevus and warts. In 1907 radium was reported to be 'in constant use' in the Skin Department and was giving encouraging results.

Massage treatment had been carried out in the Hospital since 1884, when Mr O. C. Maurice had suggested a 'rubber' should be employed to instruct the nurses. By 1900 it was usual for the male nurse to be taught massage and in 1902 sixteen nurses were receiving instruction. Certificates were issued when the course was completed.

In 1907 Mr Foster asked if instruction could be received in physical exercises for cases of lateral curvature of the spine. The Board wondered if an honorary appointment should be made but the medical staff believed it was 'neither necessary nor desirable'. Instead, Mr Tinsbury was asked to instruct suitable patients in 'gymnastic exercises', and a fee of six guineas was paid for his year's attendance.

The League of Mercy

The fund set up in 1897 by the then Prince of Wales to commemorate Queen Victoria's Diamond Jubilee in support of the Voluntary Hospitals in London had by now been renamed King Edward's Hospital Fund. A similar fund called the League of Mercy in support of the provincial Voluntary Hospitals was founded by royal charter in 1899. By 1904 a branch had been established in Berkshire with H.H. Princess Victoria its Lady President. In July that year a two-day sale was held at Buckhurst Park on behalf of the League of Mercy and half the proceeds, some £202, were afterwards sent to the Hospital.

From this time onwards the League of Mercy took a close interest in the work of the Hospital with annual inspections and donations of money. The first donation of £100 was received in 1904. In addition both Princess Victoria and Princess Christian visited the Hospital from time to time and gave encouragement to others to support its work.

The League of Mercy was particularly concerned with the nursing staff and at the inspection carried out in 1908 it was noted that: 'The duty hours of the sisters, nurses and probationers . . . are in accordance with the best managed hospitals in the country and the nursing staff is so organised as to provide that the time off duty and the leave of the nurses shall never be broken into.'

The Ladies' Linen League

A League of a different type was also established in 1904 with the formation of the Ladies' Linen League under the chairmanship of Mrs Benyon of Englefield House. The object of the League was to supply the Hospital each year with all the linen it required. Very shortly branches were established in Berkshire (with over 400 members), Buckinghamshire and Oxfordshire, and Princess Christian became its Patron. The membership steadily increased and the results were impressive, with the work of these dedicated supporters enabling the Hospital's supply of linen to be maintained without any charge to its funds.

Infectious Cases and Park Hospital

The infectious wards which had been built in 1870 were only for those cases occurring within the Hospital itself. Similar cases developing outside were not admissible as patients. The only alteration to this rule was in 1897 when it was decided that typhoid cases would be received and could be treated in the general wards, but never more than in a proportion of one case in seven. With the opening of the two children's wards, more cases of scarlet fever, measles and similar children's diseases occurred besides the occasional cases in the adult wards. These intermittent outbreaks necessitated stopping further admissions and visitors to the wards concerned, isolating the cases, and disinfecting and fumigating wards, beds and bedding.

The need for a hospital for infectious cases had been acknowledged for many years. A small wooden building erected in Bridge Street by the Town Council received a few scarlet fever patients, adults paying 9/– a week and children 7/–. They were required to provide their own medical attendants besides any necessary wines and spirits. In 1893 a corrugated building had been put up beside this Fever Hospital to take a small number of smallpox cases and on several occasions the Private Nurses were sent to work there. These buildings were far from adequate and there were constant demands for a special infectious hospital to be built.

It was not until 1905 that a ten-acre site was obtained by the Town Council at the north-west of Prospect Park and the long-awaited hospital was built. It consisted of three main blocks, one for scarlet fever, the second for diphtheria and the third for 'uncertain' cases. Altogether 40 patients could be admitted in the public wards and a further four in the single private rooms.

Park Hospital opened on May 30th, 1906. The Royal Berkshire Hospital was notified that no charge woud be made for the isolation and treatment of any member of the staff in the public wards for either scarlet fever or diphtheria, or for any inmate of the Hospital who lived in Reading. Those living beyond the Borough would be charged one guinea a week. Thereafter infectious cases both among the staff and patients at the Hospital were frequently transferred to Park Hospital. The following year Miss Mekvin, the Victoria Ward Sister, was appointed Matron of Park Hospital and from time to time members of the Private Nursing Staff were sent to work there temporarily.

Other isolation hospitals were also being built in the neighbouring towns. Smith's Isolation Hospital in Henley opened in 1901. Like Park Hospital, it was occasionally supplied with temporary nurses from the Private Nursing Department. Both these hospitals as well as the Wallingford Isolation Hospital and the Whitley Smallpox Hospital were to form an even closer association with the Royal Berkshire Hospital after the advent of the National Health Service in 1948.

Mr George May

Early in 1906 a complaint was put before the Board by Mr George May concerning the medical staff and 'their practice within the Hospital'. A committee, set up to enquire into the allegation, reported that it was 'absolutely without foundation and should never have been brought'. A Special Board decided that in view of what had happened Mr May's 'continued connection with the Hospital is undesirable'. Mr May was informed and on June 5th sent in his resignation as a Consulting Surgeon. What had happened to cause this situation was never recorded. All the emotions that had been raised in 1897, when the surgical staff had resigned in protest against Mr J. H. Walters, had been resurrected with Mr May's complaint. Many were hurt and offended.

Mr May had been associated with the Hospital practically all his life. His father had been one of the original surgeons and as his pupil he had obtained much of his early training there. In 1855 he had been elected a Surgeon to succeed his father and in 1889 he had been made a Consulting Surgeon. In 1905 he had wished to retire as he was by then elderly and deaf, but asked that his name should be retained as a Consulting Surgeon. This had readily been agreed as he was a distinguished surgeon and highly esteemed.

Like most of the honorary medical staff, Mr May was a man of many interests. Besides his work in the Hospital, he had a large private practice in partnership with Mr Isaac Harrinson and later with Dr Hurry. He was also President of the Reading Dispensary from 1876 to 1908, President of the Pathological Society from 1887–88, a Governor of the Kendrick Schools and a Director of the Electric Light Company. He was responsible for planning Caversham cemetery and, with Dr Hurry, instrumental in the restoration of St Ann's Well in Caversham.

When his death was announced in January 1909 at the age of 82, although sympathy was expressed to his widow, there was a conspicuous absence at his funeral of any representative from the Board of Management of the Hospital which he had served so long and well.

The Hospital Extensions

In 1907 it was decided to go ahead and obtain plans for the extension of the Hospital. Everything possible had been done to contain the number of out-patients eligible for treatment but the numbers still continued to rise. In 1906 there had been 20,321 attendances by out-patients besides the 6,246 casualties who had made a total of 20,640 attendances. It was believed many patients formerly treated at the Reading Dispensary were now attending the Hospital instead. Long delays were occurring once again for the admission of in-patients, with complaints of some having to wait up to 15 weeks to obtain a bed. Additional beds had been given to Mr Brooks for eye cases but even this had not been sufficient to clear his waiting list. In March 1907 Miss Gill resigned to take up an appointment as Matron to the Royal Infirmary in Edinburgh. Miss Knowles, who had succeeded Miss Philp as Assistant Matron in 1905, was appointed the new Matron.

Three months later the plans submitted by architects Charles Smith & Son of Reading for extending the Hospital were approved by the Board. The total cost was expected to be £20,000 and would entail an additional expenditure of £1,200 a year. The work would be done in two stages, with the first stage to begin as soon as possible. This involved moving the septic wards (Huntley and Palmer and Albert Wards) from the west side of the building to the corresponding wards on the east side, where they are today. A new operating theatre would be built for septic cases adjoining Albert

Extensions 1908–1909

Ward. The corresponding room below would be used to accommodate noisy patients.

The children's wards, Alice and Jubilee, would be moved to the old Albert Ward and an entirely new children's ward would be built adjoining it to the south. The old Huntley and Palmer Ward would be improved to provide a waiting-room for the Out-patients Department. While these changes were made the children would be transferred to the temporary iron building between the laundry and Victoria Ward. In August 1908 Collier and Catley's tender of £1,299 was accepted for work on the septic theatre and the room below and the work was authorised to start immediately.

The X-ray Department was now working under considerable pressure and Mr Foster informed the Board that an X-ray room was now urgently needed to bring it up to modern requirements. A MacKenzie-Davidson's localising stereoscope costing six guineas and a Wheatstone's reflecting stereoscope had been obtained in 1904 as well as an optometer costing £20. In 1905 Mr L. Bell had been engaged as the new male nurse as he was able to 'understand X-rays and photography'. To meet Mr Foster's request, new X-ray equipment was obtained from Siemens costing £95 12s 8d and the old store room in the basement was converted into a temporary X-ray room. An assistant male nurse was engaged at 20/– a week to help with the extra work. When the second stage of the extensions was complete the X-ray Department would be housed in more satisfactory conditions.

A new mortuary, to include a small chapel, was also urgently needed. In 1909 Wheeler Bros' tender of £1,367 was accepted and work started on the building at the south eastern end of the grounds. By the end of 1909 the first stage of the extension was completed with the septic wards and the new septic theatre in use. The second stage, embracing the Out-patients and Casualty Department, the ophthalmic and children's wards, was only awaiting the necessary funds for it to be started.

An appeal for funds had been launched in November 1908 and by the end of that year just over £5,000 had been given or promised to the Building Fund. Special notices drew attention to 'the pressing needs of the Hospital' and a target of £20,000 was set.

By the end of 1909, £10,361 had been received, including the remarkable sum of £2,580 raised at a three-day fete held by the League of Mercy in the Forbury Gardens. The organising committee was presided over by Princess Victoria of Schleswig-Holstein and on July 20th the fete was opened by Princess Christian. Over the three-day period 8,500 people entered the grounds to enjoy the myriad of stalls, side shows, music and other entertainments. Such an occasion had not been held in Reading before and the outcome exceeded all expectations.

With half the necessary money raised, the second stage of the building scheme was authorised to begin in 1910. The old mortuary block, the motorshed and the porter's lodge were demolished to make room for the extension to the Out-patients and Casualty Departments. It was agreed that only articles of English manufacture would be used in the new building and a 'fair wage' clause was added to the contracts at the request of the Reading Trades and Labour Council.

On May 6th, 1910 the death was announced of King Edward VII. His interest in the Hospital, first as Prince of Wales and then as Patron, had extended over many years. At a meeting held at the Town Hall on December 17th it was decided that the children's ward to be built as part of the Hospital extension should form the Royal Memorial for the County of Berkshire. The ward would be called the King Edward VII Ward and would be a fitting tribute to the King who had done so much to help hospitals throughout the country. Eventually some £5,500 was collected by the King Edward Memorial Fund to provide this new children's ward. King George V consented to take over his father's patronage of the Hospital and the coronation was celebrated on June 22nd, 1911 with a special dinner and entertainment.

Earlier in 1910 the death had been announced of the President, Major Thoyts. As in 1901, the Hospital had lost its Patron and President within months of each other. He had been President for over eight years and besides being a prominent figure in the county, he had done much to help the welfare of the Hospital. He was succeeded by Mr J. H. Benyon, whose family had now provided three of the five presidents of the Hospital.

In 1910 the Manchester Unity of Oddfellows celebrated the centenary of their Order. They had always taken an interest in the Hospital and their Lodges in the area were all annual subscribers. With the other Friendly and Trade Societies, their help in raising funds each year with the numerous Hospital Parades was greatly appreciated. The Oddfellows had suggested endowing a bed to mark their centenary but when it was found the sum available, some £200, was not sufficient they agreed to provide a room in the new Casualty Department to commemorate the occasion.

On Wednesday, February 22nd, 1911 the Foundation Stone of the new buildings was laid. The ceremony was performed with full Masonic honours by the Rt Hon. Lord Ampthill, Pro Grand Master of the Fraternity, accompanied by 400 Masonic brethren and representatives of the 26 Lodges in the Province of Berkshire. It was a colourful and impressive occasion. The long Masonic procession, in full regalia, was joined in the Hospital grounds by an assembly of local dignitaries, members of the medical and nursing staff, the Board of Management and the President, Mr J. H. Benyon.

In his address Lord Ampthill noted that part of the new building was to be the county memorial to the late King Edward VII who, besides being Patron of the Hospital, had also been the Grand Master and Patron of the Masonic Order. Another link with history was noted in the use of a special mallet for the ceremony. This had been presented to King Charles II by Sir Christopher Wren on the occasion of the laying of the foundation stone of St Paul's Cathedral nearly 250 years before. The mallet now belonged to the Lodge of Antiquity of which Wren had been the Master.

Among the coins which were deposited beneath the Foundation Stone was the first new George V penny to be issued. It had been made available to the Hospital by the Master of the Mint, who was one of the Masonic Grand Wardens that year. At the end of the ceremony the National Anthem was played and the collection that was then taken raised £254 in aid of the Hospital. All the pomp and ceremony which had been planned and then cancelled for the laying of the Foundation Stone of the Hospital in 1837 had now been realised in the founding of the new extension some 74 years later.

New Appointments

It was to be more than a year before the new buildings were completed. In the meantime the work of the Hospital continued with inevitable problems especially with the Out-patients and Casualty Departments. In May 1911 the Matron, Miss Knowles, resigned through ill health. Miss E. A. Wynne, the Matron of Lincoln County Hospital, one of 76 applicants, was appointed to succeed her. Miss Pledger, Sister of Sidmouth Ward, was appointed Assistant Matron.

Complaints were being received of long delays at the ophthalmic out-patients clinic. Typical of the problem was one girl who had attended several times and had still not been seen. She worked at the Caversham Laundry for 9/– a week and could not afford to lose her wages on fruitless attendances. Mr Brooks asked if he could have the help of a clinical

Foundation stone ceremony 1911

assistant. The present help of the Assistant Surgeon was not sufficient.

A joint committee of the Board and medical staff, set up to consider increasing the number of medical and surgical staff for the enlarged Hospital, submitted an interim report in view of the urgent problems of the Ophthalmic Department. It was decided to appoint one or more clinical assistants to relieve the situation and in the meantime to retain Dr Cotton on a temporary basis.

In January 1912 a Special Court gave its consent to the appointments advised. A Medical Registrar, Surgical Registrar, Clinical Assistants to the Ophthalmic and Aural Departments would be added to the honorary medical staff. These appointments would be made annually, the applicants should be registered practitioners and would be eligible for re-election. The clinical assistants would be responsible to the surgeons of their departments and would attend the out-patients' clinics.

The Medical Registrar would assist the physicians and deputise for the assistant physicians in their absence. He would be responsible for note taking and the annual statistical report on medical cases besides the care of medical instruments. The Surgical Registrar would be similarly employed on the surgical side, generally supervise the administration of anaesthetics and if necessary administer them himself, or instruct the resident officers.

The importance of pathology was finally recognised with the approval that a Pathologist would also be appointed for one year and be eligible for re-election. He would be a registered medical practitioner and would be required to practise pathology only and not be in general practice. He would be able to undertake private work in the Hospital laboratory, 'provided his work for the Hospital does not suffer thereby'.

Applying for a position on the medical staff was not a simple undertaking. Although only three testimonials were now required by candidates, they were obliged to provide some 65 copies of each. This daunting task, in the pre-photocopying days, combined with the interview before the large Elective Committee, could well be an inhibiting factor to candidates wishing to apply.

Nevertheless within a few weeks C. B. Baxter, M.B., F.R.C.S., L.R.C.P., R. H. Cotton, F.R.C.S., L.R.C.P. and F. H. P. Wills, L.M.S.S.A. had been appointed Clinical Assistants to the Ophthalmic Department; H. M. Clarke, M.B. and G. McMullan, M.B., Clinical Assistants to the Aural Department, G. O. Lambert, M.D., B.C. Medical Registrar and W. B. Secretan, M.B., F.R.C.S. Surgical Registrar.

The election of R. Donaldson, M.B., B.Ch., F.R.C.S., D.T.U., D.P.H., as Pathologist with a salary £200 a year completed the new appointments. The medical staff believed him 'in every way suitable', with experience in Liverpool and Sheffield and Bristol. A new laboratory would be built by adapting the ambulance shed adjoining the mortuary.

The Special Court had also altered the rules for the appointment of Honorary Physicians. In future candidates should be Fellows or Members of the Royal College of Physicians in London or a medical graduate of one of the universities of Great Britain or Ireland. Their names must also be on the medical register. Gone were the stipulations concerning surgery, pharmacy and midwifery. These changes had now opened the position of physicians at the Hospital to those in general practice. Many Governors felt this was a mistake and that a 'real' physician as opposed to one in 'general practice' should be available for consultation.

Another alteration allowed assistant physicians and assistant surgeons, after 15 years' service, to receive the titles of Physician and Surgeon respectively. The Assistant House Surgeon in future would be called the Second House Surgeon and his salary as well as that of the House Surgeon and House Physician would be £80 a year. Advertisements for this appointment noted that ladies were 'ineligible' to apply. It was also agreed that two representatives of the medical staff would be included on the Board of Management and there would be one representative on the House Committee besides the three already allowed on the Drug Committee. This medical staff representation in the administration of the Hospital was to remain unaltered until the advent of the National Health Service, with one physician and one surgeon, nominated by the medical staff each year, included on the Board of Management.

The problem of consultations on overtime patients had gradually been resolved and it had now become customary for the medical staff to discuss such cases at their monthly meetings. The actual examination of the patients concerned was limited to two or three members of the staff alone. Similarly the procedure for consultation before operations were performed had been simplified. Before an important operation the surgeon would discuss the case with one or more of his colleagues 'if in his opinion the nature of the case required it'. As the surgeons had pointed out, if the operation was straightforward there was no problem; if it was not they would discuss the case with another surgeon as a matter of course.

The original rule requiring patients on leaving the Hospital to give thanks to Almighty God and their recommender had not been free of criticism. In 1896 an article in *The Lancet* had remarked quite bluntly: 'Was ever such a monstrous rule penned by a body of presumably more or less educated men. The Almighty to be thanked if cured or greatly relieved, the subscriber to be thanked irrespective of the outcome . . .' In 1912 the Revd H. E. H. Coombes of Ipsden Vicarage drew the attention of the Board to a parishioner who had been given the usual form for returning thanks, although he would later have to be readmitted for further treatment. 'I am rather doubtful as to whether this is a case suitable for such a form . . . I am rather doubtful . . . whether they should be issued at all. I am disposed to think the better plan would be to make a recommendation to the patient and leave the matter rather more to his or her initiative.' The suggestion fell on deaf ears; the rule remained unaltered until 1947. In this matter it was not a time for change.

The Opening of the New Buildings

The new buildings were completed in the spring of 1912 and the opening ceremony was performed on May 15th by Lady Wantage. Some 400 contributors to the Building Fund attended besides the President, Vice Presidents, Board of Management and medical staff.

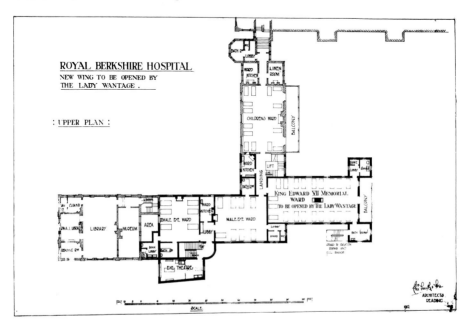

The extensions by Charles Smith and Son of Reading and built by Collier and Catley were designed to blend with the earlier work of Henry Briant and Joseph Morris. It had taken three years for the work to be completed and the eventual cost was almost £24,000. The resulting Hospital with 188 beds was now 'in accordance with the latest canons of asepsis and equipped with every modern requirement and convenience'. The Chairman of the Board proudly described it as being 'totally efficient' and 'in the front rank of County Hospitals'.

A new archway, complete with Ionic columns, had been built to form a covered entrance at the west side of the buildings adjoining Redlands Road. This led to a large waiting hall (the original Huntley and Palmer ward), physicians' and surgeons' room, a dispensary, X-ray rooms and the receiving room (given by the Oddfellows). There was also the casualty waiting hall, surgery and operating room, as well as the surgeons' rooms and dark rooms for the Ophthalmic and Aural Departments. On the floor above was the new eye theatre, with its large north-facing window, and two adjoining eye wards, one with eight beds for male patients and the second with six beds for female patients. (These are now called the West Ward and the eye theatre has become the day room for this ward.) Next to the eye wards was the splendid King Edward VII children's ward, the memorial of the County to the late King, complete with colourful tile pictures of nursery rhymes on the walls. A bronze tablet with a medallion of King Edward VII, designed and executed by Mr Alfred Drury, R.A., recorded this memorial. On the floor above were additional nurses' quarters.

On May 18th a separate ceremony was performed by Sir Rupert Isaacs to open the receiving room given by the Oddfellows. A white marble memorial tablet, designed by Mr Charles Smith and executed by Mr Jones the stonemason, was inscribed: 'As a thanks offering and in commemoration of the Centenary of the Order, the cost of this room was borne by the Reading District of Oddfellows Manchester Unity 1910.'

Later in the year the Hospital was left a legacy of £5,000 by Mrs E. R. Johnson of Bournemouth for the endowment of a special ward in memory of Douglas Johnson. It was decided that this and a further £1,000 which had been given by Miss Slatter to endow a bed in memory of Mrs Johnson would be used to endow the six-bed female eye ward. In October 1913 the brass tablets commemorating these bequests, and another for a cot by the brothers and sisters of the late Miss Theresa Miller, were unveiled by Mrs Benyon.

The hard work and generosity of a great many people had provided £18,000 for the extensions and improvements. This left a deficit of about £6,000 which it was agreed would be met by the sale of invested capital.

The improvements, with more space, better equipment and additional medical staff made all the difference to the work of the Hospital. The Nursing Department, enlarged with the addition of one sister and trained nurse for the Out-patients Department and another five probationers, was now 60 in number besides the 40 Private Nurses. Sister Treasure was sent

The new buildings. *Top*: View from the forecourt; *Centre left*: Entrance to the Ophthalmic Department; *Centre right*: The new archway; *Bottom*: View from Redlands Road

to Moorfield's Eye Hospital to receive special training before taking charge of the eye wards. The Matron was given a shorthand typist to assist with clerical work and the wage limit for out-patients was increased from 25/– to 40/– a week.

The work of the Eye Department continued to increase and an additional Saturday out-patients' clinic was started. Mr S. H. Gardiner was appointed the Hospital Optician and attended on out-patient's days. A statement by the Oxford Eye Hospital that it was the only one between London and Birmingham was strongly rebutted and the Board pointed out that the Ophthalmic Department at the Royal Berkshire Hospital was now equal to the best eye hospitals in the country.

The Aural Department was similarly busy. Mr Roberts was questioned about a complaint that patients were waiting in the room while minor operations were performed. Mr Roberts agreed that this was to be discouraged and added: 'I am very proud of this Department and the only fault I have to find is the after-treatment of the operations for tonsils and adenoids.' These patients were operated on as out-patients and sent home often far from well and being sick. Mr Roberts would have preferred that they should be admitted for one night.

Dr Donaldson took up his appointment as Pathologist on July 1st, 1912 but for the first few months his work was carried on in the main building while the new laboratories were being completed. These, designed by Charles Smith and Son and built by Collier and Catley, were opened in January 1913 by the Rt Hon. G. W. Palmer. The ceremony was attended by the Board of Management, the Mayor and members of the Town Council, the medical staff and members of the Pathological Society.

Two laboratories had been provided, one for general work and the second for special research. It was noted that few provincial hospitals could be found so well equipped for pathological and bacteriological work. There was now no need for specimens to be sent to London as facilities were available for the Hospital, public bodies and medical practitioners in the surrounding district. The work of the Department expanded rapidly and an assistant was engaged at 10/– a week. In October 1913 post-graduate classes in pathology and bacteriology were inaugurated and Dr Donaldson expressed the hope that the laboratories would be used for original research. In July of that year a paper had been read and specimens demonstrated at the meeting of the Pathological Society of Great Britain and Ireland.

By December 1912 it had been agreed that an Honorary Anaesthetist should be appointed. A total of 2,207 anaesthetics had been given that year. Such an appointment would free the Second House Surgeon to attend the Casualty Department where long delays were being experienced. The rules were amended to add that the anaesthetist should be an F.R.C.S. or M.R.C.P. or a member of one of the College of Surgeons and on the Medical Register. One or more Assistant Anaesthetists could also be appointed and they should be registered practitioners, appointed for one

Interior of the new buildings. *Top*: King Edward VII ward; *Centre*: Eye theatre; *Bottom*: The Dispensary

year and eligible for re-election. In April 1913 R. Ritson M.R.C.S., L.R.C.P., was elected the first Honorary Anaesthetist. His report for the year ending December 1913 classified the 2,150 anaesthetics administered which now included eight spinal and 244 local anaesthetics.

Dr Marriott resigned at the end of 1912 and his death was announced a few months later. Dr Freeman was elected Physician in his place and continued to take charge of the Skin Department until Dr G. F. Murrell was elected Assistant Physician early in 1913. Dr Price retired in 1913 on reaching the age of 60 and was made a Consulting Surgeon. Dr Guilding was elected Surgeon and Mr W. B. Secretan elected Assistant Surgeon. Dr G. O. Lambert and Mr J. L. Joyce were appointed Medical and Surgical Registrars respectively.

Dr Hawkins resigned in December 1913 as he had been ill for some time. His battle with the Board of Management over the allocation of beds had lasted for nearly ten years. In his letter of resignation he said: 'I so much resent the way I have been treated by the Board of Management that I wish to sever my connection of nearly 20 years with the Reading Hospital.' When two representatives from the medical staff were added to the Board in 1912 Dr Hawkins, although the Senior Physician, had refused to be one of those appointed. His death was announced in March 1914. Dr Abram was elected Physician in his place. The only change among the clinical assistants was the election of Mr L. Powell to the Aural Department to succeed Mr McMullan.

The National Insurance Act
In July 1913 the National Insurance Act, which had been passed by Parliament in 1911, came into force. This enabled workers whose income did not exceed £160 a year (later raised to £250 and then to £420 a year) to obtain insurance against sickness and unemployment by means of contributions from the State, the employer and the employee. For a weekly contribution workers could enrol on a doctor's panel and obtain medical attention free of charge.

When the Bill came before Parliament the Voluntary Hospitals, including the Royal Berkshire, were uncertain how it would affect their work and their funding. If free medical treatment could be obtained from a panel doctor, would such patients be eligible for treatment at the Hospital? Furthermore it was realised that the Hospital, as an employer, would have to contribute towards the treatment which was already given free to its employees.

There was a period of uncertainty but eventually it was decided to adopt the resolution passed by the Governors of St Bartholomew's Hospital. In-patients would be asked by a lay official if they were insured. If they were, they would be referred to a medical officer to determine whether the case was urgent or not. If they could be treated by their own panel doctor they would be referred back to him. All out-patients would be asked as far as possible to bring written statements from their medical

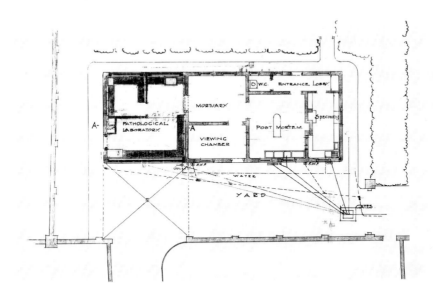

THE ROYAL BERKS HOSPITAL .
PLANS · FOR · CONVERTING · AMBULANCE · HOUSE · INTO · PATHOLOGICAL LABORATORY.

attendants and in this respect the Department would become one of referral and consultation. The 'necessitous poor' would be treated as before and all accidents and emergencies would be unaffected.

Owing to the doubts as to who could or could not receive treatment some bodies such as the Reading Industrial Co-operative Society withdrew their subscriptions for several months. It was explained that the Hospital could not accept insured people if treatment with 'equal advantage' would now be given by the panel doctors. Many people, including the dependents of insured people, would not be covered by the Act and treatment of these would be unaltered.

By the end of that year the Hospital statistics showed its income to have been relatively unaffected, although the contributions from the Reading Workpeople's Hospital Association had dropped from £700 in 1912 to £475 in 1913. The number of out-patients had dropped considerably from 7,552 in 1912 to 6,407 in 1913 and the casual patients from 5,436 to 3,689 in the same period. The Hospital expenditure, however, had increased by £156 10s for the Health Insurance contributions required on behalf of its staff.

The Request for Radium

In October 1913 the medical staff asked the Board of Management to obtain radium treatment for a patient with sarcoma in Benyon Ward. The Board's reply, that he should be sent to the Radium Institute provided the treatment cost no more than £5, came too late as the patient had already died. There was no means of treating such cases in the Hospital as the small quantity of radium available was only sufficient for superficial treatment on the skin.

A committee was set up to report on the 'advisability of the Hospital purchasing sufficient radium for the treatment of all suitable cases'. Their report in February 1914 explained what was required, what cases could be treated and suggested how the treatment should be organised. It concluded: 'The use of radium will develop on certain lines of treatment, very largely during the next few years and although in certain of the diseases specified (in the report) other treatment is available, radium appears to offer at present the only hope in many cases of inoperable malignant disease.'

Unfortunately the cost of obtaining the necessary quantity of radium would be between £2,000 and £3,000 and at that time the purchase was out of the question. It would be several years before the Hospital would be able to offer such treatment to its patients.

In February 1914 the Annual Report of the Board of Management showed that the Hospital, now with 188 beds, had treated 2,314 in-patients during 1913 (over one third more than in 1900) and 6,407 out-patients (more than double those in 1900). Over the year there had been an average of 13.5 patients per bed with the stay now reduced to 26.9 days. The re-organisation at the turn of century had proved effective and with careful management the cost per patient had remained relatively unchanged at £6 5s 9d per patient (£6 8s 11d in 1900) and 2/11¾d per out-patient attendance (2/6d in 1900). In addition much better specialised facilities were now available and a larger medical and nursing staff. The total ordinary expenditure in that period had risen from £9,800 to £13,600. Two houses called 'Lackington', adjoining those already owned by the Hospital in Craven Road, had been purchased for £1,175. They would provide a suitable site on which to build a new nurses' home when finances were available at some future date.

During the following months the work of the Hospital continued as usual. In June the annual Reading Hospital Parade brought the public and the Hospital together once again. The long procession, complete with an escort of mounted police and the Mayor riding in state on a motor fire-engine, stopped along the route in front of the Hospital to enable the five bands to play to the patients and staff. The same month when a train crashed at Reading station, the two horse ambulances with medical staff and nurses rushed to the scene and were greatly praised for their speed and efficiency. Later that month a course was arranged in the Hospital for members of the Women's Detachments of the British Red Cross Society who held certificates in First Aid and Home Nursing. In July the Hospital renewed its agreement, made each year since 1910, to provide eight nurses for Queen Alexandra's Imperial Military Nursing Service in time of war. Arrangements were made for the members of staff and nurses to take their summer break and the Board of Management decided they would not meet on the day following the August Bank Holiday.

That particular day was August 4th, 1914, the day on which the political uncertainty which had hung over Europe for the past months came to a head and war was declared between Great Britain and Germany. All too soon the life of the Hospital was to be dramatically changed.

The Hospital 1912 (Courtesy of the Francis Frith Collection)

6
THE FIRST WORLD WAR
1914 TO 1918

The outbreak of war produced two immediate problems for the Hospital: staff and supplies. Within hours of the declaration a meeting had been convened of the House Committee and four members of the honorary medical staff to consider the situation. Besides the eight nurses reserved for Queen Alexandra's Imperial Nursing Service, fifteen others were Territorial Army nurses; practically all the honorary medical staff were members of the Territorial R.A.M.C. and both gate porters had joined the Territorial Army. All were now liable to be mobilised. Provisions and groceries were likely to become scarce and additional demands for beds might suddenly be made upon the Hospital. All nurses on holiday were asked to return immediately; two tons of steam coal and a month's supply of groceries were ordered and provision was made for the opening of a further 30 beds if necessary.

One week later, when the Board of Management held its first war-time meeting, the House Committee reported that the price of bread had already risen by ½d for a 4-lb loaf, the 'amount surcharged by the millers for war-risk'; provision and grocery firms would no longer supply goods at contracted prices; it was difficult to obtain supplies of coal as the Government had commandeered output from the North Rhonda colliery; six nurses had been called for service with the Army Reserve and the fifteen Territorial nurses had been warned for call-up (two had volunteered for foreign service); the two gate porters had been mobilised but one returned unfit; Mr Madden, the second House Surgeon, had resigned as he had been ordered to report to Netley; Dr Freeman had received his mobilisation orders for the Territorial R.A.M.C. and Mr Roberts the Aural Surgeon had joined the Berkshire Royal Horse Artillery. Dr Maurice's suggestion that his son, Mr Francis Maurice, should enter the Hospital as a medical pupil was gladly accepted. He had recently taken his degree in physiology at Oxford. His services would be invaluable in the present situation.[1]

Early in August the Headquarters of the 3rd Southern General Hospital were established at the University Examination Schools in Oxford. Practically all the honorary medical staff at the Royal Berkshire Hospital were liable to be mobilised to serve at this Oxford Base Hospital. It was agreed with the military authorities that only one half of the Reading honorary medical staff would be on duty there at a time and that the periods of duty could probably be arranged for one month. This would enable them to continue to work part-time at the Royal Berkshire Hospital and also to some extent maintain their private practices. A meeting of all the medical practitioners of Reading was held in the Hospital library on August 26th to discuss the question of 'conducting the private practices of medical men absent on military service.'

The many offers of help received from local doctors enabled arrangements to be made to organise the Hospital and private work of the area. At the Hospital the consulting staff, Mr Walters and Dr Price, came out of retirement and Dr Donaldson, the Pathologist, also offered to help on the medical side. Dr Norman May of Sonning, Dr Armstrong of Wellington College and Dr F. C. Young of Twyford would assist with anaesthetics. Dr Young wrote: 'Having practised in this neighbourhood for 17 years, I have always found the resources of your Institution have been willingly and unfailingly placed at my disposal and consequently I owe it a deep debt of gratitude.' Several other local doctors offered to help in various capacities and it was arranged that Dr Hurry, Dr Chidell and Dr Armstrong would attend medical out-patients and Dr Coleman would assist in the X-ray Department.

It was pointed out that 'certain drugs would become almost unobtainable in the event of the war lasting more than two months'. All German preparations, liquid paraffin, aspirin, potassium bromide and all salicylates should be used as little as possible. Only essential X-ray work should be undertaken until a supply of tubes was assured. Extra supplies of drugs and dressings were ordered.

By mid-August fourteen nurses and four sisters had left to join the Army Reserve or Territorial Forces. Courses for Red Cross nurses were arranged and on August 25th the first three Red Cross probationers started their month's training at the Hospital.

The question of offering beds to military patients was discussed. The medical staff suggested that all the beds except a minimum number required for local residents could be made available. 'In this way the members of the medical staff could fulfill their obligations as to military service without being obliged to leave their Hospital and their private practices neglected.' At the end of August it was decided the War Office would be informed that the Royal Berkshire Hospital would make 50 beds available at once to serious cases of sick and wounded. In an emergency this number could probably be increased.

After the first month the Hospital gradually adapted to the problems of war time. Beyond its walls the patriotism of the public was reflected in the long lists printed of those who had volunteered to serve in the forces. The President of the Hospital, Mr J. H. Benyon, headed the local Prince of Wales Relief Fund. The Berkshire Branch of the British Red Cross Society, formed in 1910, was raising funds to equip its nurses and hospitals. Within a short time it had provided two ambulances, to be called 'County of Berkshire Mobile Ambulances 1 and 2', with the proviso that, should they be fit for service after the war, they would be given to the Royal Berkshire Hospital. Requests were made for clothing, tobacco and comforts for the troops, help for the Belgian refugees was invited and shortly the lists of wounded, killed and missing began to appear.

The offer of beds at the Royal Berkshire Hospital was quickly accepted by the War Office. The Hospital was formally classified as a section of the 3rd Southern General Hospital, Oxford and a charge of 3/4d per day for each military patient was agreed. Benyon Ward and the casualty waiting hall would be used to accommodate up to 50 wounded. The soldiers would be admitted as ordinary patients but subject to military discipline. There would be no interference with their treatment. Only serious cases would be accepted and no convalescent patients or German prisoners admitted. A total of £500 was spent on the necessary equipment and adapting the waiting hall into Hall Ward. By drawing on the Private Nurses a sufficient number of nursing staff was obtained and only two additional male nurses and one ward maid needed to be engaged.

Admiral Fleet, County Director of the Berkshire Branch of the British Red Cross Society, asked if the Hospital had the necessary means of conveying the wounded. Various local firms including Heelas, V. Vincent and A. Newbury had offered to help and, with private individuals, the transport of up to 73 patients could be arranged.

No military patients were received throughout October although the 3rd Southern General Hospital had telegrammed on three occasions that a convoy of 40 wounded was imminent. Throughout this period the 50 military beds were kept vacant. Civilian cases still needed to be admitted and many men were waiting to undergo minor operations to enable them to enlist. The surgical list became greatly congested and Alice Ward was made into a temporary male surgical ward to ease the pressure.

Other war-time matters arose. The Hospital decided not to insure against bomb damage; the Chief Constable said he would not be considering blackout yet and the League of Mercy's request for the admission of wounded French and Belgian soldiers had to be turned down. A letter was received from the Manager of the Reading Water Works in which he detailed the precautions being taken to prevent the water supply being poisoned by aliens. The medical staff advised that all drinking water in the Hospital should be boiled.

One of the most pressing problems was that of obtaining Resident Medical Officers. No Second House Surgeon had been obtained to replace Mr Madden and advertisements in the medical journals to fill the vacancies of House Surgeon and House Physician in October did not produce a single reply. Eventually Dr Mutsaars, a Belgian refugee, applied for the post of House Physician, but his M.D. from Brussels was not a registerable qualification. Dr Allays, an aural specialist from Antwerp who applied as House Surgeon and Anaesthetist, found his M.D. from Louvain was similarly unacceptable. It was decided that the question of registration would be overlooked and both applicants were appointed for six months at a salary of £100 a year, with the stipulation that all death certificates must be signed by a qualified British doctor. Later Dr de Neefe was appointed Assistant House Surgeon and the Board of Management gave the medical staff authority to 'make any temporary appointments necessary for carrying on the medical work of the Hospital during the present crisis'.

On October 29th a telegram was received from the Deputy Director of Military Services, Salisbury. 'Beds urgently required for reception of large number of wounded arriving from overseas. Please wire immediately number you can receive direct from Southampton.' The Hospital replied: 'We have 50 beds empty as directed for 3rd Southern General Hospital, Oxford. No others are available.' On November 3rd a further telegram informed the Hospital that 50 wounded from Oxford would arrive at Reading Station at 11.40 a.m. the following day.

This first convoy of wounded to arrive at Reading was met by a large welcoming party which included the Mayor. Major L. M. Guilding and Major G. S. Abram were there to receive the patients and outside the station various conveyances were assembled to take them to the Hospital. One of these was the motor ambulance which members of the Wellington Club in Reading had recently presented to the 2nd Battalion Royal Berkshire Regiment. Members of the St John Ambulance Brigade were also in attendance. The newspapers reported the occasion in detail, noting that the men 'mostly had their heads swathed in bandages and arms in slings but despite their condition . . . generally appeared to be of a cheerful disposition and were evidently delighted with the heartiness of their reception.' They came from many different regiments and practically all were suffering from gunshot or shrapnel wounds.

From the beginning of November the Hospital proudly flew both the Union Jack and the Red Cross flag. The total number of beds had been increased to 208 of which 158 remained available for civilians, a decrease of 20 from the pre-war period. Most of the first 50 military cases were able to leave within three weeks, and on November 21st a second convoy with 30 wounded was received at the Hospital.

The military patients were provided with hospital clothing and received a slightly better diet than that of the civilian patients. This included 6 oz of meat a day, 2 oz of jam or marmalade at breakfast and cheese as well as soup for supper on alternate days. Requests were made for books, cigarettes and tobacco and, when fit enough, many soldiers were entertained by families in the district. Experiences at the Front were recalled when visitors, appointed in connection with the Enquiry Department of the Red Cross, questioned the wounded in their search for information about soldiers listed as missing.

At Christmas is was decided the patients would be provided with a special dinner and entertainment as usual but no parties would be held for the nurses and servants that year, 'it being felt that under the circumstances they would not be desired'. Mr Brown, who had given a decorated

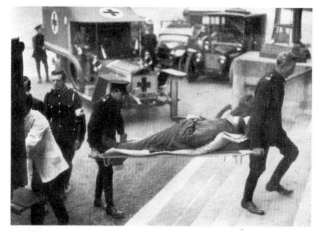

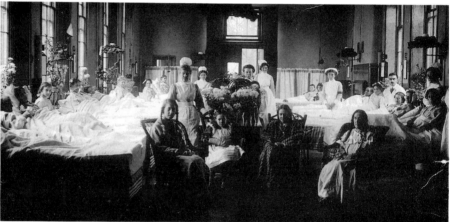

Top left: Arrival of wounded at the Royal Berkshire Hospital; *Top right*: The Red Cross joins the Union Jack; *Centre*: Victoria Ward, Christmas 1914; *Bottom*: Benyon Ward, Christmas 1914

tree each Christmas since 1895, had recently died and had left a legacy of £200 to the Hospital requesting that the custom should be continued. In the event Mr Keyser donated a tree and numerous presents were given by the public who, this year in particular, wished to express their gratitude to the Hospital and to the soldiers who had served at the Front.

1915 to 1916

The belief that the war would be over by Christmas 1914 was short-lived and by that time the military work of the Hospital was only just beginning. In February 1915 a partial blackout was ordered by the military authorities. Blinds were fitted to the theatre skylight and other windows to obscure bright lights. The Hospital decided after all to insure the building against aircraft damage. The number of Red Cross nurses accepted for instruction was increased so that six could attend at a time from 7 a.m. to 5 p.m. daily. V.A.D.s were helping in the wards, the kitchen and in the laundry and also with transport. The first bed to be endowed in memory of a fallen soldier was when Mrs Bruce of Arborfield Court gave £1,000 for a bed in Benyon Ward in memory of her grandson, Frederic de Vere Bruce Allfrey, Lieut. IX Lancers, killed in action September 7th, 1914.

In March an outbreak of cerebro-spinal meningitis (spotted fever) among civilians and the troops stationed in the town provided the Hospital with an additional challenge. The civilian cases were admitted to Park Hospital. The isolation wards at the Royal Berkshire Hospital were made available for 14 military cases and as these increased in number an adjoining marquee was erected for a further six beds. Two R.A.M.C. orderlies were provided and a request was made that the Hospital nurses who had been sent to Oxford should be allowed to return. The allowance paid by the War Office was increased from 3/4d to 7/6d in respect of these particular patients. Altogether 34 cases were admitted and the death of six, in a disease usually considered fatal, was believed to be the lowest ever recorded. The Deputy Director of Medical Services at Salisbury especially thanked the Hospital for their efficient and successful treatment.

By this time the Reading Board of Guardians and Education Committee had been approached by the War Office regarding the provision of an additional 1,000 military beds in the area. It was arranged that the Workhouse at Battle, with the exception of the casual wards and the farm, would be handed over to the military authorities. The inmates would be accommodated at various institutions throughout the district. Several council schools would also be made available. On April 22nd, 1915 the Number 1 Reading War Hospital at Battle, then equipped for 400 patients, opened with a convoy of 120 wounded from France.

More military beds were requested at the Royal Berkshire Hospital and a further 50 were made available in Sidmouth Ward. The Temporary Ward, known as the Iron Room, was refurbished to provide additional civilian beds and renamed East Ward. A total of nine extra medical beds were added in Alice, Albert and Huntley and Palmer Wards.

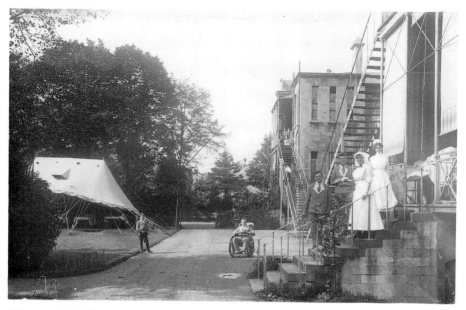

Marquee in the Hospital grounds

The first branch hospital was opened at the nearby Redlands School and the Board of Management agreed to take over the administration. The military authorities considered this would be more convenient than running it from the Number 1 Hospital at Battle. All expenses in setting up and running the hospital would be met by the War Office. A Matron and nurses were engaged, the building equipped and Dr Lambert was appointed Medical Officer in charge at a salary of £300 a year. On June 25th, 1915 No. 4 Reading War Hospital at Redlands School was opened with 120 beds. No. 2 Reading War Hospital was opened on July 1st at Battle School with 200 beds, No. 3 Reading War Hospital at Wilson School on September 7th with 300 beds and No. 5 a few months later at the Katesgrove and Central Schools with a further 200 beds. The Royal Berkshire Hospital with its 100 military beds became known as the No. 6 War Hospital. All the honorary medical staff working at the Oxford Hospital were transferred to work at the various War Hospitals in Reading. The Royal Berkshire Hospital's military wards now came under the direction of Southern Command at Salisbury.

Complaints had been received from some of the soldiers in Benyon Ward about the food and that they were having to buy sugar and eggs. It was agreed that the diets were 'insufficient in some respects' and in May they were amended to provide: Daily – bread as required, 2 oz butter, 1½ oz sugar, 6 oz milk. Breakfast – 1 pint tea; porridge on four days; 1 egg on three days. Lunch – ½ pint soup. Dinner – 6 oz meat, potatoes as required, vegetables, 8 oz pudding. Tea – 1 pint tea, 2 oz jam. Supper – ½ pint soup; 3 oz cold meat, 2 oz cheese, porridge on four days, eggs on three.

DIET TABLE

ROYAL BERKSHIRE HOSPITAL.

| | FULL DIET. | SPECIAL DIETS. | MILK DIETS. | |
			PLAIN.	FARINACEOUS.
DAILY	Bread as required. Butter, 1 oz. Milk, 6 ozs. Children, Butter, ¾ oz. Milk, 1½ Pts.	Bread as required. Butter, 1 oz.; Children, ¾ oz.	Milk, 3 Pints, divided at discretion. Children, 1½ Pts.	Bread as required. Butter, 1 oz.; Children, ¾ oz.
BREAKFAST ...	Tea, 1 Pt.	Tea, 1 Pt.		Milk, 3 Pts., divided at discretion. Children, 1½ Pts.
LUNCH	Soup. ½ Pt.	Milk, ½ Pt.		
DINNER ...	Meat, roast, boiled, or stew; Men, 4 ozs.; Women, 3 ozs.; Children, 2 ozs. Pudding, 8 ozs.; Potatoes as required.	Milk, ½ Pt. Extras as ordered, Chops, Chicken, Fried or Boiled Fish ; Pudding, 8 ozs.; Potatoes as required.		12 ozs. Pudding.
TEA	Tea, 1 Pt.	Tea, 1 Pt.		Special Beef Tea, if ordered, ½ Pt.
SUPPER	Soup, ½ Pt.	Milk, ½ Pt.		

Every Patient admitted into the Hospital is placed on Milk Diet until a Diet is otherwise ordered.

Diets ordered by the Physician or Surgeon are to be continued until changed by subsequent orders.

Extras and Special Diets are allowed for one day only, unless the Physician or Surgeon writes the word " Daily."

BY ORDER OF THE BOARD OF MANAGEMENT.

With the arrival of so many wounded in the town, various voluntary organisations were formed to provide additional help. At the end of March 1915 the first depot was opened at the Corn Exchange for the collection of eggs. This branch of the National Egg Collection covered a wide area and received donations of money as well as eggs. Three times a week supplies were distributed among the various War Hospitals in the town, including the Royal Berkshire Hospital. About the same time a Care and Comforts Committee was formed to arrange for volunteers to visit the military wards and distribute the books, cigarettes, tobacco and other items which had been collected for the wounded.

A third organisation was established later in 1915 when the Reading Chamber of Commerce formed the Reading War Hospital Supplies Depot to make and supply surgical necessities for the wounded. Like the other two, this was a purely voluntary organisation and during the course of the war expanded to provide invaluable help to the military hospitals. Started at 24, Cross Street, the Depot soon moved to Duke Street and eventually some 60 outside working parties were formed throughout the area and a branch established at Maidenhead. Bandages, swabs, splints, crutches, artificial limbs, slippers and shoes were among the items made, assembled and dispatched to military hospitals both at home and abroad. Hundreds of people became involved and the voume of their production was impressive. The Royal Berkshire Hospital with the other military hospitals in the area benefited from the work of these volunteers.

The two pre-war voluntary organisations associated with the Hospital, the Ladies' Linen League and the Samaritans' Sewing Guild,[2] continued their invaluable work throughout the war. Year after year they supplied the Hospital with an ever-increasing number of garments, articles of linen and donations of money. The support of all these voluntary organisations, besides the numerous gifts made by individuals and parishes, played a most significant part in the life of the Hospital throughout this period.

Prices were constantly rising, not only of provisions, gas and electricity, but also of drugs. Typical of this was phenacetin which had risen from 3/5d to 16/– per pound and acid acetosalicylic from 2/5d to 27/3d. Bottles became very scarce, and following an appeal in the local press in August over 7,000 were received at the Hospital.

The rise in the cost of living led to the out-patients' wage limit being increased from 40/– to 45/– a week and an increase in wages and salaries for all the Hospital employees. The Dispensers' salaries were increased by 25 per cent as they were now also dispensing for Redlands Hospital. When it was noted that the nurses employed in War Hospitals were earning higher wages, a War Bonus of £10 per year was arranged for those remaining in the Hospital. The difficulty in obtaining Resident Medical Officers was attributed partly to the low salary offered and it was agreed that in future £300 a year would be paid, the same as offered by the military authorities.

The increased work of the Hospital, now with 240 beds, put great pressure on all the staff. Most of the honorary medical staff were working at the military hospitals in the town as well as attending civilian and military patients at the Royal Berkshire Hospital. The work of the three Resident Medical Officers was described as 'one continual rush from morning to night', with little free time. The surgical work of the Hospital had increased considerably, as practically all the military patients were surgical cases. The decrease in the civilian beds had been made mainly in the medical wards. The House Physician was now undertaking surgical work, giving anaesthetics and attending out-patients and was also in charge of one of the three military wards. Apart from all their other work the Residents could expect to spend about five hours each day in the theatre. With this work load it was becoming almost impossible to keep the records properly.

Operations were usually performed in the main theatre from the afternoon onwards, with emergencies at night lasting until the early hours. The theatre staff consisted of a sister, an assistant nurse and two probationers. The sister and one probationer would be on duty at night alternating with the assistant nurse and second probationer.

The septic theatre was in the charge of the Out-patient Department Sister. This meant that no operations could be performed there until after 3 p.m. when the out-patients no longer required her presence. No operations were performed in this theatre after 9 p.m. As most of the military patients were septic cases, problems constantly arose with the theatre being required for both civilian and military operations in a very limited time.

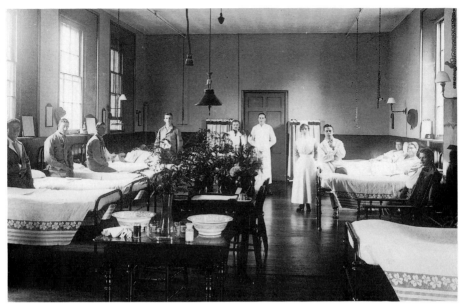

Sidmouth Ward

Among the nursing staff there was a shortage of experienced sisters and nurses. There was no difficulty in obtaining probationers, but once trained they frequently left for other posts or to join the Forces. There had been 47 nurses in 1914 and a year later this had increased to 52, in addition to the eleven sisters and one night sister. In the year since the war began a total of 65 Red Cross nurses had been admitted to the Hospital for training. This had added considerably to the work of the sisters and also had reduced the time available for training the Hospital probationers.

Many of the medical staff believed the quality of the nurses had deteriorated and complained that in some wards the sisters 'were not capable of managing their nurses or of looking after their patients properly'. Nurses were moved from ward to ward and frequently had little knowledge of the cases in their care. Inexperienced nurses and probationers were being left in sole charge of large wards at night. In the female surgical ward patients recovering from serious abdominal operations were 'frequently obliged to look after themselves' through the lack of staff. In the theatre the nurses were often not specifically theatre-trained. There was also great difficulty in obtaining male nurses and Mr L. Bell, who worked in the X-ray Department, was far from well and greatly overworked.

The Committee formed in July 1915 to consider the staffing of the Hospital recommended among other things the appointment of a fourth Resident Medical Officer. The septic theatre should be available for military operations throughout the day and should be staffed by a fully trained nurse and at least one probationer. No ward should be left in the charge of a nurse of less than three years' standing and each of the large wards should have two night nurses. Every ward with the exception of the eye wards and Hall Ward should have a nurse of three years' standing as well as the Sister and in the large surgical wards this would mean that in addition to the Sister there would now be a nurse of three years' experience and four probationers. The report of the Committee was accepted by the Board of Management. Its recommendations would be put in operation 'as and when practicable'.

As the work of the Pathology Department had increased considerably and now included Redlands Hospital, a qualified Assistant, Mr Windley, was engaged at 45/– a week and a lab boy was employed at 7/6d a week to wash bottles and run errands. A low-temperature incubator (15 guineas) freezing microtome (£6 15s) and a water-driven centrifuge (£6 5s) were obtained. Papers were read to the Pathological Society by Dr Donaldson on cerebro-spinal meningitis and slides shown of the meningococci responsible for the disease. In the X-ray Department a Charles X-ray table (£34) was purchased 'in view of the localising work required at present' and assistance obtained for Mr L. Bell, the Radiographer.

There was no conscription at this time but towards the end of 1915, when the demand for compulsory military service had become a political issue rather than a practical necessity, Lord Derby's recruiting scheme was adopted. Men of military age 'attested' their willingness to join the Forces when required and among those who did so were Mr Goss, the Hospital Dispenser, Mr Clarke, his Assistant and Mr Windley, the Laboratory Assistant. The Board of Management was asked to 'use its strongest endeavour' to retain their services. The Hospital could not afford to lose them.

During 1915 a total of 2,735 in-patients (of whom 744 were military), 6,388 out-patients, 2,235 accidents or emergencies, and 3,376 minor accidents and casualties were treated. Two thousand three hundred and twenty-six operations were performed and 2,314 anaesthetics administered. By the end of the year the rise in prices and wages had produced a deficit of £8,500. The allowance paid by the War Office for military patients, now increased to 4/– a day, no longer covered the cost. In spite of these financial problems, the purchase of 'The Lindens' in Craven Road for £750 was agreed. This property would be needed for the expected expansion once the war was over.

1916 to 1917

Fewer military patients were sent to the Hospital in 1916 but many of the 492 cases received were more severe and stayed longer. Practically all those admitted in January 1916 were suffering from frost bite or trench foot. With the decrease in the number of military patients it was possible, for several weeks at a time, to use Benyon Ward for male surgical cases and this enabled the long waiting lists for civilian admissions to be reduced. Practically every civilian admission was now entered as an 'emergency' in the Hospital registers.

Early in January there was an outbreak of typhoid fever in the town. At the insistence of the medical staff and of Dr Abram, who was also Chairman of the local Sanitary Committee, the Board of Management amended the rule which had restricted the number of cases admitted. With the 'improved methods of treatment, preventable and otherwise' no limit need now be placed on these admissions. The Medical Officer of Health, Dr Ashby, asked for the co-operation of the Hospital in this emergency and Alice and Huntley and Palmer Wards were made available for up to 30 cases. By the beginning of April only five typhoid cases remained, the maximum of 29 having been reached at the end of January. Following this outbreak, Dr Donaldson read a paper on the *Bacteriological diagnosis of the colon-typhoid-dysentery groups* at a meeting of the Pathological Society. The inoculation of the civil population against typhoid and paratyphoid was discussed and at a further meeting perforated typhoid and paratyphoid ulcers were considered. The epidemic had provided unexpected and useful material for research.

The great increase in orthopaedic cases gave urgency to the suggestion of forming a special department for massage and electrical treatment. In March Lt Col Freeman was put in charge of this new Department which would operate from the Medical Out-patients Department. Special equipment was obtained at a cost of £28 and a multostat machine connected with the mains. Nerve testing, ionic, galvanic and faradic treatment and electrolysis would come under his supervision. Miss Flanagan had already been appointed at three guineas a week to attend the military cases each day, and later in the year Miss Sydenham was appointed the first electro-therapist and masseuse for civilian patients.

After six months it was found that few of the recommendations made by the Joint Committee on staffing in 1915 had been put into operation. Inexperienced staff were still being used in the theatres and the sterilising arrangements in the septic theatre and on the wards were inadequate. The wards were still understaffed and the Resident Medical Officers found the nurses frequently 'ignorant of elementary facts with which they should be familiar'. Standards were deteriorating and many nurses were described as 'very illiterate'. In contrast, among those Hospital nurses away on military service Miss Davies of Huntley and Palmer Ward and Private Nurses Moore and Foster had been awarded the Royal Red Cross and Miss Dodd, the Out-patient Sister, was mentioned in dispatches.

The problem of obtaining Resident Medical Officers was as great as ever and no fourth man had been obtained. Some appointments were able to be extended beyond six months, others only lasted for three, and a fifth-year student was engaged at half salary. The Central Medical War Committee wrote suggesting that the honorary medical staff should take on the duties of the Residents. This was impossible as the whole staff was now engaged in military work besides their other duties at the Hospital. The suggestion that women Residents should be employed was believed to be 'impracticable owing to lack of suitable accommodation'. In July it was noted that the only applications for the post of House Physician were from 'ladies and natives of India'. Neither was engaged.

Conscription of unmarried men between the ages of 18 and 41 had been brought in earlier in the year. In the Ophthalmic Department Mr Brooks was now left with no clinical assistance and the Department was severely overworked and understaffed. There were similar difficulties in obtaining help in the X-ray Department and Mr L. Bell was now unfit to continue this work. It was some time before Mr L. Simmons was engaged as a suitable replacement with the offer of increased wages of £3 a week.

The Battle of the Somme began on July 1st and the enormous casualties suffered in that battle and in the months ahead produced a steady stream of wounded to the military wards of the Hospital. A further 16 military beds were made available in October in Benyon, Sidmouth and Hall Wards, bringing the total to 116.

By November the weather and mud produced a halt in the fighting and once again the cases of trench foot began to appear. There were practically no deaths among the military cases at the Hospital, but among those killed at the Front was Captain J. A. Ritson, 7th South Lancastrian Regiment, son of Dr Ritson the Anaesthetist. His parents gave £1,000 to endow a bed in Benyon Ward. On his birthday, November 6th, 1916 they unveiled the plaque in memory of their 'beloved and only child' who had been killed in action on July 23rd in the Battle of the Somme. He would have been 24.

1917 to 1918

In February 1917 Victoria Ward was made into a fourth military ward and in April Adelaide Ward became the fifth. This brought the total beds in the Hospital to 264, of which 156 were military and 108 civilian. For the first time the military outnumbered the civilian beds. Once again short lulls in the military admissions enabled civilian cases to be put in some military wards and the long waiting lists were reduced.

Mr Secretan was sent to France in April and did not return until September. Dr Franklin Cox took over his out-patients and Major J. L. Joyce his in-patients. In the absence of Mr Roberts, who was serving abroad, Mr L. Powell had taken over the work of the Aural Department. All three were now appointed temporary Assistant Surgeons. Conscription was affecting other work in the Hospital and appeals were made for deferment or exemption on behalf of the male staff by the Hospital Secretary. When Mr Clarke, the Assistant Dispenser, was called up, Miss Giblin, who reluctantly had been allowed to train in the Dispensary, was found to be invaluable.

Later in the year Col W. T. Maurice, who had been in charge of the No. 1 Reading War Hospital at Battle since 1916, reached the retirement age of 60. He turned down the request that he should remain as Surgeon at the Royal Berkshire Hospital for a further year and was made a Consulting Surgeon. Mr W. J. Foster was elected Surgeon in his place and Major J. L.

Joyce, who was now also working at Battle, was elected Assistant Surgeon.

The cost of dressings was constantly rising and an offer to supply the Hospital with sphagnum moss free of charge was considered. A depot had been established for the Hants. and Berks. Moss Guild by Mrs Cope at Finchampstead Place and moss dressings in a variety of sizes could be supplied. Enquiries showed that the Winchester Hospital was using large quantities of moss in place of absorbent wool for all kinds of aseptic dressings. When Miss Gill, the former Matron, now Matron at the Edinburgh Royal Infirmary, confirmed its usefulness, the Drug Committee advised 'the greatest possible use of moss should be made at this Hospital'. For the duration of the war Mrs Cope and the Guild continued their invaluable work and the supply of sphagnum moss enabled considerable savings to be made.

Additional help was asked of the Hospital when the Berkshire County Council requested accommodation for expectant mothers requiring treatment during their confinement. This could not be granted at that time. However, the request of the Red Cross for two beds for paraplegic cases and that of the Reading Disablement Committee for treatment of discharged disabled soldiers was agreed. Terms of payment were arranged with the authorities concerned and the principle of remuneration for special cases was established.

In 1916 the Local Government Board in London had asked that the Royal Berkshire Hospital in conjunction with the local authorities should provide facilities for the diagnosis and treatment of venereal disease. The war had produced an alarming number of cases and facilities were urgently needed to deal with the problem. Before the war no cases of primary venereal disease were admissible and subscriptions had been paid to the

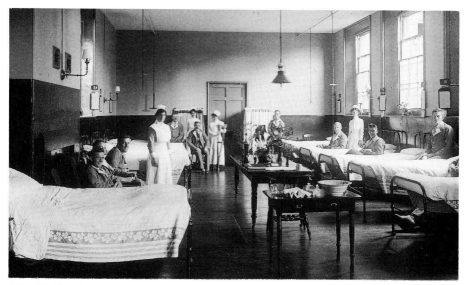

Adelaide Ward

London Lock Hospitals to enable patients to be treated there. The medical staff had suggested early in 1914 that patients with syphilis might now be admitted for salvarsan and other treatment. Some cases were received and the subscriptions to the Lock Hospitals were eventually stopped. Following discussions with neighbouring county councils in 1916 and 1917, a scheme was prepared to provide both a V.D. clinic and in-patient treatment at the Royal Berkshire Hospital. All costs of establishing the Department, its maintenance and treatment of patients would be paid for by the local authorities. Patients referred to the Hospital would require no tickets of admission from subscribers.

The former temporary Iron Ward, now re-named the East Ward, would be specially adapted for in-patients and a fourth Resident Medical Officer, to be called the Senior Resident, would be in charge of the new Department which would be supervised by Dr Guilding. At the end of 1917 a formal agreement was drawn up with the County Councils of Berkshire, Hampshire and Wiltshire and the Reading Borough Council, and arrangements were made for the Department of Venereal Diseases to be opened early in 1918.

By the middle of 1917 the financial position of the Hospital had become critical. The deficit of £8,500 at the end of 1915 had increased to £10,655 by the end of the following year and was anticipated to reach £15,000 at the end of 1917. The annual cost of each occupied bed was now £103 compared with £80 in 1914. The average cost of treating each out-patient had increased by one third from nearly 3/– in 1914 to almost 4/– in 1917. The support of the public in financing the Hospital was considerable, but demands were now being made on their generosity to help an ever-increasing number of causes associated with the war. The amount received from annual subscriptions had hardly changed since 1914. Although church collections and donations (including the League of Mercy and Hospital Parades) had increased, no income was now received from the Private Nurses Department and the contributions from the Workpeople's Association had decreased considerably. The total income was not sufficient to cover the increased expenditure caused by the enormous rise in prices and salaries. It was believed there was no alternative to closing part of the Hospital.

In July the Mayor called a public meeting at the Town Hall and launched an appeal for funds to eliminate the deficit and put the Hospital on a sound financial basis. On no account should wards be closed and the invaluable work of the Hospital be reduced. Dr H. Willingham Gell, who had just succeeded Col J. E. Broadbent as Treasurer, worked untiringly to bring the situation to the attention of the public. Considerable support was given by the local papers and within weeks the *Reading Standard* started a 'Shilling Fund' in aid of the Hospital. If each of its 100,000 readers gave one shilling, half the present debt of the Hospital could be extinguished. Week by week the total raised was published in its columns and details given of events to be held to raise more funds. Madame Clara Butt had

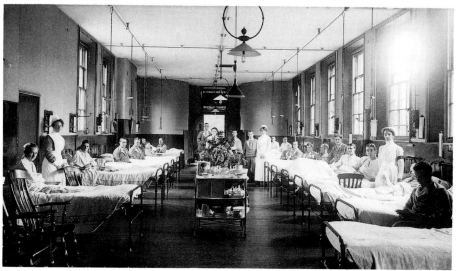

Benyon Ward

agreed to give a concert and upon popular request would sing 'Abide with Me'. The 'Snap Shots', the 30th Middlesex Regimental Concert Party, would also perform in aid of the appeal. Over £5,000 was eventually contributed by the Shilling Fund and Mr W. V. Rivers, the *Standard*'s proprietor, was made a Life Governor in recognition of his remarkable achievement. Individual donations ranging from £500 from Mr J. H. Benyon to a few shillings combined with the Shilling Fund to produce a total of £15,496 by the end of the year. The public had rallied, the crisis was averted and no ward closures would now be needed.

Altogether 896 military patients were admitted to the Hospital in 1917. By this time over 2,000 wounded were being treated in the various Reading hospitals. From July onwards the casualties in the Flanders offensive and on the battlefields of Passchendaele were almost as numerous as those on the Somme the year before. The medical, surgical and nursing staff were gaining a volume and breadth of experience they could never have obtained in normal circumstances. The advances being made in nerve and plastic surgery were described in the papers delivered by Mr Joyce at various meetings of the Pathological Society that year. In April he showed members a patient who had shrapnel removed from his brain 1¾ inches below the surface. The bone had been replaced by a bone graft from the shin and had left the patient without paralysis or deafness and completely recovered. In May he read a paper on *Operative treatment of injuries to the peripheral nerves*. He hoped to extend and expand the paper and publish the results after the war. In December he described an operation in which he had grafted two terminal phalanges of the fourth finger of the left hand on to the metacarpal bone of the thumb of the right hand in order to make a substitute thumb. The result was impressive. Mr Joyce was congratulated and it was decided the case should be published in one of the surgical journals.

Another effect of the war was to draw attention to the many groups and authorities which were now concerned with various branches of public welfare. In 1871, the creation of the Local Government Board in London had superseded the short-lived Board of Health set up in 1848. This was now the central authority for a wide variety of functions including the Poor Law, education and public health. Under its direction sanitary authorities and medical officers of health had been established and, among other developments, the isolation and treatment of infectious diseases and tuberculosis had been organised, medical inspection and treatment of school children provided as well as health visiting for mothers and infants.

Over the years, the Local Government Board had extended the authority of the Poor Law Guardians. They were now undertaking a wide variety of work associated with the welfare of those within the area of the Union but not necessarily in receipt of poor relief. County and Borough Councils had been made responsible for certain aspects of public health. Park Hospital, the Moulesford Asylum and the Reading Tuberculosis Dispensary were administered by the Borough Council. Other institutions and aspects of welfare such as health visiting and child welfare also came under the direction of the County Council and in some instances were run in association with adjoining councils. In 1914 the Berkshire and Buckinghamshire County Councils had purchased Peppard Sanatorium from Dr Carling to enable patients from those counties with pulmonary tuberculosis to receive treatment. This was now administered by the Berks. and Bucks. Joint Sanatorium Committee. The provision of treatment for venereal disease would involve several adjoining County Councils as well as the Reading Borough Council in association with the Royal Berkshire Hospital.

Insurance Committees set up following the National Insurance Act of 1911, pension funds and the many welfare organisations established during the war were all concerned with the treatment and rehabilitation of the wounded and disabled. The Hospital was becoming increasingly involved in treating such cases for which payment would be received and no letters of recommendation from subscribers would be required.

A Minister of Public Health was thought by many to be essential to sort out the various duties now performed by different bodies. The Insurance Committees in particular were agitating for change. It was widely believed that a State medical service would be established after the war. It might only be a matter of time before the Voluntary Hospitals became municipal hospitals.

These predictions were received with mixed feelings by the medical staff of the Hospital. A meeting, attended by 32 members of the medical profession in the Hospital library in March 1917, agreed that a committee should be appointed 'to consider the best means of safeguarding the interests of the profession as far as they may be affected by future legislation'. The County Council was similarly alarmed. It agreed in principle to the public health services being' unified under a Minister of Health but feared that the control of their administration might be transferred to 'non-representative bodies incapable of dealing with the matter'.

Developments were also taking place in the nursing profession. The call for State registration since the turn of the century had so far produced no result but in 1916 the College of Nursing had been established to 'secure uniformity of training and curriculum for nurses engaged in various branches of civil, military and naval practice'. Two representatives from the Hospital had been appointed to the Consultative Board of the College.

The war had accelerated the need for re-organisation and by the end of 1917 the stage was set for some fundamental changes to take place when peace returned.

1918 to 1919

The increase in military hospitals in the Reading area during the first three years of the war had been spectacular. Besides the No. 1 War Hospital at Battle and its five section hospitals, 36 auxiliary hospitals had been established. These became known collectively as the Reading War Hospital. The Red Cross staffed six auxiliary hospitals in Reading and 21 in the County besides four section hospitals in the town. The Royal Berkshire Hospital was unique, as it was administered neither by the military authorities nor by the Red Cross and admitted civilian as well as military patients. This independent status led to a disappointing oversight when the names of nurses recommended for commendation were ignored, as the Hospital came into neither category. Fortunately the omission was later rectified and the Matron, Miss Wynne, was awarded the Royal Red Cross II class in June 1918.

The 1,118 military patients received in 1918 were more than in any previous year. The 2,237 civilian admissions were practically the same as the year before the war. In February, with 50 vacant military beds and a waiting list of 95, civilians were admitted to back Sidmouth and Hall wards. Weeks later they had to be hurriedly cleared again for military cases. At the beginning of May, Southern Command gave permission for Hall Ward to revert permanently to civilian use. By this time the capitation grant had been increased to 4/9d a day with an allowance of 6d per day for each unoccupied military bed.

The new Department for the treatment of venereal diseases was opened on January 9th, 1918. Dr Bruce Gordon, M.D., F.R.C.S., the recently appointed Senior Resident Medical Officer, was put in charge under Dr Guilding. All pathological work in connection with the Department was undertaken by Dr Donaldson and his assistant. Equipment, including an autoclave and a refrigerator, was obtained at the expense of the councils concerned. A special non-resident nursing staff was engaged consisting of a Sister (salary £90 a year) and two nurses (each £75 a year). Clinics were arranged for twice a week and up to six patients could be admitted to East Ward.

Within weeks Surrey County Council asked if patients from their western region could be treated. The agreement with the neighbouring councils was extended and now included the County Councils of Surrey, Berkshire, Hampshire and Wiltshire besides the Borough of Reading. The Local Government Board officially approved the Hospital for the treatment and diagnosis of V.D. and reserved its right to inspect the Department at any time.

Resident Medical Officers were still difficult to find and when Dr Bruce Gordon resigned in February his place was taken by Dr Esterman, formerly Junior House Surgeon and qualified Assistant at the V.D. Department at Leicester Royal Infirmary. At one time he was the only qualified Resident in the Hospital, all other posts being filled by fifth-year students for a few months at a time. By the end of the year the position had improved and both the House Surgeon and House Physician were fully qualified practitioners.

One noticeable difference in recent years was that complaints were now being made of the behaviour and treatment by the medical staff rather than that of the nurses. The resident medical staff were overworked and often inexperienced. Complaints of roughness, rudeness and negligence were received and the honorary medical staff acknowledged that in most instances they were justified. Two particular complaints were noted as 'showing considerable lack of care on the part of the Residents concerned'. The procedures and duties of the Residents were tightened up and the Senior Resident instructed 'to watch the House Surgeons in their operating until quite efficient'.

Conscription continued to take its toll and in May Mr Windley, the Pathology Assistant, was called up. For the first time advertisements asked for applications from both men and women and Miss Marchal was appointed at £3 a week. When Miss Sydenham resigned to move to the newly opened orthopaedic centre in Reading, the appointment of a Sister in charge of massage and electro-therapy was advertised. Miss Waters, with a certificate from the National Hospital, was engaged at a salary of £70 a year. There were changes too in the X-ray Department and Mr A. Robotham, discharged from the army and a former electrician with the Reading Electric Supply Company, took over from Mr Simmons. His wage of £2 a week would be increased to £3 when Mr Foster found him 'sufficiently competent'. In the Dispensary it was discovered that Mr Goss had had no holiday for four years. He was given a gratuity of £25.

Prices continued to rise, particularly of meat and fish. Shortages occurred, price controls were introduced and meat was rationed. Colebrooks, who had regularly supplied the Hospital, were now able to buy only half the quantity of meat they had obtained at the end of 1917. The medical staff advised that porridge, peas, lentils and beans should be used to supplement the meat supply.

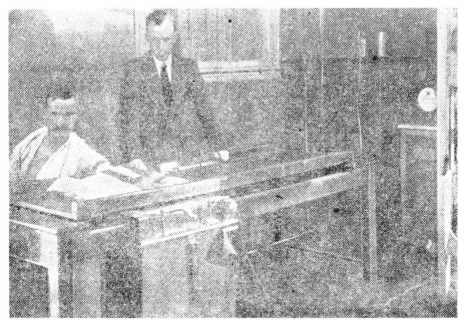

X-ray Department, 1917

Altogether 75 nurses were now employed at the Hospital and by the summer it was becoming increasingly difficult to maintain this number. There were no applications for probationers and another sister had resigned to work in a military hospital. An immediate increase in salary from £8 to £12 a year was agreed for first-year probationers. This relieved the situation temporarily and a committee was set up to look into the problems of the Nursing Department.

It was found that the salaries of the Hospital nurses had fallen behind those offered by other provincial hospitals and the Private Nurses, now only 15 in number, had received no increase for 18 years. Increases were agreed for:–

First-year probationers from the present		£12 to £17 a year
Second year	do.	£15 to £21
Third year	do.	£20 to £26
Staff nurses from the present		£28 to £34
Sisters	do.	£55 to £60

The Matron's salary was increased by £15 to £125 a year. A new agreement was drawn up for the Private Nurses and their salaries increased to £60 from the present £35 to £45 a year. It was recommended that a separate Superintendent, apart from the Matron, should be put in charge of the Private Nursing Department.

The Appeal launched in July 1917 had not been closed and eventually over £17,000 was raised. Many new subscriptions had also been obtained as well as £500 for the endowment of a cot in memory of the son of Mr and

Mrs Herbert Kingham and £1,000 for the endowment of a bed in memory of the son of Mr Astleys. The continued rise in prices and wages prompted the idea of asking for voluntary contributions from patients. The average cost of treating each in-patient was now £9 and each out-patient 5/9d. Circulars were printed to be given to all patients. It was stressed that the Hospital was funded solely by voluntary contributions and 'many would not wish or require their treatment to be a matter of mere charity'. An envelope was supplied with every circular.

The success of Mr Rivers's Shilling Fund in the *Reading Standard* had encouraged him to open another appeal to provide the Hospital with a motor ambulance. The horse-drawn ambulances were now inadequate and inefficient compared with their motorised counterparts used by the military authorities. The former Berkshire V.A.D. motor ambulance given to the Hospital by Col Thornton in 1917 was too heavy and expensive to run. It had been agreed it should be sold and a more suitable one obtained. Mr Rivers's appeal was short-lived, for in March an offer by Mr S. B. Joel of Maiden Erleigh to provide a motor ambulance was gratefully accepted.

Mr Rivers re-directed his appeal in the *Reading Standard* to raise funds for the X-ray Department. The work of this Department had increased considerably and Mr Foster had drawn attention to the urgent need for replacing the apparatus and extending the accommodation. By early in May the *Reading Standard* appeal had raised £340. A Snook X-ray apparatus was ordered from Newton and Wright for £383 3s and a new switchboard with tachometer for £16 10s. Alterations were started in the autumn to extend the accommodation with a cubicle in the receiving room and arrangements were made for the installation of the new equipment.

On November 5th, Mr Joel presented the new ambulance to the Hospital. It had been built by Messrs. Barker & Co of South Audley Street, London, with a Renault-type chassis, 20–30 horse power engine and a body similar to those of the Metropolitan Asylum ambulances. It was believed to have cost Mr Joel almost £1,000. A special garage had been built to house the ambulance and a driver obtained who would also carry out running

Presentation of the first motor ambulance, November 1918

repairs and do mechanical work in his spare time. In future the civilian patients would be conveyed in similar comfort to the military.

Within a week of this presentation the Armistice had been signed and the war was over. The whole nation expressed its relief and thankfulness that peace had come at last. Only the world-wide epidemic of influenza now sweeping the country could dampen the fervour of the rejoicing. It was estimated that one third of the population was affected by the epidemic.

The Hospital was inundated with cases of severe influenza and pneumonia and the military authorities at Salisbury agreed to release Adelaide Ward for civilian patients. During November and December, 113 cases were admitted, and among the 33 who died was one of the Hospital nurses. Their devotion to duty in the 'devastating' epidemic was especially noted by the medical staff.

Only weeks after the end of the war, the death was announced of Dr Freeman, Senior Physician and Chairman of the Medical Staff at the Hospital, Lt Col in the Territorial R.A.M.C. and Officer in Charge of Redlands Hospital. It was believed his death had been accelerated by overwork and the strain of the past four years.

Redlands Hospital, now with 181 beds, was closed at the end of December. The military wards in the Royal Berkshire Hospital were not given up until March of the following year. For over four years practically all the honorary medical staff had managed to combine their work at the Hospital with their military service at the Reading War Hospitals. The Residents, Matron, nurses and other Hospital employees had worked under extremely difficult conditions to treat an ever-increasing number of military and civilian cases. The Board of Management through the House Committee had extended its work to include the administration of the Redlands War Hospital. The public had supported the Royal Berkshire Hospital throughout in every conceivable way. Their money had rescued it from a major financial crisis and averted what had seemed an inevitable closure of wards. The decorations, presents, dinners and entertainments over the Christmas period provided a fitting conclusion to the considerable work of the war-time Hospital, its staff and friends.

NOTES

1 The rules enabled two medical pupils to attend the Hospital with each honorary physician and surgeon. The House Surgeon was allowed two 'apprentices' who would pay a fee both to him and the Hospital. Advertisements for the latter in 1841 produced no replies and in 1854 it was decided not to accept such pupils at the time. The only recorded medical pupil apprenticed to the House Surgeon was the son of Surgeon Major Rogers of the Madras Medical Establishment, who was accepted for one year in 1867. No further Hospital pupils appear to have been accepted until Mr Francis Maurice in 1914.

2 The Samaritans' Sewing Guild had been formed in 1906 in association with the Reading Workpeople's Association to provide garments to be given to patients on leaving the Hospital.

7

YEARS OF TRANSITION
1919 TO 1939

The first years of peace were a time for the Hospital to take stock and come to terms with post-war conditions. Far too much had happened over the previous four and a half years for the clocks to be turned back to August 1914. With the departure of the military patients in March 1919 civilians were readmitted to Benyon, Sidmouth and Victoria wards and Hall ward reverted to its pre-war function as the out-patients' waiting hall. The number of beds in the Hospital was reduced from 264 to 220, some 32 more than when the war began. The nursing staff, which had increased to 75 during the war, remained the same.

Demobilisation was haphazard and disorganised and it was some time before all those who had been called up were able to return to civilian life. The medical staff and nurses were demobilised over a period of eighteen months as the various war hospitals were gradually run down and eventually closed. Mr Windley, the Assistant in the pathological laboratory, was the first to return in January 1919 but within three months he had resigned to become Chief Assistant at the Wellcome Research Laboratories. Miss Thorne, Dr Donaldson's Assistant at the No. 1 War Hospital at Battle, was appointed in his place. Mr Foster was demobilised in February, Mr Secretan in April, Dr Clarke in June but Mr Baxter not until May 1920, when the No. 1 War Hospital was closed.

There were several changes among the honorary medical staff during this period. Dr Murrell, one of the Assistant Surgeons, was elected Physician in place of Dr Freeman, who had died in December 1918. He, and Dr Abram, would be the two physicians working at the peace-time Hospital. Dr Norman May, who had been a temporary Anaesthetist and Assistant Physician during the War, was now elected Assistant Physician. There were also changes on the surgical staff when Dr Guilding, who reached retirement age in the middle of 1919, was made a Consulting Surgeon and Mr W. B. Secretan, an Assistant Surgeon, was elected Surgeon. He and Mr W. J. Foster, the Senior Surgeon, were now the two Honorary Surgeons at the Hospital. Mr Baxter was then elected Assistant Surgeon, while his previous position as Clinical Assistant in the Ophthalmic Department was taken over by Mr A. E. Dorrell, F.R.C.S., on the recommendation of Mr Brooks.

When Mr Roberts, the Aural Surgeon, was demobilised he decided he would not resume his life in Reading and left to take up consultancy work in London. He had been Aural Surgeon since the Department was established and was now made a Consulting Surgeon. Mr Leslie Powell, the Clinical Assistant who had been in charge of the Department in his absence during the War, was elected Aural Surgeon in his place.

A new appointment was made with the election of Dr G. H. R. Holden as the Medical Officer in charge of the Electro-therapeutic Department. With the great increase in this work it would now be considered a special department on the lines of the X-ray Department. Two Assistant Anaesthetists, Dr F. C. Young and Dr H. Parry Price, were also elected, these appointments being considered essential in view of the great increase in the number of operations being performed.

All these appointments to the honorary medical staff were made in the usual pre-war way through the Elective Committee. The temporary war-time measure of the medical staff appointing the Resident Medical Officers was now replaced by the re-established Residents' Selection Committee.

Early in 1920 Dr Donaldson resigned to become Pathologist at St George's Hospital, London and lecturer at St George's Medical School. He had been at the Hospital since the formation of the Pathology Laboratory in 1912 and his great ability in the field of pathology and bacteriology set an extremely high standard in the formative years of the Department. His work at the Royal Berkshire Hospital, Redlands and the No. 1 War Hospital during the war had been considerable and his research into the influenza epidemic of 1918 was particularly noted. Dr A. H. Miller, M.A., M.D., M.R.C.P. was appointed Pathologist to succeed him at a salary of £600 a year, with a percentage of the fees for the work carried out for public authorities and private practitioners.

Mr Friend, who had been the Church of England Chaplain for 37 years, resigned at the end of 1919. He was succeeded by the Revd F. T. C. Gillmor, Vicar of St Giles's parish, who was appointed on a new part-time basis at a salary of £100 a year. In response to a strenuous request from the Non-Conformist Churches, the Revd W. A. Peacock was appointed in addition to be the part-time honorary Free Church Chaplain, a move which could not have been contemplated in pre-war days. Mr Richard Benyon de Beauvoir's stipulation in 1854 that a full-time Church of England Chaplain should be appointed was now believed to be inappropriate.

The war had produced many changes in attitudes. The most notable was reflected in the Parliamentary Reform Act of 1918 which, besides extending the franchise to all males over the age of 21, also gave votes to women for the first time. Their ability had been fully demonstrated in the range of work they had successfully undertaken during the war and now all those over the age of 30 were allowed to vote. The following year the long-awaited Registration of Nurses Act was passed by Parliament to be followed by the Sex Disqualification (Removal) Act which, in theory, opened nearly all professions and public offices to women. The same year the Reading Pathological Society opened its membership to women doctors. Dr Esther Carling's excellent paper on *Artificial Pneumothorax* the previous year had demonstrated the merit to be gained by their inclusion. There were, however, no women doctors on the staff of the Hospital, and for many years all advertisements for Resident Medical Officers stipulated male applicants only. It was not until 1936 that the first woman was appointed to the honorary medical staff with the election of Dr Dorothea Taylor as an Assistant Anaesthetist.

In 1919 the death was announced of Dame Edith Benyon, wife of the Hospital President, Mr J. H. Benyon. She had been awarded the G.B.E. for her outstanding work during the war. She had been Lady President of the Berkshire Branch of the British Red Cross Society, which had been formed in 1910 largely through her initiative; she had been in charge of the Red Cross Hospital which had been established at her home Englefield House; she had worked tirelessly for the League of Mercy, the Care and Comforts Committee and the Ladies' Linen League of the Royal Berkshire Hospital. She had epitomised the role which women were willing and able to assume in the post-war years. In 1923 her daughter-in-law, Mrs Violet Benyon, became the first woman on the Board of Management when the rules were altered to enable women to be elected to that body. Her influence was considerable over the years, particularly in matters concerning the nursing staff and women patients.

The anticipated Ministry of Health was created by Act of Parliament in 1919. To this new department were transferred all the powers and duties of the Local Government Board and the Insurance Commission. In October of that year the Consultative Council on Medical and Allied Services set up by the new Minister of Health under the Chairmanship of Lord Dawson was asked to consider and make recommendations for the provision of a comprehensive medical service for the country. The Royal Berkshire Hospital with the other Voluntary Hospitals waited to see how long it would be before their status was affected by further legislation.

The Introduction of Charges
The war-time rise in prices continued unabated for the first few years of peace. This, combined with increased taxation and the uncertainty of the future of the Voluntary Hospitals, led to a marked drop in subscriptions and donations. The request that patients should make voluntary contributions towards the cost of their maintenance had produced only £300 in 1919. The cost of each bed, which had been £103 15s a year in 1918, had risen to £164 18s in 1920. The cost of each in-patient in that time had risen from £8 to £12 9s, although on average each patient was still only in the Hospital for 25 days. The cost of treating each out-patient had risen from 5/8d to 7/– in the corresponding period. The resulting deficit of over £6,000 led to the decision that those patients who could afford it should now pay a

fixed amount towards their maintenance. As the Board of Management stated: 'The improved status of the industrial and labour classes make it inappropriate that they should have unrestricted access to charitable relief.' A charge of 2/– per day for adult in-patients and 1/– per day for children under ten was imposed. It was emphasised that those who were unable to pay would continue to be treated free of charge.

A new administrative post was created called the Patients' Registrar. Miss Field was appointed to make enquiries into the circumstances of patients claiming exemption from this maintenance charge. At the same time the wage limit for out-patients was raised to £3 a week for single people without dependents and £4 for married couples. Out-patients were asked to pay 1/– on their first attendance and a further 1/– every four weeks while receiving treatment. It was hoped that these charges would go some way towards meeting the deficit.

In the meantime the Hospital, besides admitting patients with subscriber's tickets, was being asked to treat an increasing number of soldiers and ex-servicemen as the various war hospitals were run down and closed. It was agreed with the military authorities and pensions committees that such cases would be received as in-patients when necessary, but no beds would be reserved exclusively for their use. Those attending the Out-patients Department would be accepted for consultation or treatment which could not be provided by the patients' own panel doctors. The authorities would be charged a fee of 7/– per day for every in-patient and the charges for out-patients would correspond to the fees charged by the panel practitioners. Additional clinics were arranged for the Ophthalmic Department and the Hospital became a centre for the supply of artificial eyes. It was arranged that X-rays for ex-servicemen would be charged to the authorities at one guinea for the whole body, and half a guinea for other cases plus a further half guinea when a photograph was required.

Another category of patient was also requesting admission. The Berkshire County Council, Reading Borough Council and Maidenhead Town Council all asked for arrangements to be made for the treatment of those maternity and child welfare cases which had now become their responsibility. A fee of 7/– a day was agreed for the admission of complicated cases of labour and pregnancy and of children under five years old. As the Hospital had not the facilities to accept ordinary maternity cases, the Reading Borough Council purchased a house called 'Dellwood' near Prospect Park in 1921 and adapted it for use as a maternity home for cases which could not safely be confined at home.

The Hospital was also asked to accept children sent by various Education Committees for operative treatment for tonsils and adenoids. Previously such cases had been admitted with subscriber's tickets, but now their treatment had become the responsibility of the Education Committees. Agreements were drawn up with the Berkshire, Reading and Oxfordshire Education Committees that children would be admitted for a fee of two guineas. All operations would be performed under general anaesthetic and the patients would be kept in overnight if necessary. The local authorities insisted that this charge would include the provision of a recovery room and the necessary nursing staff. Later they also stipulated that only a surgeon of at least three years' standing should perform these operations.

The acceptance of certain patients for whom the Hospital would receive payment for both treatment and maintenance was viewed with concern by the honorary medical staff. The Board of Management was notified that: 'Whilst the medical staff is prepared to render voluntary service to all necessitous patients at the Hospital, it declares its acceptance of the principle that in the case of state-maintained patients and those sent by the local authorities, for whom payment is made to the Hospital, an adequate remuneration should be paid to the staff, but that such remuneration should in no way be allowed to interfere with the status or terms of appointment of the staff.' When payment had been agreed by the Hospital for the treatment of discharged disabled soldiers they had asked for and obtained 15 per cent (later raised to 25 per cent) of all money thus received. Similar arrangements were negotiated when other categories of patients were admitted. This money was paid into a special Staff Fund, part of which was used for various donations and the remainder divided between the medical staff.

In October 1920 the medical staff formed a Standing Committee 'to watch the interests of the staff with regard to state payments for patients.' It was emphasised that no contract should be entered into if the

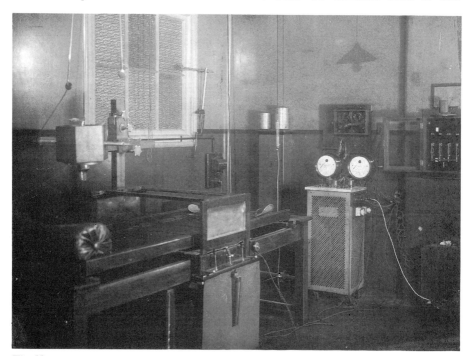

The X-ray room

remuneration was less than that received by outside practitioners. The subject of payments to staff funds featured largely in the British Medical Association meetings at that time as the receipt of payments was now the concern of all the Voluntary Hospitals. The medical staff at the Royal Berkshire Hospital were unable, however, to agree to the suggestion at one conference that patients paying anything to a hospital should contribute to its Staff Fund.

Salary Increases

In the Nursing Department probationers were still in short supply and, once again, it was found that salaries at the Hospital had fallen behind those elsewhere. When in 1920 the nurses were allowed a shorter working day, difficulty was found in obtaining the extra 12 nurses needed to raise the staff to 87. Salary increases were authorised in accordance with the scale suggested by the College of Nursing: probationers were to receive £20 a year; second-year nurses £25, third year £30, fourth year £40; Massage Sister £80; Theatre Sister £70; Ward Sister £60 to £70; Night Sister £80 to £85; Assistant Matron £90; and Matron £200. The necessary nurses were obtained, and 'Lackington', the Hospital property in Craven Road, was adapted to provide additional accommodation. It was also arranged that both the main theatre and septic theatre should now be in the charge of one Theatre Sister. She would be relieved of all night duty which would be undertaken by the Night Sister.

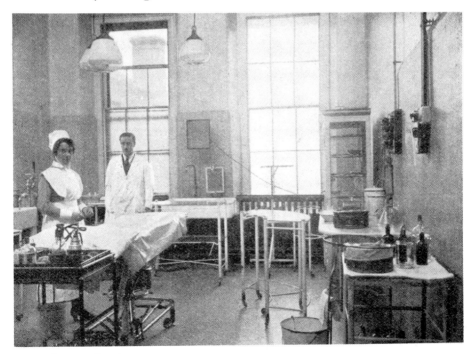

The main operating theatre

The Lady Superintendent of the Private Nursing Department was experiencing similar difficulties as the Private Nurses' salary of £60 a year was not attracting applicants. An increase to £65 for first-year, £70 for second-year and £75 for third-year nurses provided the solution. In 1921 Miss E. J. Hobson was appointed the new Lady Superintendent at a salary of £125 and the Department was reorganised under the supervision of the House Committee. The private nursing fees were increased with a standard charge of three guineas per week for ordinary cases. Massage and maternity cases could be undertaken and attendance at private operations arranged for additional fees. The Department was restructured on a better financial basis to resume its valuable pre-war work.

Post-war Donations
By this time most towns and villages were subscribing towards memorials for their dead and several made the Hospital the recipient of their collections or of surplus funds. Sir William Cain gave £1,000 to dedicate a bed in memory of the men of Wargrave. A further £1,000 was received from the United Services Fund for a bed in memory of their fallen. The parish of Bucklebury sent £200 for a memorial tablet and many 'peace donations' were received from parishes and individuals alike.

There were also unexpected bonuses with the winding up of the various war-time institutions. A considerable amount of medical and surgical equipment was purchased cheaply when Redlands and the No. 1 War Hospital were disbanded. Large amounts of surplus supplies and equipment were donated to the Hospital by the Canadian, Australian and British Red Cross Societies, and £250 was received when the War Hospital Supplies Depot closed down.

In September 1919 the British Red Cross Society and the Order of St John offered the Hospital a grant of £15,000 from their surplus funds. It was stipulated that this money should be used towards extensions to the X-ray, Electro-therapeutic and Massage Departments and towards the provision of a new Nurses' Home. The grant was conditional upon supplementary money being raised locally and the plan of the buildings being approved by the donors. It was also requested that representation on the Board of Management should be granted to the voluntary aid organisations. This magnificent offer was most welcome. All these departments had expanded rapidly and were now in urgent need of better accommodation. Mr Charles Smith, the architect, was asked to prepare plans for the scheme. Mr Stevens, the owner of the adjoining property, Greenlands, generously donated a plot of his land with a 100-foot frontage to Craven Road. This would enable the new Nurses' Home to be built immediately to the south of 'Lackington', the property already owned by the Hospital.

Various problems arose in obtaining plans which met with the approval of all the interested parties. It was not until the end of 1920 that agreement was reached with Mr Stevens on the style and building he requested for the new Nurses' Home. Plans for this and the improvements for the X-ray and Electro-therapeutic Departments were then approved by the British Red Cross Society and the Order of St John, and on January 1st, 1921 the £15,000 grant was paid to the Hospital.

In May 1921 a special appeal was launched to extinguish the accumulated deficit of 1918–20, by now some £13,726, and to raise funds to supplement the £15,000 grant. By early the following year the deficit had been erased and a start was made on the building fund. The public had rallied once again; the efforts of Mr Rivers with another *Reading Standard* Shilling Fund, the Sportsmen's Fund and the generous donation of £5,000 from Huntley and Palmer were especially noted.

The Berkshire, Buckinghamshire and Oxfordshire Regional Committee

The interim report of the Consultative Council on Medical and Allied Services under the chairmanship of Lord Dawson, which was published in May 1920, was far-sighted and far-ranging. It envisaged a comprehensive national health service available to all, embracing preventative medicine and general practitioner services as well as primary and secondary health centres, administered by a health authority in each area.

Secondary health centres would be provided by hospitals in the larger towns to which general practitioners could refer their patients for specialist and consultant treatment. The Voluntary Hospitals would not be abolished but would receive grants to assist their work.

The question of private medicine and salaried full-time consultants were among the wide range of topics covered. The method of funding, however, was not fully considered, but a national insurance scheme was envisaged as a possibility with charges for hospital treatment except for those unable to pay. Practically every aspect of the future National Health Service was included in the report, but the economic conditions immediately after the war prevented its implementation at that time. As a result, a slow step-by-step progression took place over the next 25 years and the proposals of 1920 were eventually embodied in the National Health Service created in 1948.

In 1921 a special committee, under the chairmanship of Lord Cave, was appointed by the Government to report on the financial state of the Voluntary Hospitals. Among its recommendations were included the setting up of a Voluntary Hospitals Commission with regional committees representing every county or area. Its objectives would be to encourage co-operation between the Voluntary Hospitals to improve their efficiency and reduce their financial burden. A sum of £500,000 was made available by the Government to help these hospitals.

Berkshire, Buckinghamshire and Oxfordshire were to be grouped together as one area and would include the general hospitals of Reading (the Royal Berkshire Hospital), Windsor (King Edward VII Hospital), Oxford (the Radcliffe Infirmary), and Aylesbury (the Royal Buckinghamshire Hospital). A conference of representatives from these hospitals was held in December 1921 and in March the following year the Regional Committee of the Voluntary Hospitals of Berkshire, Buckinghamshire and Oxfordshire was formed.[1]

Dr H. Willingham Gell, Treasurer of the Royal Berkshire Hospital, was appointed to represent the general hospitals of Berkshire and Col H. H. Rogers of the Maidenhead Hospital would represent the smaller hospitals in the County. In September a grant of £1,590 was made to the Royal Berkshire Hospital from the £500,000 funds of the Commission. This Regional Committee later came under the auspices of the British Hospitals Association which had been established in 1884 and which had been in the process of forming somewhat similar regional groupings when the Cave Committee was appointed.[2]

No national health service had been created nor had the municipalisation of the Voluntary Hospitals come about, but a grouping of hospitals and a system of contact had been established which was to become increasingly significant in the years ahead.

The Contributory Scheme

The money obtained from the patients' maintenance charges amounted to £3,748 in 1921. This levy not only fell far short of the amount needed but was also an additional burden to patients in times of illness. The Special Appeal Committee drew the attention of the Board of Management to a recently adopted contributory scheme which had proved most successful at the Radcliffe Infirmary at Oxford and at other Voluntary Hospitals. The regular payment of 2d per week by single people and 4d per week by families with children under 16 enabled those contributing to obtain hospital treatment when required without any further charge. It also had the additional advantage that no subscriber's tickets were needed, the only requirement being a recommendation from the patient's doctor that treatment was necessary.

A permanent committee called The Royal Berkshire Hospital Aid Committee was appointed to administer the scheme and offices were made available for its staff at 4, Craven Road. The scheme was launched at the end of 1922 with Major Wrey appointed its Organiser and Miss Field, the Patients' Registrar, the Assistant Organiser. It was hoped that the increased income obtained from this source would eventually be sufficient to cover all maintenance costs and relieve the Hospital of the need for launching periodic appeals.

The scheme was started first in the surrounding towns and villages and by the end of the first year 106 branches had been formed with a membership of over 22,000. Branches were established in Reading the following October and within a few months 9,000 contributors had joined. Four hospitals became associated with the scheme, the Henley War Memorial Hospital, the Newbury District Hospital, the Morrell Memorial Hospital in Wallingford and the Frimley District Hospital. Contributors could be admitted to these hospitals if specialised treatment at the Royal Berkshire Hospital was not necessary.

The scheme was a great success. At a stroke its members had been made independent of the old charity-related system of admission. By the end of 1924 some 40,000 cards had been issued representing nearly 100,000 people, producing an income of £19,500 that year. Early in 1925 16 members of the scheme, nominated by the branches, were elected at the Court of Governors to join the Board of Management. Ten represented the county areas, four the Reading districts and two the firms that had joined the scheme. The Board of Management now became a more representative but unwieldy body as a result.

Those who did not join the contributory scheme continued to be admitted as before. Accidents, casualties and those for whom the State and local authorities were responsible needed no subscriber's tickets. The remainder still had to obtain tickets, and no maintenance charge was required from those unable to pay.

The contributory scheme brought the work of the Hospital to the attention of the public in a way never experienced before. As a public-relations operation it was unsurpassed. Every town and village had its band of loyal voluntary collectors who week by week visited each member to receive the few pence they contributed and to encourage others to join. The members now felt identified with the Hospital, and this resulted in a remarkable expansion in the efforts to raise additional funds. It became customary for a special 'At Home' to be held at the Hospital each year to thank these voluntary collectors. Before long as many as 800 people were attending these occasions. By 1939 the membership had increased to 87,726, and was producing an income of £46,576.[3]

Nurses' Training School

In November 1922 the Hospital was recognised by the General Nursing Council as an approved institution for the training of nurses. A Preliminary Training School was established to enable probationers to take a short course of tuition before starting work on the wards. The top floor of 'Linden' in Craven Road (over the office of the Contributory Scheme) was adapted to provide a lecture room and quarters for the Sister Tutor and four probationers. At the end of a seven-week course the probationers were allowed to work on the wards, and after a further five weeks completed their initial three months' training. At the end of this they would then take a test paper and practical examination set by the Hospital before sitting their Preliminary State Examination.

The State Examinations included all the subjects on which the medical staff and Matron had previously given lectures (anatomy, physiology, medical and surgical nursing, gynaecology and bacteriology), with the additional subject of food values and invalid cooking. As this subject could not be taught at the Hospital, arrangements were made for the nurses to join a course at University College, Reading. When the first

State Examination of nurses was held in 1924 all 16 candidates from the Hospital were successful.

Approaches were made by other hospitals to obtain training for their nurses at Reading. In 1924 the Metropolitan Asylum Board asked for affiliation with the Royal Berkshire Hospital to enable probationers to be received from the Colindale Hospital, Hendon, King George V Sanatorium, Godalming, Pinewood Sanatorium, Wokingham and Highwood Hospital, Brentwood. An agreement was made to accept two second-year probationers at a time for a three-year period of training. Over the years several similar arrangements were made with other hospitals, though in many instances lack of space prevented all applicants from being accepted.

By this time the probationers from the Reading Workhouse Infirmary at Battle, who had attended all the nursing lectures at the Hospital since 1899, were no longer receiving their training there. In 1922 the Guardians had appointed a Resident Medical Superintendent and the training of the Infirmary nurses was now arranged independently of the Royal Berkshire Hospital.

Hospital Expansion

In 1923 the money raised by the Special Appeal combined with the marked drop in prices enabled tenders to be advertised for building the new Nurses' Home. That of Messrs Nicholls of Gloucester, the lowest at £18,634, was accepted. Work began in the autumn with the demolition of 'Lackington' and soon the foundations were laid for the three-storey building which would provide accommodation for 80 nurses. Once completed the adaptation of the former nurses' quarters, in the east wing, would provide better facilities for the X-ray and Electro-Therapeutic Departments at a cost of a further £3,000, thereby fulfilling both a pressing need and the conditions of the £15,000 grant.

Since the end of the war the work of every department in the Hospital had increased considerably. Additions had been made to the Pathology Laboratory and a typist was engaged to deal with the numerous reports and records. In 1922 Dr Skene Keith, the Senior Assistant at the Pathological Laboratory at Guy's Hospital, was appointed to succeed Dr Miller at a salary of £600 a year and 20 per cent of all money received by the Hospital for outside pathological and bacteriological work. He also took over the work of the V.D. Department. This too had expanded; another male nurse had been obtained and up to 12 beds were available for the treatment of in-patients. Only Berkshire County Council and the Reading Borough Council were still associated with its work as the Councils of Wiltshire, Surrey and Hampshire could now provide their own facilities.

The office of Senior Resident Medical Officer, created in 1917 when the V.D. Department was formed, was abolished in 1923. Instead the Residents consisted of one House Physician and three House Surgeons. Two of the House Surgeons would each act for one Surgeon and Assistant

The Pathological Laboratory

Surgeon, dividing the work of the Special Departments between them. The third House Surgeon would be assigned to the septic wards, act as Casualty Officer and Resident Anaesthetist. All would receive a salary of £150 a year – a reduction of £50. The appointments remained for six months duration with possible renewal for an additional maximum period of a further six months.

Great advances had been made since the turn of the century in the study of the composition and formation of blood (later to be called haematology) and in 1924 a Blood Transfusion Service was founded at the Hospital in association with the Pathological Department. The classification of blood into four groups had been made by Karl Landsteiner in 1900, and it was now possible for a donor to give matching blood to a patient, thereby avoiding adverse reactions. The experiences of the 1914–18 war had accelerated the advances being made in this branch of medicine. Although the storage of plasma was now possible, the storage of blood was not undertaken and donor to patient transfusions alone were carried out with the use of antiseptic precautions to reduce the risk of infection between donor and recipient.

Volunteer donors, obtained through the Hospital Secretary, were examined, a sample of blood was taken, grouped, and the Wasserman test (for syphilis) was applied. No one employed in the Hospital was used and only those donors with the 'universal' type of blood were accepted. These were then paid a retainer of £1 a year and re-examined every six months. Donors were paid four guineas for Hospital cases in which no more than 500cc of blood was used. A list was also kept of donors for private cases outside the Hospital. They were paid five guineas by the patient each time they were used. A further five guineas was paid to the Hospital, half of which was given to the Pathologist. To begin with only six donors were used, but by 1937 this had increased to 47.

With anaesthetics, aseptic procedures and blood transfusions much had now been achieved to combat the three problems of surgery: pain, infection and bleeding.

When Mr Brooks retired in 1923 and was made a Consulting Surgeon, Mr Dorrell succeeded him as Ophthalmic Surgeon. By the following year the Department had three clinical assistants. Its work was greatly helped by the purchase of a powerful electro-magnet (£75) which enabled metal fragments to be extracted from the eye. Local factories and the railway works at Swindon were advised that such casualties now need go no further than Reading for treatment.

The Dental Department was enlarged in 1924 when Mr Goadby retired after 26 years and was made a Consulting Dental Surgeon. Two Honorary Dental Surgeons, Mr Norman Stratton and Mr E. H. Williams, were appointed in his place. The Department was re-equipped to deal with all types of dental work, including operative work connected with fractured jaws and cleft palates, undertaken in consultation with the surgeons.

The X-ray and Electro-Therapeutic Departments were experiencing an unprecedented increase in work. In 1921 Mr Foster, who had been in charge of the X-ray Department since its establishment, asked to be relieved of his radiological work. This had increased to such an extent that it could no longer be combined with his work as an honorary surgeon. Mr Lionel Phillips, who had been appointed Clinical Assistant earlier in the year, was made Medical Officer in charge of the Department.

The following year nearly £500 was spent on new and replacement photographic apparatus. Developing tanks were obtained to enable films to be used as well as plates. It was decided that the treatment by deep therapy was 'not yet sufficiently advanced' to justify the expense of purchasing the necessary additional equipment. Major changes took place in 1924 when the Snook apparatus, obtained in 1918, had to be replaced. A new Snook was ordered and also portable apparatus for the wards and a Coin apparatus for superficial treatment. As a temporary measure, part of the casualty waiting hall was adapted for the installation of the new equipment with the special protective devices now required. A total of £840 was expended. A Senior Radiologist, Mr A. O. Forder, from King's College Hospital, was appointed at a salary of £300 a year and Mr Bunce, the previous Radiographer, became his junior at £200 a year.

The Electro-Therapeutic Department also moved into part of the casualty waiting hall and the help of another nurse was obtained. A diathermy apparatus was purchased and an electric-sun bed donated by Callas, Son and May. At the end of 1924 some 16,790 attendances had been made to these two departments during the year, 3,000 more than in the year before. Both departments would benefit from the better facilities planned for them when the nurses vacated the East Wing.

Changes had also taken place among the honorary medical staff. Dr Abram had been knighted and was now Sir Stewart Abram in recognition of his work as Mayor of Reading in 1919. Dr Murrell, the other physician, died in 1923 and was succeeded by Dr G. O. Lambert, whose position as Assistant Physician was taken by Dr T. Stansfield. Mr Foster retired in 1924 and was made a Consulting Surgeon. Mr J. L. Joyce was elected in his place and Mr H. M. Clarke (the Surgical Registrar) became an Assistant Surgeon.

On the wards there were few changes, apart from the installation of electric light in Sidmouth, Adelaide and Victoria Wards in 1923, which completed the electrification of all the wards. Complaints of the quality, quantity, preparation and serving of food and the hours of meals were investigated. There had been little change in the routine or the diet since the war and even the addition of jam was considered too costly. Enquiries to other hospitals had revealed that however good the food, 'complaints and grumbling' were still abundant. Moreover it was noted that what the Hospital could not afford to provide was frequently produced by the patients' friends and relations.

The Berkshire Federation of Women's Institutions drew attention to the very early hour of waking patients and asked if this could be later than 5 a.m. Investigation into the routine of the Hospital resulted in no change at all as it was believed this early start was necessary to enable the wards to be ready for the morning medical rounds. As the patients went to sleep at 8.30 p.m. this was not regarded as any hardship.

On the unanimous recommendation of the medical staff, in 1924 smoking was allowed on the male wards for a short time each day. Wireless receiving apparatus with loudspeakers and headphones was installed throughout the Hospital in 1925, thanks once again to the generosity of Mr Rivers and an appeal in the *Reading Standard*. Visiting days had remained the same over the years and were still restricted to Wednesdays and Saturdays from 2.30 to 3.30, and Sundays between 2 p.m. and 3.20 p.m. Children were only allowed to visit on Sundays.

In 1928 the entrance hall was greatly improved by the donation of handsome new oak doors and benches. Given by the old Cliftonians of the Reading area in memory of their fellow Cliftonian, Field Marshal Earl Haigh who had died that year, they form a practical and an attractive feature to this day.

In the Out-patients Department a refreshment stall was set up by Mrs Parsons in 1921. Her voluntary work was greatly appreciated as the increasing number of people attending the various clinics often resulted in long periods of waiting.

The New Nurses' Home

The new Nurses' Home was officially opened on April 7th, 1925 by Princess Mary, Viscountess Lascelles, in the presence of over 1,000 guests. The architect, Mr Charles Smith, had died before the work was completed but the building he had designed was a handsome memorial to his work. The bedrooms and sitting-rooms had been attractively furnished, mostly by Heelas, and there were four bathrooms to every corridor besides

Opening of the new Nurses' Home, April 7th, 1925. *Top*: Visit of H.R.H. Princess Mary, Viscountess Lascelles; *Bottom*: The new building

washing and ironing rooms and shampoo rooms with dryers. A covered way connected the Home to the Hospital and a tennis court had been constructed in the grounds behind. The total cost, including furnishing, was £25,889.

The removal of the nurses to their new Home had been expected to release accommodation in the East Wing for the X-ray and Electro-Therapy Departments. Plans had been prepared and agreed but before they could be proceeded with the medical staff had drawn the attention of the Board to a matter of great urgency. The number of surgical cases requiring operations had increased considerably and in 1924 some 3,244 operations were performed. The West Wards had been changed from isolation wards to provide an additional 14 surgical beds but the most pressing need was for another theatre. The British Red Cross Society and the Order of St John were asked if the remainder of their grant could be diverted to provide a new theatre instead of the planned alterations to the former Nurses' Home. In September 1925 this was agreed, and the plans drawn up by Mr Hutt the architect were approved. Tenders from Collier and Catley for £7,675 were accepted and the work was begun in the autumn of 1926.

To meet the now urgent need for better accommodation the Massage Department was removed from the main building into a temporary adjoining hut. The Electro-Therapeutic Department was transferred to the vacated massage room. With the X-ray Department occupying the casualty waiting hall, an annexe was built on to the adjoining west corridor to provide a waiting-room for the out-patients.

Additional surgical accommodation was provided in East Ward by removing the V.D. cases to a building erected adjoining the West Wards. The cubicles formerly occupied by nurses in the main building above the theatre were adapted to provide two six-bed wards for tonsils and adenoids cases. This enabled children to be admitted overnight and removed a difficulty which had given rise to many complaints and much acrimony.

Re-organisation of the Nursing Department
Soon after the opening of the new Nurses' Home, Miss Wynne, Matron for 14 years, resigned because of ill health. The Board of Management expressed their appreciation of her loyal and efficient service and noted this as an 'essential factor in bringing the Hospital to its present state of efficiency and high repute'. Miss Parsons, aged 43, trained at St Thomas's Hospital and Matron of the Huddersfield Royal Infirmary, was appointed in her place at a salary of £220 a year.

The nursing staff now consisted of the Matron, Assistant Matron, Home Sister, Sister Tutor, Office Sister, Out-patients Sister, Night, Massage and Theatre Sisters and nine Ward Sisters, besides the staff nurses and 70 probationers in training. Once again difficulty was being experienced in obtaining the necessary probationers and it was believed the four-year course with an entry age of 21 was deterring applicants. In 1926

East Ward

the course was therefore reduced to three years and the entry age lowered to 19. Both preliminary and final Hospital examinations would be taken before candidates entered for the final State Examination and no Hospital certificate would be given to any nurse who had not passed her final Hospital examination. The annual ceremony of presenting certificates and prizes to the nurses instituted over 25 years before continued to be held. In 1928 the first nurses' reunion took place with those trained at the Hospital coming from all parts of the country for the occasion. It became customary for these reunions to be held every two years.

The difficulty in obtaining sisters was attributed to the low salaries offered. These were now raised to £70-£80 a year for Ward Sisters, £80-£90 for Theatre Sisters, £85-£95 for Night Sisters, and £100 for the Sister Tutor and Office Sister.

By 1926 additional accommodation was needed for the Preliminary Training School and a lecture room and adjoining demonstration room were built in the garden behind 'Linden'. Ten years later the whole of the building was taken over by the Training School when the offices of the Contributory Scheme were moved to 'Thirlemere', 2 Craven Road.

The Private Nurses, now almost 30 in number, were moved back to the Hospital in 1927 from their rented accommodation in King's Road. This would bring them into closer contact with the Hospital, keep them up to date with developments in medicine and surgery and had the additional benefit of being more economical. The now vacant nurses' rooms above King Edward Ward were adapted to provide the necessary accommodation. The post of Lady Superintendent was abolished and a Sister Superintendent was appointed in her place to be directly responsible to the Matron. This re-organisation remained virtually unchanged until 1939.

In 1932 the Reading and District Branch of the College of Nursing was formed, following a meeting held in the Hospital in May that year. Miss Parsons, the Hospital Matron, was made President, Miss Carter, a former Matron of Dunedin Nursing Home, became Treasurer and Miss Carlyle, Matron of the Helena Home, Secretary.

The following year the nurses' uniform was slightly changed. The stand-up collars were replaced by semi-stiff Eton collars; the long sleeves with their stiff cuffs were changed for detachable sleeves and the shoulder straps on the aprons were removed. Still long and starchy by today's fashion, the uniform was made more practical, comfortable and hygenic.

The Maternity Ward

For some time there had been requests for the provision of a separate maternity ward. In 1925 the Berkshire Federation of Women's Institutes had sent a formal request to the Board of Management supported by letters from their various branches. They pointed out that while the child mortality rate continued to drop, that of the mothers did not. The medical staff also believed that an in-patients gynaecological and obstetric department should be formed and it was agreed that the ground floor of the old Nurses' Home in the East Wing and part of the adjoining maids' home should be assigned to this purpose.

The original idea of 16 beds was too costly and a more modest scheme with seven beds (five in one room and two single rooms) and a theatre was approved. Mr Hutt's plans were put out to tender and that of McCarthy and Fitt of £1,600 was accepted. In November 1926 Mrs Benyon presented a cheque for this amount to the Hospital. It had been raised by the Ladies' Hospital Ball Committee from the proceeds of a special concert and donations.

The ward was opened in January 1927. Sir Stewart Abram, Dr Lambert and Mr Baxter took charge of the ward in rotation. It proved a great benefit but the seven beds were far from adequate. It was decided that all Caesarian sections would be performed in the main theatre, septic cases would go to Albert Ward, cases of puerperal fever to the isolation ward, premature births after six months to the maternity ward and miscarriages to the surgical wards. A total of 40 cases were admitted to the ward during its first year and over twice that number in the following year.

Orthopaedic Cases

The admission of patients for the surgical treatment of TB bones and joints often resulted in beds being occupied for a very considerable time. As some of these cases could not be treated satisfactorily in the Hospital, arrangements were made in 1921 for the admission of children to the Wingfield Orthopaedic Hospital in Oxford.[4] In return crippled children, attending clinics associated with that Hospital, would be offered electro-therapy and massage treatment at the Royal Berkshire Hospital. At the same time an orthopaedic out-patients clinic was established in the charge of the Assistant Surgeons (Mr Joyce and Mr Baxter) assisted by V.A.D.s from the British Red Cross Society.

The great demand for surgical beds made it necessary to transfer chronic or incurable patients and those needing very long treatment to the Battle Infirmary and other institutions. In 1923 the Wingfield Orthopaedic

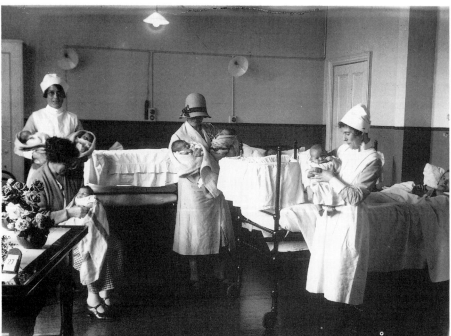

Top: Adelaide Ward, 1926; *Bottom*: The new Maternity Ward, 1927

204

Hospital Board included representatives from the Royal Berkshire Hospital and admission for adult patients from the Hospital was obtained for a charge of £2 12s 6d a week. Mr Robert Girdlestone, the Surgeon at the Wingfield who was instrumental in establishing these orthopaedic arrangements, was later appointed the first Professor of Orthopaedic Surgery in Britain. In 1940 he became the consulting advisor to the Orthopaedic Department at the Royal Berkshire Hospital.

At the end of 1926 a 5½-acre site at Calcot was purchased on which to erect a branch hospital for the treatment of surgical TB cases. The land was bought for £2,000 from the Trustees of the Blagrave estate, and Mr Harry Blagrave most generously donated £1,000 towards the cost. As the plans were prepared it was decided to enlarge the building and extend the 20 beds originally intended to 60 with provision for increasing this to 120 beds. This would enable convalescent surgical cases to be admitted, thereby releasing badly needed beds in the parent Hospital. The new hospital would be called the Royal Berkshire Hospital Blagrave Branch. Mr Hutt's plans were completed at the end of 1927 and McCarthy Fitt's tender for £23,391 was accepted in the autumn of 1928.

In 1929 the Berks, Bucks and Oxon Association for the care of cripples was formed to co-ordinate the work of the orthopaedic clinics in the area. A central body consisting of representatives from hospitals, clinics, public and private institutions was formed. One of the two representatives from the Royal Berkshire Hospital was Mr J. L. Joyce.

Extensions to the Pathological Laboratory
While the new theatre block was being built, extensions were also being made to the Pathological Laboratory. Adapted in 1912 from the old ambulance building, it was now inadequate for the great increase in work. In 1914 a total of 623 examinations had been carried out and in 1927, only thirteen years later, 4,817 investigations had been undertaken for the Hospital, local authorities and private practitioners. Advances made in treating diabetes with insulin and the new tests for sugar in the blood using the Hawkesley Colorimeter (purchased for £21 in 1924), as well as research comparing the Sigma and Wassermann tests for syphilis, were among the wide range of examinations now being undertaken. The newly formed Blood Transfusion Service also produced additional work.

A second storey was added to the building by Messrs Wheeler Bros at a cost of £1,412 and a former student from the Art Department of Reading University decorated the new stairway with murals. Shortly after the work was completed, Dr Skene Keith resigned to take an appointment at St Mary Abbotts Hospital in London and was succeeded by Dr John Bird of Manchester University and the University of Wales.

Links with Battle Infirmary
The long surgical waiting list at the Hospital had been noted by the Reading Board of Guardians. In December 1925, when asking if their

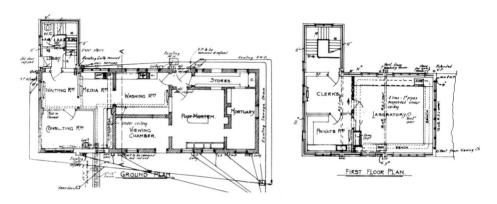

THE ROYAL BERKS HOSPITAL.
ALTERATIONS AND ADDITIONS TO
PATHOLOGICAL DEPARTMENT.

probationers from Battle Infirmary could attend the orthopaedic, aural and ophthalmic out-patients' clinics for training, they suggested that some of the Reading patients waiting for admission might be received at the Infirmary. Beds could be provided for six male and six female surgical patients and the Hospital would be charged for their admission. When accepting the probationers for training, the Board of Management arranged to inspect the offered accommodation and found that arrangements at the other hospital were 'suitable in every respect'. Agreement was then reached in principle for the transfer to Battle Infirmary of surgical cases who were residents of Reading should they be agreeable to such an arrangement.

Almost one year later in October 1926, Mr Neville Chamberlain, the Minister of Health, delivered a speech in Coventry which caused much concern to the Voluntary Hospitals and was interpreted as the first step towards the formation of a State medical service. Mr Chamberlain gave reassurance that he was at this point only asking for further co-operation between the various hospitals, including Voluntary and Municipal Hospitals, extending the ideas upon which Lord Cave's Regional Committees had been formed. There was need for 'a closer co-ordination of the institutions existing in any given area'. What had become evident by 1917 had become even more obvious ten years later. The manner in which it should be brought about was the question.

Following a letter from Mr Chamberlain to the British Hospitals Association in February 1927, a conference was arranged by the Hospital between its representatives and those of the Reading Board of Guardians and the Reading Borough Council. The subject was 'the position of Voluntary Hospitals in a co-ordinated scheme of public health service.' It was agreed that all branches of medicine were available in the area but 60 additional surgical beds were needed at the Royal Berkshire Hospital. These would be available when the Blagrave Branch Hospital was completed. In the meantime the available beds at Battle Infirmary should be used to ease the pressure. The Guardians would be paid one guinea per week for every patient belonging to the Contributory Scheme and 24/– per week for the others.

There appears to have been some reluctance on the part of both the medical staff and the patients over their transfer to the Infirmary. Its Poor Law associations were still abundantly evident and, however good the facilities might be, it was not yet considered equal to the Royal Berkshire Hospital. In February 1928 Mr Joyce, who had a very long waiting list, said he was not prepared to select any of his patients for admission to the Infirmary. When it was insisted that he should do so he produced a list of twelve who would be asked if they were agreeable to such an arrangement. In March 1928 the first transfer of six patients was made to Battle Infirmary.

The New Theatres
The new theatre block was opened by the President, Mr J. H. Benyon, on May 1st, 1928. It was a detached building to the south of the Hospital and connected to it by a covered way. Two adjacent theatres, each with its own anaesthetic room and dirty linen room, had been built to form a compact unit to include a recovery room, instrument and sterilising rooms, washing and robing rooms. Daylight was admitted through the roof and each theatre was equipped with the latest Zeiss shadowless lamps. Four back-up lights and an acetylene hand lamp were available in case of emergency. The theatres could be used either alternatively by one surgeon for successive operations or by two surgeons simultaneously.

Sixty years later, with the layout unaltered and now providing the two general theatres for the Hospital, the block has stood the test of time. An autoclave replaces the sterilisers, the roof has been lowered, modern lighting and air-conditioning installed. But the terrazzo floors and dado, the teak doors and fittings remain. Built and equipped with everything of 'proved excellence' at a cost of £10,000, it was a far-sighted addition, well ahead of its time.

Following the opening of these theatres the old theatre was assigned exclusively to the use of the Aural Department for which it remains to this day, and the septic theatre was adapted to provide lavatories for the use of the nurses. The improved methods of sterilisation and antiseptic treatment made a separate septic theatre no longer necessary.

Greenlands
'Greenlands', the property immediately to the south of the Hospital, came on the market early in 1928 following the death of Mr S. B. Stevens. Its purchase by the Hospital for £7,500 enabled accommodation to be provided for patients whose means precluded their admission to the ordinary wards but were not sufficient to pay the fees for nursing homes in the area. This was a facility that had been requested for many years.

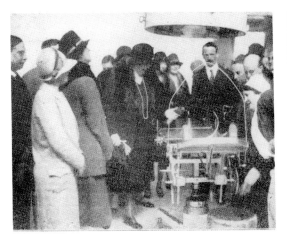

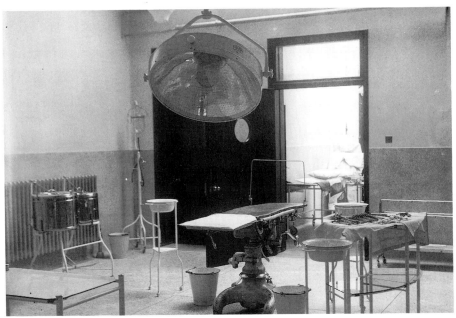

The new general theatres, 1928. *Top left*: Inspection of the operating table, May 1st 1928; *Top right*: Mr Secretan and Mr Joyce; *Centre*: Theatre and equipment; *Bottom*: Plan of the theatres

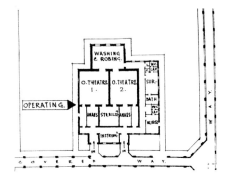

Greenlands

The days were over when all illnesses and operations could be accommodated at home and several nursing homes had been opened to which patients could be admitted who were not eligible for admission to the Hospital. Among these was the Dunedin Nursing Home in Bath Road. A convalescent home for officers during the 1914–18 war, it now offered comfortable rooms, a well-equipped theatre, X-ray facilities and good nursing. The fees of such nursing homes, as much as nine guineas a week, were beyond the means of many. The Board of Management believed the resources of the Hospital and a Private Patients Department could be combined to fill a great need which would also benefit the funds of the Hospital.

Greenlands was opened as a Nursing Home on October 15th, 1929 with accommodation for 15 patients. All the nurses were supplied by the Private Nursing Department and patients were charged six guineas per week for a single room and four guineas a week for a two-bed room. Fees for operations and treatment were arranged separately with the medical staff. Advertisements in the papers noted that it was 'designed to provide for persons of moderate means, the resources of a General Hospital with the amenities of a first-class nursing home.' Additional accommodation was provided over the years and by 1939 Greenlands had room for 23 patients and the charge for certain single rooms had risen to eight guineas a week.

One of the early patients was a young flying officer called Douglas

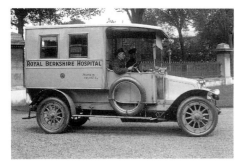

The Hospital's ambulances, 1918–1931. *Top left*: 1918 Renault; *Top right*: 1927 Daimler;
Centre left: Interior of ambulances; *Centre right*: 1929 hand ambulance (from Carter's *Patent
Ambulances 1920*); *Bottom*: 1931 R-type Morris

Bader whose plane had crashed at Woodley Aerodrome on December 14th, 1931. Following his emergency admission to Benyon Ward, both his legs were amputated by Mr J. L. Joyce and he was later transferred to Greenlands to convalesce. A combination of his own resilience, excellent surgery and Nurse Brace's skillful nursing restored him to health. In later years his bravery and success both as a war-time pilot and in civilian life became legendary and did much to show what could be achieved in the face of fearsome odds.

As well as adapting the main house, the stables at Greenlands were altered to provide accommodation for the Electro-therapeutic and Massage Department. This in turn released space in the main buildings for the X-ray Department and enabled the temporary massage hut and old garage to be added to West Ward to accommodate additional V.D. patients. In 1932 the Greenlands Lodge was adapted to provide a treatment room for private patients who did not need to be admitted to the Nursing Home.

The Greenlands garage was converted to house the Hospital ambulance. The original horse ambulance, bought in 1882, had been sold for £30 in 1919, having been made redundant by the arrival of the motor ambulance the previous year. The second horse ambulance now kept at Targett's on London Road was still in use and was not sold until 1931. A second motor ambulance had been acquired in 1927 with the gift from Sir Hugo Hirst of a 38 h.p. Daimler with 1914 engine, capable of 13 m.p.g. An ambulance body was built for the chassis by Great Western Motors; the cost of £260 was raised by private donation. Mr Ronald Harkness, a former A.A. Scout, was engaged to be the driver. A Carters Hand Ambulance was acquired in 1929 for £28 11s to enable patients to be wheeled in the open air from one part of the Hospital to the other.

Radium

In November 1928 a public appeal was launched to raise the necessary funds with which to purchase radium. In February the medical staff had sent a formal resolution to the Board of Management stating that: 'The recent advance in the treatment of malignant desease by radium impels the staff to press for improved facilities for such treatment.' It had been twelve years since the first request was made in 1914. In 1926 the Hospital had tried treatment by lead injections (choriotope); the patients had been closely monitored but the results had not been encouraging. Radium now appeared to be the best available treatment.

By January 1929 almost £5,000 had been raised and 300 milli-grammes of radium with the necessary appliances was obtained. This was put in the charge of the X-ray Department. A small store adjoining the consulting room was used to house the stock of needles in lead and steel containers safely away from the other sections of the Department.

In June the first three patients received treatment and 54 milli-grammes of radium was used. In that year a total of 69 in-patients and 19 out-patients were treated. Special rules were drawn up for the use of radium inside the Hospital and its hire elsewhere. Insurance was taken out to cover the cost of 150 milligrammes of radium needles, some £2,100, the maximum to be allowed out of the Hospital at any time. By 1938 the number of patients receiving radium treatment had almost doubled with 121 that year and 130 in the previous year.

End of the Poor Law System

The passing of the Local Government Act in 1929 brought an end to the Poor Law system. All the functions previously carried out by the Guardians would now be transferred to the local authorities; Public Assistance Committees would be established to support the needy; Public Health Committees would take over the care of the sick; the Workhouse Infirmaries would become Municipal Hospitals maintained by the rates. A co-ordinated system of health care was to be established. The County and Borough Councils were required to consult the governing bodies and medical staff of the Voluntary Hospitals in their areas when considering the provision of hospital accommodation. It was important that all branches of medical care should be provided without any unnecessary duplication of services. The Act would come into force on April 1st, 1930.

In anticipation of this the Regional Committee of the Voluntary Hospitals of Berkshire, Buckinghamshire and Oxfordshire formed three sub-committees, one for each county, with representatives from the management of the Voluntary Hospitals and medical staff of the county concerned. By the end of 1929 the Berkshire County Council and Reading Borough Council were notified that a Berkshire Committee had been formed ready for consultation on matters arising from the passing of the new Act. The County and Borough Councils formed similar committees to confer with the Voluntary Hospitals.

The Reading Borough Council on their part were required to prepare a scheme to incorporate the additional duties now devolved upon them. They already administered Park Hospital, Whitley Smallpox Hospital and Dellwood Maternity Home besides numerous clinics, dispensaries and welfare centres.[5] They now needed to assimilate the Guardians' Workhouse at Battle, a large collection of buildings in some 34 acres of land. This contained 580 beds of which 282 were for hospital patients, 59 for mental patients, 17 for children and the remainder for the use of the able-bodied destitute. The Infirmary was equipped with a modern operating theatre and sunlight apparatus. An X-ray Department was in the course of being installed. In 1928 some 103 operations had been performed at the Infirmary.

Links between the County and Borough Councils and the Royal Berkshire Hospital were already in existence with all pathological work being undertaken there since 1912, all V.D. treatment since 1918, and numerous patients admitted to the various specialist departments since the war. In recent years nurses from the Infirmary had been accepted for

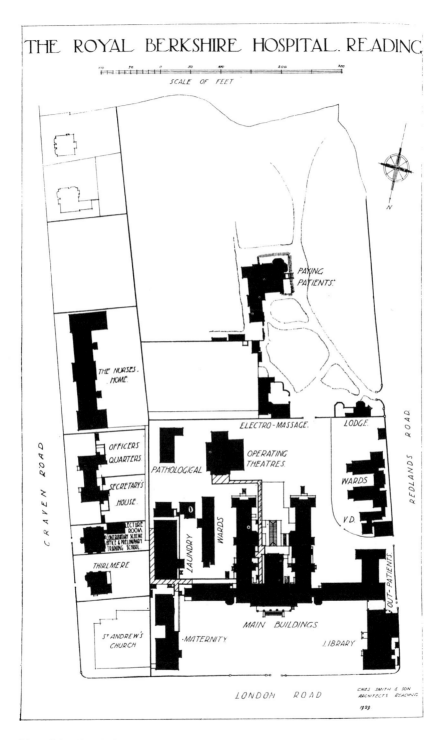

THE ROYAL BERKSHIRE HOSPITAL. READING.

SCALE OF FEET

N

PAYING PATIENTS.

THE NURSES. HOME.

ELECTRO-MASSAGE.

LODGE.

OFFICERS QUARTERS

OPERATING THEATRES.

PATHOLOGICAL

WARDS

SECRETARY'S HOUSE.

V.D.

LECTURE ROOM
CONTRIBUTARY SCHEME
OFFICE & PRELIMINARY
TRAINING SCHOOL.

LAUNDRY

WARDS

THIRLMERE

OUT-PATIENTS

CRAVEN ROAD

REDLANDS ROAD

St ANDREW'S CHURCH

MATERNITY

MAIN BUILDINGS

LIBRARY

LONDON ROAD

CHAS SMITH & SON
ARCHITECTS READING

1929

Plan of the Hospital, 1929

training in certain out-patients' departments. Conversely 82 surgical patients from the Hospital were admitted to Battle Infirmary in 1929. Specialist facilities were available only at the Royal Berkshire Hospital and it alone possessed the resources needed to provide acute medical and surgical care in the area.

The Local Government Act enabled changes to be made which would have been impossible under the Poor Law system. The old Workhouse became one hospital unit and was renamed Battle Hospital to include the Infirmary and also the former workhouse section, now maintained by public assistance. The whole now came under the administration of the Health Committee of the Borough Council. Any resident of the Borough needing treatment would be admitted. The circumstances of all were assessed and those who were able were asked to contribute towards the cost of their maintenace.

The subscriptions formerly paid by the Guardians to the Hospital on behalf of the Poor Law Unions now ceased. Instead the Hospital charged the Public Assistance Officers a weekly rate for all such patients now admitted. In 1933 the Approved Societies also stopped their annual subscription as the combination of the Contributory Scheme and the new Act now made such contributions unnecessary.

Gradually meetings came to be held regularly with the local authorities to co-ordinate the various medical services in the area. In August 1930 nurses from the Royal Berkshire Hospital were able to obtain midwifery training at Dellwood Maternity Home. Two years later an out-patients' clinic for the treatment of functional nervous disorders was established at the Hospital in co-operation with the medical superintendent of the Berkshire Mental Hospital,[6] and in 1934 a gynaecology clinic was set up at Battle Hospital with Mr Baxter appointed the visiting gynaecologist, a move which caused much concern to the other members of the Hospital honorary medical staff.

Differences still existed between the Hospital and its municipal counterpart at Battle. The Poor Laws had existed for centuries and the passing of a single Act could not dispel the aura of the past. As the Municipal Hospital expanded and extended its facilities, these differences became less apparent and gradually its association with the old workhouse system and pauperism were forgotten. It was not until 1937, however, that representatives from the Berkshire County Council and Reading Borough Council were appointed to the Board of Management of the Hospital.

The Blagrave Branch Hospital
The Blagrave Branch Hospital was opened by H.R.H. Prince George (Duke of Kent) on April 10th, 1930. It consisted of an administrative block, ward block, porter's lodge and two cottages besides a pump house with a water tower, a garage and a mortuary. It had been designed by Mr Harry Hutt and built by McCarthy Fitt and also Collier and Catley of Reading at a cost of almost £30,000.

Opening of Blagrave Branch Hospital, 1930

There were two wards with verandas, each containing 30 beds, named Willingham Gell, after the Hospital Treasurer and Rogers, after the Chairman of the Board of Management, in recognition of their great services to the Hospital. There was a small theatre with anaesthetics room, a splint room, plaster-moulding room and a surgeon's room. A Resident Medical Officer, Mr W. E. Lindeck, was appointed at a salary of £150 a year. He would also be required to help in the Pathology Department at the main Hospital. Miss Dalbiac, formerly Assistant Matron at the parent Hospital, was made Sister Superintendent.

The Hospital Chaplain, Mr Bayley, extended his duties to include the Branch Hospital and a small chapel was provided, its entire furnishings donated by well-wishers. The British Red Cross Society arranged to supply the patients with books and the Tilehurst Ward of the Aid Committee donated a wireless and loudspeakers. The provision of these additional 60 beds would do much to relieve the pressure on the main Hospital. In 1932 the Ministry of Health formally approved both the main Hospital and the Blagrave Branch as institutions for the treatment of non-pulmonary tuberculosis.

Financial Difficulties

Greenlands and the site of the Blagrave Branch had not been the only properties recently acquired by the Hospital. In 1927 'Thirlmere', 2 Craven Road, had come on the market and was bought for £1,200. Later that year three adjoining properties in Princes Street were purchased for £750 and the following year 79, Watlington Street was bought at auction for £490. All were required for the use of the Hospital staff, in addition to the earlier purchases which included Melrose Villas in London Road (bought in 1904) and the houses in Craven Road between the Nurses' Home and 'Thirlmere'.

These recent acquisitions, combined with the expense of adapting Greenlands as a Nursing Home and building and equipping the Blagrave Branch, had greatly overstretched the resources of the Hospital. In addition the number of patients continued to rise and the various departments were constantly expanding and needing new and often expensive equipment. Even the extra income obtained from the contributory scheme was not sufficient and by the end of 1930 a deficit of £25,000 had resulted.

Since the war the hard work and ingenuity of the public in raising money for the Hospital had been undiminished and fears that the success of the contributory scheme might lessen enthusiasm had proved groundless. The Hospital parades, which had stopped in some areas during the war, became more numerous as additional bands were formed and their popularity increased. An annual Hospital Ball was held from 1919 onwards and raised substantial sums; so did the Flower Day inaugurated soon afterwards. In 1923 Huntley and Palmer raised £156 from a public exhibition of the bridal cake which they had made on the occasion of the marriage of Lady Elizabeth Bowes Lyon and the Duke of York. (The Duke and Duchess of York were to become King George VI and Queen Elizabeth in 1936 on the abdication of Edward VIII.) Over 6,000 people had paid for admission besides the 7,565 employees who were admitted free.[7] In 1926 the visit of the Prince of Wales (later to become King Edward VIII) drew additional attention to the Hospital's work and welfare.

Specially organised tea dances were a new way of raising funds and so were the various annual sporting events for which many silver challenge cups had been given to the Hospital. Donations continued to be received from the League of Mercy and the Ladies' Linen League, but the Samaritans' Sewing Guild had been disbanded after the war. Several memorial beds were endowed, including one by Mr and Mrs Secretan in memory of their son, and one by the Ancient Order of Druids to celebrate the Jubilee of their Royal Berkshire Lodge. Although the generosity of people from all walks of life was directed towards the support of the Hospital, it was still not enough.

In 1931 a Special Public Appeal for £30,000 was launched to exinguish the £25,000 deficit and to establish an Endowment Fund for the Blagrave Branch. By the end of that year £12,000 had been raised in spite

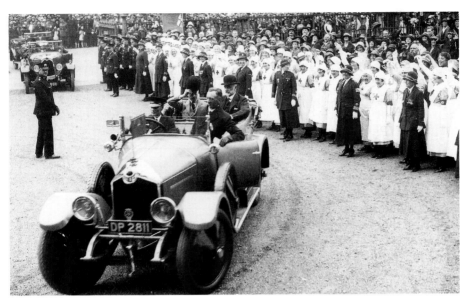

Visit of the Prince of Wales

of the prevailing economic depression. The nursing staff raised £500 to endow a cot at the Blagrave Branch; the Hospital Secretary, Mr F. A. Lyon, broadcast an appeal on the radio's 'Week's Good Cause' and many special events were arranged throughout the area. In 1931 the first illuminated Christmas tree was put outside the Hospital and numerous gifts were distributed to those who purchased tickets sold in aid of the Hospital.

By 1933 only half the target money had been obtained. The economic problems of the time were proving an insuperable difficuty in raising funds. One year later the appeal was closed and the remaining overdraft, which with interest amounted to £10,092, was liquidated by the sale of securities. The Blagrave Branch Building Fund Committee was dissolved, but immediately re-formed to become 'The Royal Berkshire Hospital Special Needs Committee'. Over the years it raised considerable sums to supply the Hospital and its Branch with special items.

The Expanding Hospital

All departments had expanded since the war, all were now benefiting from the great advances being made in medicine and surgery and the improved equipment now available. For the X-ray Department and the Out-patients Department in particular lack of space was becoming a matter of urgency.

In 1926 Mr Phillips had left Reading and was succeeded by Dr Cave as Medical Officer in charge of the X-ray Department. The deep-therapy equipment obtained in 1927 led to a considerable increase in work. The first X-ray pupil was admitted that year for a fee of 20 guineas. By 1928 the work had increased to such an extent that the balcony adjoining the

217

Casualty Hall was adapted to provide two treatment cubicles. The following year an X-ray room for casualties only was formed by partitioning off part of a corridor.

Improved equipment resulted in better pictures, including those of the heart and lungs, and the injection of Lipiodol enabled examinations to be extended to the gall bladder, urinary tract, bronchi and sinuses. In 1934 an additional radiographer was engaged for deep-therapy treatment. A successful public appeal raised the £300 necessary to provide the new equipment needed for treating breast cancer and a dosimeter for the measurement of treatment doses. Altogether some 3,868 radiographic cases using nearly 9,000 films attended the Department in 1934, besides 1,925 cases treated with ultra-violet rays, 930 by X-rays and 51 in-patients treated with radium. The cost of the Department that year was just over £1,000. In 1935 a second deep-therapy apparatus was obtained besides new portable X-ray equipment. The latest diagnostic equipment was obtained the following year which enabled serial films to be taken very rapidly.

The work of the Out-patients Department had also increased and the waiting area appeared to be permanently filled with people attending the various clinics each day. The ophthalmic clinic alone could expect to receive about 70 patients for every session and the other clinics were similarly congested. Mrs Parsons, who had run the out-patient canteen for seven years, retired in 1928 and, after a short interlude with professional caterers, V.A.D.s from the British Red Cross Society took over the work in 1931.[8] This voluntary service was greatly appreciated and continues to this day through the work of the British Red Cross Society and the W.R.V.S.

There had been several changes and additions to the medical staff. In the Anaesthetics Department Dr Ritson retired in 1926 and was made a Consulting Anaesthetist. He was succeeded by Dr H. Parry Price. Dr Bean was appointed third Assistant Anaesthetist the following year but when Dr Young retired in 1928 no replacement was obtained. Instead, an additional Resident Medical Officer was appointed as a Resident Anaesthetist, thus separating this job from that of the Casualty Officer.

The death of Sir Stewart Abram, the Senior Physician, in 1928 was a great loss to the Hospital. He had first joined the staff as an Assistant Physician in 1904 and was greatly liked and respected. Medical balconies for open-air treatment, in which he had been very interested, were built as his memorial in Adelaide and Sidmouth Wards. These were dedicated at a special ceremony in October 1930. Dr Norman May was elected an Honorary Physician and Dr H. S. Le Marquand replaced him as Assistant Physician.

When Dr John Mills succeeded Dr Skene Keith as Pathologist in 1928, Dr Le Marquand took over as Medical Officer in charge of the V.D. Department. The same year Dr Bird succeeded Dr Holden on his retirement as Medical Officer in charge of the Electro-Therapeutic Department. Dr L. M. Jennings was elected Medical Registrar in place of

Top: The office; *Bottom*: Christmas on the children's ward

Dr Bird. In 1933 Mr G. T. W. Cashell succeeded Mr Dorrell when he retired as Ophthalmic Surgeon and became a Consulting Surgeon. In 1935 Mr Secretan retired and became a Consulting Surgeon and Mr Baxter was made an Honorary Surgeon. Mr H. M. Clarke was also made an Honorary Surgeon and was replaced by Mr A. N. Hooper who was now the only Assistant Surgeon. Mr F. H. Aitken Walker was appointed Surgical Registrar in place of Mr Hooper.

A rule alteration in 1933 enabled up to two partners in a practice to become members of the honorary medical staff. The former rule now appeared unreasonable in view of the increased size of the staff. All applicants still had to submit numerous copies of their testimonials (often as many as 85, though usually about 75) unless they were already on the staff, a condition which greatly favoured the promotion of those already at the Hospital.

Additional appointments reflected the increasing work of the out-patients and specialist departments. In 1932 there were four clinical assistants for the Ophthalmic Department besides the Aural Registrar, Mr S. F. Logan Dahne; a Medical Officer, Dr Tozer, was appointed Clinical Assistant to the Out-patients Department. By 1935 there was a Clinical Assistant to the Skin Department, Dr E. E. Wheatley, and another, Dr R. A. Ratcliff, to the Medical and Children's Out-patients Department. The Resident medical staff were now seven in number with the addition of a House Surgeon for the special departments.

A Lady Almoner, Miss Christine Gurney, was appointed in 1930 at a salary of £240 a year. This new job enabled a check to be made on abuse of Hospital facilities and to arrange for the aftercare of patients. The Almoner took over the work previously done by the Patients' Registrar and was given the assistance of a clerk. This appointment enabled much of the work of the Convalescence Fund to be transferred from the Board of Management and allowed a better check to be kept on the functioning of the Contributory Scheme.

There had been questions as to whether people were eligible to join the Scheme if they paid income tax and in 1931 revised terms of membership were introduced giving limits of income. Single people over 18, without dependents, with an income of up to £260 a year, widows and widowers with children under 16 and married couples with children with an income of up to £312 would be able to join the Contributory Scheme. Those with incomes above these amounts were considered able to pay for medical treatment and could either make their own arrangements independently of the Hospital or join a separate Private Patients Scheme whereby financial assistance could be obtained towards the cost of treatment in private wards or nursing homes.

Motor Accidents and Insurance
Since the war, the increase in the number of motor cars produced another problem for the Hospital with the cost of treating accident patients. In 1924

Top: The Diet Kitchen; *Bottom*: Surgical stores

The kitchen

the Watch Committee of the Borough Council authorised the purchase of a special police ambulance to transport road accident victims to the Hospital. Two years later these accidents were so numerous that the Hospital started to record them separately. In the six months between October 1st, 1926 and March 31st, 1927, 40 in-patients and 64 out-patients were treated as a result of motor accidents and the total cost to the Hospital was nearly £500. In the whole of 1927 there were 307 such accidents, almost half of which were made in-patients, keeping the equivalent of seven beds constantly occupied and costing the Hospital £1,200 that year.

This problem was common to all the Voluntary Hospitals but the suggestion that the cost of driving licences should be increased from 5/– to 7/6d a year and the additional income used to meet the hospitals' expenses was not adopted. Instead a Motorists' Fund was formed: drivers were asked to pay 2/6d and were given a small sticker to be attached to their windscreens. In 1928 the Hospital obtained £50 from this source but the following year the Fund was closed. The Road Traffic Act of 1930 enabled the Hospital to attempt to recover these costs from insurance companies, but by 1934 less than 30 per cent was being recouped each year. This problem became an increasing burden to the Hospital and its resources as the number of motor cars continued to grow.

By 1935 a somewhat different problem associated with cars was beginning to be felt. Parking in the forecourt on visiting days was getting difficult and an attendant was employed to direct the parking. The age of bicycles and carriages was over and the problem of leaving a car at the Hospital became steadily worse.

The problem of insurance of another kind arose about the same time when the question of Hospital third party risks was considered. In 1930 a case of negligence at a London hospital had been settled out of court, leaving the hospital in question paying £200 compensation. Insuring the Royal Berkshire Hospital was considered: a premium of £25 would cover an unlimited amount with a maximum of £5,000 for any one incident. The Hospital decided not to insure, having been advised that so long as it provided the best physicians and surgeons and the best nursing staff within its power, it was not responsible for the negligence of its doctors or its nurses.

There had been a few complaints, as in the cases when a surgical needle had not been removed following an operation for excision of the breast, and some tubing was left behind after the removal of a kidney tumour. A nurse had been dismissed when the surgeons had refused to work with her after an incident in which she had failed to remove swabs. In each case the patients had been reassured, no liability admitted, and the matter was taken no further. The days of litigation had not yet arrived.

Insurance for the buildings and their contents had always been taken out and in 1935 the cost of this was just over £100 a year. The following year the Hospital reconsidered the matter of third party risks and decided to extend the insurance to cover it against possible claims made in connection with blood donors. The honorary medical staff were asked to see that they were covered in respect of patients treated at the Hospital, and all Resident Medical Officers were required to insure themselves with a Medical Defence Society. The first recorded incident in which such help was sought was when a Resident Anaesthetist, having been told to leave after complaining about the food and throwing it out of a window, threatened to sue for wrongful dismissal.

Proposed Extensions
In 1934 the improved economic condition of the country, combined with the pending Silver Jubilee celebrations, encouraged the Board of Management to consider further extensions. The expansion of the Hospital in recent years had become haphazard in response to immediate pressures and in considering the next steps more forward planning would be essential. Hospital planning had now become a special branch of architecture and with this in mind, Mr Stanley Hamp, F.R.I.B.A., was asked to prepare a comprehensive scheme for the future. He had been consulted by the Radcliffe Infirmary, King's College Hospital, London and other well-known hospitals and his work was highly regarded. He was asked to put forward proposals which would enable sections of the work to be undertaken as and when the funds became available.

The King, as Patron of the Hospital, was asked if a new wing containing the X-ray Department could be named King George V Wing to commemorate his Silver Jubilee in 1935. This could not be agreed as the granting of a Royal title could only be given to completed buildings or to those nearing completion and for which the funding was assured. As the appeal for the Blagrave Branch had been held so recently it was decided to launch the much larger appeal in 1937 in association with the centenary of the founding of the Hospital.

Mr Hamp proceeded with his survey of the Hospital and produced a variety of plans for consideration. Certain more urgent items were undertaken in 1936 ahead of the appeal and were paid for by the sale of securities. This work included the enlargement and re-equipment of the kitchens, the enlargement of the nurses' and sisters' dining-room, the construction of ramps to connect the central block of the building to the two wings and the addition of eight bedrooms to the Nurses' Home and a shed for 70 bicycles.

By 1937 the Hospital had suffered the loss of both its Patron and its President with the death of King George V in 1936 and of Mr J. H. Benyon the year before. Both had been associated with the Hospital for over 25 years. Following the abdication of King Edward VIII, the new King, George VI, was graciously pleased to become Patron and Mr A. T. Loyd, the new Lord Lieutenant of Berkshire, accepted the invitation to become President of the Hospital. To him fell the task of launching the Centenary Appeal for £150,000 at the Town Hall on April 15th, 1937.

The Extension Scheme would provide new accommodation for the Out-patients, X-ray, Ophthalmic, Orthoptic and Electro-therapeutic Departments and additional accommodation for the Aural Department. There would be a new children's unit and a new surgical ward for women, a new mortuary and post-mortem room and the addition of a bio-chemical laboratory to the Pathological Laboratory. A wing to contain 60 bedrooms would be added in the Nurses' Home.

The Appeal had raised £33,500 within three months when Lord Nuffield almost doubled the amount with a cheque for £30,000. He asked that this should be used to build a new block of four wards to accommodate children, maternity and women's surgical cases. This great generosity would enable work to begin immediately and as a result the in-patients' accommodation now took priority over all other work. With this addition of 100 beds the planned extension to the Nurses' Home would need to be started at once, followed by the provision of a third operating theatre and a new boiler and generating plant. The work on the Out-patients and specialist Departments, costing a further £50,000, would be undertaken whenever sufficient funds had been raised.

A tender of £31,700 from McCarthy E. Fitt was accepted for the new block and the mortuary and garage, complete with connecting corridors, roads and paths; another for £14,739 was accepted for the extension to the Nurses' Home. Tenders of £16,000 for the new boilers and generating plant and £4,988 for the new theatre were also approved. By the end of 1938 the Appeal had reached £81,500 and included a donation of £1,500 from Mrs

Haynes to cover the structural alterations and additions to the Pathological Laboratory. The building work, which was started in 1937, continued for almost two years.

Medical and Surgical Advances

The monthly meetings of the Reading Pathological Society, held in the Hospital library, did much to enable its members to keep abreast of medical and surgical advances. In 1924, at the suggestion of the Society, the medical staff of the Hospital gave a course of post-graduate lectures to the practitioners of the area. Although a success these lectures were not repeated.

It was not until 1931 when the first volume of the Royal Berkshire Hospital Reports was published that the work of the Hospital became more widely known. This was a collection of papers, many of which had been read at meetings of the Pathological Society, which it was hoped would 'disseminate among the doctors of Berkshire further information of the facilities of the Hospital, so that new methods of diagnosis and treatment may more quickly become available to the general public.' Edited by Dr Le Marquand, these Reports were produced until 1938 and were most favourably received by a much wider readership than originally envisaged. Enthusiastic reviews in journals such as *The Lancet* noted the range of subjects covered and the excellence of the research, more commonly found only in teaching hospitals.

Since the war greatly improved anaesthetics had made operations safer and the after-effects less unpleasant. Soon after its formation the Ministry of Health had required to be notified (with details) of all anaesthetic deaths to enable a special study to be made of the problem. Chloroform was now seldom used and had been replaced by gas and oxygen. The Shipways apparatus obtained in 1920 was replaced by the better Boyles machine in 1930 and the more sophisticated Mackesson's equipment was purchased in 1935. Spinal anaesthetics, used since the turn of the century, were now much improved. After the war advances were made in a third type of anaesthetic using intra-tracheal administration and the Hospital obtained the apparatus in 1927. The next year trials were started in the use of rectal anaesthetics. Dr Parry Price obtained a supply of 'Avertin' from the Medical Research Council to carry out research in its use at the Hospital. His paper on the subject was included in the volumes of Reports.

Work carried out with the new electrocardiograph, purchased in 1930, was described by Dr Lambert; the advances with deep X-ray therapy were recorded by Dr Cave; the treatment of detached retina with the new Moorfield's Diathermy apparatus, obtained in 1934, was described by Mr Cashell as well as the treatment of squint at the Orthoptic Clinic he established at the Hospital in the same year. In 1935 an Ophthalmic Clinic was established at the Hospital, affiliated to the Voluntary Hospitals Ophthalmic Organisation with its headquarters at Moorfields Eye

The Hospital Sunday Parade, May 1938

Hospital. Dr Le Marquand's paper on the study of endocrine disorders and Dr Mills's research on glandular fever and pernicious anaemia were included among the great variety of medical subjects. Numerous reports showed the increase in the range of surgery, from Mr Secretan's splenectomy operation to Mr Powell's drainage of brain abscesses of otitic origin.

Among the main contributors was Mr J. Leonard Joyce whose outstanding surgical ability had been noted during the war. As Surgical Registrar after the war he had drawn the attention of the medical staff to his follow-up system of cancer patients and in 1933, as an Honorary Surgeon, he gave details of its method of operation which was adopted in the Hospital. That year he received a great compliment when Professor Gask brought his surgical unit from St Bartholomew's Hospital to Reading to see him operate. The Hospital Reports record the wide range of his work, which included a study of 94 cases of malignant disease of the colon, peptic ulcers, melanotic sarcoma of the retina, a study of 71 consecutive operations on the thyroid gland and treatment of breast cancer. His sudden death in 1939 at the age of 57 removed one of the most able surgeons of the time. The operating theatre to be built in association with the new block of wards was to be dedicated to his memory and to his outstanding work in the Hospital.

A Period of Crisis

Several changes took place in the two years during which the new extensions were being built. Miss Parsons resigned as Matron in 1937 after eight years, as her deafness was proving an increasing disability. Miss Mutimer, aged 45, Assistant Matron of Guy's Hospital, was appointed to succeed her at a salary of £300 a year. At the same time the system of subscribers' tickets for the admission of patients was abolished. After almost 100 years they had now become unnecessary.

The forthcoming Centenary prompted the idea of writing the history of the Hospital and this was undertaken by various members of the medical staff and the Hospital Secretary with Mr Ernest W. Dormer, as editor, co-ordinating their contributions. *The Story of the Royal Berkshire Hospital* was published in 1938 and sold at 6/– a copy. Application was made to the College of Heralds for a grant of arms for the Hospital and this was also obtained in 1938.[9] In addition a grand fete, opened by H.R.H. the Duchess of Kent at Englefield House in June 1938, attracted over 10,000 people and raised £3,081 for the Centenary Extension Fund. Arrangements were made for a Centenary Medal to be struck and special celebrations were planned to be held October, 1939.

The Sankey Commission set up to enquire into the position of the Voluntary Hospitals and to make recommendations for their future published its report in 1937. For almost two years its contents were the subject of much discussion. Co-operation, rationalisation, the payment of medical staff and the formation of regional boards were among the items to the fore. In 1938 the Berkshire, Buckinghamshire and Oxfordshire Regional Committee of the British Hospitals Association met to discuss the proposals. The outcome of this was the decision that the Royal Berkshire Hospital would join the Oxford and District Joint Hospitals Board which had been formed in 1935. Early in 1939 three members of the Hospital were appointed to this body.

Over everything hung the cloud of events in Europe. Meetings were held in 1937 to discuss air-raid precautions. An advisory body was set up to consider the medical services of the Borough in case of war. The Blood Transfusion Service at the Hospital was put on a voluntary basis. Few donors had accepted payment but it was feared that should they do so the Hospital could not afford the additional expense. The number of donors on the register increased from 45 to 107 that year.

The Deputy Director of Medical Services, Southern Command, was informed in April 1938 that the Blagrave Branch had been placed at the disposal of the Secretary of State in case of war. Nurses had once again been promised for the Army and Queen Alexandra Nursing Service. The events of 1914 seemed to be happening all over again.

On September 20th, 1938 the Hospital was notified that in the event of a national emergency it would be required within 24 hours to provide for the admission of 180 patients to be evacuated from London. Over the next few days extra supplies and dressings were ordered, additional A.R.P.

The Hospital ambulances 1934–1939. *Top left and right*: 1934 Rolls Royce; *Bottom left and right*: 1939 Austin ambulance

measures taken and Huntley and Palmer Ward made gas-proof. One week later, at the height of the Munich crisis, the forewarned evacuation of patients took place. The Hospital records state that: 'On September 28th, acting on instructions from the Ministry of Health, accommodation for receiving 180 patients from London was made by evacuating patients from the Royal Berkshire Hospital. Large numbers of patients were taken home by friends, and owners of private cars offered their services.' Fortunately the outcome of the political negotiations avoided further disruption. No patients were evacuated from London and within days the patients were able to return to the Hospital.

Although war had been avoided the country had been shaken and put on further alert. Gas masks were issued for patients and staff. The gift of an iron lung by Lord Nuffield coincided with the arrival of sandbags at the Hospital. The decision to apply for recognition as a Radium Centre for the treatment of cancer (under the provision of the 1939 Cancer Act) came at the same time as an agreement to provide medical facilities for troops passing through the area. A new 18 h.p. Austin ambulance[10] was purchased with funds raised by the Special Needs Committee while black out and emergency fire-fighting squads were organised.

The Nuffield Block

Opening of the Nuffield Block
The Nuffield Block and the extension to the Nurses' Home were formally opened on June 4th, 1939 by Princess Alice, Countess of Athlone, in the presence of Lord Nuffield and a large assembly of guests. The new block had been built to the south of the theatre block and was linked to both it and the main building by a covered way. The wards were bright and airy, a modernised version of the original wards with the additional advantage of side wards and cubicles. The ground floor contained the new children's ward, later to be called Kempton Ward, and Nuffield I, the women's surgical ward. On the floor above were the obstetric and gynaecology wards, named Nuffield II and III. An up-to-date theatre with all the ancillary accommodation had been built adjoining these first-floor wards. The Hospital could now provide 315 beds for patients and a Nurses' Home for 150 nurses besides the accommodation at the Blagrave Branch.

At the south-western end of the grounds a new mortuary and ambulance block had been erected and on the east side the Pathological Laboratory had almost doubled in size and now included an up-to-date Bio-chemical Laboratory adapted from the old mortuary.

Additional nursing and medical staff would be needed when the new wards were occupied at the end of September. Mr Baxter had become the

Top: Extension to the Nurses' Home; *Bottom*: The new mortuary block

Senior Surgeon following the death of Mr Joyce. Mr F. H. Aitken Walker was now elected Honorary Surgeon, and his place as Surgical Registrar was taken by Mr F. E. Wheeler. A new temporary appointment of Assistant Obstetrician and Gynaecologist was made with the election of Mr A. N. Hooper (formerly Assistant Surgeon) to be responsible for this new Department under the Senior Surgeon. An additional House Surgeon was also appointed specially for the Department. Mr G. O. Tippett was elected to the new appointment of Assistant Surgical Registrar. The Casualty Department would now come under the charge of the Surgical

The iron lung, with Princess Alice, Mrs V. Benyon, Lord Nuffield, the Bishop of Reading and the Matron, Miss Mutimer

and Assistant Surgical Registrars. In addition three Honorary Assistant Anaesthetists were appointed, making five altogether. With the earlier appointment of a Radiotherapist, Dr H. C. Simchowitz, at a salary of £500 a year and a Bio-chemist, Dr Mawson, at £400 a year, the Hospital had now obtained the additional medical staff that would be needed for its greatly increased size.

Throughout the summer of 1939 the Centenary Appeal remained open and reached £82,650, sufficient to cover the first stage of expansion. The building which had housed the Electro-therapeutic and Massage Department and the Orthoptic Clinic had been demolished to make way for the new Nuffield Block. These were now housed in temporary accommodation, and with the other special departments were waiting for further funds to enable the second stage of development to begin.

Developments of a very different kind were taking place with 100,000 sandbags protecting the buildings, blackout material and adhesive tape obtained for the windows, a covered trench dug to store the gas and oxygen cylinders and A.R.P. training being given to all the male staff.

On August 29th, two months after the opening of the Nuffield Block, the Hospital was once again alerted for a 24-hour warning for the reception of patients to be evacuated from London.

Admission to the Hospital was limited to emergencies only, a large number of patients were sent home, and others were transferred to the

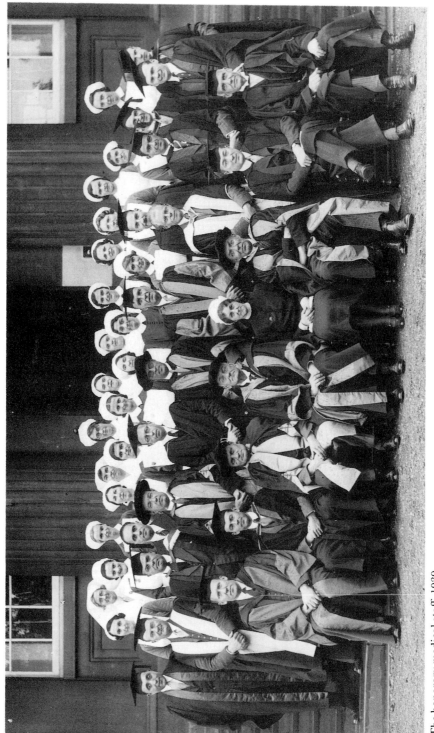

The honorary medical staff, 1939

Blagrave Branch. Altogether 180 beds were vacated. On Friday, September 1st the emergency plans were put in force and by 8 p.m. that evening 166 patients evacuated from hospitals in London were admitted to the wards of the Royal Berkshire Hospital. On Sunday, September 3rd, in his historic broadcast the Prime Minister, Mr Neville Chamberlain, informed the nation that it was now at war with Germany. Once again the life of the Hospital was to be dramatically changed.

NOTES

1 The Regional Committee consisted of two representatives from each of the County Councils, one from each Borough Council, six hospital representatives (two from each County, one of which was to be from the staff of a general hospital and the second from the smaller cottage hospitals), six medical representatives (two from each county, one of which was from the staff of a general hospital and the second from general practice) and five other members nominated by the Commission.

2 The original Regional grouping of the British Hospitals Association included Berkshire with Surrey.

3 By 1939 the Contributory Scheme had been extended and in addition included Fleet and District Hospital, Odiham Cottage Hospital, Wallingford and District Hospital, Yateley and District Hospital. There were also arrangements with seven different orthopaedic clinics and many Red Cross and St John Ambulance Brigades throughout the area.

4 This hospital, developed from the Wingfield Convalescent Home (established in 1872), became known as the Wingfield Morris Orthopaedic Hospital in 1931 following donations from William Morris, later to become Lord Nuffield. In 1955, after rebuilding, thanks to generous donations from Lord Nuffield, the Hospital was renamed the Nuffield Orthopaedic Centre.

5 The Berkshire Mental Hospital at Moulesford was administered by a Joint Committee of the County and Borough Councils. The Peppard Sanatorium was administered by a Joint Committee of the Berkshire and Buckinghamshire County Councils.

6 In 1933 agreement was reached for patients from the Boroughcourt Hospital (established in 1930) to be treated at the Ophthalmic Outpatients Clinic.

7 A similar exhibition was held in 1934 on the occasion of the marriage of Princess Marina and the Duke of Kent.

8 The V.A.D.s were allowed on the wards in 1930, from which time they looked after the distribution of library books for the patients.

9 The Hospital's coat of arms are: 'Sable on a Cross Argent between in the first and fourth quarters a Hart trippant and in the second and third quarters an Escallop or a Cross Gules charged with a Sceptre in pale gold.' The red cross symbolises medical aid, the Royal Sceptre marks the Hospital's royal foundation in 1837 and its Royal Patronage; the Hart (or stag) its connection with the Royal County of Berkshire and the Escallop shell the continuing work of caring for the sick of Reading dating from the foundation of Reading Abbey in 1121. Motto: 'Serviendo fidem tenemus' – 'in service we keep faith'.

10 The old 1918 Renault ambulance was sold in 1931 when an R type de luxe Morris ambulance costing £425 was purchased. In 1934 a Rolls Royce chassis was provided with an ambulance body for £100 by the Reading Garage Company, all given by Mr and Mrs J. H. Scrutton. The 1927 Daimler ambulance was then sold for £5.

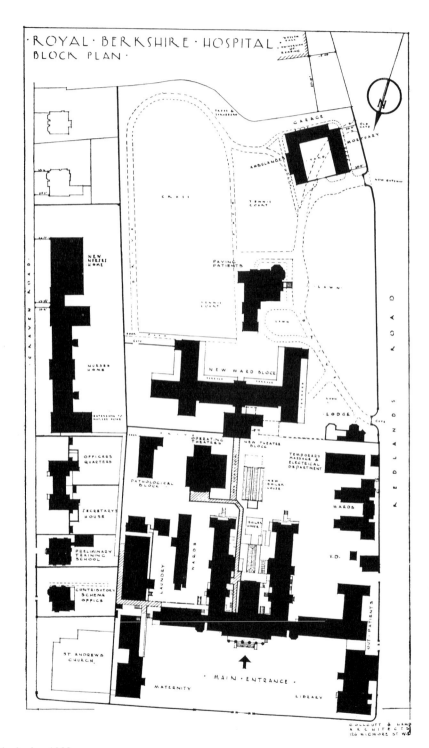

Block plan 1939

234

8

THE SECOND WORLD WAR
1939 TO 1945

The role of the Royal Berkshire Hospital in the Second World War was largely determined by its position as the main general hospital in a town 40 miles west of London. As early as June 1937, on instructions from the Home Office Air Raid Precaution Department, the Reading Borough Council, in common with other local authorities, had drawn up plans to protect the civilian population should war be declared. The following year the Ministry of Health became responsible for hospital and casualty services in case of war, and planning on a mammoth scale began.

It was believed that the country would suffer enormous casualties through air raids quite apart from those sustained by the armed forces in any sphere of battle. The Ministry of Health conducted a survey to establish the available hospital facilities throughout the country. Reading was regarded as a 'safe area', unlikely to suffer aerial bombardment. As part of a national scheme, the town was notified that in the event of war it would receive some 400 patients to be evacuated from London hospitals, besides 25,000 children and non-combatants.

An Emergency Hospital Scheme (E.H.S.), also known as the Emergency Medical Service (E.M.S.) was prepared whereby hospitals in each region were grouped together and graded according to the type of work they could undertake in time of war. A corps of salaried doctors was formed who would be available to serve anywhere in the country as needed and a Civil Nursing Reserve was established which included untrained volunteers known as 'nursing auxiliaries'. A central Medical War Committee was set up with local committees to monitor the supply of doctors to the armed forces and to the hospitals. Hospital officers were appointed to co-ordinate the work in the regions. In the hospitals themselves plans were made to have beds available for immediate occupation in case of emergency for both civilian and service casualties. By the time war was declared the E.M.S. had been fully organised and the Royal Berkshire Hospital had agreed to participate in the scheme. Assurances had been given that this would not affect its administration in any way. By September 3rd, 1939 the Hospital had received 166 of the 400 London patients evacuated to Reading and the town itself began to receive the thousands of evacuees it had been warned to expect.

Externally the Hospital took on a new look. Strapping was put on windows; sandbags, later replaced by blast-proof walls, protected the front entrance and ground-floor windows; the word 'Berkshire' was obliterated from the front of the building so that no useful information could be gained by enemy agents. The question of camouflaging the roof was discussed with the R.A.F.

Inside the Hospital the problems of obtaining an efficient blackout were immense. Some windows were painted over and others were covered with thick curtains. Lights were dimmed and covered with dark shades. The lack of light and ventilation was found particularly trying.

Instructions were given to patients and staff on safety measures to be taken in case of air raids. Special protection was given to the glass roof of the general theatres. Tonsil operations were temporarily abandoned as the tonsil wards were situated in a vulnerable position above the Aural Theatre. All patients unable to wear gas masks or recovering from anaesthetics were transferred to Huntley and Palmer and Albert Wards, both of which had now been made gas proof. All radium treatment was stopped and the Hospital's supply of radium was sent to Mount Vernon Hospital for safe keeping.

A special Hospital A.R.P. Committee had been formed under the Steward, Mr Richards, as Air Raid Warden. He was in charge of sandbagging and also supervised the squads of porters and works staff who had been instructed in fire fighting. Regular blackout patrols were organised and during air raid alerts fire-watching duties were carried out using first the tonsil wards above the Aural Theatre as a watch post and later a spotter's tower, specially constructed on the roof of Nuffield Block.

All thoughts of celebrating the Hospital's centenary which had been planned for October 11th, 1939, had to be abandoned. The opening of the new Nuffield Block and Nurses' Home by Princess Alice the previous July would be the only reminder of that notable anniversary. Instead, the Hospital was working under greatly changed conditions, ever alert to the possibility of air raids and the casualties they might produce.

Under the E.M.S. scheme the Hospital had agreed to make 100 beds available for military and air-raid casualties. Of these 80 were to be kept empty and ready for emergency use and the other 20 would be capable of being vacated at short notice. The Ministry of Health would pay the Hospital for the 100 beds made available whether in use or not. Additional payments would be received when the beds were occupied. After much rearranging it was eventually decided that Benyon Ward would be kept available for air-raid casualties and other beds in the old building would be used for E.M.S. cases in preference to the new Nuffield Block.

Besides service patients and civilian casualties, the E.M.S. scheme included the provision of treatment for the police, auxiliary services and school children evacuated from London. As well as paying the Hospital for all these categories the Ministry of Health also arranged that the medical staff attending them would receive payments for treating both in-patients and out-patients. By the end of 1939 some 140 service patients had been treated and £5,040 received by the Hospital from the Government towards the E.M.S. scheme. This arrangement was to prove both lucrative to the Hospital and useful to its honorary medical staff, who would now receive a small but regular income.

In addition to providing facilities for the E.M.S. patients and treating the normal population of the area, the Hospital was also looking after the innumerable people who had been evacuated to the district. Within eighteen months the population of Reading had increased by almost 50 per cent and the strain on the Hospital's resources was considerable. Apart from children evacuated by the Ministry of Health under the E.M.S., others were voluntary evacuees who had left London with their parents. In addition various Government departments had been sent to Reading, and the B.B.C. monitoring service had established itself at Caversham Park. Factories were turning over to war work and increasing in size as they took on extra staff. Ordnance depots were established at Burghfield and Theale and the Phillips and Powis aircraft factory at Woodley expanded beyond recognition, eventually becoming Miles Aircraft Ltd and employing several thousand workers.

The Almoner's Department was overwhelmed with additional administrative procedures, sorting out who was liable to pay for whom, filling in forms for the special records now needed by the Government and Army authorities and making arrangements for convalescent patients and the supply of surgical appliances. All this was in addition to the usual flow of contributory and non-contributory patients and the various groups for whom payment was made by the local authorities. The Almoner's Office in the out-patients' waiting hall was extended to accommodate this vast increase in paper work and additional staff were recruited.

Many of the 166 patients from the London hospitals were soon transferred to other institutions. This enabled more local patients to be admitted, and the opening of the four wards in the Nuffield Block later in 1939 eased the pressure on admissions. However, with 80 E.M.S. beds kept unoccupied this was still insufficient and by the end of 1939 less than 250 of the 327 beds in the main Hospital were available. A waiting list of over 500 resulted.

Mr C. B. Baxter, the Senior Honorary Surgeon, and Dr H. Parry Price, the Honorary Anaesthetist, were called up within weeks of war being declared. Members of the non-medical staff including an ambulance driver, three stokers and the window cleaner were soon to follow. A great shortage of domestic and laundry staff developed. On the wards, auxiliary nurses and V.A.D.s belonging to the British Red Cross Society and the St John Ambulance Association were providing much-needed additional help. Members of the Red Cross were also helping in the Out-patients Department canteen and the St John Ambulance Association was providing stretcher bearers.

It had been agreed with the B.M.A. that any appointments to the honorary medical staff would be considered temporary appointments for the duration of the war. Under this heading Dr Ruth Plimsoll was appointed Assistant Anaesthetist, Mr A. H. Hooper and Mr F. E. Wheeler Assistant Obstetricians and Gynaecologists. Mr Wheeler was also appointed Surgical Registrar in place of Mr Elliot-Smith who had accepted the post of acting Assistant Surgeon at the Radcliffe Infirmary shortly after war was declared.

Dr Fidler was appointed a full-time Anaesthetist under the E.M.S. scheme at a salary of £250 a year, paid by the Ministry of Health. Mr J. L. Griffiths was appointed to the new post of Emergency Surgical Officer (E.S.O.) created in view of the casualties that were anticipated and 'to ensure the maximum efficiency in dealing with them'. The E.S.O. was put in charge of the other eight Residents and in 1940 this title was changed to Resident Surgical Officer (R.S.O.). To strengthen the orthopaedic facilities and the links between the Hospital and the Wingfield Morris Hospital in Oxford, Professor G. R. Girdlestone was appointed Consulting Adviser to the Orthopaedic Department.

Special arrangements were made by the medical staff to organise the surgical work of the Hospital. Two firms (teams) were formed, one under Mr Hooper and Mr Wheeler and the second under Mr Aitken Walker and Mr Bohn. Emergency surgical duties were arranged to provide a complete seven-day cover. The surgical lists were growing rapidly and in September 1939 it was noted that one operating session in the general theatres started at 8.50 a.m. and continued until 7.30 a.m. the following morning. An additional porter was engaged so that there would always be one on duty continuously in the theatres during operations. By the end of the year, when the children's and maternity wards had been transferred to the Nuffield Block, tonsils operations were resumed with those children now being admitted to King Edward Ward.

The great increase in work affected all departments but especially those dealing with children and maternity cases. The Orthoptic Department met the demand by remaining open every day besides continuing its evening sessions for adults. The X-ray and Pathological Departments also recorded a considerable increase in their work. The blood donors' register had increased to 180 names through much publicity and press advertising and by the end of 1939 an emergency donors' register of some 1,576 people had been established.

One side effect of the blackout was a great increase in motor accidents. With no street lighting and greatly reduced apertures for the headlights, motorists were finding night driving extremely difficult. In June 1940 arrangements were made so that accidents in the east side of the Borough would be treated at the Hospital and those occurring on the west side would be taken to Battle Hospital.

Co-ordination of Hospital Services
The E.M.S. scheme brought about co-ordination of the local hospital

services never possible in pre-war days. A Hospital Officer, Dr Dykes, had been appointed by the Ministry of Health to oversee the work of the region. Dr Lambert, the Senior Honorary Physician, had been appointed Group Officer of the Reading area with authority among other things to transfer patients from one hospital to another. This would enable the Royal Berkshire, graded an A1 hospital, to make best use of its resources for treating acute medical and surgical cases. Green labels were attached to patients able to be moved to Battle Hospital and elsewhere, care being taken to explain the reason for their removal. Members of the surgical staff agreed to operate, if necessary, on cases in other hospitals. In 1940 the Oxford and Reading Groups were amalgamated under one Group Officer and Major General Sir Robert McCarrison took over from Dr Lambert.

The local Medical War Committee included both Dr Lambert and Mr Aitken Walker as representatives of the Hospital. All doctors up to the age of 41 were liable to be called up and this Committee, under the Central Medical War Committee in London, would review all applications for deferment, agree the levels of medical staffing at the various hospitals and arrange the transfer of medical officers between hospitals as required.

Quite independently of this, other moves to effect co-operation between the various hospitals were taking place which were to become increasingly significant in the next few years. In December 1939 Lord Nuffield established the Nuffield Provincial Hospitals Trust (N.P.H.T.) with an endowment of one million shares in Morris Motors Ltd. His interest in the Voluntary Hospitals had already been demonstrated to the Royal Berkshire Hospital with the gift of £30,000 to build the Nuffield Block and the donation of an iron lung earlier in the year. He was now keen to promote the recommendations of the Sankey Commission for the co-ordination of the work of the Voluntary Hospitals throughout the country on a regional basis under regional councils.

The Berks, Bucks and Oxon Regional Committee of the British Hospitals Association, set up as a result of the Cave Committee in 1921, had met regularly but its influence and effectiveness was limited. Lord Nuffield hoped the establishment of the Nuffield Provincial Hospitals Trust with its administrative and advisory councils and financial resources would help to bring about the regionalisation suggested by the Sankey Commission and would obtain the necessary co-operation of the various public health authorities.

In April 1940 the Berks, Bucks and Oxon Regional Hospitals Council was formed with representatives from the Nuffield Trust, the University of Oxford, the Ministry of Health, 37 Voluntary Hospitals and the five major local authorities of the three counties. Mr A. T. Loyd, President of the Royal Berkshire Hospital, was appointed Chairman. Funding of the work of the Regional Council would be obtained from local authority subscriptions and contributions from the N.P.H.T. Two advisory committees were formed, one medical and one administrative, besides three divisional councils grouped round the key hospitals of Oxford, Windsor, Aylesbury and Reading. The first Divisional Council was the already existing Oxford and District Joint Hospital Board which had been set up in 1935 and which the Royal Berkshire Hospital had agreed to join in August 1939. The second was the Bucks and East Berks Divisional Hospitals Council which consisted of the previously established South Bucks and East Berks Voluntary Hospitals Council. The third was the specially established Reading and District Joint Hospitals Council, based on the Royal Berkshire Hospital as the key hospital and including the Voluntary Hospitals of Newbury District and Cold Ash and the Cottage Hospitals at Frimley and Camberley, Henley, Odiham, Wallingford and Yateley. The four Hospital representatives on this Council were the Chairman of the Board of Management, the Chairman of the House Committee, the House Governor and Mr G. T. W. Cashell (Ophthalmic Surgeon). With the formation of this Council an administrative structure had been established which in a few years would be used to form the basis for the future development of a unified scheme of hospital services.

Financial Difficulties

By the spring of 1940 financial problems were once again confronting the Hospital. A decrease in income combined with the abnormal increase in prices, wages and the number of patients had produced a deficit of over £11,000. The Hospital property was used as security to obtain a bank overdraft and plans were made to close 107 beds, almost one third of the total. But before taking such a drastic step the Hospital approached the local authorities, invoking certain powers granted to them through the Public Health Act of 1936. This enabled the local councils to subscribe a sum equal to 1⅓d rate each year to the Voluntary Hospitals in their area. Through the newly established Regional Hospitals Council, the Berkshire County Council agreed to grant £6,000 under these powers, of which £5,000 was to be earmarked for the Royal Berkshire Hospital. The Reading Borough Council agreed to a similar grant of £1,000.

The Reading Borough Council decided, however, to require the Hospital to meet certain conditions for the acceptance of this money. They wanted more influence in the running of the Hospital, including the power of veto on some financial and administrative matters. This was considered totally unreasonable by the Hospital and 'an undue encroachment' upon its independent status. After much negotiation involving both the Regional Hospitals Council and the British Hospitals Association, the conditions were modified. The grants would be made in exchange for additional local authority representation of both the County and Borough Councils on the Board of Management and, for the first time, also on the House and Finance Committees. Financial necessity had made a significant inroad on the Hospital's independence. By the end of that year, the local authority grants in addition to the £19,012 received under the E.M.S. scheme and an increase in public support returned the Hospital to solvency. These local authority grants were received annually from that year onwards through

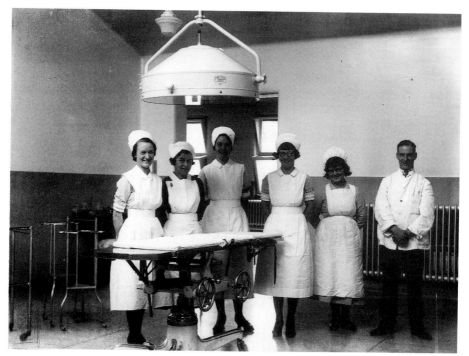

The Gynaecology Theatre, Nuffield Block

the Regional Hospitals Council. In 1945 over £7,000 was made available to the Hospital from this source.

Preparing for Bombardment

Overshadowing all the financial problems of 1940 was the deteriorating war situation. The advance of the German army through Europe with the evacuation of the British army from Dunkirk in May and the subsequent occupation of France left Britain isolated and preparing for invasion. The Hospital had been advised that it was unlikely Reading would receive military convoys. Instead it should make further preparation for the reception of air-raid casualties. The daylight raids of the German air force in the summer months of the Battle of Britain were followed throughout the winter by incessant night bombing of London and other cities. Even more people were arriving in the Reading area to escape the Blitz and the town itself was eventually declared closed to further incomers.

The Hospital air-raid precautions were reviewed and improved. A further 30 beds were made available at Blagrave, making 94 in all and, at the request of the Ministry of Health, a further 100 beds were provided at the Hospital, bringing the total to 417. At the same time in Nuffield Block the new Gynaecology Theatre, which for financial reasons had never been opened, was now equipped and brought into service on the urgent request of the medical staff and Hospital Officer. With the opening of additional

Top: The war-time Hospital; *Bottom*: Building the Decontamination Unit

surgical beds all possible theatre capacity was needed. Tonsil cases, if admitted, were to be transferred to the playroom of the children's ward with instructions to use the space in front of the Gynaecology Theatre in case of air raids. Additional emergency anaesthetic services were promised by eight local G.P.s and Dr H. Neville Smith was appointed temporary Assistant Casualty Officer (non-resident) at a rate of two and a half guineas per week.

The Ministry of Health had regionalised all the blood transfusion services in the country. Oxford, with a Regional Transfusion Officer, became the centre of the region incorporating the Reading area. Dr John Mills, the Hospital Pathologist, was in charge of the local blood transfusion service and through him was organised the bleeding of donors and the sending of blood to the Oxford depot for storage in the regional blood bank or for conversion to plasma. The British Red Cross Society and W.V.S. provided invaluable help in obtaining a regular supply of donors and local firms co-operated in allowing workers to attend to give their blood. Sir Robert McCarrison, the Group Officer, advised the appointment of an additional Resident under the E.M.S. scheme to assist with blood transfusions.

The Pathological Laboratory was experiencing a similar increase in work and in September 1940 it was agreed it should become part of the Emergency Public Health Service which had been organised by the Medical Research Council (M.R.C.). Dr E. H. Gillespie was appointed Bacteriologist, his salary of £500 being partly paid by a grant of £150 from the M.R.C.

In case of a gas attack, a Decontamination Unit was constructed in the Hospital forecourt, incorporating part of the old maternity ward in the East Wing. This was staffed by outside nurses under the direction of Dr May. It also became the headquarters of the Mobile First Aid Unit presented by the American Ambulance Association later in the year. A third use was made of the building in November when a weekly mass collection of blood from donors was arranged.

Other changes to the forecourt included a trench dug to house the inflammable materials usually kept in the Dispensary and also half the Hospital's supply of electric light bulbs. At the western end a public air-raid shelter was constructed capable of holding 200 people. The removal of the Hospital's railings and entrance gates the following year for the manufacture of munitions completed the war-time transformation of the exterior of the Hospital.

The Private Nursing Department, established over 60 years before, had gradually been run down and by August 1940, with only four elderly nurses remaining, it was agreed it should now be closed. Their work over the years had proved invaluable but in wartime conditions it was now impracticable to continue. Sister Skey was offered the post of Assistant Housekeeping Sister and the other nurses were given a pension of £1 a week to supplement their State spinster's pension of 10/-. The accommodation thus released above the eye wards could be used to house the Greenlands nurses, now in Melrose Villas. This building was converted, with the aid of £2,500 from Lord Nuffield, to provide ground-floor offices for the Contributory Scheme and two flats to be rented by Hospital employees. The former Contributory Scheme Offices at 2 Craven Road were then used by the Matron and senior nursing staff which released 4 Craven Road for additional staff accommodation.

Changes of a somewhat different nature took place when the Aliens War Service Department withdrew permission for three German nurses and Dr H. C. Simchowitz, the Radiotherapist, to work in the Hospital. Aliens would no longer be allowed to work at a hospital which provided treatment for members of H.M. Forces. Dr Simchowitz was subsequently interned and his position as Radiotherapist was taken by Dr Kerby, at a salary of £400 a year.

The Reading area was fortunate as it suffered few air attacks and the numerous emergency casualties the Hospital had been warned to expect had not materialised. On November 5th a bomb which landed near the Blagrave Branch Hospital only damaged the boiler house and caused no casualties. A time bomb some 30 feet away necessitated the temporary evacuation of 40 patients to the main hospital and this was conducted smoothly and efficiently. At the end of the year the Ministry of Health asked the Hospital to make arrangements for the evacuation of all the patients, staff and equipment at short notice 'should the necessity arise'. The threat of bombardment and invasion was not yet over.

The difficulties of 1939 and 1940 became even more acute in the following three years. Although the E.M.S. beds were reduced to 80 in February 1941, and the total beds in the Hospital reduced to 268 with another 74 at Blagrave, there was no decrease in the number of cases requiring admission and out-patient treatment. Food and petrol rationing, combined with the constant rise in costs and wages and the difficulty in obtaining sufficient staff, produced almost insuperable problems. The employment of maids from the Foundling Hospital in London had not proved satisfactory. In an endeavour to obtain more domestic staff, wages were increased from 7d to 9d an hour for full-time workers and 10d an hour for those on part-time. Application was made to the British Legion at Watlington House to see if porters could be obtained; the employment of conscientious objectors in this capacity was already in hand. An additional Assistant Almoner was appointed at £200 a year and a clerk at £2 5s a week. More clerical helpers and typists were required but were increasingly difficult to find. Great reliance was placed on the many voluntary helpers who were now helping in all capacities throughout the Hospital.

On the wards, Mr Bourne, the Church of England Chaplain and Mr Willis, the Free Church Chaplain, had been joined by Father R. E. Scantlebury, the newly appointed Roman Catholic Chaplain. In addition it had been agreed that officers of the Salvation Army should be given similar facilities for visiting patients to those of the clergy.

Gifts of all descriptions were still being sent by the public including thousands of eggs collected throughout the area during the Annual Egg Collection organised by Miss Benyon. The Ladies' Linen League continued its invaluable work and the Special Needs Committee was raising increasingly large sums through the Sunday Parade and Flag Days and other efforts. The League of Remembrance was providing thousands of dressings each year. The Hospital Ball, however, had been abandoned, the victim of rationing and the blackout.

No sooner had plans been approved for the emergency evacuation of the Hospital than a revised scheme was required for the reception of air-raid casualties. Mr Aitken Walker had visited Coventry in the aftermath of the bombing and learnt of the experiences of the hospitals there. This information, with that of arrangements made at the Radcliffe Infirmary and St Bartholomew's Hospital in London, provided the basis of the scheme to be adopted at the Royal Berkshire Hospital. Benyon Ward was equipped for the reception and resuscitation of casualties and would remain closed and ready for emergency use. An operating theatre and X-ray equipment were installed at the Blagrave Branch so that it could be used as a casualty clearing station and an overflow if needed for the main Hospital. An emergency water supply was installed and additional protective measures carried out, including the extension of the decontamination unit. The cost of this was met by the Ministry of Health. As an additional measure the Hospital would keep all upper-floor baths full of water each night.

Precautions of a different sort were taken with the disposal of the valuable medical books from the library to the safety of Bradfield College. In addition numerous specimens from the Hunterian collection belonging to the Royal College of Surgeons, which had been sent for safety to the Hospital, were now given to various members of the medical staff to provide a 'safer and more permanent storage place'.

In July 1941 the Reading Pathological Society celebrated its centenary. Since its formation in 1841 the Society had held practically all its meetings in the Hospital library. To mark this auspicious occasion the Board of Management presented the Society with the Hospital's notable collection of books. Among these were included those formerly belonging to the Reading Medical and Chirurgical Society which had been formed in Reading in 1824.

The Staffing Crisis

Nineteen forty-two was a year of crisis with medical staffing and financial problems. The entry of the United States into the war following the Japanese attack on Pearl Harbour in December 1941 had extended the sphere of hostilities and although the German attack on Russia had lessened the possibility of invasion, Britain was still undergoing aerial bombardment. For the first time the Ministry of Health and the Central Medical War Committee were requiring a reduction in Hospital staffing levels with greater mobility in order to meet the urgent needs elsewhere.

Dr Parry Price, the Honorary Anaesthetist, was released from military service for medical reasons in December 1941, but by the middle of 1942 he had resigned to take up another post. Dr Basil Hill was elected Honorary Anaesthetist in his place, his military call-up having been successfully deferred in view of the Hospital's urgent need of anaesthetists. With Dr Holden's resignation the previous year, only two Assistant Anaesthetists remained and the retention of the post of Resident Anaesthetist was now in question in view of the requested reduction in the number of Resident Medical Officers. The Hospital Officer had recommended a reduction of three and, in addition, the Central War Committee was imposing limitations on the period the various grades of R.M.O.s could be employed in the Hospital.

In April Professor Fraser, Director of the E.M.S., informed the Hospital that a further 1,200 medical men would need to be recruited by the end of the year. This in effect would mean the call up of practically all registered medical practitioners who were physically fit. A compromise was obtained over the number of R.M.O.s with the reduction of one being accepted. The duties of the House Surgeon to the special departments would be divided between the other two House Surgeons. The post of House Surgeon to the Pathology Department was not to be allowed. Instead, Dr Lynette Dowsett, formerly R.M.O. and Assistant Pathologist at the Blagrave Branch, was appointed Assistant Pathologist under the E.M.S. scheme at a salary of £500 a year. For the duration of the war she provided invaluable help to Dr Mills.

With the demobilisation of Mr C. B. Baxter in March, it was decided to proceed with the appointment of the Honorary Obstetrician and Gynaecologist and Honorary Assistant Obstetrician and Gynaecologist, which had been deferred since 1939. At the same time Dr Gordon Lambert retired and was made a Consulting Physician and Cardiologist. He had worked at the Hospital since 1913 when he had been appointed Medical Registrar, eventually succeeding Sir Stewart Abram as Senior Physician in 1923. For the past eight years he had been in charge of the Cardiological Department. It was particularly noted that 'he had visited the patients daily throughout his long association with the Hospital'. In May he was elected a Fellow of the Royal College of Physicians.

Dr Lambert's retirement produced an almost unprecedented number of changes in the honorary medical staff. It was agreed that in the present wartime conditions, candidates from outside the Hospital would be required to submit only six copies of their testimonials instead of the usual 65. Dr Le Marquand (Assistant Physician) was elected Physician and Dr Jennings (Medical Registrar) Assistant Physician. Mr Baxter (Surgeon) was elected Obstetrician and Gynaecologist and Mr Hooper (acting Assistant Obstetrician and Gynaecologist) Assistant Obstetrician and Gynaecologist. It was subsequently noted that Dr Stansfield had been an Assistant Physician for 15 years and, under the Hospital rules, should have automatically become a Physician. His resignation through ill health came before this was rectified and in May he was made a Consulting Physician.

Mr G. L. Bohn (Assistant Surgeon) was elected Surgeon in place of Mr Baxter and Mr F. E. Wheeler (Surgical Registrar) was elected Assistant Surgeon. Mr R. G. Reid was appointed Surgical Registrar and his post as Assistant Surgical Registrar was left vacant. Dr W. J. Tindall replaced Dr Jennings as Medical Registrar. In addition, Mr R. G. Hunt Williams was elected Assistant Aural Surgeon and Dr A. H. Price was made Medical Officer in charge of the Electro-therapy and Massage Department. Dr Bird would succeed Dr Lambert as the Medical Officer in charge of the Cardiological Department.

The Ministry of Health had meantime notified the Hospital that a list was required of medical staff who would be available for temporary transfer to other areas in case of emergency. This list was to include one physician, surgeon and anaesthetist, one member from both the Ophthalmic and Aural Departments and one Resident Medical Officer. Contingency plans were also to be made for the temporary transfer of 10 per cent of the nursing staff, one third of whom should be fully trained. Two nurses the previous year had been transferred under the E.M.S. scheme to work at Winchester. Independently of this, during the year four sisters and one staff nurse joined the Royal Nursing Service.

The call-up of experienced R.M.O.s combined with the recruitment of members of the honorary medical staff was to leave the Hospital greatly understaffed and overworked. The Central Medical War Committee would not sanction the appointment of an R.M.O. with previous experience to the Obstetrics and Gynaecology Department. The Blood Transfusion Officer had been called up and was replaced by a woman with a general science degree. By September Mr Cashell, Mr Wheeler and Mr Reid had all left for military service to be followed shortly by Dr Le Marquand and Mr Bohn. This loss of staff, particularly on the surgical side, would be sorely felt for the rest of the war.

Mr R. P. Brooks agreed to take charge of the Ophthalmic Department in Mr Cashell's absence. He and Mr Dorrell, the other Consulting Ophthalmic Surgeon, would be on call in emergencies. Mr R. Foster Moore, Consulting Ophthalmic Surgeon at St Bartholomew's Hospital, agreed to attend one day a week to operate. Of necessity the work of the Eye Department was greatly curtailed but that of the Orthoptic Department continued, although the training of students was suspended. Dr A. J. Reed of Peppard was appointed Clinical Assistant in the E.N.T. Department where Mr L. Powell, the Aural Surgeon, was now without his Assistant, Mr Hunt Williams. Through the co-operation of various local G.P.s the level of out-patient clinical assistance was maintained on a satisfactory level for the remainder of the war.

It was during this period that the enclosing of the ward balconies was started, prompted by the difficulties of blackout and the need to gain more space in the wards.

The Hospital nurses, 1943

Another Financial Crisis and the Bombing of Reading

In June 1942 the Revd H. W. G. Thursby resigned as Chairman of the Board of Management, a position he had held for nine years. Col C. B. Krabbé, the Treasurer, was elected the new Chairman and Mr H. H. Wilder was made Treasurer in his place. This change in office came at a most demanding and critical period of the Hospital's financial life. The total annual expenditure had risen by over 60 per cent since before the war, the staff had increased from 283 employed in 1938 to 407 in 1941, and the wages alone had increased from £23,638 to £38,700. Prices and wages were continuing to rise and the expenditure in 1942 was expected to be some £95,000. By the end of that year there was a deficit of £54,270 and no further help from the bank could be obtained. An appeal was launched and the public once again was asked to come to the help of the Hospital. If sufficient funds could be obtained it could resecure its property and stocks now being held against the overdraft and obtain financial security for the years ahead. A massive effort was made throughout the following year to realise this objective.

The events of Wednesday, February 10th, 1943 dramatically brought the work of the Hospital to the attention of the public. At 4.35 p.m. a lone German aeroplane within minutes dropped five bombs and strafed the town, leaving a trail of destruction, killing 41 people and injuring over 100 others. Of the 86 casualties taken to the Hospital, one was found dead on arrival, 42 were admitted to the emergency Benyon Ward and the remainder were treated in the Casualty Department. Altogether 31 cases required operations, including two amputations, and six people were so seriously injured that they required urgent blood transfusions.

A report of the event was given by Mr Aitken Walker who noted the 'fortunate chance' that both Mr Secretan and Dr Astley Cooper were in the Out-patients Department at the time helping with clinics. The plans so meticulously prepared for such an event swung into action. Three surgeons operated continuously and within seven and a half hours at 1.30 a.m. all the casualties had been dealt with, at 3.00 a.m. the reception ward was ready for further cases and by 10.30 a.m. the operating theatres were restocked for the normal daily sessions. All the Hospital supply of blood had been required and the following day the donors were recalled and the stock replenished.

The Hospital and staff were congratulated, the Mayor, in particular, thanking them for their services and the Regional Commissioner of the E.M.S. commended them for their efficiency. A meeting was held to discuss future arrangements in the light of the events of that night. In the words of Mr Aitken Walker: 'The experience has been very valuable and in the event of further raids we shall have greater confidence and . . . increased efficiency.' Fortunately such an occasion was not to be repeated.

Throughout 1943 outstanding efforts were made on behalf of the Hospital Appeal by individuals, groups, towns and villages alike. By August the required £54,270 had been raised. A Thanksgiving Ball was held on September 24th. On July 1st, 1944 the Bishop of Reading conducted a service in the chapel on the occasion of the dedication of 12 beds and 21 cots named in respect of donations made to the Debt Reduction Appeal. A tablet placed in the entrance hall records this notable fund-raising achievement, made all the more remarkable in view of the prevailing war-time conditions. The work of Mr H. H. Wilder, the Treasurer, and Mr B. Leaney the Hon. Secretary of the Appeal, was recorded in the inscription with 'lasting gratitude' in association with the generosity of the subscribers. The Hospital could now continue its work relieved of the anxiety of debt, high interest charges and insufficient funds. The Debt Reduction Appeal Committee would in future be known as the Hospital Appeal Committee, its objective now being to increase the income of the Hospital and to act as a liaison between it and the public.

Planning of the Post-War Hospital Services

Since 1939 much work had been undertaken on both national and regional levels to improve hospital and ancillary medical services. In spite of the war plans were also being made for their post-war development.

In October 1941 the Minister of Health, Ernest Brown, made a statement on post-war hospital policy. This aspect of the Ministry's work had been given added impetus by the pioneering work of the Nuffield Provincial Hospital's Trust (N.P.H.T.) and the formation of the various

Regional and Divisional Councils. The Minister announced that after the war a comprehensive hospital service would be available to everyone. No detailed plans had yet been made but central government funding to local authorities combined with patients' contributions was envisaged. Hospital 'areas' would be established which would be larger than those of the individual local authorities. The links between the Voluntary and Local Authority Hospitals would be 'placed on a more regular basis'. In the meantime the Ministry of Health would conduct a survey to obtain information on the existing hospital facilities, assess their adequacy in connection with future planning and advise on their co-ordination and possible expansion. The country was divided into ten areas and the work of the surveyors began.

The publication of the Beveridge Report in December 1942 cut right across all previous thinking on post-war hospital planning. National Insurance and National Health were to be inextricably linked. A much wider stage had now been set and the public debate that this produced, with the widely divergent views of the many parties concerned, was to occupy the medical profession, the hospitals and the politicians for several years to come. The vision of the Dawson Committee in 1920 for a comprehensive system of health care was to be combined with the complete re-shaping of the Insurance Act of 1911 to produce a National Health Service available to everyone, regardless of their means.

In March 1943 Professor Gask (Emeritus Professor of Surgery at London University and Chairman of the Regional Medical Advisory Committee), Mr Bevers (from the Radcliffe Infirmary and Chairman of the Regional Administrative Advisory Committee) and Professor R. H. Parry (Medical Officer for Bristol) visited the Royal Berkshire Hospital in connection with the Ministry of Health's survey of the hospital services in the Berks, Bucks and Oxon area. With the agreement of the Minister, this and many other provincial surveys were organised and financed by the N.P.H.T. and later published under the title *The Domesday Book of the Hospital Services*.

The conclusions of the Berks, Bucks and Oxon Survey differed little from those of other areas. The medical services were not adequate, the accommodation was often poor, the number of specialists, staff and beds too few. The surveyors' comments on the Royal Berkshire Hospital in particular were blunt and to the point:

> 'The buildings are antiquated and inadequate (with the exception of the new Nuffield Block and the Pathological Department). The number of beds is too small and in consequence the waiting lists are long. There are some good men on the medical staff, but they are too few and the appointments to the staff are not made in such a way as always to secure the best man for the post.'

The indignation of the Board of Management to this final point was predictable. Over fifty years before a similar criticism had been made in *The Lancet*. Little had changed in this respect in the intervening years.

Turning its attention to the second hospital in the town, the survey pointed out that Battle Hospital, belonging to the Borough Council, was the only general hospital in the survey area to have been built by the local authorities. Its 580 beds were available to residents of the Borough alone and of these 152 were used for the chronic sick and 270 were for public assistance cases. Since the war 155 of the latter had been used as E.M.S. beds. The survey described the hospital as 'not up to the standards of modern hospitals'. Its staff was small and: 'For specialist services the Hospital has to rely on the assistance of the staff at the Royal Berkshire Hospital.'

In conclusion the survey noted that Reading, 'an active growing town', was second only to Oxford as a medical centre in the region. Neither the Royal Berkshire Hospital nor the Battle Hospital sites were adequate for the needs of the present population. Future hospital facilities should 'provide most of the needs of the people in the area and for that purpose must be adequately staffed by specialists in most branches of medicine and surgery'. Medical and health centres would also be required, 'the services of which would radiate from the main hospital centre'.

While a National Health Service was being planned at Governmental level the Berks, Bucks and Oxon Regional Hospitals Council (R.H.C.) and its three Divisional Councils were undertaking two distinct but integrated types of work. The first was a series of investigations with recommendations into various aspects of hospital administration and medical treatment with a view to co-ordinating the services of the Region. The second was the formation of proposals for the development of the post-war hospital service in the Region. In 1943 the three Divisional Councils each appointed a planning committee. It was hoped that their work in association with the Regional Hospitals Council would produce proposals which could 'fit into the framework of a national scheme', thereby enabling 'much time to be saved at a later stage'. The work of these committees in 'assessing the available resources' and 'estimating the probable needs of the area' was greatly assisted by the mass of information obtained by the Survey conducted by the Ministry of Health.

Between this time and the advent of the N.H.S. in 1948, a remarkable amount of work was undertaken by the Regional Hospitals Council and its various committees. Their reports and recommendations were to play a most important role in the development of the work of the Royal Berkshire Hospital both before and after the formation of the N.H.S. Equally important was the fact that many members of their committees were the principal administrators and medical officers of the Hospital. Their influence was to become increasingly important in the years to come. Col J. Norman Walker, Mrs V. Benyon and Mr F. H. Aitken Walker were all members of the R.H.C. The Regional Administrative Advisory Committee included Mrs Benyon (Chairman of the Royal Berkshire Hospital House

Committee throughout the war), Dr H. S. Le Marquand (Senior Honorary Physician) and Mr H. E. Ryan (Royal Berkshire Hospital Secretary). The Regional Medical Advisory Committee included Dr Le Marquand and Mr G. T. W. Cashell (Ophthalmic Surgeon at the Royal Berks.). The 1943 *Report on the E.N.T. Services of the Region* was made with the advice of Mr L. Powell (Aural Surgeon, Royal Berkshire Hospital), that of the Ophthalmic Services was under the chairmanship of Mr Cashell and the report on *A Regional Orthopaedic Service* was made by Professor G. R. Girdlestone.

The changes made at the Hospital during this period reflected the work of these committees and incorporated many of their proposals, all of which would help in the standardisation and co-ordination of the hospital services of the Region. On the financial side a costing system was introduced in 1941 on the recommendation of the N.P.H.T. The out-patients' registration procedures were improved and an appointments system introduced in 1943. This was followed by a reorganisation of the work of the Almoner's office, some of its duties being transferred to the administrative staff. Plans were made for the improvement of the Out-patients Department and a grant of £1,000 obtained from the N.P.H.T. for this purpose. No progress could be made, however, until the necessary building licences were obtained from the Ministry of Works.

A Group Preliminary Training School was established at the Hospital in 1943 and for a time this was also attended by nurses from Battle Hospital. A 24-hour ambulance service was obtained through the services of the Mechanised Transport Corps in 1942. Their loan of an ambulance and driver in 1941 to supplement the work of the Hospital's ambulance had been gratefully accepted. They would now provide two ambulances and drivers at a cost of £6 a week. The Regional Council's hope of co-ordinating the ambulance service was not achieved but with the aid of a £200 grant an Ambulance Bureau was to be established at the Hospital in 1945.

On the medical side advice was obtained from the Nuffield Professor of Anaesthetics at Oxford University and a regular system of inspection of anaesthetics equipment was introduced. Wartime conditions, which prevented the implementation of change in several departments, had given impetus to developments in the Pathology Department. In 1943 it became an Area Laboratory under the Ministry of Health E.M.S. and branch laboratories were opened at Battle Hospital, Peppard Sanatorium and the Newbury and District Hospital. The Blood Transfusion Service was re-organised and the Reading Service incorporated with the Army Blood Transfusion Service.

In January 1944, following the resignation of Dr Gillespie on being appointed Pathologist at Rotherham, Dr Patrick Kidd was appointed Bacteriologist under the Emergency Public Health Laboratory Service, his salary of £900 per year being paid by the Medical Research Council. With the extension of his work to include the public health bacteriology in the county and the borough, plans were discussed for the extension of the Pathology Laboratory.

The Radiotherapy Department had not been so fortunate. Although a £1,000 grant from the N.P.U.T. in 1942 enabled the replacement of the obsolete superficial therapy plant, the work of the Department had to be suspended for a year. Dr Kerby, the Cancer Registrar and Radiotherapist, left to become Radiotherapist at the Royal Cancer Hospital, London in August 1943 and his replacement did not start work until September 1944.

The Psychiatric Department also had problems. For the first time beds had been made available for convulsive therapy under Dr Astley Cooper but within a year the clinic had to be closed temporarily when he was called up for military service.

In February 1944 the Government published its White Paper on the National Health Service. Its proposals concerning the Voluntary Hospitals met with instant criticism. Partial government funding without adequate representation on the administrative councils would not be approved. Sir Bernard Docker, the Chairman of the British Hospitals Association, quickly expressed its objections to the Minister himself. Within days the Hospital was faced with another problem when the Ministry of Health asked it to plan for a restriction on civilian admissions. Preparations were being made for the invasion of France and additional Service accommodation was required in anticipation of the heavy casualties that might be suffered. Over the following weeks the debate on the N.H.S. proposals

View from Alice Ward, 1944

coincided with a 50 per cent reduction in civilian beds and only the most severely ill could now be admitted. The Pathology Department organised a greatly increased supply of blood. On June 6th, the Allies landed in France. With D-Day the final phase of the war had begun.

The Last Year of the War
The limitation on civilian admissions was not completely withdrawn until October 1944, although more beds had been made available within a month of the invasion. In June and July the Hospital sent supplies of blood to the Winchester, Southampton and Portsmouth hospitals for the treatment of service casualties. Of the 700 servicemen admitted to the Hospital that year, few were directly connected with the landings in France. The resources made available at the Hospital had hardly been required and the casualties suffered in establishing the second front had not been as heavy as had been feared.

The debate on the National Health Service continued as the proposals contained in the White Paper were considered. The Board of Management, like those of other Voluntary Hospitals, was in agreement with the principle of a co-ordinated hospital and consultant service available to all. They could not agree, however, on the proposed financial and administrative arrangements which they believed would erode their independence and would be detrimental to both the Hospital and its patients. Concerted action through the British Hospitals Association, the Regional Council of the B.M.A. and local M.P.s was made to register these objections. The medical profession was equally unhappy with various aspects, particularly those concerning the abolition of private practice.

In the meantime the Regional and District Hospitals Council continued their work. The Post-war Planning Committee of the Reading and District Joint Hospitals Council, under the chairmanship of Mr Aitken Walker, published its interim report early in 1945. It believed provision should be made for a population of 300,000 in an area to include Reading, Bradfield, Wokingham, Henley, Newbury, Hungerford and Wallingford. There was a shortage of over 1,000 beds of every type including 782 beds for the acute sick. In Reading alone the present 524 acute beds should be doubled to 1,052; 800 surgical beds were needed and in addition 75 obstetric beds should be provided. A medical staff of 79 would be required. For comparison, the Hospital at that time with 411 beds had a medical staff of 39, of whom only the eight Resident Officers, four Pathologists and one Radiographer were employed full-time. Included in the Interim Report were three others covering 'Proposed Future Anaesthetic Service of the Reading Division', by Dr Basil Hill (the needs of the Reading, Newbury, Henley and Wallingford Hospitals were all considered), the 'Scheme for a Comprehensive Radiological Service' by Dr Cave and a 'Pathological Service' by Dr J. Mills. Whatever the outcome the hospital services and staff of the district would need to be increased beyond all recognition.

Acute staff shortages dogged the Hospital for the rest of the war. The

Ministry of Labour refused to direct labour to institutions which did not adopt the scale of wages recommended by the Hetherington Committee. This required additional expenditure of £2,000 a year. The acceptance of the Rushcliffe Report on nurses' salaries and conditions of service would cost a further £6,000. Additional staff would be needed to implement the 96-hour fortnight, 28 days paid leave and the minimum of one complete day off each week. At that time this just could not be achieved. Many nurses were not completing their training and advertisements for midwives offering high salaries did not produce a single reply. This resulted in further delays in opening all the maternity accommodation in Nuffield Block with little chance in proceeding with plans to obtain the additional beds now needed. Waiting lists had soared, and by the end of 1944 nearly 800 people were awaiting admission besides a further 490 tonsils cases.

During this period of debate and speculation two valuable developments took place within the Hospital: the provision of rehabilitation treatment in association with the Physiotherapeutic Department and the renewal of discussions on the formation of a cancer centre in Reading.

In 1943 Dr Henry Price had laid the foundation of a rehabilitation service after visiting Horton Hospital in Epsom. The Department Sister took a course there to study the methods and on her return physical exercises were introduced to the patients at both the Hospital and Blagrave Branch. The introduction of this treatment was noted as producing 'most satisfactory' results, enabling patients in many instances to shorten their period of convalescence. Financial constraints prevented the introduction of all the types of treatment wanted but in October 1944 Mrs H. Davies was appointed the first Physical Training Instructor at a salary of £280 a year and in January 1945 Miss M. Cleave was appointed the first Occupational Therapist at a salary of £250 a year.

Plans for a Cancer Centre
Plans for the establishment of a cancer centre at Reading under the Cancer Act of 1939 had been shelved due to the war and it was not until the autumn of 1943 that the subject was raised again. At that time all the Hospital's supply of radium was still in store at Mount Vernon Hospital, and with no replacement for Dr Kerby the Department was without a Radiotherapist and temporarily closed.

Early in 1944 a meeting was arranged through the Medical Advisory Committee of the Regional Hospitals Council to discuss the organisation of the radiotherapy services of the area. A representative from the Ministry of Health attended as well as representatives of all the key hospitals, including Dr Cave on behalf of the Royal Berkshire Hospital. It was noted that the departments at both the Radcliffe Infirmary and the Royal Berkshire Hospital were closed. The former had a medical officer but no apparatus, the latter had apparatus but no medical officer.

Following this meeting a sub-committee made recommendations to the Medical Advisory Committee which were immediately adopted by the

R.H.C. Cancer centres should be established at Oxford and Reading. Suggestions were made concerning their organisation, the number of machines, technicians and beds which would be needed to provide the service required in the area.

In March 1944 Dr Joyce Mulvany, second Chief Assistant in the Radium Department at St Thomas's Hospital, was appointed Radiotherapist at the Royal Berkshire Hospital. Before starting work in September she underwent four months' work at the Christie Hospital and Holt Radium Institute in Manchester. Mr Forder, the Radiographer, also spent several weeks at the Christie Hospital studying mould-room techniques. With the appointment of a part-time physicist, Mr C. C. Butler (Demonstrator in Physics at Reading University) at £100 a year, a night Radiographer and a full-time Secretary, the Department was now in a position to resume its work.

In October 1944 a new KX 10 Superficial Therapy Unit was installed and at the same time the Hospital's supply of radium was returned from Mount Vernon Hospital. While this was being reloaded the treatment of cancer was continued with the loan of 171 milligrammes of radium from the Radium Commission. With the return of the radium in new platinum containers, with each needle giving an even dosage along its length, the Hospital became the first in England to have its stock brought completely up to date.

In parallel with these events, plans were being made to extend the recommendations of the 1944 Committee to enable a co-ordinated cancer service to be provided for a much larger area. The Radium Commission believed such a Cancer Region should be based on a teaching hospital and serve an area of at least two million people. By including Northampton with Oxford and Reading such a Region could be established with Oxford as its centre. Representatives of the Northampton General Hospital, the County and Borough Councils of Northampton were co-opted to the Regional Hospitals Council for matters concerning cancer treatment.

The Medical Advisory Committee of the Regional Hospitals Council formed a new committee to report on a 'cancer service for Berks, Bucks, Northants and Oxon' under the chairmanship of Professor Gask. Among its 24 members were Mr Aitken Walker and Dr Joyce Mulvany. Its report was published in 1945 in association with the N.P.H.T. It covered the existing services in the Region, those needed to provide a central organisation of the cancer services, noting the place of the G.P.s, diagnostic and preliminary investigative centres, pathological services, records and transport as well as radiotherapy treatment.

The Royal Berkshire Hospital at Reading with Oxford and Northampton would provide the three centres in the extended Region. Every facility of the Radiotherapy Department at the Hospital would have to be increased. The 321 milligrammes of radium (plus the 171 milligrammes on loan) should be increased to 555 milligrammes. The two sets of equipment should be doubled to four. The existing staff of a senior radiotherapist, part-time physicist, radiographer and secretary should be enlarged to include a junior radiotherapist, a full-time physicist, a house surgeon, sister and three technicians. In addition 25 hospital beds and 15 hostel beds should be provided. At that time there was none. In the short term, 1,690 sq. feet of space was needed and in the long term 5,781 sq. feet.

The report was sent to the Minister of Health for consideration. In the meantime the Radium Commission, in recognising the Hospital as a centre for the treatment of cancer, emphasised the urgency for increased space for the Radiotherapy Department. Plans were prepared and approved for a new block of buildings behind the existing Department. This would be used temporarily by the Radiotherapy Department and eventually would become part of a new Out-patients Department. It would include an operating theatre, mould room, physics department and three treatment rooms. The cost would be £8,100. The stage was now set for the formation of a cancer region with the Royal Berkshire Hospital performing an important role in the co-ordinated service. Unfortunately wartime conditions and building restrictions were to delay the implementation of these plans.

In the autumn of 1944 the long-awaited building licence was obtained for carrying out the alterations so urgently needed to the Out-patients Department. A special Almoner's Office was built adjoining the west wing to correspond to the permanent part of the decontamination centre in the east wing. The archway leading from the forecourt to Redlands Road was filled in to provide additional clerical and clinical records offices. By January 1945 the work had been completed and the increased space created for the out-patients' clinics was to prove of great assistance.

Among other developments of the period was the transfer to lay hands of the housekeeping and Matron's secretarial appointments formerly held by members of the nursing staff. A Food Services Sub-committee was formed, a Catering Officer and later a fully qualified Dietitian were appointed. Following an inspection by the Ministry of Health, it was recommended that patients should not be disturbed earlier than necessary and breakfast should be served after 7.30 a.m. The request of the Women's Institute some 20 years before had at last been granted.

Probably the most important event of all was the arrival of penicillin. Discovered by Sir Alexander Fleming in 1928, this miraculous antibiotic was developed clinically by Professor Florey and Edward Chain at Oxford University during the war. By 1943, with American help, supplies were first made available to the services. Its use for civilian cases was not sanctioned until later in the war when modest supplies were made available to Dr Mills, the Pathologist, for distribution. Although enquiries were made in December 1944 about its use for the treatment of syphilis and general and surgical cases, it was not until March 1945 that increased supplies became more readily available for civilian use. Another milestone in the treatment of infection had been reached.

Following the death of Dr Norman May in June 1944, Dr L. M. Jennings (Assistant Physician) was elected Honorary Physician and Dr G. B. Mitchell-Heggs, Physician in charge of the Dermatological Department. As Dr Mitchell-Heggs was still on active service, Dr E. D. Page assumed responsibility for the Department in his absence. No second Assistant Physician was appointed. In January 1945 Mr Conrad Latto was appointed Resident Surgical Officer. The appointment of an F.R.C.S. to this post led to the Board of Management agreeing that the salary should now be increased from £250 to £400 a year, rising to £550. In February 1945 the reservation of Benyon Ward for air-raid casualties was withdrawn and two months later the E.M.S. beds were reduced to 50 in number. The war was nearly over.

The surrender of the German army in May 1945, followed by that of Japan in September, brought peace once again. For almost six years the Hospital had worked in extremely difficult circumstances, but as in the First World War, with the great support of the public, it had risen to every challenge. The E.M.S. had introduced a co-ordination of hospital services never possible before the war. The proposals for a National Health Service combined with those of the Regional Hospitals Council were offering an exciting, demanding and much wider concept of the Hospital's role than ever previously considered. The return of peace would herald the radical changes envisaged but never implemented a quarter of a century before.

9

TOWARDS
THE APPOINTED DAY

Within weeks of the German surrender a general election had been called for July. No National Health Service Bill had been drafted by Winston Churchill's wartime coalition government and the proposals contained in the White Paper, even with amendments, envisaged a scheme of alarming administrative complexity. The incoming Labour Government under Clement Attlee, with Aneurin Bevan the Minister of Health, was left to reassess the situation and produce a workable alternative.

The National Health Service Bill of March 1946 embodied the earlier amended proposals within a much simplified administrative structure. The Voluntary Hospitals and their honorary medical staffs were reassured by the changes and the former danger that the needs of the patient would become subservient to those of administration had, it was hoped, been avoided. In December 1946 the Bill became law and the 'Appointed Day' for the Act to come into operation was fixed for July 5th, 1948.

Under the National Health Service Act a system of comprehensive medical care, free 'at the point of delivery', would be available to everyone regardless of their means. All hospitals, including voluntary, municipal and public assistance institutions, with their equipment, would be nationalised. The Minister of Health would become responsible for hospital and specialist services including blood transfusion and public health laboratories.

Health centres, clinics and domiciliary services would be adminis-tered by County and Borough Councils. Executive Councils would assume responsibility for general practitioner, dental and pharmaceutical services.

Hospital services would be organised through the establishment of Regional Hospital Areas. Each would be associated with a university medical centre and be administered by a Board appointed by the Minister of Health. These Regional Boards in turn would appoint Hospital Management Committees (H.M.C.) responsible for groups of hospitals, and House Committees would be formed within these groups. All staff would be employees of the Regional Board, those of consultant or specialist status would be appointed by the Board itself, the remainder by the H.M.C.s. Consultants would choose to be either full-time or part-time employees.

The Hospital, June 1945

The hospitals would be funded by the Government from block grants to the Regions. The provisions of the separate National Insurance Act would enable part of the revenue to come through national insurance contributions which would also provide pensions, sickness and unemployment benefit. The remainder of the N.H.S. funding would come from the Exchequer through general taxation. Except at Teaching Hospitals, all hospital endowments would be pooled and allocated to the appropriate Regional Board. Gifts and legacies would still be received, though not for use on maintenance. Two types of pay beds would be available: amenity beds, providing free service with a charge for additional comforts, and private beds for which both treatment and accommodation would be charged.

In the first three difficult post-war years the Hospital strove to resume its peacetime work until the advent of the National Health Service. Uncertainty combined with alarm for the Hospital's future gave way to the necessity for developing its services and effecting a smooth transfer on the appointed day.

It was a year before all the external evidence of the war was removed from the Hospital and the public air-raid shelters and blast-proof walls were dismantled. It was almost eighteen months before all the medical staff returned from military service. Mr Wheeler had been mentioned in dispatches and awarded an M.B.E. for his work with the Field Service in

Italy. Dr Le Marquand, as the only neurologist in the area, had been greatly missed while on active service. In his absence, his book *Endocrine Disorders in Childhood and Adolescence*, written with Dr Tozer, had been published in spite of the paper shortage. In 1946 he was elected a Fellow of the Royal College of Physicians. At home Mr Secretan, who had come out of retirement to help in the Surgical Out-patients Department in the latter years of the war, was presented with a silver salver and thanked for his great help.

Retirements resulted in many changes. Mr Hooper succeeded Mr Baxter in 1946 when he became a Consulting Obstetrician and Gynaecologist. The following year Mr Hooper himself retired and was succeeded by Mr F. E. Wheeler. This lead to the appointment of Mr R. G. Reid and Mr C. Latto as Honorary Assistant Surgeons, the post of Surgical Registrar being left vacant. On his retirement after 20 years Mr D. T. G. Dickens was made a Consulting Dental Surgeon and was succeeded by Mr H. M. Archibald in 1947. Dr Ogden, the Medical Superintendent of the Berkshire Mental Hospital, took over Dr Astley Cooper's work in the Psychiatric Department.

Miss Mutimer, Matron for ten years, was succeeded in 1945 by Miss K. I. Cawood, formerly Matron of the General Hospital in Birkenhead. At the Blagrave Branch Miss A. L. Reynolds was succeeded by Miss W. J. Pavier. The work of both Matrons during the war years had been especially difficult and Miss Mutimer in particular had earned the high appreciation of the Board of Management with her organisation of the main hospital. Mr Goss, the Chief Pharmacist, retired after 38 years and was succeeded by Mr E. A. Burton, his Deputy. All had worked tirelessly in their various capacities and were thanked for their valuable services.

In November 1944 the death had been announced of Mr A. T. Loyd, Lord Lieutenant of Berkshire, Chairman of the Berks, Bucks and Oxon Regional Hospitals Council and President of the Hospital since 1935. His great service to the Hospital in those nine years would be sadly missed. It was not until July 1945, with the election of Mr H. A. Benyon, the new Lord Lieutenant of Berkshire, that the office was filled again. Mr Benyon had been a Trustee since 1923 and a Vice President since 1935. He was the fourth member of his family to hold this office. The name was synonymous with service to the Hospital since its foundation.

In September 1946 the E.M.S. beds were reduced to 40 in number. During this period, far from returning to normal the Hospital, like all others, was suffering the most severe shortage of domestic and nursing staff ever experienced. In the laundry alone 12 of the 25 jobs remained unfilled. By June 1946 one third of the beds had been closed, all tonsils operations suspended and the waiting list had risen to over 1,000 with another 400 on the tonsils list. Benyon Ward had never reopened since its release as a casualty ward at the end of the war. The eye wards had been closed in July 1945 and were not to reopen for over a year. In the meantime patients requiring admission were referred to the Oxford Eye Hospital or the Royal Eye Hospital in London. The closure of Huntley and Palmer Ward enabled the Preliminary Training School to move in temporarily, thereby easing the congestion at 'The Lindens' in Craven Road.

A concerted drive on a national level was made to encourage the recruitment of nurses. With such a shortage it was impossible to implement the 96-hour fortnight and the lack of domestic staff was resulting in many nurses having to carry out additional non-nursing jobs. National standards of pay and working conditions to cover domestic and allied staff were gradually being introduced through the formation of the National Joint Council, and through the Joint Negotiating Committee to cover almoners, pharmacists, physiotherapists and radiographers. The Rushcliffe Committee's recommendation would cover the nurses and midwives. A fully trained staff nurse would be paid £120 rising to £180 per year; a ward sister £160 rising to £260; enrolled nurses £90 to £160. For the student nurse the 96-hour fortnight would include time spent on lectures and tutorials.

The Ministry of Labour's 'Nursing Campaign' started in Berkshire in the autumn of 1946. In the meantime a nursing exhibition had been arranged at Heelas, the Reading department store, with the Hospital showing a theatre unit, fracture beds and demonstrating drip saline treatment. Further exhibitions, films and circulars were used to encourage recruitment and gradually the numbers began to rise. Although 32 additional nurses had been obtained by the end of the year another 90 were still needed and 100 beds remained closed. The employment of part-time nurses enabled Albert Ward to be re-opened as a tonsils ward in the spring of 1947. Miss Cawood's recruitment of twelve part-time nurses to do the work of four full-time nurses, employed entirely on one ward, was believed to be the first time such an experiment had been tried. The use of part-time nurses throughout the Hospital was invaluable to keep the services running until sufficient full-time nurses could be obtained. By the appointed day the number of nurses had risen to almost 200.

With the implementation of the 96-hour fortnight more nurses and additional accommodation would be needed. There was already pressure on accommodation for the Preliminary Training School and at the end of 1946 the Hospital accepted an offer to lease part of Joyce Grove at Nettlebed. During the war this large house had been used by St Mary's Hospital, Paddington, and the Westminster Hospital for their Preliminary Training Schools. As the Westminster no longer needed these facilities the Hospital was able to move the Senior Sister Tutor and 17 student nurses to their new accommodation in March 1947. At the same time the Ministry of Pensions Hospital at Stoke Mandeville became affiliated with the Royal Berkshire Hospital and during the following year 16 of their nurses received training there. Additional accommodation was obtained for 11 staff nurses at 56 London Road, purchased for £3,000 in June 1947, and the following month Orwell House in Craven Road was obtained for £6,500. Plans were also prepared for the extension of the Nurses' Home.

As the E.M.S. was gradually run down, arrangements were made by the Government to enable those Voluntary Hospitals in financial difficulty to receive grants to tide them over until the appointed day. The hospital survey had pinpointed the need for modernisation, expansion and long-term planning. It was essential that this should not be unnecessarily delayed in the period of transition. The payment of visiting and specialist medical staff should be continued and the development of services should not be shelved through lack of funds. When the Hospital's own capital funds had been exhausted the Government would provide financial support.

The E.M.S. scheme had provided the honorary medical staff with a small but regular income. In addition, payments received on behalf of the various local authority patients had increased with the implementation of the 1944 Education Act. There was, however, great reluctance on the part of the honorary medical staff to accept Government reimbursement in lieu of their E.M.S. payments and only three were prepared to receive an honorarium in respect of their services before July 5th, 1948. Dr S. F. Logan Dahne, with his decision in 1947 to dissolve his private practice, specialise in aural surgery and accept a temporary post as Assistant Aural Surgeon at a salary of £800 a year, was the first member of the honorary medical staff to break from one system to another. His appointment was also the first to be made with the help of a specially appointed 'assessor' working in conjunction with the Elective Committee. With reluctance the honorary medical staff and Board of Management had accepted the criticism of the Ministry of Health's survey and agreed to a method of appointment more in tune with the times.

By the end of 1946 the Elective Committee had confirmed as permanent those temporary appointments made during the war. However, Dr Basil Hill, whose call-up had been deferred throughout the war, was told to enlist for military service in 1947. His position as Honorary Anaesthetist was temporarily filled by Dr T. R. M. Bristow, one of the three Honorary Assistant Anaesthetists.

The return of medical practitioners from the forces prompted the Hospital to run refresher courses for G.P.s at the various clinics and in addition a series of two-week post-graduate courses was arranged. Oxford University had inaugurated a special scheme of post-graduate education for medical officers released from the forces. Through this the Hospital was able to obtain specialist trainees whose salaries of £1,000 a year were paid by the Ministry of Health. With the appointment of Dr J. J. Kempton, M.B.E., Assistant in the Medical Dept., Mr T. Rowntree, Accident Room Surgeon, Dr K. Bryn Thomas, Anaesthetist and Dr J. A. Rankin, Assistant Radiologist, a new group of salaried medical staff had arrived.

Plans for the Post-War Hospital
Plans had been drawn up in 1945 to meet the most immediate needs of the post-war hospital. Top priority was the erection of a block of buildings in which the Radiotherapy Department would be temporarily housed. These

buildings would eventually form part of the new Out-patients Department for which plans had been made before the war. This and the modernisation of Benyon and Sidmouth wards were the most urgent needs at that time. Difficulty in obtaining the necessary licence, however, deferred the start of the work until March 1947 and constant delays resulted in the building not being completed before the appointed day.

Other improvements were also required and a list was drawn up for approval by the Ministry of Health. Plans for increased accommodation for the nurses providing 104 additional bedrooms and a new building for the Preliminary Training School; extension to the nurses' dining-room; long overdue improvements to the West Ward block; the provision of four prefabricated huts for the ophthalmic, otolaryngological, gynaecological and physiotherapeutic out-patients' clinics as well as another hut for the Orthoptic Department were all approved. This last was particularly needed as the Orthoptic School and Clinic were now temporarily housed in the old Decontamination Centre. Disbanded during the war, the School was re-established in 1946 as a Joint School of Orthoptics run in conjunction with the Oxford Eye Hospital and sharing the services of a full-time Orthoptist. Delays prevented all but the orthoptic hut and the extensions to the nurses' dining-room (started in February 1948) being undertaken at this time. Other plans, including extensions to the Pathology Laboratory, desperately short of space with its newly created Haematology Department, were not considered sufficiently urgent to warrant the Ministry of Health's approval.

Developments not requiring structural changes were also taking place. A hearing-aid clinic was established by Mr Hunt Williams and agreement obtained for the appointment of an audiometrician to be trained in London. Branch ophthalmic clinics at the Newbury, Wallingford and Henley Hospitals were formed, thus carrying out some of the recommendations of Mr Cashell's Committee of 1943. Additional medical and technical staff were obtained for most departments although the appointment of a full-time electro-cardiographer and also a clinical photographer was deferred for the time being. The first Home Visitor was appointed part-time at a salary of 50/– a week attached to the Almoner's Department. The Radiotherapy Department, with plans of expansion when the new building was completed, had to close for several months between the resignation of Dr Mulvany in November 1946 and the appointment of Dr W. G. Evans in April of the following year. In all departments more up-to-date equipment was obtained, the new X-ray and deep-therapy apparatus being especially expensive.

The peace-time ambulance service had been greatly improved through the establishment in 1945 of the Ambulance Bureau which provided 24-hour cover. The presentation the same year of a 26 h.p., four-stretcher Austin ambulance by the American Ambulance Association of Great Britain improved the quality of the transport. With the sale of the old Morris ambulance for £100, the 1939 Austin ambulance and the American ambulance would now provide the Hospital's ambulance service until this was taken over by the local Health Authority under the N.H.S.

The voluntary car pool, organised by the W.V.S. during the war, ended in July 1945. In its place a Hospital Car Service was formed by the British Red Cross Society, the St John Ambulance Brigade and the W.V.S. This provided transport for sitting patients at a charge of 3d (later raised to 6d) a mile. The Hospital paid any charges not recovered from patients.

Work began on establishing the boundaries of the proposed Hospital Regions as soon as the N.H.S. Bill became law in December 1946. Reading would be in the Oxford Region, based on the City of Oxford with its University Medical Centre. The Region would include the counties of Berkshire, (with the exception of the Boroughs of Maidenhead and New Windsor, the Rural Districts of Cookham, Easthampstead and Windsor), Buckinghamshire, (with the exception of the Boroughs of High Wycombe and Slough, the Urban Districts of Beaconsfield, Chesham and Marlow and the Rural Districts of Amersham, Eton and Wycombe), and the whole of Oxfordshire and Northamptonshire including the Boroughs of Northampton, Oxford and Reading. These boundaries were almost identical to those recommended by the Berks, Bucks and Oxon Regional Hospitals Council. Of the eight Districts to be formed within the Region, the Reading District would be the largest, extending to Henley, Newbury and Wallingford and including some 18 voluntary, municipal and public assistance hospitals.

While the structure of the N.H.S. was being decided on at national level, a considerable amount of planning was being undertaken by the Berks, Bucks and Oxon Regional Hospitals Council. However the administrative structure was eventually arranged, the N.H.S. envisaged a system of comprehensive medical care and therefore the needs of the area and the methods of supplying them had to be determined.

The *Report on the Planning of Hospital Services in the Berks, Bucks and Oxon Region* was submitted to the Ministry of Health and published in January 1947. Among the twelve Committee members producing it were Mr Aitken Walker and Col C. B. Krabbé. Its recommendations were far-reaching, covering every aspect of the hospital services in the future N.H.S. Oxford Region and its various Districts. Much information had already been obtained regarding the Reading District from an earlier Report published in April 1946 by the Reading and District Joint Hospitals Council. This Committee had included Mr Aitken Walker, Mrs V. Benyon and Mr Ryan (the Hospital Secretary). Included in both the 1946 and 1947 reports were those published in the Interim Report of 1945 by Dr Basil Hill on the Anaesthetic Service, Dr Cave on the Radiological Services and Dr Mills on the Pathological Service required in the Reading Division.

The 1947 Report emphasised the deficiency of nearly 6,500 beds in the Region. In the Reading District alone the present 3,283 beds should be doubled and include 1,500 beds for the acute sick. At that time, including the Royal Berkshire Hospital, Battle Hospital and Newbury District

HOSPITALS AND INSTITUTIONS IN READING
AND DISTRICT IN 1947

Hospital	Category	Present number of beds	
Royal Berkshire Hospital, Reading including the Blagrave Branch.	Acute Sick, General. Maternity	446 15 ———	461
Battle Hospital, Reading.	Acute Sick, General. Maternity and Diseases of Women. Chronic Sick.	168 61 155 ———	384
Newbury District Hospital	Acute Sick, General.		90
Wokingham P.A.I., Berks. (Wokingham Hospital)	Chronic Sick.		111
Wallingford P.A.I., Berks. (St Mary's Hospital)	Chronic Sick.		117
Newbury P.A.I., Berks. (Sandleford)	Chronic Sick.		111
Henley P.A.I., Oxon. (Townlands)	Chronic Sick.		87
Woodleys P.A.I., Reading.	Accommodation for aged and infirm only.		———
Park Isolation Hospital, Reading.	Infectious Diseases. Tuberculosis.	78 26 ———	104
Whitley Smallpox Hospital.	Infectious Diseases.		22
Wallingford Joint Isolation Hospital.	Infectious Diseases.		34
Smith Isolation Hospital, Henley	Infectious Diseases.		36
Whitelands Smallpox Hospital, Henley.	Infectious Diseases.		12
Peppard Sanatorium.	Tuberculosis.		260
*Berks. County Mental Hospital, Wallingford.	Mental Diseases.		964
Borocourt Institution.	Mental Defectives.		400
Dellwood Maternity Home, Reading.	Maternity.		16
Cold Ash Children's Hospital, Newbury.	Children's (long-stay cases).		36
Wallingford Hospital.	Cottage Hospital.		17
Henley and District War Memorial Hospital.	Cottage Hospital.		21
	Total		3,283

An additional 110 beds are provided at Hungerford P.A.I., leased by the Visiting Committee from the Berkshire County Council.

Hospital, less than half this number were available. A programme of great expansion was needed to provide the necessary facilities and also a corresponding increase in all categories of medical, surgical, nursing, technical, administrative and domestic staff.

ESTIMATED TOTAL REQUIREMENTS OF READING AND DISTRICT

	Beds
Acute Sick	1,500
Long-stay Cases: the Chronic Sick	750
Infectious Diseases (assuming existing accommodation to be adequate)	182
Tuberculosis: Sanatorium requirements for whole region	523
Other	26
Mental Diseases	1,036
Mental Defectives: (requirements for the whole region)	2,200
Maternity	180
Convalescence	186
Cottage Hospitals	85
Total	6,668

Taken from 1947 *Report on the planning of Hospital Services in Berks, Bucks and Oxon Region*

The Royal Berkshire Hospital, on its present site, could only be enlarged to provide 700 beds and problems were envisaged for the enlargement of Battle Hospital. The Report recommended that a new hospital with 1,052 beds should be built in Reading to serve as the key hospital for the District providing specialist services for a wide area. In the meantime full use should be made of both Battle Hospital and the Royal Berkshire Hospital.

Co-operation between the two hospitals had been maintained during the war through the E.M.S. Since the war the Borough Council had embarked on a scheme to up-grade its municipal hospital and bring it more in line with the facilities available at the Royal Berkshire Hospital. It had been agreed that 'the closest possible co-operation of services rendered by both hospitals should be effected'. Members of the Hospital's honorary medical staff had been appointed consultants at Battle Hospital and other public assistance institutions in the area and in an emergency the Resident Anaesthetist would attend at Battle.

The announcement that the University of Reading would be moving to Whiteknights Park and that additional land might then become available adjacent to the Hospital site prompted an addendum to the 1947 Report: 'Contrary to earlier expectations it may be possible to acquire several acres of land adjacent to the Royal Berkshire Hospital. In this event the erection of the proposed new hospital on the Royal Berkshire site is brought within the bounds of possibility.'

The Town Planning Committee agreed all University land on the east of Redlands Road should be earmarked as 'Hospital property' and the University agreed to sell it 'when it became available'. In June 1948 Dr Maitland, the Chief Medical Planning Officer to the Ministry of Health, inspected the site and recommended its approval for the future key hospital of the area.

The Oxford Regional Hospitals Board was formed a year before the appointed day and included Col C. B. Krabbé, Chairman of the Hospital's Board of Management. Mr Cashell, Mr Aitken Walker and Dr Le Marquand were appointed to its Medical Advisory Committee. The Regional Hospitals Board met regularly each month from the time of its formation, maintaining regular communication with the Board of Management until the appointed day. The inclusion on this Board of those familiar with the Hospital who had also been instrumental in planning the future hospital services of the area provided continuity and would enable a smooth transfer from one system to the other.

When the Reading and District Hospital Management Committee (one of 15 in the Region) was formed in April 1948, ten of the eighteen members were on the Hospital's Board of Management, six of whom were also members of the House Committee. Several members had also been on the various post-war planning committees of the Regional Hospitals Council. Col C. B. Krabbé was appointed Chairman, Mr W. McIlroy, Vice Chairman and Mr Ryan (Hospital Secretary) Secretary. Other members included Mr H. H. Wilder (the Hospital Treasurer), Mrs V. Benyon (former Chairman of the House Committee), Col J. Norman Walker (present Chairman of the House Committee), Mr Aitken Walker, Dr Le Marquand, Mr G. T. W. Cashell, Lady Palmer and Lady Mount. This new administrative body was a compact edition of the Hospital's Board of Management which by this time included some 69 members.[1] In June 1948 seven House Committees were established for the Reading District. House Committee No. 1 for the Reading area would oversee the work of the Royal Berkshire Hospital and Battle Hospital. After so many years the work of the two hospitals would now be inextricably linked.

Changes in Financial Support

During this period the loyal support of the public for their Hospital continued, but the amounts donated gradually decreased as the appointed day approached. In 1945 donations and subscriptions amounting to £19,000 had been received. In 1947 this had decreased to £12,500. Since the war the total average cost per in-patient for the whole of their stay had more than doubled from nearly £10 in 1939 to £21 15s in 1947. In the corresponding period the cost of each out-patient attendance had risen from 2/8d to 4/7d. The increase in out-patient attendance charges from 2/– to 2/6d in 1943 and to 3/– in June 1947 had not kept pace with the continual rise in costs.[2]

The increase in salaries and wages, the great rise in the drug account (which doubled in 1947, largely through the cost of penicillin), the price of instruments and equipment, all combined to produce a deficit of £46,000 that year. In addition the sale of securities to finance alterations, building and the purchase of property, had exhausted the Hospital's capital resources.

The Ministry of Health's financial support was obtained in September

1947 with the proviso that the Hospital must endeavour to maintain its income from other sources until the appointed day. Furthermore the Minister should be consulted on all matters such as increases in salaries, wages and capital purchases. From that point, to all intents and purposes, the term 'Voluntary' was no longer applicable to the Hospital.

While plans were being made for the future of the Hospital and the various committees were being formed to take over its administration, the great volume of voluntary work built up over the years was gradually being run down. For almost 110 years the Hospital had relied entirely on the generosity of the public. Built, maintained and enlarged by public subscription, the original Hospital with 50 beds had increased eightfold. The advances of science and medicine had brought equipment, instruments and treatments never envisaged in 1839. Generations had grown up knowing that their support was necessary for the maintenance of the Hospital. Annual subscriptions, church collections, parades and flag days combined with hundreds of events throughout the area to provide the Hospital with the funds it needed year by year. All this was now to end.

In his last Annual Report delivered at the 109th Annual Court of Governors in March 1948, Col Krabbé thanked the numerous voluntary workers and fund raisers for their unfailing support. The Reading Townswomen's Guild, the W.V.S., the British Red Cross Society and the League of Remembrance had all provided invaluable services for the Hospital. Among the many fund raisers the Reading University Students Union had raised £1,355 as a result of their last Rag Day. Lady Palmer and the Ball Committee had raised the record sum of £672. Mrs Benyon's organisation of the egg weeks had produced some 7,688 eggs and £130. The Ladies' Linen League had collected £319.

The Special Needs Committee, formed in 1927 from the Blagrave Branch Building Fund Committee, disbanded on its 21st anniversary in February 1948. Over the years it had raised over £12,000 for the Hospital and, among other things, had provided the 1939 ambulance, re-equipped the out-patients' canteen and given £1,790 to the Debt Reduction Appeal. Through it the first Hospital Flag Day had been organised in 1936.

The last formal meeting of the Ladies' Linen League held in April 1948 was attended by over 100 members with their Chairman, Miss Vera Palmer. Formed in 1904 by Mrs Benyon (later to become Dame Edith Benyon), their object had been to raise sufficient funds each year to provide the Hospital with all its linen. The members were thanked for their great work at a special meeting held at the Hospital in May.

The work of two contributory schemes, the Reading and District Workpeople's Hospital Fund Association formed in 1902, and the Royal Berkshire and Associated Hospitals' Contributory Scheme, founded in 1922, also came to an end. The latter held its last annual meeting in May. Throughout its 26 years it had created an enormous amount of good will and interest in the Hospital and its hundreds of helpers had brought its needs to the attention of every town and village in the area. In 1947 its members had produced an income of £71,000. It was possible that the work of its private patients' scheme would continue and a National Providential Scheme backed by the Nuffield Trust might be inaugurated.

The Convalescent Fund, formed in 1841 by the Hospital Chaplain, later administered by the Board of Management and then by the Almoner's Department, had provided surgical appliances and help for convalescent patients for over a century. Its income from donations had eventually proved inadequate and since 1936 it had been principally funded by charitable bodies, approved societies, the Contributory Scheme and local authorities. From July this invaluable work would be financed by the State.

The League of Mercy, founded in 1899 by Royal Charter for the support of Voluntary Hospitals in the provinces, had made generous annual donations to the Hospital since 1904. In winding up their affairs the sum of £1,050 was sent to the Hospital. This was placed in a new account called the Hospital Endowment Fund. A sub-account called the Royal Berkshire Hospital Welfare and Comforts Fund would be opened to which all donations could be made to the Hospital after the appointed day. It was hoped that this new fund would enable the links forged over many years between the Hospital and the public to be maintained in the future.

The Nuffield Provincial Hospital Trust had also helped the Hospital financially since its formation in 1939. Its support and financial backing had enabled the fundamental work for the development of the future N.H.S. Hospital to be carried out. The organisation of hospital services on a regional basis had been achieved and the future work of the Trust would now be directed to developing those services to which the N.H.S. did not extend.

The Berks, Bucks and Oxon Regional Hospitals Council, with its three Divisions, ended its work in March 1948. With its final *Report on Child Health Services* published in May, it had produced in its eight years a most comprehensive and valuable set of reports on many aspects of medical services. These included ophthalmic, E.N.T. and orthopaedic in 1943, anaesthetic, pathological and radiological in 1945, cancer in 1945 and maternity in 1947. In addition their various reports on the planning of hospital services had provided the basis on which the future N.H.S. Hospital could be developed.

The most outstanding and fundamental of all the voluntary work had been that of the honorary medical staff. Since the original appointment of three physicians and three surgeons at the great election held at the Town Hall in 1839, the members of the honorary medical staff had always been in general practice, working part-time at the Hospital. Few had been consultants in the modern sense but over the years with the formation of departments many had specialised in one particular branch of medicine or surgery. The advent of the N.H.S. would end this system at a stroke.

The various Hospital administrative committes had also been made up entirely of voluntary members, each making his or her particular contribution, often representing special bodies associated with the Hospital. Week by week the Board of Management and the House Committee had guided the development and work of the Hospital in all its aspects. In this alone the N.H.S. would be unchanged, with the Regional Boards and Hospital Management Committees remaining purely voluntary bodies.

In April Miss Cawood resigned to take up her appointment as Matron at the Alder Hey Children's Hospital in Liverpool. Miss Aldwinkle, A.R.R.C., aged 46, at one time the Senior Home Sister, now the Assistant Matron, was appointed in her place. She would take up her duties when the Hospital became part of the N.H.S. in July. No one was appointed to replace the Revd C. Bourne, Chaplain since 1932, who had resigned on becoming Rural Dean of Reading. This decision would be left to the House Management Committee after the appointed day.

The final meeting of the Board of Management was held on June 29th. The proceedings were short and businesslike. Mr Wilder would make up the accounts to the appointed day for submission to audit. Col Krabbé's resolution was then passed unanimously.

'At this their final meeting, the Board of Management wish to record their profound gratitude to the Medical, Nursing, Administrative and Technical Staff for their devotion to duty whereby the Hospital has received the proud and respected position it holds today. They also offer their heartfelt thanks to all those individuals and organisations, who by their interest and efforts on behalf of the Hospital, have contributed so greatly towards the achievement of so honourable a result.'

An underlying fear was not expressed. Would the N.H.S. Hospital become too big and too impersonal? Would the greatly prized relationship between patient and doctor disappear? Would compassion and dedication become subservient to efficient administration? Would the soul of the voluntary system be lost in the rush for progress and expansion? Time alone would tell.

NOTES

1 The Board of Management had gradually increased in size from the original 18 members with the President, Vice Presidents and Treasurer as ex-officio members. Since 1901 the Lord Lieutenant of Berkshire, the High Sheriff and the Mayor of Reading had also been ex-officio members. The Workpeople's Association, Contributory Scheme, British Red Cross Society and Local Authorities had all gained representation over the years. Although eventually 69 people were eligible to attend the meetings, usually only about 25 appeared.

2 These figures include both the Hospital and Blagrave Branch. For the Hospital alone in 1939, 5,003 in-patients were treated, 4,148 operations performed and the average duration of stay was 17.07 days. In 1947 there were 6,848 in-patients, 5,612 operations and the average duration of stay in the Hospital had decreased to 13.06 days. The daily cost of an in-patient had risen from 11/5d in 1939 to 12/7d in 1942, to 17/1d in 1945 and to £1 7s 7d in 1947.

Hospital frontage in the 1960s

1

THE COMING OF THE NATIONAL HEALTH SERVICE

When the Royal Berkshire Hospital became part of the National Health Service on July 5th, 1948, that day, as predicted by Col Krabbé, was no different to the day before. All the planning of the previous years, the formation of the Oxford Regional Hospitals Board and the Reading and District Hospital Management Committee had ensured a smooth change-over from the Voluntary Hospital to one now to be maintained by the State.

The New Structure
The Royal Berkshire Hospital was accepted as the key centre of 22 hospitals now controlled by the Reading and District Hospital Management Committee (R.&D.H.M.C.), and in representation on the Committee it fared very well. Following Ministerial policy, the Chief Administrative Officer, House Governor Mr H. E. Ryan and Accountant Mr J. H. Kitchen were appointed respectively Secretary and Finance Officer to the R.&D.H.M.C. Col Krabbé, as Chairman, still presided over many old hands from the Royal Berks Board of Management. Lady Palmer, Lady Mount, Mrs Benyon, Col Norman-Walker, Mr McIlroy and Mr Wilder had all been appointed to the Committee by the Oxford Regional Hospital Board, together with Surgeons Cashell and Aitken Walker and Physician Le Marquand.

In May 1948 they were all welcomed to the first Management Committee meeting with the news that, owing to a clerical error at Oxford, the papers giving the particulars of the task in hand had only reached them that morning. What misgivings must have been shared by the administrators, lay members and medical men on the new Committee! No nurse, however, heard this disturbing portent of National Health Service administration; the Hospital's Board had never included a nursing member and none was appointed to the Management Committee. It would be 1961 before just one, the Chairman of the Area Matrons, gained admission as an 'officer in attendance'. The Matrons of the Royal Berks, Battle, Park Isolation, Wokingham, Newbury and Peppard Hospitals were 'granted attendance' at the meetings of the Nursing Sub-committee, but of the many sub-groups formed to make recommendations to the Reading and District Hospital Management Committee, that was the weakest, serving more to receive information and directives than to influence events.

For the Royal Berkshire Hospital, the most relevant sections of the National Health Service Act were Sections 3 to 7. Section 3 required the Minister to provide hospital accommodation and services; Sections 4 and 5 allowed for amenity beds and private beds; Section 6 vested in the Minister all hospitals not run for profit and Section 7 transferred the Endowments of Voluntary Hospitals to a central fund. Later sections defined the functions of the Regional Boards and Management Committees. The Oxford Regional Board would, according to the Act, guide and control the planning, conduct and development of the service in its area, retaining the ultimate power of 'laying down the manner in which the various functions are to be performed'. The Reading and District Hospital Management Committee and its sub-committees would undertake the 'ordinary local administration and management' of its hospitals. The day to day administration would be devolved further to various House Committees.

The most powerful of the sub-committees was the Financial and General Purposes Committee which approved all expenditure, and its composition was very close to the old House Committee of the Voluntary Hospital. All promotions, and posts other than Regional appointments (for example the consultants), were the concern of an Establishment and Development Sub-committee, which rapidly promoted itself from a recommending role to one of executive power. This Committee also had a majority of people strongly linked to the Hospital. Again there was no nurse and, perhaps more surprisingly, no medical member either.

This Sub-committee, the Financial and General Purposes Committee and the Management Committee itself all relied heavily on a Medical Advisory Sub-committee of 12 doctors. Here the Hospital was again to the fore with Geoffrey Cashell as Chairman, Aitken Walker his Deputy and Dr Le Marquand a very active member. The pre-eminence of the Royal Berks was further acknowledged in what for the times was a major concession. In October 1949, the Matron of the Hospital was granted permission to attend the Medical Advisory Committee meetings 'when matters having a bearing on nursing staff were under consideration'. The key Hospital's interests were obviously well looked after in discussions by the Medical Advisory Committee on the staffing, provision of facilities and the clinical functions of the various hospitals in the district. But these dozen doctors could not alone provide a coherent voice for the many medical staff of widely disparate hospitals now brought together by a geographical grouping. A pattern of representation had to be developed, and a good start was made when the old Honorary Medical Staff Committee of the Royal Berks agreed to form a Joint Staff Committee extending to all the hospitals in the Reading area.

This proposal was readily adopted by the R.&D.H.M.C. and in February 1949 the Visiting Medical Staff Committee was formed, which is still an active forum of medical opinion. The specialties soon sorted themselves into Area Departments, so that by 1951 the Medical Advisory

Committee and the Management Committee were getting not only general reports from the V.M.S.C., but specific advice from Area Departments of Obstetrics and Gynaecology, Paediatrics, Anaesthetics, Pathology, E.N.T. and Ophthalmology – representing the Area, but all firmly based at the Royal Berkshire Hospital.

The day-to-day management of the Hospital rested with House Committee No. 1, whose responsibility consisted of the Royal Berks and its Blagrave branch, Battle Hospital, Park Isolation Hospital (Prospect Park Hospital in 1951), Whitley Smallpox Hospital (closed in 1959), Grove Maternity Home (closed in 1951, becoming part of Highdown School) and Dellwood Maternity Home. On this crucial Committee, Col Norman-Walker as Chairman with Lady Palmer, Mrs Benyon, Mrs Dahne, Mr Cashell, Mr Aitken Walker and Dr Le Marquand weighed the balance heavily on the Hospital side in debate with Vice Chairman Alderman Clark and the seven members from Reading Borough Council, who were naturally protective of the hospitals previously in the charge of the Local Authority.

Staff Appointments
With such strong support on all the important committees, the Royal Berks pressed confidently ahead with new facilities, improved staffing and increased services. There was no directive for economy. Additional medical equipment, office furniture and building improvements were all readily approved. The Establishment and Development Committee upgraded posts, raised salaries and created new positions in a wide range of hospital activities. The first heady year of the N.H.S. saw an increase in receptionists, clerks, typists and secretaries. An extra porter was appointed to make 18 strong this team of mostly long-serving members. The Head Porter, Mr Dibley, had started at the Royal Berks in 1916 on £3 8s per week. He now received a 5 per cent pay rise bringing his income to almost double that amount. The porters, in their new uniform of serge trousers and white jackets, exemplified the tradition of proud loyalty which was carried by most of the hospital staff into the National Health Service.

Many of the staff newly appointed under the N.H.S. would also serve long and loyally. Positions of permanence were filled in maternity, nurse tutoring, orthoptics, audiometry and physiotherapy. The basement Electro-cardiograph Unit created in the 1930s by Dr Lambert and Radiographer Forder got its first ECG technician. Since the cardiographs were recorded on photoplates, a photographer was appointed – Evelyn Aust, who later became a liberalising Warden of the Nurses' Home before her retirement in 1983.

All the honorary medical staff of the Voluntary Hospital joined the N.H.S. The custom of appointing general practitioners to the honorary staff was by then finished, the returned service doctors having brought home the message that specialisation to a high standard was essential. This policy was firmly endorsed in the N.H.S. appointments. The staff were subjected to a Regional Board Review to determine their correct status – Consultant, or the lesser post of Senior Hospital Medical Officer. Great reliance was placed on local consultation, with Mr Aitken Walker as a key figure. External assessors were also used and the outcome was well accepted, with a couple of disappointed Senior Hospital Medical Officers but no major grievances.

At first, due to the backlog of paperwork, the consultants were employed on temporary sessional contracts, but within a year most had signed a contract with the Regional Board which gave them tenure till retirement. Those with no private practice chose a full-time contract of eleven sessions; many selected the maximum part-time option of nine sessions, and a few who wanted more spare time signed on for six to seven sessions. The salary scale of £1,400 to £2,750 was not ungenerous. The 1949 contract for one of the consultant anaesthetists detailed eight half-day sessions (seven at the Royal Berks and one at Battle) with on call and extra duties to make up the ninth session. He was paid £1,576 apart from any distinction award, and this income could be increased by fees for domiciliary visits, for example to attend a home forceps delivery.

Despite the early fears of many, and possibly the reality for some metropolitan consultants, the income of Reading's hospital doctors was not in general lowered. Only the gynaecologists and general surgeons had very lucrative private work, and this scarcely altered after the appointed day. Greenlands stayed full, Dunedin Nursing Home, which Gordon Bohn and Aitken Walker had allowed to run down, had to be brought back to standard when it became obvious that the private patients were staying. The physicians and other specialists gratefully took up high session contracts which more than compensated for their middle-class patients having consultations under the N.H.S., and still allowed sufficient time for their limited private work. The amenity beds, single rooms which (under Section 4) could be asked for if available on payment of a small fee, were seldom taken up. Then, as now, the prime concern of the paying patient was choice of doctor rather than of bed. Rarely, in fact, have amenity beds been available, because of the overall shortage.

New junior medical posts were advertised on upgraded salary scales of £150 to £300 per annum to attract young doctors from the teaching hospitals. An added inducement was the generous free time. With a junior staff establishment raised to 25, weekends off duty were increased from four to six every six months. The senior medical staff for a long time just continued their usual activities. When the delicate negotiations were concluded in allocating Senior Hospital Medical Officer status to selected general practitioners on the staff, other G.P.s were granted clinical assistant sessions which were either paid (necessary for staffing) or honorary (for post-graduate instruction). The specialists themselves were pleased to accept their contracts as Consultants and to carry on their clinical sessions for a welcome financial reward. Many were surprised that in accepting payment they did not lose any freedom; indeed, they practised with less interference than before. Constant scrutiny of the provision of its medical services had been a feature of the Voluntary Hospital, always mindful of its responsibility to subscribers and benefactors.

The ticklish matter of salaries for the senior administrative staff was decided at the first meeting of the Finance and General Purposes Sub-committee which was held a month before the 'Appointed Day', and was attended by the Treasurer of the Regional Hospital Board. Henry Ryan, the Secretary, was transferred at a salary of £1,600 per annum, well above the minimum on the new scale, to match his income from the Voluntary Hospital. J.H. Kitchen, the Finance Officer, was transferred at the minimum salary of £995, rising by increments to £1,275, plus residential accommodation valued for the purposes of superannuation at £85 per annum.

At the same meeting a sum of £250 received from the Regional Board for petty cash purposes was used to open an account in the name of Reading and District Hospital Management Committee at Lloyds Bank Ltd, Market Place, Reading. On June 29th, authority was given for a Finance Officer's imprest account to be opened up to a sum of £40,000, disbursements to be reimbursed monthly in respect of expenditure on weekly wages, monthly salaries, imprest cash floats and urgent accounts (involving discounts). Payment of staff from this account was curiously assorted. A ward maid for instance received £3 15s per week, telephonist £4 3s, and gardener £5 4s. The theatre orderly was paid 2/6½ per hour which is just over £1 for 8 hours, while a porter only received 2/2½ per hour. A laboratory technician earned £279 per annum, just £1 less than the Second Assistant Matron, although she also had residential accommodation. A radiographer was paid £310 and the Chief Pharmacist did well at £725 per annum.

Clinical Services

Until 1953, the consultants continued to keep the Overtime Book. This referred not to medical attendance, but to prolonged patient stay. The book was circulated at Visiting Medical Staff Committee meetings and the clinical management of long-staying patients was seriously discussed. This was less bureaucratic inquisitiveness than assessment of clinical work by colleagues of equal status, which today would be applauded as 'peer review' in the quest for 'quality assurance'. Discreetly, no record was made of comments on the cases in the Overtime Book.

The Attendance Book was a different matter. Most of the senior staff had, since the war, refused to sign themselves in and out, so the Management Committee wisely resolved to 'discontinue the practice'. They had little choice, since 'their' consultants no longer belonged to the Hospital, but were appointed officially to the Oxford Region.

The many hospitals now connected with the Royal Berks under the control of the Reading and District Management Committee meant increased work loads, but also some opportunities for expansion of clinical services. The work of the Pathology Department adapted easily to the

N.H.S. Dr John Mills, while not an outstanding pathologist, was a good organiser. During and after the war he had run one of the best blood transfusion services in the country. This was now taken over and expanded by the new Regional Blood Transfusion Service in Oxford. The general surgery service fused at once with Battle, and peripheral medical, surgical, E.N.T., gynaecology and ophthalmology clinics and operating sessions were soon established variously at the Newbury, Wallingford and Henley Hospitals. These were most important and valuable, since at the Royal Berks none of the changes under the N.H.S. had brought more beds. Indeed, with a persistent shortage of nurses, wards were still frequently closed.

Today the deficit in beds is largely due to population pressure and inadequate funds. Forty years ago the chief problems were lack of nurses which kept wards closed, and the presence of the long-stay patients. Many conditions were treated by prolonged bed rest; leg ulcer patients might stay for months and the elderly sick even longer. Most of these chronic patients were happy, but many of the population, despite the new freedom from the worry of hospital costs, were not keen to go into hospital, where it was believed 'they' practised on you and cut you. In contrast, the out-patient clinics were bursting. The first rush for free treatment under the N.H.S. was not to the hospitals but to the general practitioners, for medicines, spectacles, dentures and certificates. Later came the demands on the hospital ancillary services – for X-rays, blood tests and physiotherapy.

The local G.P.s did well in controlling the flow to the Royal Berks clinics, but until 1957 every patient requiring, for instance, an X-ray had first to be seen by a hospital doctor. As was the case before the N.H.S., the degree of congestion in the out-patient clinics depended on the efficiency and attitude of the doctor in charge. Some preferred a large crowd as evidence of their popularity. Most ran appointments systems. In Gordon Bohn's clinic, women were given times from 2 p.m. onwards, and the men after 4 p.m. so that they would miss less of their day's work.

At the end of each clinic, the doctors' notes were dictated to a secretary skilled in shorthand. The clerical staff had already been boosted in anticipation of the N.H.S. Mary Russell was for three years until mid 1947 the doctors' secretary. She was then, in modern terminology, 'head hunted' by Peter Wheeler and Hunt Williams for their private practice, and was replaced, she recalls with some pride, by six secretaries.

Major capital expansion was now beyond the jurisdiction of local committees. The grandiose plans of the Centenary Appeal for replacement of West Ward with an entirely new Out-patients Department had long ago faded. Structural alterations at the end of the war had closed the archway from Redlands Road to gain a little more out-patient space and a larger office for the almoners, whose work was then rapidly increasing.

The title of Lady Almoner had been lost when Mrs Osmond retired in 1944. Her replacement, Miss Platt, was possibly the first among the staff of the Hospital whose work was immediately benefited by the N.H.S. No longer were patients required according to the 1947 Hospital Rules 'to contribute towards the cost of their maintenance according to their means'. Thus relieved of responsibility for financial assessments, the Senior Almoner and her assistants could concentrate on their real work among the patients flooding in, many with social rather than medical problems. They now had reasonable space, but the general congestion on the ground floor of the West Wing was becoming intolerable, with multiple clinics fighting for the same facilities – eye testing, for instance, competing for space with gynaecology changing. Chief Pharmacist E. A. Burton was also desperate to expand his overworked Dispensary. More room was needed at once.

Pressure for Expansion
By 1951 the priorities agreed in 1948 by the Ministry had evolved into an ugly row of five huts with a linking corridor, separated by the even uglier old physiotherapy huts from the still undemolished West Ward block. These huts were originally for physiotherapy, gynaecology, E.N.T., ophthalmology and orthoptics. From the start, they were a temporary expedient and few would have anticipated their continued heavy usage in the Hospital's 150th year.

The key Hospital was already overdue for a carefully planned massive expansion. The catchment area population of 290,000 would not long remain at that figure, while advances in medicine and technology were of themselves demanding more facilities, more beds and more staff. A clear sign of the pressure to come was the transformation of radiotherapy from a small section of the X-ray Department to a vigorous new specialty. Dr W. G. Evans had taken up duties as Director in 1947. His new Department was squeezed in alongside the diagnostic X-ray premises. By 1949 he had a new 250 KV Victor Maximar Therapy Unit, a new fire-proof safe for radium, and 12.9 cwt of lead for staff protection. This staff now included an assistant radiotherapist, a physicist, D. V. Mabbs, plus his own technician, and two radiographers. Dr Evans also negotiated some precious in-patient beds and persuaded the administration to purchase a radiotherapy hostel – 37, Upper Redlands Road, later to be named Parkside House. The compressed Radiology Department meanwhile was staggering under the burden of demand for free X-rays, and many other consultants were bidding for significant developments in their specialty.

Mr Wheeler submitted an aggressively worded report on the needs of the Obstetric and Gynaecology Service; Mr Cashell a more moderate, yet firm argument for a new Eye Department. The surgeons had been quick to claim beds and operating lists in Henley, Wallingford and Newbury, but the physicians disliked peripheral clinics and wanted many more beds in their main Hospital. In addition, the resignation of Mr Rowntree and the appointment in December 1948 of Mr C. M. (Mike) Squire as Accident Surgeon presaged a rapid expansion of the trauma and orthopaedic services. Now was the time for major decisions on a rational scheme for capital development.

It was also the time of the first chill winds of financial stringency. The Regional Board at the end of the first year had demanded that revenue costs be reduced by 10 per cent – the start of a dreary pattern of repeated financial disappointments, with enforced economies frustrating logical plans and the clinical services only just being maintained in a delayed and disjointed building programme. A splendidly designed and efficient acute District General Hospital could have been developed on the one central site, but over the next 20 years the opportunity was lost.

Forecourt in the 1960s

2

PLANNING AND POLICY CHANGES

Fundamental to the development of the hospital services in Reading would be the relationship between its two major institutions, less than three miles apart. The Royal Berkshire and Battle Hospitals, although totally different in origin and background, were now providing similar services. Battle had followed the path of many Poor Law institutions, changing in the First World War from the Oxford Road Workhouse to Reading War Hospital No. 1, and after the war maturing into Battle Infirmary. In the 1930s, co-operation between the Voluntary Hospital and this rapidly progressing Local Authority rival was good, probably well in advance of the times, and the 1939–45 conflict brought a considerably closer liaison.

The wartime spirit of sharing was continued when the Health Committee of Reading Borough Council immediately after the war strove to upgrade the facilities and the status of Battle Hospital. In 1946 the Royal Berks had appointed four representatives to help in this endeavour, Mrs Benyon, Col Norman-Walker, Mr Aitken Walker, and elder statesman E.N.T. Surgeon Powell who had been Aural Surgeon from 1915–19 at Reading War Hospital. It was agreed that there should be the closest co-operation, and the Hospital had contributed in great measure, particularly with laboratory, technical and X-ray services, but also in less obvious fields such as nurse training and anaesthetics cover.

In March 1948, just prior to nationalisation, an important concession had been made. When none of the Battle visiting anaesthetists was available, it was agreed that the Resident Anaesthetist of the Royal Berks might be called upon to deputise at Battle. Paradoxically, with these intertwining relations and Battle's obvious improvements, the old rivalries intensified, particularly concerning the quality of medical service. The National Health Service brought these competing factions under the one House Committee and soon produced the definitive breakthrough – appointment of the first Resident Medical Officer with designated duties at both hospitals.

Under the N.H.S., the position of Medical Superintendent had become anomalous and Dr J. C. Harvey, the incumbent at Battle, resigned in 1949, leaving the way clear for full amalgamation of the two establishments. The medical staffs, by now already linked within the

Visiting Medical Staff Committee, were agreed that complete fusion was the only sensible policy, the combined hospitals between them forming a District General Hospital. There was no argument that a single specialist service should be provided and little doubt that this should be based, together with major facilities such as the laboratory and radiological services, at the Royal Berks. But the distribution of departments and clinics, and especially the allocation of beds, were understandably subjects of great contention.

Plans and counterplans were discussed in private and in committee. The least controversial was the Tuberculosis Service, then in its infancy of chemotherapy and still of primary importance. When the diagnosis of TB was confirmed, all patients would be transferred to Peppard Sanatorium as soon as possible. Also undoubtedly, the public assistance patients would be removed from Battle to provide more beds. It was fully accepted that both hospitals would have acute medical and surgical beds, the problems of such duplication not yet being realised. Apart from these certainties, a bewildering array of options and schemes were argued back and forth between the differing specialties.

All out-patients would be seen at the Royal Berks; a small casualty service would be retained at the Hospital and the Accident and Trauma Department would move to Battle. Beds thus freed would allow gynaecology to be concentrated at the Royal Berks and some would also be taken up by the physicians. Physical medicine would be divided, with therapeutic management at the Royal Berkshire and rehabilitation at Battle.

Plans for maternity were even more complicated because the Grove Maternity Home was being lost to the Education Authorities. A proposal was firstly made to purchase the nearby Chiltern Maternity Home in Peppard Road, then switched to the leasing of just half a dozen beds. Dellwood Maternity Home could continue to service the southern side of Reading, but where would the major obstetric unit be?

Eventually a Hospital Planning Sub-committee was formed, which cut through all these discussions with a brief simplifying report presented by Geoffrey Cashell in late 1949. Only Maternity, the Accident and Orthopaedic Department and a Geriatric Unit should be based at Battle. All out-patients (except orthopaedic), all paediatrics, acute medicine and surgery would go to the Royal Berks. This was simple and logical, but it was offered only as a temporary solution. The second half of the Planning Committee Report considered at length a plan for the future development of the Hospital which had been prepared by Mr L. G. Pearson, architect, for the Oxford Regional Hospital Board. This aimed for an eventual 500 additional beds using land still awaiting acquisition from the University. The Hospital Management Committee had already decided that: 'The RBH site was correctly situated and suitable for the enlargement of the Hospital so that one main general hospital for the area can be situated in Reading.'

The Cashell Sub-committee agreed with this clear, if clumsily phrased policy, but found the Pearson plan unacceptable. Instead of delay, they urged that 'a new block of 500 beds be erected forthwith on the existing site', with provision for future developments on the extended site at a later date.

Here, in 1949, was a bold and far-sighted policy. The Accident Service, Orthopaedics and Maternity would come back to the Royal Berks to concentrate all acute services on the one site. Battle would provide the complementary services of convalescence, geriatrics and rehabilitation. It certainly could have been done. There was enough space for a tower block at the Royal Berks. The obvious problems of recruiting and keeping staff for the less glamorous work at Battle could have been solved by rotational programmes, training courses, housing benefits and similar inducements, given sufficient adminstrative will and imagination.

In the event things turned out very differently. The hospitals certainly united. The Local Authority patients left Battle, the last of the old people going in 1953. The acute medical beds formerly at Battle also went, but to Prospect Park instead of the Royal Berks, so creating a third site of acute clinical activity. Transfer of Mike Squire's Accident and Orthopaedic Service was slow and piecemeal. His allotted task was gigantic – to create an Area Accident Service based on Reading and with his Oxford training at the Wingfield Morris Hospital, to provide the new specialisation in orthopaedics as part of a Regional service. With only ten male beds in Victoria Ward and a few female beds in Nuffield, he first used Battle as a convalescent hospital, shipping the post-operative patients across as soon as possible. As further facilities were provided at Battle he was able gradually to move more patients, then the operative work and eventually all out-patients. Casualty remained in its congested area adjacent to the old Redlands Road archway until fully transferred in March 1954. Meanwhile the entire Royal Berks Maternity Unit had moved to Battle in 1952. Peter Wheeler accepted this on two counts. Firstly, it freed the upper Nuffield Wards and Theatre for the rapidly expanding gynaecology service. Secondly, the conversion in 'C' (Thames) Block at Battle provided very reasonable maternity facilities to carry on with, while he built up his case for a definitive unit on the Royal Berks site.

With this gradual transfer of many services to Battle there came a significant level of staff sharing, not just confined to those doctors with split responsibilities. The pioneer of this trend was Chief Pharmacist E. A. Burton who, even before the N.H.S., had created with Treasurer Kitchen's enthusiastic support a Group Pharmacy Service to take advantage of the economies of centralised buying. Olive Clark, Superintendent Physiotherapist, followed this lead when the Orthopaedic and Accident Service moved to Battle. She completely amalgamated the Royal Berks and Battle Departments and became Group Superintendent Physiotherapist, using this position to improve the service in both hospitals. Previously, the physiotherapists had worked mainly in their own departments and gymnasium. Now the group policy was to bring them into the wards, to the benefit particularly of those surgical patients liable to post-operative chest infections.

New staff were now being appointed to a Royal Berks/Battle/Prospect Park conglomerate. Within this grouping Blagrave could also lay some claim to a separate identity, since from 1950 it accepted patients from Battle and was no longer exclusively an annexe of the Royal Berks. Whatever the arguments of in- and inter-dependence, a name was needed for the hospital group. 'The Reading United Hospitals' was suggested but faded in 1952 with the establishment of 'The Reading Combined Hospitals Training School for Nurses'. Despite this official accreditation, no unifying name ever became popular and the commonest term still used is the non-specific 'Reading Group of Hospitals'.

At the Royal Berks, the hoped-for progress proved to be snail like. The 1950s and early 1960s saw only the new out-patients huts, behind them the Social Club and Audiology Unit, and some significant extensions to the laboratories. To the rear of Huntley and Palmer Ward the carpenter's hut, previously E.N.T.'s East Ward, was demolished and replaced by Public Health Service cytology and microbiology laboratories. At the same time a Haematology Department was fitted into the space between the main pathology building and general theatres. But these were all single-storey huts, and the optimistic plan of 1949 for a master building had degenerated into prolonged discussions about a succession of add-on units. Expansion of the Hospital territory was delayed until the mid 1960s when the Wessex Hall site was eventually purchased in deals with the University, including 'friendly' compulsory purchase to overcome some restrictive covenants. The remaining house owners on the hospital side of Craven Road were persuaded to sell, so there was now the full island site of some 19 acres, but no unifying plan of development.

A new Hospital Planning Sub-committee was formed to advise on all the proposals. Geoffrey Cashell and Gordon Bohn became Chairman and Vice Chairman of this vital Committee which continually urged the importance of creating a centralised hospital of adequate size. They were gradually dragged into agreement with the Oxford Regional Board that this development would be completed in phases. Phase I was to be Mr Cashell's new Ophthalmology Block, which would bring together on two floors the out-patients, eye casualty, the Orthoptic Clinic, adult and childrens' eye ward and a modern Ophthalmic Theatre. Below would be Pharmacy and a Pilot Central Sterile Services Department; above, a private patients' ward to replace Greenlands, scheduled for demolition. Phase IIa was a Nurse Education Centre plus an extension to the Nurses' Home, IIb was the transfer of laundry and transport services to Battle. Phase IIIa was Peter Wheeler's long-awaited obstetrics and neo-natal block. Its planned six floors would include the Midwifery School, modern clinics and their ancillary services, ante-natal and post-natal wards, individual delivery rooms, an adjacent suite of operating theatres and a Special Care Baby Unit. The main development would be Phase IIIb.

'One District General Hospital'

Once again the Hospital Management Committee and the visiting medical staff held hopes for a 1,400-bed hospital on the Royal Berks site, and a major row now surfaced as to the nature of this 'main development'. The Visiting Medical Staff Committee in 1962 observed with regret that in Enoch Powell's Command Paper No. 1604, *A Hospital Plan for England and Wales*, 'The Minister adheres to the view that there should be two District General Hospitals in the Reading area.' Whose decision this was, and why, remains something of a mystery. The only reason given in writing to the local medical staff was the smallness of the Royal Berks site, but a large tower block could resolve that problem or a single District General Hospital could have been based in the vast grounds of Battle Hospital.

Possibly it was just the inflexible application of the Hospital Plan which called for D.G.H.s of up to 800 beds, without recognition of local factors or attention to local advice. It is interesting, however, that seven years later when the Bonham-Carter Report recommended D.G.H.s of 1,000 to 1,750 beds, Regional Boards were asked to keep their planned hospitals below 1,100 beds, finance being one of the determining factors. By 1980, a consultation paper on the future pattern of hospital provision had swung back to the small D.G.H. of less than 600 beds with strong government approval because of the economies involved.

In 1962 Dr Oddie, Deputy Senior Administrative Medical Officer at Oxford, argued fiercely with the Reading Group Secretary that the locally proposed development would be too large to manage as a single District General Hospital. Geoffrey Weston, who went on to become Deputy Health Commissioner for England, Scotland and Wales, disagreed then, and 25 years later still believes that a great mistake was made. Perhaps one factor was the fear of an atomic attack in that time of international tension – the era of spy plane incidents, Russian atmospheric nuclear tests and Polaris missiles coming to Britain. If this was the reasoning for two acute hospitals it was surely flawed since one nuclear explosion with a weapon of the 1960s would have destroyed both.

At first, in the face of an onslaught of vehemently expressed local medical opinion, the Regional Board compromised. There would be only one District General Hospital but the Royal Berks would be limited in size to 1,000 beds up to 1975, and a further 500 beds would be provided at Battle! 'For what purpose?' the Reading staff wished to know and were given no direct answer.

On this unsatisfactory basis the Hospital Planning Committee met monthly to formulate details of the three agreed phases. An unexpected bonus was the sudden provision of finance for two temporary projects to ease some of the pressure on the general hospital until completion of Phase III. It was agreed that at the firmly restricted cost of £100,000, an Interim X-ray Department be built behind the east wing of Nuffield Block. Consultant Radiologist George Burfield and his colleagues, with recent experience of creating a new department at Battle, rapidly designed a two-floor unit which efficiently used two clusters of four X-ray rooms. This X-ray Department was completed in 1966. At the same time an 'Interim Out-patients Block' was constructed on the Redlands Road site of the old Greenlands gate lodge. Built according to the standard Ministry design for out-patient departments, its three storeys rose incongruously above the still-persisting line of temporary huts along the Hospital's western boundary. These two 'interim' buildings and the Nurses Education Centre, completed in 1968, were all of a similar box-like appearance. Their scattered disposition at the points of a triangle about the older hospital buildings effectively destroyed any likelihood of future developments bothering about coherence of architectural style. If not aesthetically, they were functionally very successful in reducing severe congestion in three departments while Radiotherapy benefited at once by expanding with Dr Mabb's Physics Department into the vacated Surgical Out-patients and the old X-ray rooms.

The Ophthalmic Block opened in 1967 and at its rear the Maternity Block in 1968. Geoffrey Cashell and Peter Wheeler both had reason for pride. These were two impressive buildings, which from the start functioned efficiently and as their designers had planned, with equipment and facilities which were right up to date. Each also was of pleasant appearance, but again there was no architectural relationship to any other Hospital building, nor indeed to each other.

The Planning Committee had spent much time 'finalising details', which was to say agreeing economies, with the Regional Board as these two blocks were equipped. They also organised the use of vacated space. The old ophthalmic ward would be used by radiotherapy patients from West Ward, which could then accommodate an expanded Medical Records Department and the medical social workers. The ophthalmic and orthoptic huts would switch to E.N.T. out-patients, photography and ECG. Phase IIa was also extended by some additions to the Pathology Laboratory and a new telephone exchange to be placed on the south side of the Nurses' Home. These were important, but only sidelines to the chief planning effort which was of course the main development of Phase IIIb.

By 1963 the arguments over the proposed development had been resolved and a draft plan had been generally agreed. Phase IIIb would be a 14-storeyed block with ten ward floors, each of 60 beds, including a self-contained private unit. There would be ten operating theatres. Accident, out-patient and diagnostic departments would be in a three-floor extension from the main block connected by concourses at ground and first-floor levels. Services and supplies would be at lower ground-floor level giving access to the existing hospital, and by a tunnel to the new Maternity Unit. (Herein lies the explanation of the original labelling of lift buttons in the Eye Block, which perplexed thousands of patients and visitors in its first 20 years.) All out-patient services were planned to be on the same level which would be designated 'ground floor', irrespective of the sloping site. The Eye Clinic, although one floor up, was therefore reached by pressing button 'G'.

A first suspicion that the tower block might never be built came in 1964 when the target date was postponed from 1972 to 1975. Mike Squire responded immediately. With the rapidly rising population of Reading and the increasing number of traffic accidents, his Accident and Emergency Department facilities at Battle were now more congested than they had previously been at the Royal Berks. He demanded, with much support from the clinical staff, that the Accident and Emergency Department be given priority and built alone, ahead of this prolonged time scale. Meanwhile, to give some relief from the mounting pressure on beds at the Royal Berks, it was decided not to demolish Greenlands, but to upgrade it, the first floor becoming a medical investigation unit and the ground floor to have surgical day beds.

In 1965 the Ministry of Health, now with Kenneth Robinson as Minister, published its document HM(65)37 which reviewed the general Hospital Plan and, catastrophically for the Royal Berks, firmly applied the financial brakes. Doubtless a Conservative government would have done the same, in response to the unexpectedly high costs of the building programme.

For those involved in acute hospital planning 20 years later, the phrases of this document have a familiar ring. Match schemes to resources, geriatric and psychiatric services to get their due share, start redevelopments with a core of department, leaving existing wards to be replaced at a later date . . . The Oxford Regional Board also had a new set of figures for its population estimates. In 1981, Reading would have a population of 220,000 and the catchment area 450,000. The Board used these figures again to justify assuming that Battle would need to become a second District General Hospital to provide the 1,500 beds demanded by this population. Again, no convincing argument was advanced but spending plans would thus be scaled down at the Royal Berks and spread between the two hospitals over a longer period.

The Royal Berks projects were totally and spectacularly recast. The Maternity Unit was going ahead, but its position, originally near Addington Road, had to be moved closer to the main buildings to entirely circumvent the last restrictive covenants. This sped up the timetable of purchase of University land which led to even greater pressure on development finances. The all-important Phase III was slashed to become just the Maternity Block; the group laundry at Battle and a new boiler house at the Royal Berks were allocated to Phases IV and V. The 14-storeyed tower block was discarded. On to the planning boards came Phase VI, incorporating Accident and Emergency, four theatres, some out-patients, X-ray and Pathology and just 120 beds. Phase VII, the main ward block with the second stage of diagnostic and treatment departments, would not be discussed even in outline until 1967.

Proposals for an 'Export Hospital'
The ensuing flood of disapproval spilled over into the local press,

culminating in October 1965 with a series of outspoken articles in the *Evening Post* surreptitiously fed to the newspaper by a prominent Royal Berks consultant. All to no avail, and the Planning Committee reluctantly accepted this decimated programme 'provided there should be no parallel development at Battle until all the acute development at the RBH was completed'. Almost in riposte, the Regional Board announced in April 1966 that Reading, convenient to London and to travellers by air, had been chosen as the site for a new Export Hospital. This was to be a showpiece of British design and technology to attract buyers from overseas. It would be of 200 beds, cost £2,000,000 and be built at Battle.

Here was a dilemma of classic proportions for the beleaguered hospital doctors of Reading. Desperately short of equipment, finance, space and beds, they were being offered on a platter a showpiece acute hospital, but not where they wanted it. At Battle, still somewhat enshadowed by its workhouse past, Administrator Les Parcell and Matron Gladys Morgan were understandably jubilant. Their staff had been dejected by the certain loss of the Maternity Unit back to the Royal Berks and the likelihood of the Accident and Emergency Department following. Now they would have an acute unit so ultra modern that the plans even included a helicopter pad. Frank Naylor, the new Group Secretary, helped the Planning Committee compose a tactful, purposely vague and rather optimistic response to what so far was a rather woolly proposal. The concept was accepted of the eventual need for two District General Hospitals in Reading. The major development at the Royal Berks should proceed as planned, while the new hospital should function as a separate unit. When its showpiece purpose was fulfilled it should be 'adapted to meet local requirements'. In passing, the Committee noted that with the provision of eight day beds in the new hospital, the ground floor of Greenlands could be used for nursing and administration offices.

Within the month, the Chairman of the Regional Board Mrs Graham-Bryce, together with six other representatives, came to Reading to clarify the position to the Management Committee and senior medical staff. They explained that the British Hospitals Export Council had persuaded the Ministry of Health to support the project to help the export drive. A number of consortia of architects, consulting engineers, building and equipment suppliers were to be invited to submit proposals for the design, construction and equipping of the project. The completed building would serve to demonstrate their joint capabilities and be a shop-window for export trade. The necessary finance would be quite separate from and additional to funds already promised for development, and would in no way delay or affect the development of the Royal Berkshire Hospital as planned.

With this guarantee, the support of the Reading doctors and Management Committee was enthusiastic. It seemed too good to be true – and it was. The design consortia quickly backed out and the Regional Board were asked to recruit their own design team. Their architects decided 'because of the ground conditions at Battle to develop a single storey layout'. The equipment consortia then declined to tender. The equipping would therefore be undertaken by normal procedures and the Export Council lost all interest in the project. The Board still had the allocated Government funds, however.

A final vigorous effort was made by the Management Committee to have these surplus funds applied to progress on the Royal Berks site and to abandon the development of Battle for acute cases. The Visiting Medical Staff Committee pointed out that the new unit could be placed on the Royal Berks site without disrupting the development of Phase VI. But the Regional Board stood firm. Thus in November 1967 the unanimous opinion of those best qualified to advise on local hospital development in Reading was finally rejected. A typically compromised policy was cobbled together by the Management Committee and the Board. This stated that 'the whole complex of the Reading Hospitals can be regarded as providing the services of a single District General Hospital,' that 'the Royal Berks shall continue to be the major acute unit' and that 'the development of Phase VII is of paramount importance in order to provide supporting beds for Phase VI'.

The 'Export Hospital' became the Abbey Building, opening in 1972 with acute medicine (transferred back from Prospect Park), paediatrics, thoracic surgery (from Peppard Sanatorium) and acute surgery. The Planning Committee having been forced to accept an acute unit at Battle, Gordon Bohn determined that it would be successful. He, who had served on every surgically related committee at the Royal Berks from Records to Sterilising Services, totally changed his allegiance, bringing his own surgical unit to the Abbey Block, where he worked tirelessly to improve the Battle clinical services. Only after his retirement in 1978 did Bohn again actively support the Royal Berks by renewing his musical studies and playing the organ for special occasions in the chapel.

By 1969 there was still no sign of Phase VI. The Visiting Staff Committee voted 'No confidence' in the current plans and yet again demanded a high-rise solution to the ever-increasing congestion of clinical activity. Some functional modifications were made to the plans, but no material alteration in shape or size of Phase VI, while the proposals for Phase VII were still quite vague. The Accident and Orthopaedic Service would get all 120 of the Phase VI beds. Consultant Oral Surgeons David Mackenzie and Ken Ray won a fight to include a new Dental Department alongside the trauma and orthopaedic out-patients, some recognition of their efforts in coping with an escalating workload; a reward perhaps also for Mackenzie's invention, with the assistance of the Applied Physics Department at Aldermaston, of a widely acclaimed splinting device for facial fractures – the Royal Berkshire Hospital Halo. The physicians asked for a cardiac monitoring unit in Phase VI which would service their beds in Phase VII. Until those beds arrived, it was agreed that medical emergencies referred by G.P.s would bypass the Accident and Emergency

Department and go direct to the existing medical wards. The planning team formally requested the Board to include a new E.N.T. Department in the development programme, but with little real hope that the Phase VII plans would be expanded.

The target date for Phase VI receded to 1971, then to 1974, but at the beginning of 1974 the new building was just a steel framework in a sea of mud. Phase VII, which had already been postponed to 1982, was now postponed indefinitely. So a multi-facility specialist block was under construction, with no likelihood of provision of the back-up beds and facilities for which it had been designed.

The clinicians relying on Phase VII were aghast. They tried in increasingly acrimonious discussions to change the accident and ortho-paedic clinical monopoly of Phase VI, but the strong bids of physicians and general surgeons for beds were unavailing. In any event, Phase VI was not completed until 1978 and, newly named as South Wing, stood empty for a further year because no funds were available for its activation. Even then, commissioning was gradual, as the new staff dining-room, kitchen, pathology and medical records slowly moved in. Having fought off its competitors the Accident and Emergency Department had the Battle theatres declared unsafe. With this convincing stimulus to transfer, the Unit at last came home to the Royal Berks in June 1980. Mike Squire, who had created the service, moved the Department to Battle and master-minded its return, had retired in 1979 and it was Patrick Chesterman who triumphantly brought the orthopaedic patients and staff into wards whose names he personally had chosen. He shrewdly judged that in honouring surgeons eminent in the history of orthopaedics, the very names of Hunter, Lister, Hey-Groves, Gauvain and Trueta would help dissuade any future proposers of change in the use of South Wing wards.

Once again, the provision of new facilities meant alterations in the function of some older buildings. The mortuary was taken over by the Works Department, medical electronics moved into part of the now deserted Pathology Laboratories, and photography to the Public Health Laboratory. The Cyril Taylor Intensive Care Unit was closed after ten successful years. This Unit had been financed and built adjacent to the general theatres within six months of the mention of its need by Conrad Latto to a local manufacturer and benefactor, C. F. Taylor. In contrast to this speedy, albeit small-scale private enterprise, South Wing having been years in the planning, delayed in commissioning and then deprived of its vital complementary ward block, could not in the end be fully used. Two of its new operating theatres remained unopened and only one half of the splendid cardiac monitoring/intensive care unit was brought into operation by Anaesthetist David Price and the skilled nurses from the C. F. Taylor Unit.

In this unsatisfactory, unfulfilled state South Wing has remained, with no follow-up development. It is a reflection on N.H.S. financing that apart from ward upgradings and the small Day Bed Unit originally attached to a corner of Greenlands, the few major building projects since the commencement of Phase VI have relied mainly or entirely on non-exchequer funds. The medical Post-graduate Centre was heavily subsidised, the Ken Thomas Appeal raised £1.25 million for the scanner unit built in 1981 next to Burfield's 'interim' X-ray Department. Now a complete redevelopment of the old West Wing for the Radiotherapy Department is being made possible by the Appeal for £1.5 million in celebration of the Hospital's 150th anniversary. Meanwhile, the acute services remain wastefully split between the Royal Berkshire and Battle Hospitals. No amount of charitable effort can be sufficient to implement the unheeded 1949 advice 'to concentrate all the acute services on one site.' Persuasion of the Government is required, and rationalisation of the extensive hospital properties in the West Berkshire health district. The local community, loyal and generous to their favourite hospitals, must understand and accept this vital necessity. It is the greatest challenge to the current holders of responsibility in a repeatedly changing system of local hospital administration.

Pathology Laboratory, 1960s

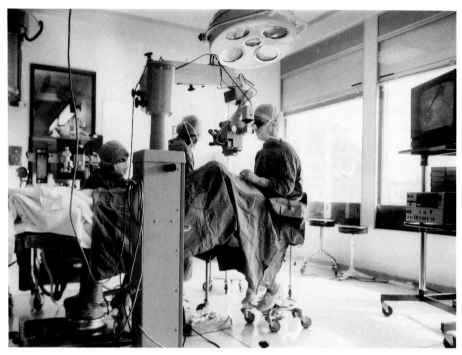

Eye Theatre showing 1980s' equipment in the Ophthalmic Block

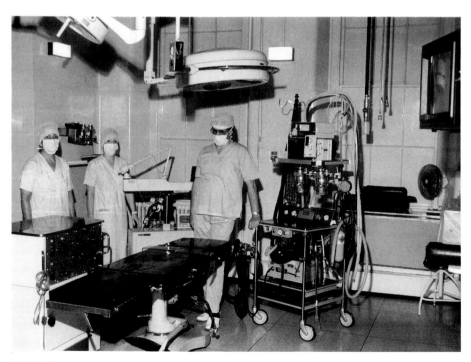

E.N.T. Theatre

THE ADMINISTRATIVE
STRUCTURE

For more than a century the Royal Berkshire Hospital had been managed by stable, conservative committees whose membership was long serving and loyal, if not particularly innovative. The first 40 years of the N.H.S. have seen this stability replaced by a succession of dramatic changes in the practicalities and the philosophy of its administration. Particularly since the N.H.S. reorganisation of 1974, diverse groups and individuals have, with the best of intentions, modified many times the routine of daily management and the course of the Hospital's development. Although inadequate funding has certainly been the main cause of falling morale during this era of the National Health Service, many dedicated hospital workers have deeply resented crucial decisions being made by staff for whom the Royal Berks has been not a career, but one concern of many, or a stepping stone on the swift path to promotion. The fault has not lain with the hard-pressed administrative staff themselves. Rather consider the rationality of a system which forced many of them to move so quickly to other posts, and withheld from those who were most knowledgeable and sensitive to local difficulties the finance and the authority to resolve them. The political realisation is yet to come that a District General Hospital is not equivalent to the local branch of a national business enterprise.

At first the Reading and District Hospital Management Committee and its subsidiaries maintained many of the old traditions. The monthly meeting of the Management Committee was always held at one of the hospitals for which it had responsibility, most frequently, of course, at the Royal Berks. Until 1966 the meetings were usually followed by a tour of inspection of the host hospital. The Sub-committees relating particularly to the Royal Berks met as often as weekly. These various meetings nearly always took place in the library. Its splendid high Victorian ceiling, imposingly solid furniture and walls lined with leather-bound historical volumes must have influenced those deliberating the Hospital's future to be mindful of the values of the past. For readers in the library, however, these frequent and often lengthy meetings became an increasing irritation. General practitioner members of the Reading Pathological Society complained, and so did the Visiting Medical Staff Committee. The consultants were concerned on their own behalf but more especially for their juniors. Rapid attainment of post-graduate diplomas and wide reading towards research and publication were becoming vital in the increasing competition for good consultant appointments.

This minor conflict between the Committees and a section of Hospital staff was finally resolved by the building of the Post-graduate Centre, and was in fact a rarity. The hallmark of those early Committees, of their officers and members alike, was the successful working together with genuine personal concern for all the staff and the patients, and with a fierce pride in their Hospital. Long service on the Committees was still common, although changes were coming.

In 1950 Col Krabbé resigned to become Vice Chairman of the Oxford Regional Hospital Board. His place as Chairman of the Management Committee was taken by Mr W. E. C. McIlroy. Some titles were also changing. Chief Administrative Officer Henry Ryan was redesignated Group Secretary in 1952. Mrs Stride, the Administrative Officer of House Committee No. 1, left the N.H.S. in that year. Mr A. D. C. Williams, her successor, was appointed with the title of Hospital Secretary, but stayed only two years before departing for Kuala Lumpur. He was followed by Ron Penney, who became in actuality the Hospital Secretary of the Royal Berkshire Hospital when the House Committee faded to informal status during the 1960s. Mr Penney served in this capacity until the 1974 reorganisation and is universally remembered with admiration and respect. He was fortunate in having direct responsibility and immediate access to three most able Group Secretaries.

Henry Ryan retired in 1956, 21 years after joining the Hospital as House Governor. His Assistant Secretary from the start of the N.H.S. had been Geoffrey Weston, who was now promoted. He served nine years as Group Secretary before becoming Regional Administrator of the North West Thames Health Authority. Mr Weston was in turn succeeded by Frank Naylor, who came new to the Reading District from High Wycombe. Mr Naylor settled easily into the Group Offices which were still adjacent to the Hospital at 3, Craven Road, and was able to continue the close, harmonious relationship with Ron Penney and the Royal Berks. In a significant pointer to future trends, Mr Naylor took early retirement at the 1974 reorganisation, and was immediately recruited to Dunedin, the private nursing home which Gordon Bohn and Aitken Walker had planned to close down in 1948.

Role of the Management Committee
The lifetime of the Reading and District Hospital Management Committee from 1948–74 was in general a happy and effective one. Despite financial pressures, shortage of nurses, the traumas of the 'Export Hospital', continued arguments over the question of one or two District General Hospitals and the agonisingly slow development of the ill-fated Phase VI – despite these and all other difficulties, the relationships between medical and nursing staff, lay committee members and administrators remained

excellent. The Hospital Secretary and the Group Secretary were always available and pleased to talk to any consultant with a problem. The Chairmen following Col Krabbé and Mr McIlroy – Mrs (later Lady) Benyon, Aitken Walker, David Woodrow and John Parkes, all provided leadership of quality. Mr Woodrow indeed left the Committee in 1972 to become Chairman of the Oxford Regional Board. Finance Officer Kitchen, who served every Chairman of the Hospital Management Committee, was always able to cope with his funding difficulties, although in retrospect these were trivial compared with the problems awaiting David Smith a decade after his appointment to the Treasurer's post in 1972. Active and enthusiastic lay members such as Lady Mount, Lady Palmer, the Hon. Mrs Lorna Palmer, Mrs Cashell, Mrs Dahne, William Pettit and ex-Treasurer Wilder served on numerous specialised sub-committees.

In addition to the official H.M.C. inspections, Committee members and co-opted volunteer Hospital Visitors regularly visited different departments of the Hospital to see for themselves what was happening and to give staff and patients a chance to let off steam. The Management Committee formed a Special Liaison Committee for junior medical staff, which continually battled for improved conditions and accommodation. Mrs Palmer was particularly alarmed by the block of flats of one and two bedrooms, built in 1969 in Addington Road. She vigorously denounced their inadequacies as family residences and personally took on the choosing of their furniture and fittings. Senior medical staff were equally well supported by the Committees. Peter Wheeler and Geoffrey Cashell received every encouragement in their fights for the Maternity and Ophthalmology Blocks.

Within the R. and D.H.M.C. the doctors themselves had a powerful voice. Geoffrey Cashell, Aitken Walker, Gordon Bohn and Consultant Pathologist Frank Hampson, successive Chairmen of the Medical Advisory Committee, were active and influential long before 'Clinicians in Management' became a political catch-cry.

The Salmon and Cogwheel Schemes

During this time the Hospital's administrative reputation matched its impressive medical standing. In 1967, the Reading Group was one of the first in the country to be selected for piloting the introduction of the new Salmon structure of nursing administration. The Salmon Report shifted the organisation of nursing from the individual hospital to the Group. When Miss Aldwinckle retired – the last purely Royal Berkshire Matron – in 1966, Rosemary Bromley was appointed Group Matron. Her job in essence was Matron of the Royal Berks with a supervisory responsibility for the other hospitals in the No. 1 Group. Under the Salmon structure, she became No. 10, or Chief Nursing Officer, now in charge of nursing in all the hospitals of the Reading and District Management Committee. The title of Matron of the Royal Berkshire Hospital had already gone; the title of Group Matron had also now disappeared and nursing at the Hospital

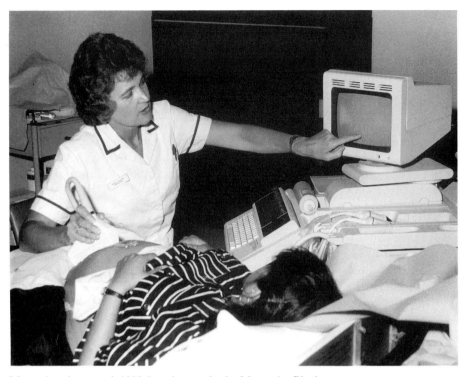

Maternity ultrasound: 1980s' equipment in the Maternity Block

became divided and weakened by unnecessary administrative tiers from No. 9, Principal Nursing Officer, to lowly No. 6, the Ward Sister, who should have been the key figure in the new system. But the Reading changeover was smoothly organised and functioned well according to the Salmon Scheme.

The following year, 1968, saw a major change in the system of medical advice and administration. The old Medical Advisory Committee was replaced by a Hospital Medical Services Committee, with Hampson still as Chairman. Again the Royal Berkshire had been chosen to set up one of the first such Committees following the Cogwheel Report on the *Organisation of Medical Work in Hospitals*. The inaugural meeting of the new H.M.S.C. was not held until February 10th, 1969. The first representatives of the clinical divisions were interestingly varied – a serious endeavour was being made to avoid narrow sectional interests or bias. Medicine was represented by Paediatrician David Stone and Geriatrician Sam Vine, surgery by Robert Reid and Anaesthetist Martin Bristow, obstetrics and gynaecology by Peter Wheeler, pathology by E. H. Hemsted, and radiology by George Burfield, with Dr C. R. Haines of the junior medical staff completing this first Royal Berks Medical Services Committee. Initially they met twice monthly at 3 Craven Road.

Subsequent experience increased the number of specialties represented as Divisions and halved the number of meetings, which reverted to the old library when the new Post-graduate Centre library became operational. The original Committee started well, being used sensibly and responsibly by the different Divisions. It was a tribute to Frank Hampson's administrative ability and to the friendliness and co-operation of the medical staff that this new venture was so smoothly and quickly established. The Cogwheel and the Salmon Central Committees later visited the Royal Berks to assess the impact of their Schemes in a well-organised District General Hospital and its ancillary institutions. The Management Committee had every reason to take pride in its staff, its hospitals and in its own stewardship.

The 1974 Reorganisation
This efficient, cohesive and highly regarded administration was abolished in the ill-fated first major reorganisation of the N.H.S. Sir Keith Joseph's 1974 scheme had developed from Green Papers by Kenneth Robinson and by Richard Crossman, who in 1968 had become the first Secretary of State in the new Department of Health and Social Services. Pushed through by Sir Keith Joseph to coincide with the reorganisation of local government, the N.H.S. reorganisation ironically had to be implemented by a less than enthusiastic Barbara Castle. The hospitals were united with the Community and Family Practitioner Services, and administration became three-tiered, with 14 Regional Health Authorities, 90 Area Health Authorities and 205 Districts. This was the start of a regrettable distancing of hospital management from its major sphere of responsibility.

The new Berkshire Area Health Authority, with Ian Islip as Administrator and Sir John Hedges as Chairman, was located in the warren of rooms and corridors of the old Great Western Hotel opposite Reading Railway Station – ideal for office commuters and for visiting bureaucrats and dignitaries. With no parking facilities, however, visiting by consultants and other key hospital workers was extraordinarily difficult, and the HQ administrative staff were rarely to be seen at the Royal Berks.

The concept of a West Berkshire Health District and the appointment of District Officers did little to help the Hospital. Integration of hospital, general practitioner, public health and social services was not obviously successful; repetitive committee meetings often proved ineffective and time wasting for the Hospital representatives. Many of the well-established systems were by-passed, particularly in Departments such as Pathology, Radiology and Catering which provided a district service. Stewart Hinder, promoted from Deputy Group Secretary to District Administrator, fought hard to make consensus management efficient, but to the Hospital staff it seemed that many important decisions were unduly delayed or were never made at all.

Within the hospital service eccentric functional divisions and administrative boundaries confused a previously simple organisation. Ron Penney successfully applied for the new post of 'Support Services

Manager'. He was replaced not by a Hospital Secretary, but a Sector Administrator. This was Geoff Part who had been seconded from his post as Hospital Secretary at Newbury to join the Joint Liaison Committee for the reorganisation. Mr Part's new position carried responsibility for the Royal Berks, Battle, Prospect Park, Blagrave and Dellwood Hospitals – shades of Mrs Stride and House Committee No. 1. Nursing management in these same hospitals under the Salmon Scheme added further complications. Division 1 contained the Royal Berks (except for its maternity services) plus Battle Hospital; Division 2 included Dellwood, Prospect Park and Blagrave; the Maternity Division covered the peripheral units as well as the Royal Berks Maternity Block, while the Education Division impinged on all sites.

Little wonder that this period was marked by confusion, misunderstandings and irritation, particularly among the medical staff who were less interested in the status of administrative and nursing posts and their boundaries of responsibility than in bringing together scattered services for the improvement of efficiency and patient care.

The Reorganisation of 1982
Barbara Castle's consultative paper 'Patients First', and the subsequent reorganisation of the N.H.S. in 1982 came as no surprise and received a cautious welcome. The essentials were the loss of one administrative tier as District Health Authorities took over from their Area Health Authority, and the arrangement of their services into 'Units of Management'. The Royal Berks staff were pleased to have their Hospital back as a single entity, albeit with this soulless designation. Those with clinical commitments in both the Royal Berks and Battle Hospital had some qualms about dual control, but hopes were very high for benefits from a return to genuine local management. The Hospital acquired yet another system of administration – the Unit Management Group. Simon Strachan was appointed Unit Administrator, the Directors of Nursing and Midwifery Services, Miss J. Ingram and Miss I. Waterhouse, automatically took their places, and the first Unit Medical Representative was Consultant Anaesthetist Marshall Barr, no election being necessary since all other consultants were too wary of this new position to accept nomination.

Major setbacks came immediately. Mr Strachan, who had proved to be confident, energetic and popular, after just a few months moved to Brighton in the absurd roundabout of administrative appointments. The new West Berkshire Health Authority soon lost the confidence of its major hospital, although there had been no similarly disruptive staff changes at Great Western House. Dr Hampson, who had been made Chairman of the Area Health Authority in 1979 during his last year as a Royal Berks Consultant, was now Chairman of the new Authority. Ian Islip had moved to become District Administrator and David Smith to District Treasurer.

Apportionment of the budget between individual units was the matter of disagreement with these old allies of the Hospital. The share for the Royal Berks was disastrously inadequate. The governmental policy of reduced spending for the acute services was being implemented, and despite the strongest protests of the fledgling Unit Management Group, its effect was exaggerated by imbalance of provision between the Royal Berks and Battle Hospitals. As so often in the past, it was only the inability to recruit a full establishment of nurses which gave some budgetary saving and at least temporary protection from financial chaos. Martin Hawke, the second and the last Unit Administrator of the Royal Berks, joined a Management Group which was completely swamped by the problems of underfunding.

Retrenchment and More Reorganisation
Most of the departments of the Royal Berks initially supported their management's call for a realistic exercise in belt tightening. Some inefficiencies were corrected and wasteful practices controlled. But it was soon obvious that these were of almost trivial consequence compared with the level of underfinancing in relation to the work load of the Hospital. Annual savings amounting to hundreds of thousands were being demanded of the Royal Berks, while paradoxically its catchment area was booming. New housing developments at Earley and westwards towards Newbury were accommodating the large influx of a youthful population which brought its own contribution of a rapidly rising birth rate.

Against this increasing demand for health care, justified new developments were refused, previously accepted projects were shelved, necessary maintenance work was neglected and worn-out equipment was not replaced. In common with hospitals up and down the country, the Royal Berks now entered a gloomy phase of apathy, or in some cases antipathy, to the N.H.S. Deterioration in the clinical services was now inevitable. The previously harmonious Hospital Medical Services Committee became an assemblage of factions and of bickering discontent. Among senior consultants the talk in the corridors was not of new plans but of early retirement. Morale in more junior medical and nursing ranks was further lowered by a series of niggling constraints. Free beverages were stopped for the operating theatre and intensive care staff. Out-of-hours catering was reduced to inadequately stocked dispensing machines. Junior doctors working through the night had to scurry across the London Road to the recently opened 24-hour service station in order to get some reasonable food – a disgraceful situation which was bitterly resented. The concurrent redecoration and carpeting of the recently vacated junior doctors' Mess and dining room for use as new administrative offices hardly improved the situation.

Fresh hopes came with the Griffiths Report and the appointment of the Hospital's first General Manager in 1986. Ian Gornall was recruited from industry, coming in his own phrase 'with fire in the belly'. He was given the authority but not the finance to correct the glaring deficiencies and undertake the tasks whose necessity was even more obvious to a newcomer in the hospital service. He was able to clean up the general untidiness; he made significant staff changes and he simplified the management system. The administrative offices were relocated yet again; the start of a domino movement in which Admin. went to Greenlands and its attached Day Bed Unit, Sister Heading shifted her Day Beds to the Anaesthetics Department (previously the C. F. Taylor Unit), and the anaesthetists very happily took over the upgraded front offices, where years before many of them had dined and partied in the Residents' Mess.

Within the Authority there now came two changes in key personnel. Frank Hampson, dedicated servant to the Hospital and the Health District since 1959, reached retiring age and was replaced as Chairman by Dr Peter Phillips in 1986. Within a year the District General Manager had also gone: Ian Islip, still tragically young, died of an inoperable brain tumour. He had functioned efficiently throughout this period of increasing difficulties until his first symptoms and immediate hospitalisation, and to the end he remained lucid and cheerful – a brave episode, but a reminder of the potential hazard when illness strikes at those holding positions of responsibility.

The new District General Manager was Michael Taylor, who came with outstanding recommendations from the 'spies' of the Royal Berks in the City of London Hospitals. The consultants hoped for urgent action and Mr Taylor did not fudge making a difficult decision. Having studied the projected overspend of £1.3m by the Health Authority, he proposed a large package of economies which mainly affected the Royal Berks. The proposals began with the closure of four surgical wards and the loss of some 25 operating sessions per week. The Visiting Medical Staff Committee, which since 1949 had functioned mainly as a safety valve, allowing consultants to air their divergent views and complaints without any executive action, reacted immediately and with a vigour never previously suspected.

The consultants foresaw the disapprobation which would follow these cuts, when the loss of beds and theatre time for elective surgery propelled patients into the private sector. They wanted to make clear to the public their total opposition to measures which would improve medical income, but dismantle the local acute health service. Led by the Chairman, Cardiologist John Bell, the Committee placed a full-page advertisement in the Reading *Evening Post* of September 10th, 1987, pointing out the consequences of the proposed cuts and the unanimous opposition of the consultants to the proposals.

This unprecedented direct communication by fully united consultants to the local populace attracted national attention. It was reported in major newspapers, on television and radio as well as in the prestigious *Lancet* and the British Medical Association's *News Review*. Similar advertisements were subsequently placed by the general practitioners of West Berkshire and by other hospital doctors in different districts throughout England. In future years this advertisement by the Reading consultants may come to be seen as a significant event in changing the policy of financing the National Health Service.

In the short term the cuts were approved at a stormy meeting of the Health Authority. Ian Gornall resigned after two years of endeavour, before yet another reorganisation took place. He departed in December 1987 in a blaze of media publicity which must also have increased the mounting pressure for better Health Service funding.

This next reorganisation was in fact the return of an old idea – realignment of Battle with the Royal Berks, the two to be managed as one acute unit. The District Manager and Health Authority Chairman both strongly favoured this scheme. More importantly, they committed themselves to striving for the ideal of all acute services on one hospital site. Dr Alun Jones was appointed Acute Services General Manager in mid-1988. His task is daunting, but a rejuvenated Health Service and a united, determined local Administration may yet see the goal achieved.

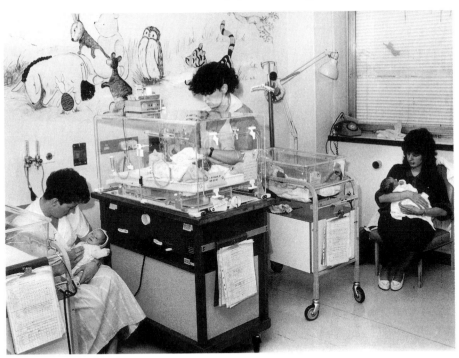

Buscot Neonatal Ward in the Maternity Block

4

EDUCATION AND TRAINING

In the narrow sense of affiliation to one particular medical school with academic medical staff holding Honorary Consultant appointments, the Royal Berkshire Hospital has never been a teaching hospital. Nonetheless, through arrangements which started in the 1950s, it has helped to teach a steady stream of medical students from Oxford and the London Schools of St Mary's, the Royal Free and St Bartholomew's. With ultra specialisation in the teaching hospitals, and in many cases considerable loss of their local catchment population, the University Faculties have come to rely heavily on attachments to District General Hospitals of acknowledged excellence.

At the Royal Berks experience is most commonly provided in general medicine, paediatrics, surgery and obstetrics. Academically cocooned students are astonished by the numbers of patients treated and the variety of conditions. The Reading consultants have the challenge of questing minds, and the opportunity to assess potential recruits to the junior medical staff. Rarely are schemes devised of such mutual benefit.

Proposals for a Medical School
There have been three formal attempts to establish a medical school at Reading University with the Royal Berks as its main teaching hospital. In 1966 a first proposal failed to gain inclusion in the recommendations of the Royal Commission on Medical Education. A Joint Liaison Committee of the University and the Reading and District Hospital Management Committee was then established to prepare a more detailed submission. Bryn Thomas and Eric Cox represented the Royal Berks medical staff on this Committee, with Naylor and Woodrow from the R.&D.H.M.C. and Dr Oddie from the Oxford Regional Hospital Board. The Vice Chancellor, Bursar, Senior Assistant Registrar, Dr Cumming, Professors Curnow, Graham (later replaced by Professor Kaplan) and Tyler comprised the enthusiastic University team. Their planned programme of teaching was very modern, with elimination of departmental barriers and particular emphasis on training for general practice. Stress was laid on the proximity of the two sites. The University was prepared to make available a considerable area of its London Road premises, which would be separated from the Hospital only by Redlands Road. It was hoped to have this major thoroughfare converted to a precinctual road and thus have the two institutions virtually united.

A twenty-page paper *Proposal for the Establishment of a Medical School at Reading University* was published in November 1969 – and rejected by the University Grants Committee. The Joint Liaison Committee continued to meet for several years and another bid was made in 1974, which met with no greater success. Unless one of the financially squeezed London schools makes a move westwards, there seems little likelihood that Reading will ever have its own medical school.

For many, this is no bad thing. Full-time undergraduate education is very consuming both of time and of staff. The strength of the Royal Berks as a Voluntary Hospital and as a District General Hospital has always been in direct clinical care – the practical management of vast numbers of patients by high-quality staff – coupled with a determination to maintain standards by continuing education at the post-graduate level. This policy has been in evidence from the earliest deliberations of the Reading Pathological Society to the lectures, seminars and group meetings of the modern Post-graduate Centre. Young doctors on the staff have always worked long hours, gaining a wealth of experience under immediate supervision or with the back-up of consultants on call. Their seniors, with few exceptions, have constantly striven to remain up to date in knowledge and technology. In consequence, the Royal Berks has developed its enviable reputation as a training ground for both specialists and general practitioners.

Post-graduate Training

The post-basic educational role has been strongly supported by the University of Oxford Post-graduate Medical Education Committee ever since 1949, when Gordon Bohn was able to announce plans for the Royal Berks and Battle to provide teaching facilities for all doctors in the Reading area. Matters were formalised in 1962 with a grant from the Nuffield Provincial Hospitals Trust. Dr R. I. Meanock, Consultant in Physical Medicine, became the first Area Post-graduate Clinical Tutor. The library received an annual grant for books and journals plus the salary for a Secretary/Librarian. Projection facilities were also provided, which helped to persuade some far-sighted consultants of the need for a Department of Clinical Photography. The Management Committee were readily convinced, and speeded its establishment by the application of Endowment Funds. Lionel Williams was appointed Senior Medical Photographer in 1964. He built up a Department of Medical Illustration which has grown steadily during 25 years, has undergone three changes of venue, and made perhaps the most consistent contribution to post-graduate education at the Hospital.

The new educational activity of the 1960s centred naturally on the library where, as we have seen, frequent committee meetings were already a problem. Bryn Thomas, as Honorary Librarian of the Reading Pathological Society, was caught between enthusiasm for advances in post-graduate education and further encroachment on the function of the library. His part-time helper Una Spanner took on the extra responsibility of Secretary/Librarian and at first was able to cope with both roles, using as her base just the small office in the far corner of the library. At that time the current holdings of subscribed journals were so few that they also shared this tiny area. Things changed quickly with expenditure of the Oxford funds. The stocks of journals and texts rapidly increased; the library grew busier and the post-graduate administrative work multiplied. Ian Meanock appropriated a room at the foot of the library stairs. This became the Post-graduate Office; Mrs Spanner reverted to her purely library duties and Mrs Kathleen Street was appointed as the first Post-graduate Secretary.

The original plan was to take over more of the ground floor rooms when out-patients, the almoners and Dispensary all moved to their respective new quarters. It was conceived that eventually the entire West Wing would constitute a Post-graduate Centre. On the eastern side of the Hospital, however, the new Nurse Education Centre was being planned, to be built adjacent to the Nurses' Home. It was logical that the Medical Education Centre should be linked to this development, but logic would be expensive. There would have to be demolition of 2/4 Craven Road and construction of an entirely new building rather than a modest conversion in the West Wing. Furthermore, the complex must include a new library, since ready access to an up-to-date library has always been the first essential of post-graduate education.

After much discussion, grants were obtained from the Oxford Regional Health Authority and the Hospital Management Committee, while to raise the balance required for a first-class centre, a Medical Education and Research Trust was formed. The original Trustees were Ian Meanock, Frank Hampson, Haemotologist David Robertson-Smith, Physician Viscount Waverley and David Woodrow from the Hospital Management Committee. G. W. Cashell volunteered to chair the Appeal Committee which, with some professional help, soon had money flowing. There were financial complications when C. F. Taylor, who offered to build the centre at cost, became ill and was ordered to rest. The Regional Board accepted his designs and appointed their own architects and quantity surveyors. As costs increased from an estimated £160,000 in 1970 to £210,000 in 1972, the Region contributed more, the District increased its grant from Free Monies and the Trust's Appeal Committee intensified its efforts. The doctors and dentists of Reading naturally contributed to the benefit of their own continuing education, but many local business firms and families were also generous to the cause. Major benefactors sponsored rooms, and their names are recorded on the plaques distributed through the Centre. The Lilly Lecture Theatre, Marks and Spencer Reading Room, W. H. Smith and Son Refectory, the Huntley and Palmer and the Mid-Southern Hospital Contributory Seminar Rooms, and the Behrens Bar are all suitably identified, as are rooms co-sponsored by several firms which range from national companies to local enterprises.

Ian Meanock, who had worked for years towards the establishment of a formal Post-graduate Centre, retired from the Tutorship in 1970, and Geoffrey Cashell took on the last of his quite remarkable list of extra duties in the service of the Royal Berks. As his consultantship in ophthalmology drew to a close, he became the new Post-graduate Tutor, guiding the development of the Centre until its official opening in 1975.

The linked nursing and medical centres heralded a new era for the Hospital in ways far beyond the important fact of their establishment. Four of the original properties in Redlands Road were lost. By a strange quirk the Nurses' Centre replaced the doctors' quarters of Craven Villas and St Denys, while Thirlmere, the Matron's Home and Lindens, the now-redundant Nurses' Training School, were demolished to provide the site for the new Medical Building. Bryn Thomas and the Reading Pathological Society jealously preserved the old library in the West Wing to house the historical collections, to serve as a quiet reading room and to continue as the home of the Society. The small library office now holds the historical records and memorabilia of the Reading Pathological Society. An archives room for the hospital itself was established by Bryn Thomas in the original Post-graduate Office downstairs, when a hoard of old hospital records was

The old library in the 1960s

A corner of the new Post-graduate Library

discovered in the damp coach house of 23 Craven Road (Orwell House). The archives are not complete, but do fully record the foundation of the Hospital and most of the significant changes in its progress through 150 years. The most recent advance, the redevelopment of the Radiotherapy Department in the West Wing, demanded another move for the archives. Now they are stored appropriately in a basement room of the original Hospital building.

While the historical library and archives room preserve the Hospital's past, Bryn Thomas's new library was from the outset looking towards the future. In 1976, perhaps sensing that his time was now short, he recommended the Pathological Society to elect his fellow anaesthetist Marshall Barr as Honorary Librarian. When he died two years later, the library was named by popular consent 'The Bryn Thomas Memorial Library' – a tribute to his 27 years of dedicated service.

Over the next decade many important changes were made in the medical library service. Successive professional librarians Stephen Town and Enid Forsyth began a formal integration with the nurses' library, now just a corridor away. Computer technology was introduced, and on-line facilities rapidly developed. These revolutionary advances were offered not only to the doctors and now the nurses, but to all professional hospital staff. The library thus contributed to the gradual breaking down of the haughty isolationism of the hospital doctors, a process in which other aspects of the Post-graduate Centre played their part.

The Post-graduate Centre has therefore had a marked influence on the hospital buildings, on the preservation of its history, advances in its library service and integration of different groups of staff. Of course, its prime function has always been the provision of facilities for continuing education.

If a focal point is sought in the medical life of the Hospital, it is the Thursday Midday Grand Round for which the Post-graduate Lecture Theatre is regularly filled. New Zealander Ken North inaugurated this most successful programme in 1975. He became Post-graduate Tutor when Geoffrey Cashell retired from his five years' final term of service for the Hospital. North was replaced in turn by E.N.T. Surgeon Roger Parker and Radiologist Tom Walker. Each Tutor, with a different specialist background, has brought new ideas for the continued improvement of medical education at the Royal Berkshire Hospital. Exhibitions, seminars, G.P. training schemes, interdisciplinary meetings and specialty courses have all flourished. Mrs Pat Austin, the second Post-graduate Secretary, has guided the successive tutors throughout this period of expanding activity with quiet efficiency. Her promotion to Centre Administrator in 1981 gave proper recognition to her role, and to the key importance of the Post-graduate Centre in the modern Hospital. Within the Centre, the astonishing contributions over 50 years by one man were recognised when the Common Room was allocated for committee meetings and in 1988 given the name Cashell Room.

Nurse Education
In 1947 the General Nursing Council made its first post-war inspection of the Royal Berkshire Hospital and was 'happy to continue its recognition as a Complete Training School for the General Part of the Register'.

Earlier in the year the Preliminary Training School had moved to Joyce Grove, Nettlebed, a property which had been shared by St Mary's and the Westminster Nursing Schools from London since the outbreak of war. The Westminster now withdrew and the Royal Berks took the opportunity of renting the second floor and sharing the training facilities with St Mary's. Forty-seven nurses attended the eight-week P.T.S. courses in 1947, hardly the numbers needed if the Hospital was to be fully staffed by its own trainees. Previous affiliations with Bideford, Bexhill and Stoke Mandeville Hospitals were all terminated by the time of nationalisation, and in 1948 the Royal Berks, including Greenlands and Blagrave Branch, had a total of 241 full-time nurses, of whom 134 were students. The revolutionary social changes leading to general acceptance of the working wife and especially of the married nurse were still to come; only 28 part-time nurses were employed at the start of the National Health Service.

Living accommodation for the single nurses was a major problem, tackled as we have seen in direct representations to the Ministry. So also was space for tuition, despite removal of the Preliminary Training School from Lindens. This house, adjacent to Matron's residence, was quite inadequate as the centre of nurse training. A long wooden classroom was added behind, and much later a hutted practical room was built between Lindens and Thirlmere, but these were merely stop-gap measures until a proper nursing school could be built. An immediate demand for expansion came in 1952 with the establishment of the Reading Combined Training School incorporating the Royal Berks, Battle and Prospect Park Hospitals. The Pupil Nurses' School, running the shorter course for State Enrolled Nurses, stayed at Battle.

Properties were purchased in the Bath Road, strategically central to all three hospitals, and were converted for accommodation and for teaching. Paxton House and its neighbour Pendragon, acquired respectively in 1950 and 1952, became the new Group Preliminary Training School for 40 students. The sale description for Pendragon House included as an asset 'a well-equipped theatre'. This prompted a Department of Health query. Geoffrey Weston was invited to explain why the property being purchased had an operating theatre already, and why it should be paid for. The explanation was that it was a different type of theatre, the curtains, lighting and stage equipment all being purchased using Endowment Funds. It did prove useful. A changing room behind the stage served as a Practical Room; the theatre itself was used as a lecture hall, but also for entertainments such as concerts, and performances by the then active Hospital Dramatic Club.

Visit of Douglas Bader in 1957 with Matron Brace in the foreground

The Bath Road Preliminary Training School was constantly being repaired, decorated and expanded in its first few years. Until the official opening in 1956 Sister Lawrence, the P.T.S. Tutor, had to teach against the difficult background of builders' noises and the understandable interest of the workmen in her student nurses.

At the Hospital itself there were different problems. Apart from overcrowding, the amalgamation of two schools had brought together two Principal Tutors of equal status but very different attitudes and personalities. When Sister Ellement retired, Mrs Doreen Thomas, originally the Battle Principal Tutor, had sole charge of training. The ultimate responsibility, of course, still rested with Miss Aldwinckle who as Matron of the Royal Berks was also Matron of the Group Training School.

In 1957 a highlight for nurses and staff was the visit of the celebrated war-time flyer Group Captain D. R. S. Bader C.B.E., D.S.O., D.F.C. He came on April 27th for the annual presentation of certificates, badges and prizes. He heard speeches from Mrs H. A. Benyon C.B.E., retiring Chairman of the Hospital Management Committee, and from Lady Palmer, Chairman of the Nursing Sub-committee – the Benyon and Palmer families being as active in the affairs of the Royal Berks as when he had been a patient there. This occasion brought back many memories for Douglas Bader and he spoke of his deep gratitude to the Hospital and its staff. He most keenly regretted that Leonard Joyce had not lived to see his youthful patient fly again and to fight. The many photographs taken and kept as a record of this prize-giving event show how popular he was and how infectiously enthusiastic. The official programme records that of more than 50 nurses awarded certificates and prizes only three were male and only four of the ladies were married. There was certainly a youthful and appreciative gallery when the war hero embraced the Greenlands Sisters of 1931, and had Thornhill and Brace, now eminent Matrons both, giggling like schoolgirls.

The long-awaited Nurses Education Centre was by now being seriously discussed. A site next to the Nurses' Home was agreed and it became Phase II of the slow-moving official development plans. The Centre was eventually completed in 1969, but without any prestigious opening ceremony. Having four major developments on its hands, the Hospital Management Committee were most uncharacteristically indecisive in considering official names for the buildings, and plans for their formal opening. Lack of finance was certainly an important factor. One proposal for a Royal visitor to perform some sort of combined opening ceremony was quietly dropped, and the Eye Block, X-ray Department, Maternity Unit and Nurses Education Centre all came into use with a minimum of fuss or expense. Perhaps fortunately – Cashell had hoped that the Ophthalmic Block would be called 'The Queen's Building', which might today invoke mirth rather than patriotism. The Nurses Education Centre opened with that bare title exactly indicating its function. This was pleasing enough for the Nurse Tutors; at last they were together, with modern facilities, space for classrooms and practical teaching, and a library instead of a book cupboard.

The coming of this Centre also marked a transition period in nursing at the Hospital. The old Nursing Advisory Committee was dissolved in favour of a Nurse Education Committee, chaired by the Hon. Mrs Gordon Palmer. This group made significant decisions on such things as the minimum age of recruitment, and useful recommendations on many educational matters.

By far the most important change, however, was the introduction at this time of the Salmon Structure of Nursing Administration, whose divisive numbered posts removed good nurses from their clinical work and robbed the ward sisters of their autonomy. On the positive side, 'Salmon' did improve senior salaries and the status of the nurse teachers, and hastened the demise of traditional rigid nursing discipline, which was certainly authoritarian enough at the Royal Berks. Today, junior nurses do not wait trembling outside Matron's Office to report a broken syringe or thermometer. Nor do their tutors have to present themselves to Matron before taking leave and again on their return.

The old system of authority based on Matron, ward sisters and tutors did have good aspects, including simplicity and clarity of purpose. It could be adopted again but would have to take account of the vast changes in nursing duties and attitudes, and would have to adjust to the proliferation of tutors with a very different educational role. Miss Pat Hunt, the Director of Nurse Education, now has 24 tutors in the West Berkshire School of Nursing. The newer medical technologies have demanded wider education of her nurses, to a higher standard, and with more open discussion on controversial issues. Major teaching commitments include refresher courses for married nurses and continuing education for the permanent staff. The grand new Education Centre of 20 years ago is now too small and has overflowed. Once more there are nurse teachers trying to cope in cramped, uncomfortable accommodation – a small corner retrieved from the deserted Pathology Laboratory next door. This structurally sound building with ample space is being wasted because of shortage of funds, while the high standards of Royal Berks nurse education are threatened. Yet again the fundamental issue is finance.

The Royal Berks nurse educators are looking more and more to Project 2000, the revolutionary plan of the United Kingdom Central Council for Nursing, Midwifery and Health Visiting. This aims to give trainee nurses genuine student status with a foundation academic course up to two years, to have the students supernumary to N.H.S. staffing establishment, and to improve post registration continuing education. In mid 1988, John Moore has given his blessing. But where will be found the huge number of extra nurses and the vast sums required?

Midwifery training (which is very different from general nursing training, as midwives are fond of pointing out) returned to the Royal Berks with the opening of the Maternity Unit in 1968, just before the Nurses

Education Centre. Here was Peter Wheeler's real triumph. The horrendous days were gone of the hospital physicians who were basically general practitioners, or their inexperienced juniors, trying to cope with complicated maternity cases at first in Adelaide Ward and later in the East Wing. He had steadily advanced midwifery care through Nuffield 3 and the interim unit at Battle Hospital to this completely modern unit, built at his favoured site and fully staffed by specialists with trainees in support. Previously, the only training recognised by the Central Midwives Board had been at Dellwood Maternity Home. In 1950 Dellwood had an establishment of Matron, four staff midwives, and eight pupil midwives who spent six months there for the intern experience of normal deliveries for their Part II training.

The Reading Combined Hospitals Maternity Unit which opened in the Thames Block at Battle in 1952 had hoped for recognition for the more advanced Part I training, but this was not granted until the opening of the new unit. Here, with the strong support of Consultant Obstetricians Wheeler, Frewen and Stallabrass, two midwifery tutors ran the full one-year course. Today five tutors pack into an 18-month course the practical work and skills required by the modern midwife who has to cope with a range of demands from natural childbirth to computerised monitoring and Caesarean section under epidural anaesthesia. Yet the student numbers for years have been too small, leading to a serious shortage of midwives. And here controversy rages, which must be resolved. Will trained midwives continue to have duties in the small peripheral hospitals at Henley, Wokingham and Newbury or will centralisation of obstetric services at the Royal Berkshire Hospital be permanent and complete?

Other Departmental Training Schemes

Many departments of the Hospital other than medical and nursing have a proud history of education, training and research. Three units caring for particular aspects of the mouth, the eyes and ears perhaps deserve special mention.

The Department of Oral Surgery and Dentistry has gained a high reputation for clinical training of senior house officers. More recently, this departmental reputation has been further enhanced by Orthodontist Keith Isaacson, author of a standard text book, whose practical courses in the Post-graduate Centre attract attendance from countries throughout the world.

The Orthoptic School, opened in 1935 and combined with the Oxford School of Orthoptics in 1947, had a fine reputation, despite being sited first in the old Greenlands stable block, the Hospital East Wing and then the end hut in Redlands Road. It closed in 1956 due to staff shortage, as did the Oxford School in 1964. With the coming of the new Eye Block, the School reopened in 1967, with Miss Yvonne Maurer as the Principal. Today it is more active than ever; Principal Pauline Bagley has three part-time teachers, and the continued enthusiastic assistance of the ophthalmic

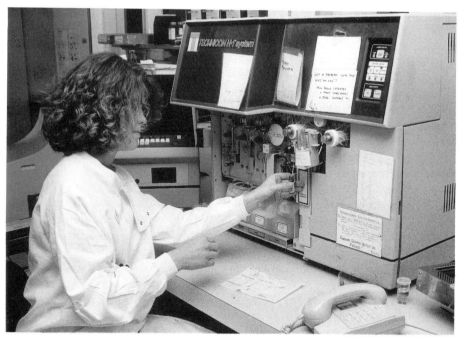

Haematology Laboratory, showing the auto analyser

medical staff. The dozen or more orthoptic students know they belong to one of the best schools in Britain.

The Audiology Unit was started in 1958 with the help of a Nuffield Foundation grant, mainly for research into the development of speech and hearing in the first two years of life. Under the direction of E.N.T. Consultant Hunt Williams and with Dr. K. Murphy as Research Scientist, it became a world-renowned centre. Its work has expanded to involve a major commitment for patients of all ages. Now in the charge of John Bamford, with E.N.T. Surgeon Tom Heyworth as Consultant, the Unit remains at the forefront in research, and gives theoretical and practical instruction to Linguistics students from the University. Its most vital educational role, however, is the training of patients, their families, and those doctors and nurses involved with the care of the deaf.

On a much broader canvas, the Hospital laboratories have for many years coped with mounting service commitments while becoming increasingly involved with education of their own staff and of students from Reading University. Currently there are some 25 undergraduates and postgraduates in training. In 1979 the Department of Pathology was recognised as an Associated Institution of the University of Reading. Frank Hampson was honoured with a Visiting Professorship and others in haematology, bacteriology and biochemistry became honorary academic staff. Andras Tarnoky, Head of Clinical Chemistry, organised a clinical course for third year Patho-biology B.Sc. students which is a continuing success. In

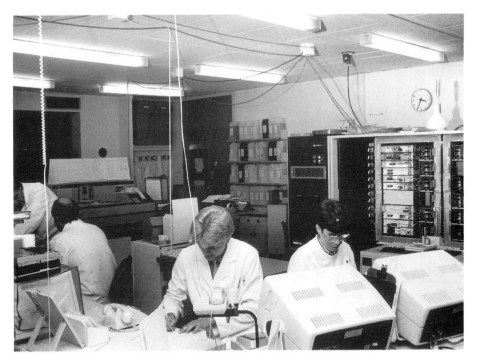

Screening Laboratory, Bio-chemistry Department

retirement, Dr Tarnoky became an Honorary Research Fellow at the University, continuing his research on protein variants which in 1964 had led to the Americans naming one of his discoveries 'Albumin Reading'.

Many other departments have in ways big and small contributed to the general recognition of the Royal Berks as a centre of training excellence. In 1956 the Group Pharmacy was approved for student training. The Catering Department in the same year began participating in the Whitley Council Apprenticeship Scheme for cooks. The Engineers have run apprenticeships and training programmes, continually adapting to their fast-changing technologies.

An excellent modern training programme for Operating Department Assistants, organised by Senior O.D.A. Patrick Sheehy and Senior Theatre Nurse Gill Griffiths is the end result of a remarkable transformation whereby a group of willing, but untrained helpers in theatre have become skilled professionals. In the 1960s, theatre orderlies were still members of the general portering staff. Following an Operating Theatre Attendants' Course run part-time in the evenings at Oxford, J. Amor, J. Ploszynski and C. W. Blanchard were regraded in 1964 to Operating Theatre Attendants (O.T.A.s) Class 1. Other Royal Berks porters were then similarly upgraded for other theatres. When day-release courses were created to standardise such training nationally, the Royal Berks sent its men, and new grades were established to recognise the high quality of the modern O.D.A.

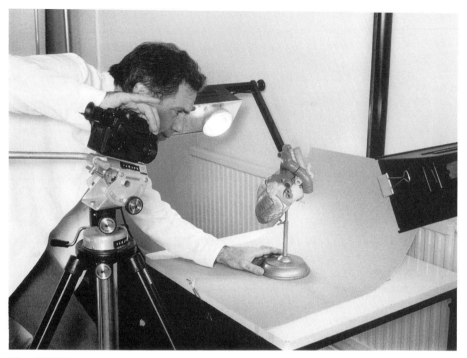

Lionel Williams, Head of Department of Medical Illustration

'George' Ploszynski, now Senior O.D.A. in general theatres, is the only Royal Berks porter to have been involved throughout this complete educational metamorphosis.

The new Hospital Administration of the 1980s has itself been active in education of its staff, particularly in the provision of middle management courses, an example of how the needs and aims of training are subject to change, and how the Hospital has adjusted. Compare lectures on management theory with a course which was last successfully run at the Royal Berks in 1957, when nine students sat and passed the City and Guilds Specialist Examination for Hospital Steam Stokers.

5

SOCIAL LIFE
IN THE HOSPITAL

Since the 1939–45 war the Royal Berkshire Hospital has undergone social changes possibly even more dramatic than its physical expansion. As with similar institutions throughout the country there has been accelerating progress towards a freer, more relaxed hospital community. Senior doctors have lost their god-like status, low-paid workers have gained in experience, skills and confidence, multiple nationalities and ethnic styles of dress have been accepted. Most importantly there has been a social intermingling of groups which previously were almost completely segregated.

The first stirrings of these changes probably came during the war, as the diminished staff were brought together in patriotic effort and shared hopes and griefs. The most significant instance of this new camaraderie was the Hospital firewatchers' group which developed into a sort of informal club. A fire guard of twelve assembled nightly on the roof above the E.N.T. theatre, their base and rest room now being the theatre nurses' changing room. The guard was drawn from all walks of hospital life. There was plenty of time during the night watch for cups of tea, cards and conversation since Reading was little troubled by the Luftwaffe, and it was decided that after the war a hospital social club should be established. Table-tennis was started in 1944 but for many years this was the only real leisure and social facility for the hospital staff.

Eventually, in 1956, the administration, perhaps a little influenced by Geoffrey Weston's secretary – Rosemary Powell was a member of the ladies' table-tennis team which became County Champions – agreed to provide a recreation hut. This was done by using a specific legacy from America, an amount which was sufficient only for the material and the plans. Building Supervisor Harry Sellwood and his team constructed the building in their own free time.

The new building was in line with the out-patients' huts and directly across the driveway from the private patients in Greenlands. Its use was strictly controlled by the Hospital Secretary; noisy activities and alcohol were strictly forbidden. In effect, it functioned merely as a large games room, particularly for the table-tennis players. Harry Sellwood remained the enthusiast and the driving force, so that when he retired with a well-earned British Empire Medal in 1962, recreational interest dwindled and other hospital activities began to encroach. Meetings of the Red Cross and similar organisations were held there, and the Reading Pathological Society began to use the room for examining patients at clinical meetings.

In 1968 a young laboratory worker eating her sandwiches was ejected by medical staff preparing for such an occasion. John Dykes, Chief Technologist in Haematology was incensed. He decided there and then to organise a proper social club for the hospital staff. He harangued and cajoled until interest was aroused, had himself elected Club Secretary, obtained a loan from the Morlands Brewery, negotiated lengthily with the Administration and at last on May 29th, 1969 had the great satisfaction of opening a genuine Club with appropriate facilities and a licensed bar.

The Social Club prospered, but in 1981 this building burned down. Following a temporary move to the site of the old cafeteria at the front of the East Wing, a permanent site was found at 22 Craven Road and the new Social Club opened in September 1986, where it continues to expand. Its membership, which now exceeds 3,000, includes many doctors and nurses. This coming together socially of medical and nursing staff with the technicians, engineers, porters and all other grades of employment represents one of the greatest changes in attitudes within the Hospital.

Changing Standards
Until the 1960s, the younger student nurses all lived in the Nurses' Home under the watchful eye of Sister Borrell, a heroine of the siege of Malta. No male was admitted and porters attending on official duties were rigidly chaperoned. The doors were locked at 10 p.m. and a midnight pass was obtainable just once a month. The medical residents' quarters were strictly out of bounds. Secretive late returns via fire escape and unlatched windows were not unknown, and many took the calculated risk of attending the parties next door at St Denys; but it was a stifling social existence for the young nurses, who in practice mixed only with their own training set.

The Greenlands Private Nursing Staff had lived quite separately in comfortable and secluded flats above the old ophthalmic ward and theatre in West Wing. When the Private Nurses' distinction was lost, this select accommodation was from 1962 given to the Childrens' Nurses from Great Ormond Street Hospital who came to do their general training.

Today, the Nurses' Home and 'Greenlands Flats' have a freely mobile mixture of residents, male and female, including paramedics and other non-nursing staff. There are still two resident maids, both Spanish, a reminder that in days not so distant – until the early 1950s – almost the entire East Wing formed the maids' quarters. The many occupants then were basically of two nationalities, English or Irish.

The old social divisions were well illustrated by a rigid classification of dining areas. The nurses' dining-room was in the basement below Victoria Ward, where the third years and staff nurses had an elevated section of their own, but all the nurses had their meals served by maids. Adjacent, but quite separate, was the maids' own room while the sisters dined on the opposite side of the kitchens, beneath Benyon Ward. Upstairs, the junior doctors had their own dining area next to the Mess.

In 1951 a cafeteria was provided at the front of the East Wing, when the Orthoptic Department moved to their hut. This cafeteria, or canteen, was specifically for the use of 'non-resident staff other than nurses', whose habit of eating in their work places was a cause of worry about hygiene. Consultants were included in this clientele but they were as a matter of course given a separate room. Class distinctions even extended to the crockery, until shortages caused an intermingling of the patterns, which matched the changing social attitudes.

In 1988, the maids' old dining-room houses the Hospital archives, the sisters' sanctum is part of the Medical Photographic Department; the canteen and temporary Social Club stands empty. The nurses' old dining-room is now called North Wing Dining, and caters in tandem with its huge South Wing counterpart for all hospital staff. This includes the few doctors who choose to breakfast at the Hospital – a very low proportion, and indicative of another remarkable change, which is in the lifestyle of the Hospital junior medical staff.

In 1949 there were three Senior Registrars, ten Registrars and 12 House Officers. All were male. The salary for a House Officer was £350. Annual leave was only two calendar weeks and for most of these young men their hospital was 'home'. The Casualty House Officer on call slept next to the Mess and placed his shoes outside the door for the porters to clean. The porters also tended the Mess fireplace, the last coal fire in the Hospital, and doubtless sampled the contents of the free firkin of beer which was still provided from a private legacy. The young doctors played tennis on the Greenlands lawn court while the nurses were restricted to their own hard court behind the Nurses' Home.

Accommodation for the juniors was splendidly idiosyncratic, but uncomfortable. It steadily improved during the next decade as increasingly outspoken and better organised Residents demanded more facilities in the quarters of Melrose Villas, 56 London Road, St Denys, and later 22 Craven Road. A complete transformation came in the 1960s with rapidly rising staff numbers. Standardised flats were built for them in Erleigh and Addington Roads and an attractive group of houses in the Mount were purchased for the benefit of a new phenomenon, the older 'junior' hospital doctor with not only a wife, but several children. Living standards for the junior staff were also improving in other ways.

In 1962 a meeting of Resident Medical Officers obtained approval amongst other things for refreshments at night, a hot cupboard in the dining-room, different papers and journals, a wine cupboard, the formation of a Club and the holding of Mess Dinners. The Club and Mess Dinners continue, if rather sporadically. In 1988 the junior staff number almost 90, of whom nearly half are female and most are married. For many the Royal Berks is just part of a rotation around several hospitals. These transients usually reside at a distance and live in only when on call. For others, the hospital-provided accommodation is home, its network of flats and houses forming a type of village, discontinuous and geographically scattered, quite different from the old domestic atmosphere within the Royal Berks itself. Even the 20 or so doctors now living in the refurbished maids' quarters have no real communal life in the East Wing.

When the Hawke Administration of the early 1980s sought more offices at the front of the Hospital, no great objections were raised by the junior doctors to the removal of their traditional Mess. They were no longer dining separately, but in South Wing or the Post-graduate Centre. The common room and mess facilities were moved across to 15 Craven Road, which in the new style of hospital life was a much more suitable location, central to and part of the residents' 'village'. But the new Mess is rarely the scene of parties such as a previous generation held, and off-duty Residents tend more and more to gravitate to the Social Club opposite.

The consultants have fought two delaying actions against the general advance of social democracy in the Hospital. The traditions of the Reading Pathological Society have been jealously preserved, and in 1960 an even more elitist club was founded. This was the Royal Berkshire Hospital Club, a social arm of the Visiting Medical Staff Committee and therefore almost entirely restricted to consultant membership. Recently appointed Anaesthetist Tom Boulton was its chief instigator. The Club was granted use of the old museum room next to the library and each member had a numbered key to this sanctuary, which for a while became a miniature gentlemen's club.

This pleasant, convivial aspect of hospital life for the senior doctors lasted only a few years. Tom Boulton moved on to St Bartholomew's, pressure of work reduced attendance and the introduction of the breathalyser significantly hastened the Club's decline.

The concept was revitalised in 1974 with the opening of the Post-graduate Centre. 'The Reading Medical Club' took over the refectory, bar and leisure activities of the Centre. There was now a much broader membership, including junior doctors and G.P.s, but the Club was still essentially confined to medical and dental practitioners. Some die-hard consultants kept their numbered key to the quiet den next to the old library, but all eventually gravitated to the Post-graduate Centre. When Ian Gornall made use of the old consultants' room for V.I.P. luncheon meetings, few even knew their retreat had been invaded.

The new Club at the Post-graduate Centre was immediately popular, but restrained drinking habits have persisted and the bar trade does little to boost the Treasurer's balance sheets. Most use of the Club has been for 'medical only' lunching, where interestingly a voluntary segregation persists at the long refectory luncheon table. The consultants and general practitioners occupy the top end nearest the food, while the junior doctors sit at the opposite end, next to the telephone. The closed nature of the Reading Medical Club is on the whole understood and accepted, although it is certainly against the trend, and many consultants who have most valued their Club privileges have elsewhere been active in dismantling divisions within the Hospital.

The Royal Berkshire Hospital Dramatic Club was founded in 1951. Geoffrey Cashell was the Chairman, Jack Kempton and Geoffrey Weston early enthusiasts, together with Evelyn Aust, Bryn Thomas and many others. Treasurer Kitchen became Business Manager and Conrad Latto was readily persuaded to perform. This group of assorted players and helpers had a very successful few seasons. Their first year's presentations were 'On Monday Next' and 'Quiet Weekend', performed in the Nurses' Home. But work loads were already increasing. It became impossible to get the cast together for adequate rehearsal time and in 1956 the Club came to a halt. It is doubtful if the Hospital clinical staff will ever again be able to take major roles in drama productions – and certainly not twice a year.

A revival of show business came in 1974 when newly appointed Consultant Surgeon David Goodwin, his Senior Registrar Ian Hutton and Sister Maggie Bird organised the first of a highly popular series of Hospital Christmas Shows. These were even more successful in bringing together talent from all sectors of hospital staff. First act after the interval was invariably conjurer and magician 'The Great Goodwini', whose talent in both operating and revue theatre led to a performance before an audience of millions.

In 1987 the B.B.C., in a widely admired TV series on the history of surgery, made use of an array of talent from the Royal Berkshire Hospital. Consultant Anaesthetist Steve Allen became an adviser, provider of Hospital historical equipment and bit-player. Many Royal Berks nursing and surgical staff also appeared, but it was the imposingly built David Goodwin who featured in the title sequence of 'The Courage to Fail' – changing in fashion, whiskers and protective clothing from the pre-anaesthetic slashing amputator to the modern scientist/surgeon. Only Art Themen, Consultant Orthopaedic Surgeon, has outdone this level of TV exposure as an internationally acclaimed jazz saxophonist.

Before his TV stardom, Mr Goodwin had initiated another entertainment of greater specific importance to the Hospital. Nineteen eighty-two saw the beginning of a sporting tradition – the consultants versus junior medical staff cricket match. The standard of cricket varies, but is usually high enough to surprise spectators and some new players.

In celebration of the 125th anniversary of the foundation of the Royal Berkshire Hospital, a *Reading Hospitals' Journal* was published in 1962, edited by Anaesthetist Donald McWilliams. This was a well-presented publication which, although popular and well supported by local advertisers, faded like the Dramatic Club and for the same reason – the ever-mounting clinical workload. The seventh issue, of Christmas 1964, was also the last. Its more modest successors came 20 years later, the newsletters *Roundabout, Management Brief* and *Messenger*. These have been produced by hard-working enthusiasts on the administrative staff to improve information on the increasing activities and to boost staff pride in the Hospital.

No such boosting was necessary in 1962 when Secretary Ron Penney and his Assistant Norman Parker devised the first Royal Berks tie, which sold in great numbers from the Administrative Office. The widespread and increasing depression of staff in recent years has been a new phenomenon in the history of the Hospital – the culmination of repeated disappointments with the building programme, underfunding, overwork and episodes of adverse publicity. The betterment of social relations between different groups of Hospital staff with the opportunity of airing complaints to a wider audience has certainly not countered this malaise. Probably the contrary has been true, as doctors have grasped the genuine despair of their most loyal nurses, different workers have compared their own grievances with other groups often in a worse situation – and all have become aware that improvements for one section has usually meant less for the others, and for services to patients.

The Place of the Church

In past years, the Church would probably have provided the backbone of support for such a disenchanted staff. But the decline of practising Christianity has been another marked change in the social fabric of the Hospital. The Anglican, Free Church and Catholic Chaplains are as dedicated as ever, bringing great comfort to patients and their relatives. The beautiful, centrally situated chapel is still a focal point of hospital life, its special services of thanksgiving and remembrance still well attended. The annual lighting of the Christmas trees remains a religious occasion and the Hospital Christmas is not crassly commercialised. Yet the influence of the Church on the daily life and attitudes of most staff has dwindled almost to insignificance. As long ago as 1953 some urging was required to revive enthusiasm for an old-style Hospital Sunday, which it was hoped would help nurse recruitment. The tradition of an annual Hospital Sunday service is continued, but the uncomfortable reality is that today more nurses might attend a union rally than a Hospital service.

The Hospital's closest neighbour is St Andrew's Church, which still occupies the north-east corner of the island site, and between the two there has been an interesting social relationship. When the old church was condemned as too expensive to maintain and to heat, the Hospital Management Committee tried hard to purchase the property. In 1964, the Church authorities were prepared to build elsewhere and £65,000 was asked. The Ministry, through the Oxford Regional Board, thought this too expensive 'for landscaping and car parking'. Planning for the new Education Centre began shortly afterwards, as did demolition of the old church. There was some interest in a joint planning venture with a physical link and shared facilities between the new buildings of church and Postgraduate Centre, but the plans fell through and the only permanent sharing has been of the adjacent parking areas – daytime for the Centre, evenings and Sundays for St Andrew's.

Another opportunity for closer relations was a shared Hospital and church crêche which started in 1973 with a hut on the Hospital side, a gap made in the dividing stone wall and a caravan in the church car park. Four years later the crêche was closed. Eighteen staff members were bringing their children but the annual cost of £11,000 was felt to be too great. It seems a short-sighted decision: a permanent hospital/church crêche would be a much more effective recruiting enterprise than any number of Hospital Sundays.

There has been little inclination, then, to turn to the Church for help in combating the troubles of a Hospital society which, freed largely from the old distinctions of class and work, nevertheless has become grievously dispirited. Funding is yet again the key, but a new hope is detectable. A pay rise of 15 per cent has given a personal boost to the nurses; its 'guaranteed' central funding gives a hope of some availability of Health Authority funds for the acute services. The 150th Anniversay is gathering interest and enthusiasm. It will be celebrated by a staff who, if not fully contented, are at least more informed, more tolerant and show a greater understanding of each other than at any time in the Hospital's history.

The Hospital chapel

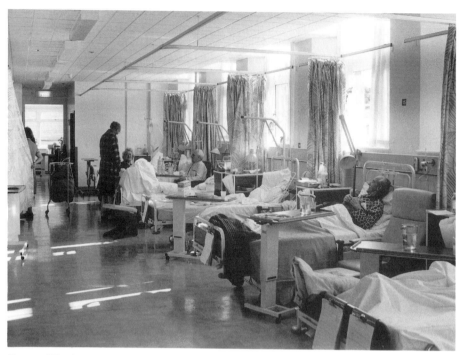

Benyon Ward

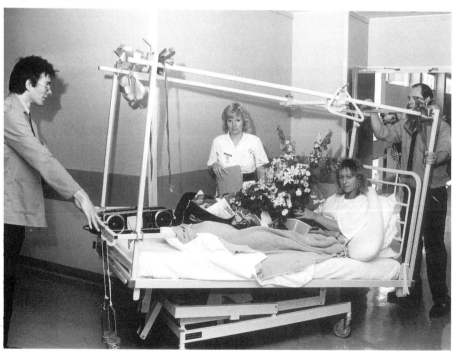

Patient transfer in South Wing

6

THE PATIENTS' VIEW

Once their Hospital was assimilated into the National Health Service, further changes in the administration of the Royal Berks were of little concern to the patients. Nor were they greatly interested in educational activities, altered social attitudes among the staff or even the inter-hospital rivalries for funding and advancement. The to-and-fro shuttling of the Maternity and Orthopaedic Services, and the other new building developments have, of course, been important to the patients directly using these services. However, for many 'The Royal Berks' is still the pre-NHS Hospital and to them the most noticeable changes have not been the massive new blocks, but alterations to the areas they have always known.

Changing Aspects

What patients and their visitors critically observe are everyday things – the outlook and the general appearance of familiar surroundings, and the routine activities within. Improvement or deterioration in the facilities provided obviously feature prominently in the public's awareness of their Hospital, second only to changes in the quality of medical and nursing care. The sum of such physical and functional changes at the Royal Berks, more recently against a background of increasing dependence on charitable fund raising, has determined the character of the Hospital over the first 40 years of the National Health Service. Except for those few whose only experience of the Hospital has been in the new buildings south of the Nuffield Block, this character has retained its historical roots while steadily evolving under the influence of medical and social demands and sometimes of decorative whims.

The sense of historical continuity has largely depended on the preservation of the original Hospital buildings and their still pleasing aspect when viewed from the London Road across the broad forecourt. Once the wartime disfigurements required for air-raid protection were removed, the traditional first impression of the Hospital for visitors remained, and subsequent alterations to the frontage have happily had little deleterious effect. The blast-proof walls and air-raid shelter made their final contribution in providing rubble for a stronger forecourt foundation, soon needed to bear the postwar increase in hospital traffic. In 1951 the dwarfed front boundary wall was capped with slab paving, and its low guard rail was added two years later. In 1957 the eroded bases of the hospital entrance columns were repaired with Portland stone. During this period there were more grandiose plans for a park-like front courtyard with statuary, a fountain, footpaths and ornamental seats to allow convalescent patients and their visitors to enjoy the lawns and gardens. Instead, as the finances worsened and car parking problems increased, the modestly restored gardens were reduced to a single centre plot while the expanse of tarmac for parking spaces was extended. By 1967 in order to guarantee accessible parking for medical staff travelling between hospitals, an automatic barrier was installed.

Despite these depredations, the Hospital frontage has remained imposing and dignified, a tribute to Henry Briant's architecture and not a little to the gardeners who have always managed to set off the entrance with an immaculate display in the small island bed. In 1958 Conrad Latto provided and maintained another garden behind the main building. This was for the benefit of his patients in Huntley and Palmer Ward, whose rear outlook was being blocked by the Laboratory extensions. This small green patch has remained despite the increasing congestion of new buildings and the encroachment of vehicles into every available space.

The proliferation of parked cars has been one of the most obvious and unhappy changes in the general appearance of the old Voluntary Hospital. Those who complain today of parking difficulties should know that in 1964 it was planned that 'the public should be forbidden from parking in the Hospital' and again in 1972 that 'the island site should be used for clinical purposes only'. Car parks off site and on site, overground, underground, single and multi-storeyed have all been mooted without the problem being resolved, while each year patients and their visitors have had more difficulty in getting to their ward or clinic. For those attending Speech and Hearing Therapy, the twin problems of financial constraint and crowded parking are immediately apparent. This busy clinical unit functions in the temporary hut erected by the builders of the Ophthalmic Block, which 20 years later still stands alone behind the Eye Block, as an island in a sea of parked cars. Not for much longer perhaps, if the public respond to an Audiology Unit Appeal for £200,000 for a modern replacement building.

This dilapidated hut is just one of many unsightly changes in the outlook to the rear of the old Hospital buildings. Several developments related to the energy supply have particularly occasioned unfavourable comment. Few were sorry when the coal heaps stockpiled during the war along the Redlands Road frontage were finally used up. This made space for the row of out-patient huts which themselves did little to improve the view. The switch to oil-firing then brought an ugly bank of fuel tanks and a standby diesel generator behind Benyon Ward.

Meanwhile, the old boiler house was allowed to deteriorate since a new power plant was due for installation at the southern end of the site. For years now it has stood with peeling paintwork and cracked windows, unloved and unused, a huge defacement of the rear quadrangle area behind the old kitchen. Completion of the South Wing power complex also made

The Audiology hut

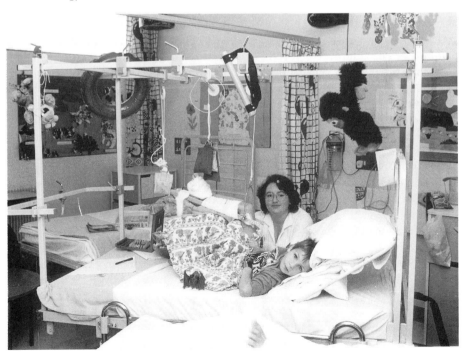

Young patient in Gauvain Ward

the oil tanks and generator redundant. They in turn were replaced by a tall calorifier and plant services building, whose jutting rooftop water tower disrupted the western skyline of the old Hospital. More harmoniously, the dominating feature on the eastern side has remained the chimney of the old laundry. Its original purpose was lost when steam from the main boiler house was piped in. The laundry itself was converted to most handsomely vaulted nurses' changing rooms when all laundry services were transferred to Battle in 1968.

Nevertheless, the old chimney still occasionally startles passers-by when noxious waste is incinerated in its small furnace, and dense black smoke suddenly belches forth. Most incineration now is done in the South Wing power block, its smoke better dissipated by the towering modern concrete chimney. This, the tallest structure by far on the Hospital site was in embarrassing public view when it required some early rebuilding work, pointed comparisons being made with the long-lasting chimney of the Victorian laundry.

Another sight of some public interest was the mortuary, which for years occupied the south-western corner of the main Hospital grounds. Its morbidly discreet comings and goings became less obvious when the central yard was roofed over, but the new roadways to the Hospital's southern developments brought many more people past its doors. There was general relief that the new mortuary of South Wing was well hidden in the basement. When the pathologists moved to this new facility, the Building and Works Department took over the old mortuary premises without any qualms.

One of the more remarkable features of the Royal Berks is that despite its considerable age, and the British tradition of hospital ghosts, there has never been any truly eerie or gloomy building. Occasionally odd things have been reported. There were times when the Adelaide Ward doors would open by themselves in the night, and sensible senior nurses have reported seeing a Grey Lady shimmer through the closed doors of Sidmouth Ward. Sister Pickering, who was Night Superintendent for over 20 years, retired in 1974 never having seen the Grey Lady of Sidmouth, but with one splendid ghost story from that period. In Benyon Ward a little old lady made a dying will, leaving everything to her devoted friend. Following her death, the family contested the will and successfully claimed the estate. One night soon afterwards a third-year Irish nurse came shivering and crying to Sister Pickering. She had seen a strange small woman limp slowly from a cubicle in Benyon Ward – and disappear. This nurse had no knowledge of the events months before, yet she described in exact detail the stooped gait, nightdress and shawl, and the figure had come from the cubicle in which the old lady had died. Such happenings, exceptional in former years, are today almost unheard of. Criminal intruders are the modern fear at night, visitors and nursing staff alike particularly detesting the long, lonely and bare passageway to South Wing.

Within the original Hospital the atmosphere is of warmth, and a comfortable sense of the past. Over the years, the addition of balconies and annexes, and the upgrading of wards to modern standards, have not seriously affected this pleasant ambience which largely derives from the more public areas of entrance hall, stairway and corridors. Changes here are immediately obvious and may significantly affect the attitude of patients and visitors towards the Hospital. In 1954 for instance, after six years of the Health Service, a reminder of the historical past was provided when the commemorative oak panelling was unveiled above the first flight of the main staircase, recording the names and dates of the office bearers and the medical staff of the Voluntary Hospital from 1839 to 1948. The reception area was greatly altered in 1970 when Endowment Funds were used to install a counter, letter racks, shelving and a second oak bench. This work was done with admirable taste and markedly improved the functioning of the busy entrance hall.

In 1977 an attempt to improve the appearance and efficiency of the main corridors went sadly wrong. Because of wall damage due to increased hospital traffic the long glass-fronted panels recording the Hospital's Benefactors and Subscribers were summarily removed to permit a protective redecoration. This consisted of a synthetic pallid veneer, floor to ceiling, punctuated at corners and at trolley height with strips of funereal black. This awfulness, so out of keeping with the mellow surroundings, was perpetrated with almost no objection from staff or visitors, which says something about the apathy and materialism of the times.

The 1960s telephone exchange, to be replaced in 1989

Not all the redecorative programme was so disastrous. The corridor to Nuffield Block certainly was improved by its wall treatment, and the sharp corner into this corridor was opened out to relieve a site of severe congestion. Space for this widening came at the expense of a magnificent Victorian water closet, traditionally used as a private lavatory for the consultants. However, even the most reactionary of the older medical staff conceded the sense of this action, which further benefited patients and visitors when the League of Friends later funded the installation of a much-needed public telephone in the vacated corner space.

Life on the Wards
On the wards, everyday life at the Royal Berks has changed completely in the last 40 years. The long-staying patients, who previously required little attention and often acted as nursing assistants, have all but disappeared in response to changing fashions of hospital treatment, the expanding role of the G.P. and District Nurse and the provision of homes for the elderly. The rigid disciplines of nursing routine have been relaxed in the urgency of coping with too many acutely ill patients competing for too few beds. The conflict between old-fashioned standards and modern demands has increased over the years as overstressed nurses have dealt with many more and much sicker patients, changing methods of treatment and galloping advances in technology. Many patients will have personally witnessed the transition from an era of 'six weeks' strict bed rest' and cold compresses to computerised monitoring equipment and ambulatory syringe pumps. So swift has been the progress in electronic gadgetry, it is difficult to believe that at the Royal Berks the first Electronics Technician was appointed to the engineering staff as recently as 1969. Even more astonishing is the fact that the change from hospital generator power to mains electricity was only made in 1955.

With their modern clinical activities, the nurses have gradually relinquished many traditional roles. Domestics now do the routine cleaning. Ward clerks, first suggested for the Royal Berks by Jack Kempton in 1960, cope efficiently with much of the reception work, telephoning and routine administration. To the patients, the most important change has probably been in the system of hospital catering. The old kitchen, with its ancient but reliable gas oven, previously prepared bulk meals which the ward nurses then served from a heated trolley. In the older wards this continued until 1975, although a switch to plated meals had begun with the opening of a new kitchen in the Maternity Unit basement. In 1972, the Ganymede system of electric tugs and trolleys was introduced to expedite delivery of the prepared meals, but since then staff shortages have often resulted in the patients receiving lukewarm food. For several years the cook-chill method of mass catering has been under serious consideration and may shortly be introduced. Florence Nightingale would not be pleased.

Hospital meals have always been difficult, but the personal serving of individually presented meals was once an important part of nursing care.

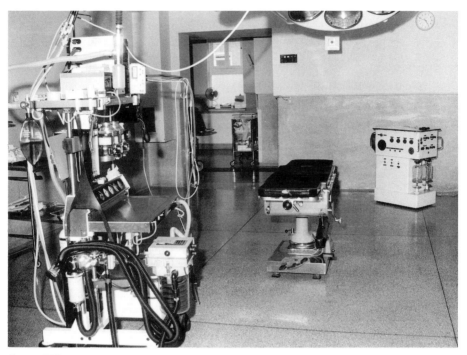

General Theatre

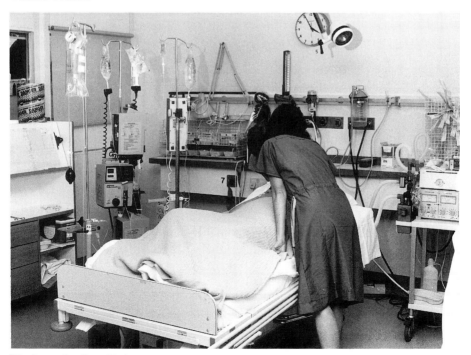

The Intensive Care Unit

Only the children in Kempton Ward now have this privilege, while the Maternity Wards have not even the facilities to serve a freshly boiled egg. Despite these strictures, in a general nutritional sense the meals have greatly improved, particularly through the 1980s, as District Dietitian Kathy Debenham has succeeded in her motivation of both patients and staff towards a healthier style of eating.

In a ranking of patients' interests, food would probably be first, with visitors second and, until recently, smoking may have been third. At the Royal Berks in 1947, visiting was permitted on Wednesday and Saturday afternoons between 2.30 and 3.30 p.m. and for an extra 15 minutes on Sunday. The children, who were believed to be better off without distraction by their parents, were allowed only one hour a week, on Saturday afternoon. The task of controlling the Visiting Day crowds belonged to the porters who, with a gate on each side of the columns in the entrance hall and a rope strung between, held back the impatient visitors until exactly 2.30 p.m. As a trial in 1966 visiting hours in Huntley and Palmer Ward were extended to 2.30 to 6.30 p.m. daily. By 1968 common sense and humanity had at last triumphed. All wards accepted visitors for several hours each day and until 8 p.m. to allow visits after work, while in Kempton the visiting of children became completely unrestricted.

The Royal Berks was more ahead of the times in its attitude to smoking. By 1956, the dangers and the influence of medical example were already being realised. Byelaw 23 stated that no smoking by the Resident Medical Officers could be allowed in the wards or corridors of the Hospital. In 1963 a trial was started of 'no smoking by patients in the acute wards'. This was referred back by the Hospital Management Committee, which obviously included several smokers, for 'less stringent rules'. It was then left to the individual clinician in charge to advise on smoking – an unsatisfactory state which resulted in confused rules and variable degrees of restriction. The quarter century since has seen gradual success for the health campaigners and smoking is becoming a rarity in hospitals. Despite small pockets of resistance among the staff, objections by union representatives and the undoubted distress of addicted patients, the Royal Berks may well become a non-smoking hospital in its 150th anniversary year.

Medical Services
It is customary for hospital histories to record, not always with complete accuracy, a continuous parade of medical brilliance and benevolence. For the Royal Berkshire Hospital under the N.H.S., it is unquestionably true that the patients have consistently enjoyed a quite exceptional quality of medical care. Battle Hospital, in its parallel development, has achieved identical standards because of the splitting of clinical services and the sharing of staff. Indeed, so-called 'Royal Berks patients' have been just as likely to receive treatment at Battle in particular specialties or on emergency calls.

The Second World War freed the Royal Berks from the custom of appointing general practitioners to the honorary staff. The returned service doctors carried home a firm commitment to specialisation and they and the later N.H.S. consultants brought to the Hospital remarkable standards of skill and experience. At least as importantly, they developed a tradition of mutual help and co-operation which is the admiration of many District General Hospitals burdened with a faction-split, in-fighting medical staff. As specialisation increased, the Royal Berks doctors assisted each other's endeavours, avoided duplication of effort and strove to provide the most up-to-date facilities and equipment for their patients. More and more this provision has depended on their turning to local charitable effort.

In general medicine the new era began in 1969 when Lord Waverley established coronary monitoring in Sidmouth Ward. Eric Cox and Ken North developed special services in gastroenterology, diabetes and endocrine disorders. Ramesh Naik was appointed in 1981 as the first Physician with Special Interest in Renal Medicine. He battled for years until in 1987 he was able to offer ambulatory peritoneal dialysis to patients with kidney failure, and to establish a chronic haemodialysis unit at Dellwood, which since 1981 had functioned only as a cottage-type hospital for general practitioners.

Reading's specialist paediatric service officially began in June 1948 when Jack Kempton was given the position of Assistant Physician in Charge of Children, in accordance with a recommendation of the Nuffield

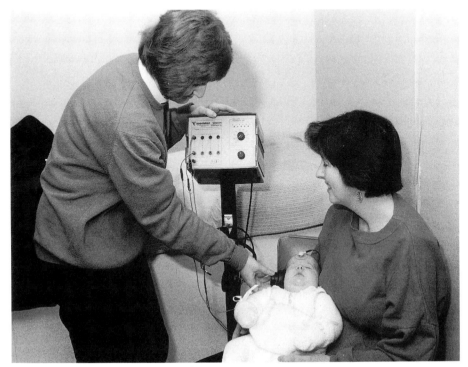

Testing for hearing

Provincial Trust Child Welfare Service that a specialist paediatrician be appointed. Joyce Burke and David Stone, the most gentle and caring of children's doctors, continued Kempton's pioneering work while greatly expanding the Department's facilities. With considerable help from C. F. Taylor, a dayroom for Kempton Ward plus overnight accommodation for parents was provided, and extensions were built to the isolation unit and the Out-patients Department. A plan to convert the Craven Road Nurses' Home into a comprehensive Children's Department, which would have centralised paediatrics on the one site, unfortunately came to nothing.

The Special Care Baby Unit began as an integral part of the Maternity Block when 50 per cent of babies were still delivered outside the Hospital. At that time the major concern was isolation and treatment of infected new born. Increasing centralisation and specialisation of obstetrics led to the demand for advanced techniques of monitoring and intensive care for tiny patients. These came with the appointment of Chris Newman in 1977, and charitable donations have provided more than half of the expensive equipment now essential to the Unit. The skilled staff of the S.C.B.U. bring new hope for parents of the very premature and ill babies who are now surviving, thanks to the expertise and advanced technology of the modern obstetricians.

Surgery in Reading has the highest of traditions, from George May in 1839 to Leonard Joyce 100 years later. Since the Second World War their talented successors have continually improved the service and unselfishly encouraged the development of special surgical interests. These have been typified by Norman Rothnie's Vascular Clinic, the work of Harvey Ross on parathyroid problems and of David Goodwin in treating melanomas. At least two specialist surgeons at the Royal Berks have gained world recognition – Dick Welham as as authority on surgery of the tear ducts, and Orthopaedic Surgeon Steve Copeland as a shoulder specialist and the inventor of a new type of artificial shoulder joint.

Surgical patients of the Royal Berks were among the first in the country to receive the benefits of safe day-stay surgery, when Anaesthetist Tom Boulton, now returned from St Bartholomew's, was invited to create a formal Day Bed Unit in 1973. The patients, without knowing it, have also had increasingly safer operations due to persistence of the surgical and anaesthetic staff in demands that the older operating theatres be provided with recovery rooms. This was a long drawn-out struggle, since a new multi-theatre suite was for years confidently anticipated, while upgrading old theatres is expensive financially and in the loss of operating time. Staffed recovery rooms came to general theatres in 1963, as part of the E.N.T. Theatre extensions in 1969 and finally to the Nuffield Gynaecology Theatre in 1978.

Anaesthesia itself has become much safer in the last 40 years and considerably less unpleasant. The entire Royal Berks specialist anaesthetic staff in 1946 consisted of Basil Hill and Martin Bristow, two experts in the techniques of the times. Over the next 40 years the smell of ether gradually disappeared as increasingly sophisticated apparatus came into the theatre areas, together with a whole new range of anaesthetic techniques. Children in particular have been better looked after, injections are now less often used for premedication; parents are usually welcome in the anaesthetic room, and management of post-operative pain has greatly improved.

The numbers of consultant and trainee anaesthetists have multiplied at a rate disconcerting to other specialties. Here, too, individual consultants have been encouraged to follow special interests. David Price fathered intensive care which remains a responsibility of the anaesthetic service. Steve Allen established a Pain Clinic in 1981; others have become particularly involved in areas such as obstetric anaesthesia, eye surgery and cancer treatment for children. Tom Boulton, a world authority on anaesthesia in difficult situations and a past President of the Association of Anaesthetists of Great Britain and Ireland, has attracted a constant stream of overseas visitors to the Department. A more unusual contribution to the Health Service has been made by Donald McWilliams, who currently serves as Chairman of the East Berkshire Health Authority while an Anaesthetics Consultant in the major hospital of West Berkshire.

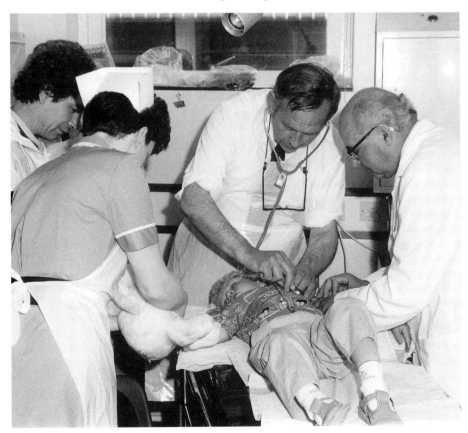

Dental anaesthesia in the Day Bed Unit

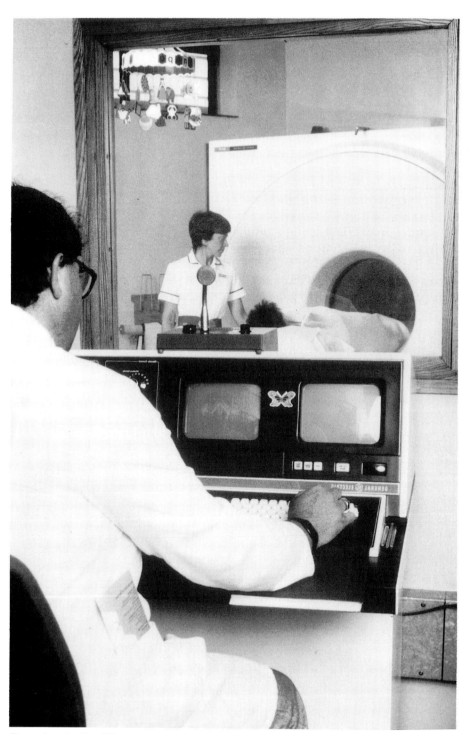

Operating the Ken Thomas scanner

The X-ray Department was emotionally brought into the public consciousness when the dying cancer patient Ken Thomas orchestrated the Scanner Appeal, which his friend Michael Wood successfully carried to completion. £1.25m was donated to purchase, install and maintain the Hospital's first Computerised Axial Tomography (CAT) Scanner Unit. No specialty at the Royal Berks has advanced as quickly as radiology. Dr Cave retired in 1958, just missing the sensational technical developments which have expanded the consultant numbers to nine and changed the function and the name of the Department to 'Diagnostic Imaging'. Even this title is no longer adequate, since with the modern techniques of interventional radiology, the Department takes an active part in the actual treatment as well as diagnosis of conditions such as concealed abscesses, kidney stones and blocked arteries.

In contrast, two departments of the Royal Berks were much slower in their development than the general pace of hospital progress, although they have since been rapidly catching up. A separate Accident and Emergency Department was not established until December 1986 when Paul Ferrugia and Shanti Soysa became the first A & E Consultants appointed to the Royal Berkshire Hospital. They are coping with a task comparable with Mike Squire's in 1948 and for the same reason – too many people seeking to use the front-line service of the Hospital. The much-publicised complaints of previous years have dwindled, but the staff and modern facilities in the South Wing are already overloaded.

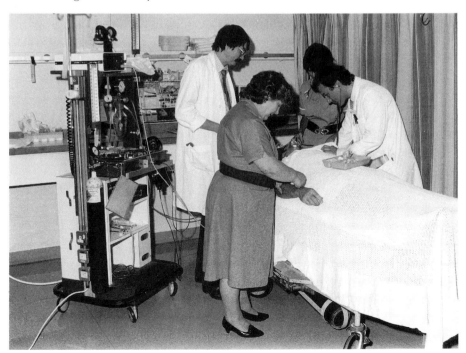

Resuscitation in the modern Accident and Emergency Department

If the Casualty Department is the Hospital's front line, the V.D. Department was for years its backdoor Clinic, tucked away in a succession of odd corners. Unused beds in the old West Ward Unit led to a swap, with medical records getting more space in West Ward and its wooden annexe, while the V.D. Clinic was squeezed into the Records Department in the West Wing, and later upstairs into two small rooms above the enclosed Redlands Road archway. The swinging sixties and a rising workload demanded another transfer, this time downstairs to occupy the vacated pharmacy premises, where the Clinic remained for the next 20 years. It was never popular with the medical staff. Horace Le Marquand took it on to supplement his income with the payments from the Local Authority. When he went into the army in 1942, the Clinic was run by Dr Neville Smith, a gentleman-doctor of independent means who decided to 'do his bit' by abandoning his shooting and fishing to become the Royal Berks Casualty Officer and then taking over the Special Clinic. After the war, Dr Le Marquand could not wait to hand over responsibility when Hugh Calvert was appointed Consultant in Dermatology and Venereology in 1950.

Dr Calvert continued the Clinic with two sessions per week, Wednesday and Saturday, at first assisted by Neville Smith, followed by General Practitioner Pat McIlvenna. The latter became so experienced that he was appointed Medical Assistant and Dr Calvert was content to revert to nominal status only. Dr McIlvenna then ran the Unit almost single handed.

On his retirement and after much debate (mostly financial), it was agreed to appoint the first Consultant in Genito Urinary Medicine to the Royal Berks Hospital. Jenny Isaacson took up the position in 1981, bringing a new name for the Clinic as well as for the specialty. The Florey Unit during the next few years moved from a backwater to join the mainstream of acute medicine, just in time to expand in response to the epidemic threat of AIDS. In 1987 the Unit moved yet again, this time to gain further space in the old Public Health Laboratory Service building between Huntley and Palmer Ward and the general theatres. The once backdoor Clinic has thus gained a central position within the Hospital, to match its new-found clinical importance.

Cancer Treatment

The relocation of the Florey Unit, so desperately needed because of the explosive increase in work, was actually precipitated by the plans in association with the Hospital's 150th Anniversary to redevelop the Radiotherapy Department to the standards first visualised in the 1944 conference on Regional cancer care. Dr Evans in his temporary new building of 1947 had waited a further two years to get a new X-ray therapy machine, and he was able before his retirement to supervise the installation of a modern Cobalt Unit. This was in 1960, and made possible only by an anonymous donation of £10,000. John Bunting, his successor as Head of Department, continued the battle against financial restrictions, persuading the Region to fund a second Cobalt Unit in 1970 and, another decade later, a Linear Accelerator. Dr Bunting also negotiated successfully in 1968 to take over Geoffrey Cashell's original Eye Ward as a new West Ward for radiotherapy patients, and conversion of the old surgical out-patients to become the Radiotherapy Clinic. The lot of the cancer patients was thus improved with modern management in a close-knit unit of clinic, treatment areas and ward, in an atmosphere of family togetherness.

By the 1980s however, advances in radio- and chemotherapy, the associated increase in patient attendances and in the numbers of staff (now led by three consultants), had transformed the Department into a congested, uncomfortable clutter of modified old rooms. There was little privacy for the patients and a threat to safety standards in the Physics Laboratory. The Region was prepared to supply a more modern Linear Accelerator by 1989, but no N.H.S. funding was available to correct the inadequacy of the routine facilities. For its 150th Anniversary, the Hospital therefore decided to launch an Appeal for £1.5 million to bring its treatment of cancer patients up to first-class standards. The public's immediate response allowed work to begin on an imaginative design to redevelop completely the ground floor of the West Wing. A new mezzanine floor would provide some much-needed space. More would come from the first phase which opened in May 1988, being a new out-patient and chemotherapy section to replace the old Florey Unit.

In 1973 the Radiotherapy Department was actively seeking a facility nearby for continuing care of the cancer patients. Parkside House, in Upper Redlands Road, used as a hostel from 1949–76 was not suitable, being mainly for overnight stay by patients having radio isotope diagnostic tests. The National Society for Cancer Relief were approached, but had no funds available at that time for developments in the Reading area. Interest was revived by the successful Scanner Appeal and the continued local enthusiasm for cancer care demonstrated by immediate support for the 150th Anniversary Radiotherapy Appeal. Cancer Relief Macmillan Fund joined forces with the Anniversary Appeal under the auspices of the West Berkshire Health Authority to create the West Berkshire Macmillan Cancer Care Appeal.

This Appeal will raise a total of £3m – for the Radiotherapy Department, for Day Centres at Wokingham and Newbury and for a Macmillan Green Cancer Care Centre at Dellwood Hospital. This innovative, comprehensive scheme to improve the initial treatment and the aftercare of cancer patients and their families will be studied and almost certainly copied by many Health Authorities wanting to give their patients a comparable standard of service.

These huge appeals are the most notable development in the movement back from total government funding to a greater reliance on local charitable help. As a purely voluntary Hospital the Royal Berks was eventually unable to maintain its standards of patient care. It is now obvious that, in contrast to initial optimism, the N.H.S. could never completely fund the escalating costs of modern medical advancement. On the other hand medical staff of the quality attracted to the Royal Berkshire Hospital would never accept yesterday's standards of diagnosis and treatment. The only path for maintaining local medical progress has been a return to funding from the community. Similarly, comforts and amenities for patients and staff could only be maintained and improved by reverting to local goodwill.

Voluntary Agencies

In 1957 the League of Friends of the Reading Hospitals was formed. Miss Vera Palmer, the last Chairman of the Ladies' Linen League, became the first Chairman of the new voluntary organisation. The contributions made by charitable organisations such as this and by service and voluntary groups from the local communities have been immense – tens of thousands donated annually plus the incalculable value of a cheerful host of voluntary hospital helpers. The British Red Cross Society, the W.R.V.S., the Townswomen's Guilds, the Lions, Round Table and Rotary – these and many other dedicated organisations and individuals have without any doubt played a vital part in maintaining the Hospital's standards of equipment and patient care. Operating microscopes, ophthalmic equipment, cardiac monitors, emergency trolleys, neonatal ventilators, syringe pumps, ultra sound and laser machines, radios, TV and special beds for the patients are just a few of the medical advances and amenities funded by

Top left: The Red Cross shop; *Top right*: League of Friends shop; *Bottom left*: W.R.V.S. canteen; *Bottom right*: Waiting area in South Wing

local charity in response to pleas from the Reading specialists and the nursing staff.

Perhaps most ironic has been the donation of fibre optic endoscopes. When Professor Harold Hopkins was pioneering the science of fibre optics in the Physics Department of Reading University, he frequently consulted with clinicians at the Royal Berkshire Hospital on their potential use in medicine. Commercial development went overseas, with the result that the Royal Berks doctors have had to rely mainly on charity to obtain vital foreign-made instruments which are based on a Reading invention.

New types of medical equipment will always be needed, but some things at the Royal Berks have seemed never to change. There has always been a shortage of beds, of nurses and of money. For a brief period there was a dimunition of community interest in the Hospital, and more recently a serious disillusionment among the staff. The 150th Anniversary has revived interest and pride in the Hospital's history, and the Appeal has highlighted the renewed relationship between the Royal Berks and its community.

In the 44th and last year of the Ladies' Linen League, Mrs Benyon commented that under nationalisation the Government would provide necessities but no frills. There would still be room for voluntary societies to fund these amenities. Mr Wilder, the Honorary Treasurer of the Royal Berks noted in his final report that even after the 'Appointed Day', personal support would still be necessary in some form. How right they both were!

Patient Care Today
Has the N.H.S. worked for the patients of the Royal Berkshire Hospital? The answer undoubtedly is 'yes'. For 40 years their medical care has continuously improved. At no direct personal cost, they have benefited from all the major advances in the treatment of conditions such as resistant infections, cancer, high blood pressure, glaucoma and skin diseases. The consultants have learned to assess and apply expensive medical innovations in a responsible fashion. Staff committees and watchful monitoring by the Hospital pharmacy have curbed premature therapeutic enthusiasms. Individual consultants, when certain of the value of a new technique, have successfully crusaded within and without the N.H.S. to bring the benefit to their patients. Those needing more specialised skills or services have been rapidly referred to appropriate centres in London or Oxford, where links forged during the system of medical training in the Health Service have been maintained between the consultants of the District General and the Teaching Hospitals.

Under the N.H.S. the pattern of patient care between the Royal Berks and local general practitioners has also changed for the better. The relationship between G.P. and consultant has improved, less through official channels than through individual contact, and by the programmes of the Post-graduate Centre and meetings of the Reading Pathological

Society. Except for difficult psychiatric and geriatric problems, domiciliary visits by consultants have become much less common. The older formality of G.P. addressing consultant by title and being in turn called by surname gradually disappeared with the arrival of the young consultants of the 1960s. General practice was meanwhile becoming a specialty in its own right, with many trainees cementing bonds with the Hospital by rotating through several senior house officer posts at the Royal Berks before joining practices in the catchment area.

Over the years, the local general practitioners have taken up the care of those patients previously long staying at the Royal Berks or decanted to Blagrave, Prospect Park or Battle – the convalescents, chronic sick and the elderly. Prospect Park has ceased functioning as a hospital though serving a useful new role as an accessible District Administrative Headquarters. Blagrave's sale was finally determined in July 1988. Rationalisation of services has also closed the Henley War Memorial Hospital and the G.P. beds remaining at the old TB hospital at Peppard.

In contrast, the general practitioners and their patients in the Wallingford area were well served by the opening in 1973 of the first purpose-built Community Hospital in the country. Its links with the Royal Berks lessened, however, when the Reading and District Hospital Management Committee lost it to Oxfordshire in the 1974 reorganisation. A few G.P. hospital beds are still available at Townlands in Henley, at Newbury and at Dellwood, and indeed at the Royal Berks, whose Maternity Unit now includes the G.P. maternity beds previously provided at Dellwood. But is in their own homes and in the Social Services' homes for the elderly that the 'overtime' patients of the early N.H.S. years are now to be found. The general practitioners enjoy greater personal contact with their patients, they have fewer financial constraints than their hospital counterparts, recruit the best of junior staff and are able to offer them a correspondingly bright future. Little wonder that some consultants, bitter about the Government's diversion of funding from the acute hospital sector, now view their G.P. colleagues with some envy.

Within the Hospital, the high proportion of G.P. trainees among the juniors is just one feature of a continually evolving pattern of medical staffing. The largest change with the coming of the N.H.S. was the provision of more resident doctors, making the hours of work not quite so unreasonable, and lessening the hazardous doubling up of duties such as the house physician acting as occasional anaesthetist. For many years overseas doctors were relied on to staff the increasing number of junior posts. This is now decreasing, although the Orthopaedic, E.N.T., Obstetric and Anaesthetics Departments all continue a long tradition of training doctors from overseas. The implementation of recent national agreements will reduce the junior rotas to a maximum of one night in three, and adjust the numbers to match career posts available. Increased involvement by consultants in everyday (and night) patient management is the certain trend for the future to the equally certain benefit of the patients.

The patient/staff relationship has also been evolving. Since the patients' stay is now so brief, they are less well known by the staff, yet frequently called by their Christian names. They are much better informed medically and probably in consequence have less respect for the doctors. A few unfortunately are coming to believe that 100 per cent health is their right and anything less might be grounds for litigation. More legitimate current complaints certainly include the waiting times for out-patient appointments and for elective operations. Difficulties of access to the Hospital by public or private transport also cause dissatisfaction. The Ambulance Service, shuttled from the Hospital to Local Authority in 1948 and back to the Health Authority in 1974, copes brilliantly with the transport of emergencies, but is grossly over committed and wrongly employed in moving patients whose requirement is rather for just a taxi-type service or a bus. Similarly, the Hospital has a major problem in the continued demand of the public to be seen in the Accident and Emergency Department for conditions which are neither accidents nor emergencies. Sorting out these problems, and streamlining the system of patient administration is a major task which technology may largely overcome.

In 1987 a main-frame computer was installed in the old pharmacy storeroom of the Eye Block. This will eventually link communications on patient services throughout West Berkshire. But clinical care does not yet rely on the silicon chip. Happily for most patients their Hospital provides an effective, modern service which still, it is to be hoped, has not lost the personal touch.

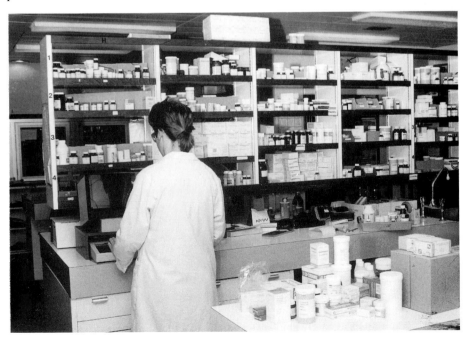

Section of the Pharmacy

Redevelopment of Radiotherapy Department in association with the 150th Anniversary Appeal: artist's impressions. *Top*: The Redlands Road entrance; *Centre*: New waiting area; *Bottom*: New consulting rooms

EPILOGUE

by

MARGARET RAILTON

From 50 beds and one operating theatre to some 645 beds and 12 theatres; from four untrained nurses to a nursing staff of over 900; from an honorary medical staff of three physicians and three surgeons to a salaried consultant staff of almost 100; from an annual expenditure of £2,000 to one of £21.8 million – these are the bare statistics of a century and a half of growth and development.

There can be few institutions to compare with a hospital where history so closely mirrors prevailing attitudes and social conditions. The Voluntary Hospital was built and maintained entirely through the generosity of the public. For over 100 years this support enabled the advances in medicine and surgery to be applied for the benefit of the poor and needy in Reading and the surrounding neighbourhood. With the increase in medical and scientific knowledge came a greater awareness of the links between health and environment, and the treatment of sickness both inside and outside the Hospital developed in parallel with the maintenance of health within the community.

Two world wars brought many changes in attitude and a more egalitarian outlook replaced the rigid social divisions of the pre-war days. The evolution of a National Health Service embodied this thinking. Its title, as opposed to a 'National Hospital Service', illustrated the need for hospitals to become part of an integrated system which included secondary care, primary care, and ancillary services. The fact that this service would be available to all regardless of their means was a mammoth step and one which, for almost 40 years, could be sustained with reasonable efficiency.

On July 5th, 1948 the Royal Berkshire Hospital opened its doors to the rich and poor alike. All could now obtain treatment 'free on the point of delivery'. The Hospital became part of a large administrative system where local needs were considered in relation to a Regional plan within a national strategy.

The organisation of the N.H.S. at that time had divided the country into 'Hospital' regions. Great emphasis was placed on developing the hospital and specialist services and resources were directed in large measure towards this end. The Royal Berkshire Hospital, in the Oxford

Region, was required to be enlarged and developed to fulfill its envisaged role as the key hospital of the Reading District, with a catchment area of some 300,000 people.

Forty years later a very different structure has emerged. By 1965 the idea of one large 1,052-bed hospital on the Royal Berkshire Hospital site had been abandoned. Instead, two General Hospitals, the Royal Berkshire Hospital and Battle Hospital, would provide the acute services originally planned for the one key hospital. This decision coincided with an increasing awareness that the three divisions of the N.H.S. (hospitals, G.P.s and ancillary services) were developing without co-ordination, and the finance which had been directed to expand the hospital service had been at the expense of family practitioners and community medicine. Integration of the three divisions was now believed to be essential.

The reorganisation in 1974 replaced the Regional Hospital Boards with Regional Health Authorities and added an 'Area' tier of administration in order to integrate the three divisions of the N.H.S. Further reorganisation in 1982 produced the structure which exists to this day. The Oxford Regional Health Authority is responsible for planning and administering the N.H.S. in Berkshire, Buckinghamshire, Oxfordshire and Northamptonshire. In size it has not changed significantly from the original Hospital Region created in 1948 and it covers a population of 1.6 million.

The West Berkshire District of the Oxford Region is concerned with the local administration of the N.H.S. It serves a catchment area of some 445,000 people and covers the local government authorities of Newbury, Reading and Wokingham District Councils and part of South Oxfordshire District Council. The Royal Berkshire Hospital with 645 beds and Battle Hospital with 406 beds provide the acute services for the District. The planning in 1947 for 1,052 acute beds serving a catchment area of 300,000 has not altered greatly in the 40 years.

The expansion which has taken place at the Royal Berkshire Hospital since 1948 could never have been funded through the voluntary system. The cost of the additional staff, combined with the high-technology equipment now employed, could not have been met through public subscriptions alone. Although only 300 additional beds have been provided at the Hospital in the past 40 years, the advances in medicine and surgery which have enabled patients to be treated more efficiently and discharged earlier have resulted in an impressive increase in the number of patients treated each year. Since the reorganisation in 1899 great emphasis has been placed on the length of stay, the number of patients per bed per year and the cost of treatment. The following table will show at a glance the enormous strides which have taken place over the years and how the beds doubled in number between 1898 and 1947, and doubled again between 1947 and 1987. The number of in-patients in the corresponding periods increased from four to five-fold as medical and surgical advances reduced their length of stay dramatically.

On a national scale, statistics for 1986/87 demonstrate the high

HOSPITAL TRENDS 1898–1987

	1898	1900	1947	1986/87
Beds	160	160	326	645
In-patients	1,300	1,667	6,841	33,600 + 2,570 day cases
Operations	844	1,516	6,510	23,000
Average length stay in-patients	42.7 days	30.2 days	13 days	4.6 days incl. maternity
Av. length stay general medical patients	43.2 days	29.9 days	—	7.3 days
Av. length stay general surgical patients	42.2 days	30.5 days	—	5.4 days
No. of patients per bed per year	8	12	—	59 incl. maternity
Cost per in-patient per day	—	—	£1 7s 7d	£117.46
Total average cost per in-patient	£7 3s 5d	£6 1s 5d	£21 5s 0d	£539.12
No. of new out-patients	2,008	2,334	20,445	49,600
Cost per out-patient attendance	—	—	4/7d	£26.55
No. of out-patient attendances	—	—	103,283	171,700

turnover per bed obtained at the Royal Berkshire Hospital and, for an acute hospital, the low cost per patient treated. The severe financial constraints imposed in September 1987 therefore appeared to the Hospital to be especially hard and an unwarranted penalty for efficiency. In an area with an increasing population, the Hospital believed its work should be expanded and not curtailed.

By the time the N.H.S. reached its 40th anniversary in 1988, the national debate on its future role and structure was at its height. The financial crisis, which was affecting hospitals throughout the country, had made a fundamental review imperative. Every aspect of the National Health Service came under scrutiny. The hospital services, accounting for some 60 per cent of the total N.H.S. spending, became the central issue. The level of national funding, the system of regional administration, the requirements of local management and links with the private sector all became matters of intense debate. Proposals for greater independence and flexibility at hospital level were considered; medical audits, clinical budgets and internal markets were examined. The life appointment of consultants and their terms of employment came into open discussion, as did the suggestion for geographical variations in nurses' pay. The importance of the quality of patient care was emphasised with the need to provide a service that was efficient, effective and compassionate.

In its smaller voluntary days, the Hospital had suffered frequent financial crises. These had been handled by its Board of Management with direct appeals to the public for help. Wages and salaries had also been determined by the Board who were in a position to take action quickly when difficulty in staff recruitment was discovered to be the result of low pay. On being released from the responsibility of raising its own funds, the N.H.S. Hospital had lost its previous autonomy to a large central administration. Similarly wage and salary awards became the concern of national negotiation and union pressure. By 1988 not only had the Hospital reduced its beds by 20 per cent compared to the previous year, closed wards and cancelled operating sessions to keep within its budget, but it was also having great difficulty in recruiting sufficient staff. Low pay, in an area of high wages and little unemployment, had left some departments grossly understaffed and overworked. Among the nurses it was hoped that the salary increases awarded in association with a restructuring of their clinical nursing posts would help to boost both morale and recruitment.

As the Hospital has expanded it has inevitably become more impersonal. The feeling of unity, which in its smaller, pre-N.H.S. days the Matron, Hospital Secretary and Board of Management were able to provide, has to a large extent been lost. This detachment has extended to the patients. Although much better facilities have been made available and safer and more effective treatment provided, efficiency and rapid turnover has left little time for communication. In many instances patients may still find it difficult to obtain the information and reassurance which they and their families so often need. The fears which arose in 1948 concerning the future of the N.H.S. Hospital have not altogether proved groundless.

The links between the Hospital and the general public which had supported it in its voluntary days were initially almost completely severed with the arrival of the N.H.S. This isolation gradually lessened over the years, and the voluntary interest slowly became re-established. The combination of the Hospital's financial problems and the 150th anniversary being celebrated in 1989 has resulted in an unprecedented demonstration of good will and generosity. The concern of the general public for its Hospital is as strong as it has ever been. The redevelopment of the Radiotherapy Department in association with the 150th Anniversary Appeal will be a memorial to this fact.

It is easy to forget just how greatly the Hospital has expanded and to underestimate the extent of the development of its services to the patients. From Victorian times the skill and dedication of the medical and nursing staff have enabled the advances of pathology, anaesthesia, radiology and their allied sciences to benefit the work of every department. Over the last 40 years this progress has been spectacular, and the direction of recent research points to even greater advances in the years ahead.

Whatever the outcome of the next reorganisation of the N.H.S., the Hospital in celebrating its 150th anniversary can justifiably be proud of all it has achieved.

INDEX

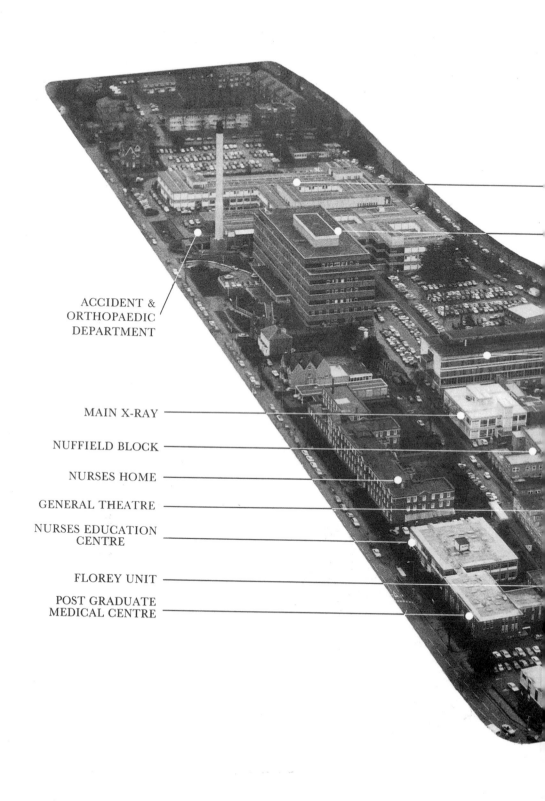

ACCIDENT &
ORTHOPAEDIC
DEPARTMENT

MAIN X-RAY

NUFFIELD BLOCK

NURSES HOME

GENERAL THEATRE

NURSES EDUCATION
CENTRE

FLOREY UNIT

POST GRADUATE
MEDICAL CENTRE